HOUSE OF COMMONS

DEFENCE COMMITTEE

Third Report

THE FUTURE OF NATO:
THE WASHINGTON SUMMIT

Report and Proceedings of the Committee
with Minutes of Evidence
and Appendices

Ordered by The House of Commons *to be pri...*
31 March 1999

LONDON: THE STATIONERY OFFI...

£20·50

The Defence Committee is appointed under Standing Order No 152 to examine the expenditure, administration and policy of the Ministry of Defence and associated public bodies.

The Committee consists of 11 Members, of whom the quorum is three. Unless the House otherwise orders, all Members nominated to the Committee continue to be members of it for the remainder of the Parliament.

The Committee has power:

(a)   to send for persons, papers and records, to sit notwithstanding any adjournment of the House, to adjourn from place to place, and to report from time to time;

(b)   to appoint specialist advisers either to supply information which is not readily available or to elucidate matters of complexity within the Committee's order of reference;

(c)   to communicate to any other committee or sub-committee appointed under the same Standing Order (and to the European Scrutiny Committee, to the Committee of Public Accounts, to the Deregulation Committee and to the Environmental Audit Committee) its evidence and any other documents relating to matters of common interest;

(d)   to meet concurrently with any other committee or sub-committee appointed under the same Standing Order for the purposes of deliberating, taking evidence, or considering draft reports, or with the European Scrutiny Committee or any of its sub-committees for the purpose of deliberating or taking evidence.

The membership of the Committee is as follows:

Mr Bruce George   Mr Jimmy Hood
Mr Crispin Blunt   Mr Mike Hancock CBE
Mr Julian Brazier TD   Mr John McWilliam
Mr Jamie Cann   Mrs Laura Moffatt
Mr Harry Cohen   Ms Dari Taylor
Mr Michael Colvin

Mr Bruce George was elected Chairman on 16 July 1997

Mr Menzies Campbell was discharged, and Mr Mike Hancock was added, on 1 February 1999.

TABLE OF CONTENTS

Page

THIRD REPORT

The Defence Committee has agreed to the following Report:—

THE FUTURE OF NATO: THE WASHINGTON SUMMIT

INTRODUCTION

1. 4th April 1999 marks the fiftieth anniversary of the signature of the North Atlantic Treaty, the basis for the establishment of the North Atlantic Treaty Organisation (NATO). NATO will celebrate its anniversary at a Summit to be held in Washington DC on 24th and 25th April 1999. This Summit should be marked by the publication of NATO's new Strategic Concept, a document which will outline NATO's purpose, missions and roles and from which NATO's future military planning will be derived.

2. At the time at which we agreed this Report (31st March), NATO forces had been engaged in air strikes against the armed forces of the Federal Republic of Yugoslavia for a week. The purpose of Operation Allied Force is, in the words of the Foreign Secretary, to prevent—

> ... the present humanitarian crisis from becoming a catastrophe ... by taking military action to limit the capacity of Milosevic's army to repress the Kosovar Albanians.[1]

The UK is among 14 NATO nations currently contributing to NATO operations in support of United Nations (UN) resolutions in the Balkan region. This operation is the culmination of ten months' work by NATO and the international community to attempt to find a peaceful and lasting solution to the problems of Kosovo, including diplomatic efforts, enhanced Partnership for Peace activities with Albania and the former Yugoslav Republic of Macedonia, air demonstrations over the region and the deployment of an extraction force to safeguard unarmed international verifiers in Kosovo. Operation Allied Force, in pursuit of humanitarian goals, represents the first instance in its 50–year history of NATO military action against an independent state.

3. The future form and outcome of NATO's actions in the Balkans is uncertain, and it would be inappropriate for us to draw wider conclusions at this juncture. However, current events have thrown into sharp relief many of the pressing questions that NATO faces at the Washington Summit. Kosovo provides a compelling example of instability on the borders of NATO and of the type of conflict in which NATO may expect to become more involved in the future. While ground troops have been deployed to the region, as yet none have been involved in either combat or confrontation. It is possible, however, that we shall in the near future see NATO troops deployed within the Federal Republic of Yugoslavia in support of any peace deal, as presently envisaged by NATO, and it is at that point that it will become clear whether or not the lessons of NATO's involvement in Bosnia and Herzegovina have been learned.[2] However, there are those who argue that ground troops will have to be deployed against opposition in pursuit of NATO's military goals. The debate on NATO's mandate for such operations, until now mainly theoretical, has been overtaken by events; although it still rages between those who would wish to see an unambiguous UN mandate for NATO's actions and those who are satisfied that, as 'an exceptional measure to prevent an overwhelming humanitarian catastrophe',[3] the operation is justified under international law.

4. NATO can now peer into its future by examining the present. The political and the military lessons of recent and current operations in Former Yugoslavia are already beginning to be learned, and they may have to be brought to bear on the drafting of the new Strategic Concept. We must hope that the Washington Summit is not completely hijacked by the Kosovo crisis, however grave it is, and however critical the juncture it may have reached by the end of April. It would be regrettable if NATO planners were forced to delay the preparation of the new Strategic Concept. However, there are many competing and pressing demands for attention

---

[1] HC Deb 25 March 1999, c 538

[2] See eg First Report, Session 1997–98, *Peace Support Operations in Bosnia and Herzegovina*, HC 403

[3] MoD document *Legal Basis for Operation ALLIED FORCE*, available on the Internet at www.mod.gov/news/kosovo/legal.htm

currently faced by NATO's International Staff. It will be for the Heads of Government to decide whether the new Strategic Concept can be fully promulgated at the Summit, but NATO will still need to map a path to the future.

5. The North Atlantic Alliance was founded in April 1949 to counter the power and influence of the Soviet Union and to provide mutual defence guarantees to its members. Its founding members were Belgium, Canada, Denmark, France, Iceland, Italy, Luxembourg, the Netherlands, Norway, Portugal, the United Kingdom and the United States; Greece and Turkey joined the Alliance in 1952, the Federal Republic of Germany in 1955 and Spain in 1982. The Washington Summit will also be the first Summit that the Czech Republic, Hungary and Poland will have attended as full members of the Alliance since their accession on 12th March 1999. NATO invited these countries to become members of the Alliance at its Madrid Summit in July 1997. Between that time and the formal ratification of the protocols of enlargement by NATO's member states, intensive debate occurred about the merits and disadvantages of this and further enlargement of the Alliance.

6. The Defence Committee's contribution to that debate was an extensive inquiry into NATO enlargement. The Committee reported its findings to Parliament in March of last year.[4] Our Report outlined the run–up to enlargement, noting that the possibilities for Central and Eastern European countries of becoming full members had led to real improvements in the security of Europe as a whole, by providing incentives for these countries to improve the structure and control of their militaries, to enhance democracy and to resolve border disputes and internal problems with ethnic minorities.[5] We recognised the misgivings that Russia has about enlargement, but concluded that in this case they were outweighed by those advantages.[6] We approved the choice of candidates,[7] but urged that any further enlargement should be approached with caution.[8] The Report also discussed the financial ramifications of enlargement, concluding that, despite widely varying estimates of cost, enlargement offered value for money.[9]

7. After the publication of our Report into enlargement, we agreed to continue our inquiry into the future of NATO to consider the development of NATO's new Strategic Concept and the prospects for further enlargement, with the intention of publishing a Report to inform Parliament before the Washington Summit. In this Report we explore the purpose of a new Strategic Concept; NATO's new roles and missions and its mandate for those missions; NATO's relationships with other international organisations and with non–NATO countries; the development of a European Security and Defence Identity (ESDI) within NATO; and the progress of the current round of enlargement together with the prospects for further accessions to the Alliance.

8. This Report looks at issues likely to be debated at the Washington Summit, and the conclusions likely to emerge within either the new Strategic Concept or the Washington Declaration. We consider the strategic issues that underpin the need for a new Strategic Concept, and ask how NATO should formalise its new roles and missions and what priority it should accord its 'traditional' self-defence function. We evaluate the debate on the transatlantic relationship, examine new initiatives on European defence and discuss the implications of these for Europe, North America and the various security organisations of the Euro–Atlantic area. We explore the issue of NATO's global reach and discuss where it can expect to be involved in operations in the future, and examine the question of the mandate for NATO operations. We also examine the potential for NATO's outreach and cooperation programmes with its former Cold War adversaries and those countries who now aspire to NATO membership. We will look at the process that led up to the accession of NATO's new members and discuss how the Washington Summit is likely to address the hopes and concerns of the remaining aspirant members. This Report is addressed primarily to Parliament and the UK government, but we hope that a wider

---

[4]Third Report, Session 1997–98, *NATO Enlargement*, HC 469
[5]*ibid*, para 33
[6]*ibid*, para 42
[7]*ibid*, para 98
[8]*ibid*, para 108
[9]*ibid*, para 88

readership will find it useful. **The debate on defence and security issues, both within Parliament and the media, is often muted and sometimes ill-informed, and has been for many years now. The future shape and scope of NATO is fundamental to the future stability and security of the UK, Europe and the world at large. It should be of concern to us all. We hope that Parliament will be given an opportunity to debate this issue in advance of the departure of Ministers to the Washington Summit.**

9. Over the last six months we have taken formal evidence from the Secretary of State for Defence, the Minister of State for Foreign and Commonwealth Affairs, officials of both the Ministry of Defence (MoD) and the Foreign and Commonwealth Office (FCO) and experts in peacekeeping operations and academics. Following on from our formal meetings with the Prime Minister and Minister of Foreign Affairs of the Republic of Hungary and the Polish Minister of National Defence during our last inquiry, we took formal evidence from the Minister of Foreign Affairs of the Republic of Slovakia and the Chairman of the Bulgarian National Assembly's Foreign Policy Committee. We have met informally with many others to discuss NATO's future, including Ambassador Thomas Graham of the Lawyers' Alliance for World Security. In November we divided into two delegations and visited Bulgaria, Hungary, Romania and Slovenia; in January we visited Paris, NATO Headquarters and the Supreme Headquarters Allied Powers Europe; and in March we visited the Federal Republic of Germany, the Russian Federation and Ukraine. Our itineraries are published as annexes to this Report. The Ministry of Defence, academics and other interested parties provided us with written submissions, many of which are published with this Report. We are most grateful to the many people who have assisted us with this inquiry, including our specialist advisers: Professor Michael Clarke of the Centre for Defence Studies, King's College London; Rear Admiral Richard Cobbold of the Royal United Services Institute; Professor Keith Hartley of the Centre for Defence Economics, University of York; Dr Beatrice Heuser of the Department of War Studies, King's College London; Dr Colin McInnes of the Department of International Politics, University of Wales Aberystwyth; and Mr James Sherr of the Conflict Studies Research Centre, Royal Military Academy Sandhurst.

NATO'S NEW STRATEGIC CONCEPT

Why a new Strategic Concept?

10. 1989, the year of NATO's fortieth anniversary, saw the end of the post-war division of Europe and the Cold War. NATO's reaction to the change in Europe's security situation was contained in the 1990 London Declaration on a Transformed Atlantic Alliance, followed by the adoption at the 1991 Rome Summit of the Alliance's New Strategic Concept. Nearly ten years on, the political, economic and security situation in Europe has again changed beyond any prediction. Many of these changes were outlined by the Committee in our Report on the government's Strategic Defence Review last year,[10] and it would be superfluous to repeat them here. NATO can take much of the credit for the positive changes in Europe's security environment.[11] Over the past years it has embarked on initiatives aimed at increasing stability and security—such as the Euro-Atlantic Partnership Council (EAPC), Partnership for Peace (PfP), the NATO-Russia Founding Act and the NATO-Ukraine Charter—well beyond those envisaged in 1991. NATO has become, in the words of the Prime Minister at the opening of a recent Royal United Services Institute (RUSI) Conference celebrating NATO's 50th anniversary, an "exporter of stability"[12] and it made possible the Dayton Peace agreement which brought an end to the civil war in Bosnia and Herzegovina.[13] So it is that, in the words of the MoD's Policy Director, the 1991 Strategic Concept is now looking "highly dated".[14] It did, however, point to a number of the new directions that NATO has subsequently taken, and—

> ... was not a bad response at the time because exactly how the world was going to develop was not entirely clear.[15]

The Alliance resolved at the Madrid Summit to devise a new Strategic Concept, to be valid for the next ten to fifteen years; the drafting process is still going on[16] and the new Strategic Concept is to be adopted at the Washington Summit. Events in Kosovo will influence the debate and may delay its adoption.

11. Amid all the remarkable changes of the past eight years, two trends stand out as particularly important to Europe's security. One is the increasing tendency for the United States to pursue its interests unilaterally where it has become frustrated with its allies, disillusioned with the limited operational competence and political compromises of the United Nations,[17] and when it is fired with an urgency to take on international problems, such as the proliferation of weapons of mass destruction within Iraq and North Korea. This has had an increasing impact on NATO's strategic environment, and has shaped the terms of debate within the Alliance about the future of the 'transatlantic bargain', burden–sharing, military structures, new roles for the Alliance, and much besides. NATO's response has been to work towards reconfiguration around a new self–image: that of 'separable but not separate' capabilities for the European and North Atlantic Allies. The Alliance's development of a European Security and Defence Identity is discussed further below.[18]

12. The other major trend is Russia's fluctuating response to collective Western security policies. The best prediction that can be made about Russia is that it will remain unpredictable. It is still an open question as to whether Russia's humiliated armed forces will be reconciled to the civil state and reformed, whether they will melt away into private enterprise and criminal pursuits, or whether they will become a focal point for domestic and regional instability. Dr Mark Smith of the Conflict Studies Research Centre outlined for us four possibilities for Russia's future: the optimistic, that Russia will become a fully functioning market democracy;

---

[10]Eighth Report, Session 1997–98, *The Strategic Defence Review*, HC 138
[11]Ev p 97
[12]Royal United Services Institute, 8–10.3.99. Conference website www.nato50otan.org
[13]See First Report, Session 1997–98, *Peace Support Operations in Bosnia and Herzegovina*, HC 403
[14]Q 6
[15]Q 6
[16]See paragraph 24
[17]Ev pp 102, 122
[18]See paras 62–95

the likely, that it will continue to 'muddle through'; the pessimistic, that it will disintegrate into its constituent parts; or the disastrous, that an undemocratic, aggressive, anti-Western regime will come to power.[19] Whatever political direction it takes, for the foreseeable future it is hardly likely that Russia will have the motive or the capability to resurrect conventional theatre–wide military threats to the Euro–Atlantic area;[20] indeed, we think it implausible that Russia would seek to threaten *any* of NATO's 19 members by military means. But we do not rule out the possibility that a less friendly Russia could, for example, apply pressure to Partner countries and reduce stability in NATO's area of concern.

13. NATO cannot and will not grant the one thing that would bolster Russia's great power aspirations—a veto over the decisions of the North Atlantic Council. Despite all the initiatives for consultation between Russia and the West—many of which have been successful, including the NATO–Russia Founding Act[21]—and despite numerous aid programmes that have aimed to help the domestic reform process along, there is only so much that Western powers can do directly to reverse its economic downturn and repair the disarray within its domestic politics. Some of Russia's political élite continue to hold to an agenda that inhibits cooperation with Europe and the USA. Events in Kosovo have reinforced these perceptions. Relations between NATO and Russia absorb considerable political resources, and are clearly central to the wider security of Europe. We discuss these issues further below.[22]

14. It should not, however, be taken that the post-Cold War period is the first to see major debates about NATO's roles and structures. The Alliance has a history of diffusing internal dissent using compromise, concession and, on occasion, fudge. We may see many of these techniques utilised in the coming formulation of the Alliance's new directions. Many current internal debates have their roots in the early days of the Alliance: the transatlantic burden sharing question (which we discuss further later in this Report[23]) has been revisited many times since 1960, when President Kennedy first raised the idea of a 'twin pillar' NATO. Often disagreements have been between the American and European powers, including differing views on the role of West Germany in the early 1950s. The blow to France of that country's rearmament and accession into the Alliance was softened by the prohibition imposed—and self-imposed—on German development of weapons of mass destruction. Later that decade Europe had serious doubts on the apparent US monopoly on nuclear decision-making; again the eventual solution was a compromise. US missiles were deployed to Italy, Turkey and the UK under a 'dual key' arrangement and the strategy of flexible conventional and nuclear response was adopted to accommodate differing US and European interests.

15. The out-of-area debate is also nothing new. Though today often characterised as the US pushing to extend NATO's reach with the Europeans dragging their feet, initially the American Allies were ranged against the Europeans' desire to reassert control over former spheres of influence. For example, Portugal attempted to incorporate its African territories within the NATO area. We discuss the current out-of-area debate further below.[24] There have also been many internal divisions about action taken by Allies outwith the Alliance, from the Suez through Vietnam to the Gulf.[25]

NATO's Strategic Interests

16. The definition of NATO's broad strategic interests that will be enshrined in the new Strategic Concept, will have to be debated before and at the Summit. Four factors stand out as key issues in this debate. First, NATO will have to continue to be capable of honouring its mutual territorial defence commitments under Article 5 of the North Atlantic Treaty,[26] now along

---

[19]Private briefing
[20]See Eighth Report, Session 1997–98, *op cit* para 106
[21]See para 98
[22]See paras 95–116
[23]Para 69
[24]Paras 58–61
[25]*NATO's Evolving Role from Cold War to the New Security Environment*, Mark Stenhouse, in Jane's NATO Handbook 1991–92
[26]See Appendix 1

a new set of borders after enlargement. This remains the Alliance's core function,[27] despite the fact that the Article 5 guarantee has never been triggered, and even though Article 5 threats are unlikely to come from the same source as they did in the past.

17. Second, NATO has a strategic interest in developing effective policies towards a very broad range of security challenges: from 'new' security issues, such as terrorism, information warfare or the proliferation of weapons of mass destruction, including to sub-state groups; through contingencies such as the need to provide crisis management, humanitarian aid or provide forces to enforce or monitor peace deals, such as we may see in Kosovo;[28] to enabling cooperation on issues such as the need to deal with environmental degradation or the military implications of the 'millennium bug' as contributions to stability in countries outside the Alliance that are important to European security. We examined the issues of asymmetric threats, the Revolution in Military Affairs and Information Warfare in our Report on the Strategic Defence Review.[29] It is clear that NATO will have to develop strategies to address these developments. It is evident that there have been differing views over how far NATO should go in these directions. However, NATO will in the longer term have to grapple with the problem of how broad a range of security concerns it is prepared to take on, and what resources its members are prepared to devote to them. Although the Alliance must maintain its ability to provide collective defence for all its members, their territorial integrity seems unlikely to be directly threatened in the near to medium term future, and coping with the other diverse challenges to European stability and prosperity will be an immediate preoccupation.

18. Third, NATO must develop a firm strategic purpose along its borders: NATO has policies in relation to individual countries and in dealing with their requests for membership, but it is difficult to discern a strategic purpose in terms of policies towards the sub-regions of Europe, in particular, and most urgently, the Balkans. However, the Alliance cannot afford to allow the current focus on its eastern borders (where most of its new members are likely to come from) to distract it from its other borders.

19. The current crisis in Kosovo indicates the continuing instability of south eastern Europe and the increasingly evident dangers of destabilisation spreading into the Former Yugoslav Republic of Macedonia, Albania and even further afield, perhaps as far as the former Soviet Union territories. This raises the risk igniting old conflicts between other states in the region.[30] This crisis demonstrates even more vividly than the 1992–95 Bosnian war that instability in one part of Europe constitutes a threat to European peace in general.

20. NATO has already established a strategic purpose to the North and South of its membership area. Although recently emphasis has shifted towards the 'arc of crisis' encompassing the Balkans and middle East, and NATO's interaction with the South has slowed somewhat, a new approach has been outlined towards the Western Mediterranean to help maintain stability in North Africa and address the immediate security concerns of France, Spain and Italy;[31] in the Eastern Mediterranean NATO's purpose is to contain tensions which threaten its unity.[32] The recent rebuff of Turkey by the European Union makes the former's relationship with and engagement within NATO all the more important. Our predecessor Committee looked at many of these issues in the last Parliament[33] and emphasised the importance of NATO's dialogue with its southern neighbours, including military cooperation and liaison.[34] NATO will clearly have to continue its efforts to engage in the Mediterranean region, particularly in the light of increased instability in the Balkans.

---

[27]Ev p 89

[28]QQ 356–399

[29]Eighth Report, Session 1997–98, *ibid*, paras 164–172

[30]QQ 374

[31]NATO's Mediterranean Dialogue: Brussels Summit Communiqué 8.12.98, para 10. The non-NATO states participating in the Mediterranean Dialogue are Egypt, Israel, Jordan, Mauritania, Morocco and Tunisia

[32]See also *NATO's Role in the Mediterranean*, Report by the Mediterranean Special Group of the NAA, 25.8.97, available on the Internet via www.naa.be, and Defence Committee's Third Report, Session 1995–96, *NATO's Southern Flank*, HC 300

[33]Third Report, Session 1995–96, *op cit*

[34]*ibid*, para 41

21. In the North, the effects of the end of the Cold War have certainly been felt, though in the context where Norway and its Scandinavian partners still have to live close to an overwhelmingly bigger power—Russia. NATO's strategic purpose in relation to Northern Europe remains consistent, and its strategic interests are little changed from the days of the Cold War, though they can be pursued in a rather more relaxed way at present. Nevertheless, the delicacy of addressing issues surrounding the future security of the Baltic states should not be underestimated. NATO's relations with the other non-aligned states in this area—Finland and Sweden—must also be handled with great care. The trend of events in the Northern region may—in the light of NATO's 'open door' policy—demand resolution in more definite terms in the not too distant future.

22. Fourth, NATO must remain capable of managing security in Europe. NATO's role in building a solid security order across the continent is central, but not exclusive. As the Supreme Allied Commander Europe (SACEUR) described to the audience at the recent RUSI conference on NATO's 50th Anniversary,[35] the range of actors with which NATO is required to cooperate has vastly increased since the end of the Cold War. It must therefore provide the necessary cement to keep its members bound together in a deepening 'security community', while helping them individually to work with other security organisations, individual countries and groups of countries, for the benefit of European security as a whole. This is a far more challenging task than was the case during the Cold War as the rationale for NATO is extended beyond collective defence, in a continent of multi-layered and overlapping security arrangements. Failure to meet this challenge would be just as serious as a failure to address any of the other three broad security interests mentioned above.

23. The MoD outlined the government's overall approach to the drafting of the new Strategic Concept in a memorandum to the Committee, reiterating comments made following our Report on the Strategic Defence Review. The government, we were told, wishes to see a NATO which—

- embodies and maintains the transatlantic relationship;
- prevents renationalisation of defence;
- contributes to managing other key relationships and engages Russia;
- remains an effective and flexible military instrument for dealing with threats and challenges to our security;
- through engagement with other countries in the region, spreads stability and democratic values; and
- acts as Allies' primary forum for consultation on all issues of security concern.[36]

Process of drafting the new Strategic Concept

24. The Council in Permanent Session—made up of Allied countries' permanent representatives in Brussels—was tasked at NATO's Madrid Summit with examining and updating as necessary the 1991 Strategic Concept, with the assumption that the resulting work would—

> ... confirm our commitment to the core function of Alliance collective defence and the indispensable transatlantic link.[37]

In the autumn of 1997, terms of reference were developed, which were approved in the ministerial meetings of the North Atlantic Council that December. The process itself involved the identification of passages in the 1991 Strategic Concept that were in need of 'updating' because they had been rendered obsolescent by changes in the strategic environment or subsequent events. There followed a long series of 'brainstorming' sessions, as a result of which a draft of a revised Strategic Concept was presented by the International Staff in the late summer

---

[35]Speech at the Royal United Services Institute, 9 March 1999
[36]Ev p 89
[37]Madrid Declaration, para 19

of last year.[38] The final document is intended to provide a clear guide as to the Alliance's purpose for the next ten to fifteen years, as well as to guide NATO's central military planners in the drafting of their major planning document.

25. While originally most members had pleaded for minimal revisions, stressing the remit of 'updating *as necessary*', enthusiasm for a much more thorough revision grew markedly in some quarters, particularly as several fundamental issues were raised. These include:[39]

- the balance between 'old [Cold War] missions' and 'new [post-Cold War] missions', or, in the words of Sir Michael Alexander, the balance between collective defence and collective security missions;

- the mandate under which NATO might take action, other than in a clear Article 5 situation;

- the definition of the area in which NATO might in future operate;

- relations with non-members of NATO;

- the structural adaptation of NATO to new missions and enlargement; and

- the strengthening of a European Security and Defence Identity (ESDI) within NATO.

We discuss these issues more fully below.

---

[38]Private briefing, NATO HQ
[39]Ev p 119

NATO'S NEW ROLES AND MISSIONS

The New Roles

THE BALANCE BETWEEN THE OLD AND NEW ROLES

26. Article 5 of the Alliance's founding document, the North Atlantic Treaty,[40] has always been at the very core of the Alliance,[41] committing the Allies to agreement that—

> ... an armed attack against one or more of them ... shall be considered an attack against them all.

The Foreign Office told us that—

> There will be no dilution, obviously, of the Article 5 element envisaged in the Strategic Concept, but there will be some discussion and paragraphs concerning the sorts of actions outside Article 5 in which NATO might anticipate being involved in the future.[42]

The necessity of NATO continuing to have an Article 5 capability was described by the US Deputy Secretary of State—

> NATO must maintain its capability to deter, and if necessary defeat, what might be called classic aggression. Even though such a threat does not exist today, two facts remain: first, it could arise in the future; but, second, it is less likely to do so if NATO remains robust and ready.[43]

In the past the Organisation's energies were directed to having the military capacity to fulfil its Article 5 commitments with its strategy and force structure designed to repel a Soviet attack on its territorial integrity. This is a scenario which now "does not form part of [NATO's] day to day thinking",[44] and all commentators agree that in the future—

> NATO ... will find itself ... having to deal more with non–Article 5 problems than with Article 5 itself.[45]

Hence NATO's attention is becoming increasingly focussed on crisis management involving military actions in support of the *interests* of the Allies (under Article 6 of the Treaty) or to ameliorate humanitarian crises. NATO is therefore moving in a similar direction to the UK in the post–Cold War world; as the Secretary of State said in his introduction to the SDR, 'we must be prepared to go to the crisis, rather than have the crisis come to us'.[46] Issues such as the nature of NATO's 'core' and 'peripheral' military missions and defence planning processes for these missions have been crucial in the formulation of the new Strategic Concept. As we were told by the MoD's policy director—

> ... there is a quite animated theological debate going on about just how much emphasis is placed on which mission and what the practical consequences of that are.[47]

27. The Foreign and Commonwealth Office's Director of International Security told us that the new Strategic Concept should "encapsulate the idea of NATO as an all–purpose organisation for dealing with security challenges relevant to Europe".[48] He later said that, in relation to the new Strategic Concept—

---

[40]See Appendix 1
[41]Ev p 89
[42]Q 3
[43]Royal United Services Institute, 10 March 1999
[44]Q 11
[45]Q 288
[46]The Strategic Defence Review, *Modern Forces for a Modern World*, Cm 3999
[47]Q 12
[48]Q 3

I think NATO will avoid, for example, any attempt to define a geographical area or a particular size or nature of a conflict which will automatically call for or rule out a NATO response. I think it will include a lot of generic language about the sort of situations, challenges to regional securities, threats to stability, humanitarian situations which could promote a NATO response.[49]

28. Within NATO, the eastern states, including the three new members, are particularly concerned about the possibility of erosion of the mutual defence function of the Alliance.[50] The MoD's Policy Director told us that—

For very understandable reasons the three invitees show a strong interest in the collective security dimension,

(but that, "I have not seen them avoiding the new missions".[51]) Other states want to see non–Article 5 activities given the same strategic emphasis as territorial defence, or to see new activities which could fall under Article 5 but have not featured previously given greater prominence, such as measures to counter the proliferation of weapons of mass destruction, or combatting terrorism.

29. Sir Michael Alexander told us that much of the debate can be boiled down to two diverging requirements on NATO, one to provide for collective defence, the other to provide for collective security measures. There remains a concern that NATO is currently straddling two horses which are vigorously pulling in opposite directions,[52] and that even the most skilful and inventive riders will not be able to stay on top of both indefinitely. However, not all of NATO's non–Article 5 activities will necessarily be military–led; Dr Beatrice Heuser told us that such tasks could include outreach activity, the projection of stability through the Euro–Atlantic area and the exchange of information with non–Allies.[53] These tasks have not been forced on NATO,[54] and many are not 'new'. We have seen the UK armed forces progressively be reconfigured to provide capability for a wide range of tasks, and hope that NATO forces will be able to demonstrate a similar flexibility. We were encouraged by the Minister of State at the Foreign and Commonwealth Office's statement that—

We are coming now to a sensible balance between the ['old' and 'new' roles], which is based on the pragmatic role that NATO will have.[55]

We wish to see the new Strategic Concept outline a new direction for NATO for the years ahead. New roles must be outlined and prioritised. The changing security environment means that new challenges must be faced, and new roles and responsibilities taken on. NATO has already done well to reconfigure itself to meet post–Cold War challenges. However, its core function of territorial defence must not be undermined by its new missions, and NATO must retain its military capability to fulfil Article 5 tasks, however remote such threats may seem.

NATO's Force Structure

Conventional Forces

30. Sir Michael Alexander also told us that—

... the military requirements of the two roles [of collective defence and collective security] are different: over a period providing the force structures, the planning and the equipment

---

[49]Q 59
[50]Ev p 95
[51]Q 16
[52]Q 103
[53]Q 111
[54]Q 111
[55]Q 292

needed for crisis management and humanitarian tasks will tend to downgrade the provision made for defence tasks.[56]

31. However, the Policy Director of the MoD told us that—

... as we concluded in our national debate about the Strategic Defence Review, for the foreseeable future the types of forces that we believe are necessary both for ... a collective defence scenario and for responding to crises on the periphery ... are the same ... essentially.[57]

NATO is undergoing the same debate on so–called 'high intensity' versus 'low intensity' capabilities that the UK faced during its Strategic Defence Review. On that question, we concluded that, despite the changed nature of operations in which the UK is likely to become involved—

... it is essential to retain well–equipped forces capable of fighting and winning in the most demanding types of conflict.[58]

The same conclusion, that we must retain the capability to engage in high-intensity warfare as well as to participate in less intensive operations, is applicable to NATO's force structure, although we regretfully may have to accept that some members will continue to have conscript forces primarily configured for Article 5 operations that will not be deployable for less intensive operations.

32. The MoD described the military capabilities the Alliance must have available to it to fulfil the full range of its new missions. In particular its forces need to—

> ► be structured, trained and equipped for combined, joint missions;

> ► be held at readiness levels which will allow the full range of missions to be undertaken in a timely manner;

> ► have the sustainability necessary to support extended and possibly concurrent operations; and

> ► be structured to permit, where necessary, longer term military capability to be built up by reinforcement, regeneration and reconstitution.[59]

These are very similar to the capabilities required of the UK armed forces under the SDR. **We are encouraged to note from our meetings with them that many of our Allies have observed with approval the reconfiguration of the British armed forces since the end of the Cold War and the SDR; and that many are either actively reconfiguring their armed forces for precisely the types of capability that NATO is likely to require in future, or putting in hand review processes which are likely to lead to this conclusion. We hope that other Allies will follow.** As the MoD told us, while retaining an overall capability—

The Alliance should continue to plan for the full range of missions through a single defence planning process and a single spectrum of military capabilities,[60]

---

[56]Ev p 119·
[57]Q 14
[58]Eighth Report, Session 1997–98, *op cit* para 205
[59]Ev p 89
[60]Ev p 89

33. The new Strategic Concept's definition of NATO's future roles will feed into NATO's defence planning[61] via the revision of the Alliance's top–level, central military planning document (the current one being MC400/1). **Thus the new Strategic Concept must provide a clear steer as to the capabilities required by the Alliance over the next ten to fifteen years.**

34. NATO has already been moving towards a more mobile, joint and modern force structure, for example through its Combined Joint Task Force (CJTF) concept.[62] A new Command Structure for NATO is to be implemented in 2002–03. It will involve a major reconfiguration of commands, including a reduction from 65 headquarters to 20, designed to deliver better joint operations. Two strategic commands, Strategic Command Europe, based in Mons, and Strategic Command Atlantic, based in Norfolk, Virginia, are responsible for overall planning and direction and conduct of all Allied activities within their areas. Strategic Command Europe will have two subordinate regional commands, Regional Command North, based in Brunssum, and Regional Command South, based in Naples; Strategic Command Atlantic has three, Regional Command West, also based in Norfolk, Regional Command SouthEast, based in Lisbon and Regional Command East, based in Northwood. Reporting to the Regional Commands in Europe are eleven Component Commands and Joint Sub-Regional Commands (including Component Command Nav North based in Northwood). Reporting to SC Atlantic are two additional headquarters, HQ STRIKFLTLANT and HQ SUBACLANT. Significant force reductions, including a 25 per cent reduction in the total number of Alliance ground combat units, a reduction of over 45 per cent in the peacetime strength of NATO's land forces in the Central Region, a reduction of over 10 per cent in the number of naval combat units assigned to NATO and a decrease of over 25 per cent in the total number of combat aircraft assigned to NATO have been made.[63] NATO has moved from its original 'layer cake' strategy of deploying international corps along the former inner German border. According to General Klaus Naumann, the Chairman of the Military Committee—

The overriding imperative in developing a new structure was that it be mission oriented. It needed to provide NATO with the capability to cope with the full range of Alliance roles and missions, from its traditional mission of collective defence to new roles in changing circumstances.[64]

We approve the Alliance's moves towards restructuring its forces for the modern world; as the Secretary of State for Defence said—

... it is only by getting force planning right that we give ourselves the option of really being a force for good in the world.[65]

35. But while applauding the modernisation initiative, we note that under the process the UK has lost a major Command: Allied Command Channel. Nevertheless, the command of the Allied Command Europe Rapid Reaction Corps (ARRC), the sharing of the posts of DSACEUR and Chief of Staff at SHAPE with Germany, and the UK's holding of the post of DSACLANT[66] should ensure that the UK continues to have a strong and appropriate influence on the Alliance's military structure.

---

[61] Q 24

[62] CJTFs are intended to facilitate crisis management and peace support operations by providing the necessary flexibility for short-notice deployment of specifically-tailored forces.

[63] NATO Factsheet: NATO's New Force Structures

[64] *NATO's New Military Command Centre*, General Klaus Naumann, in NATO Review, Spring 1998

[65] Speech at the Royal United Services Institute, 10 March 1999

[66] Letter from MoD, 5 March 1999

NATO's Nuclear Posture

36. Nuclear weapons remain a key element of NATO's strategy. Alliance nuclear policy since 1977 *had* been to ensure that nuclear weapons in NATO's armoury were held to the minimum number necessary for deterrence.[67] All decisions on nuclear capabilities were taken with an eye to the east: in 1983 Alliance policy was to—

> ... preserve the peace through the maintenance of forces at the lowest level capable of deterring the Warsaw Pact threat.[68]

However, by the dying days of the Cold War, the Alliance's 1989 *Comprehensive Concept of Arms Control and Disarmament*[69] was arguing that—

> ... the fundamental purpose of nuclear forces—both strategic and sub–strategic—is political: to preserve the peace and to prevent any kind of war.[70]

Although under START I and in the context of the 1991 Strategic Concept nuclear forces have been greatly reduced, and their role less emphasised, this valuation of the Alliance's nuclear forces as essentially political has prevailed to this day,[71] and the 1991 Strategic Concept reiterated that—

> The fundamental purpose of the nuclear forces of the Allies is political: to preserve peace and to prevent coercion and any kind of war.[72]

37. The redrafting of the Strategic Concept has been seen by some, including the new German government, as an opportunity for the Alliance to reassess its nuclear policy in the light of the changed strategic circumstances. Some proponents of disarmament argue that while nuclear weapons are irrelevant to most of the threats that NATO may now face, nuclear proliferation might yet pose a threat to Allied countries. They argue therefore that non–proliferation should be paramount among NATO's security objectives, and that NATO's emphasis on the political value of nuclear weapons is counter–productive. Ambassador Thomas Graham of the Lawyers' Alliance for World Security argued that the goal of non–proliferation could be best pursued by NATO lowering the political importance of nuclear weapons by adopting a 'no first use of nuclear weapons' policy.[73]

38. However, declared policy on the use of nuclear weapons may in fact be secondary to the question of how the Alliance, no member of which possesses chemical or biological weapons, would respond to any attack on its territory with these categories of weapons, although it is possible that any such attack would not come directly from another state. One proposal is to adopt a 'no first use of Weapons of Mass Destruction' policy (which would allow NATO a nuclear response if attacked with chemical or biological weapons). Ambassador Graham in a meeting with the Committee argued that for NATO to attack with nuclear weapons any of the non–nuclear states that are signatories to the Nuclear Non-Proliferation Treaty (NPT)[74] would

---

[67]*NATO's Evolving Role from Cold War to the New Security Environment*, Mark Stenhouse, in Jane's NATO Handbook 1991–92

[68]The Montebello Decision, October 1983

[69]Adopted by the Heads of State and Government at the meeting of the North Atlantic Council in Brussels May 29-30, 1989

[70]Comprehensive Concept of Arms Control and Disarmament, para 23

[71] NATO's strategy is no longer centred on the possibility of the nuclear escalation of conventional war, or directed against a specific threat. Between 1991 and 1993, NATO reduced the number of sub–strategic weapons available for forces in Europe by 80%; under START I and II, the Alliance's strategic weapons will also be vastly reduced. NATO declared in 1996 that it had no intention, no plan and no reason to deploy nuclear weapons on the territory of new member countries, nor any need to change any aspect of NATO's nuclear posture or nuclear policy, and that it did not foresee any future need to do so.

[72]1991 Strategic Concept, paragraph 54

[73]This idea has also been pursued by the German Foreign Minister, Joschka Fisher.

[74]The Nuclear Non-Proliferation Treaty (NPT) commits nuclear weapon states to engage in disarmament and not to use, or threaten to use, their nuclear weapons against non-nuclear signatories; and commits those non-nuclear signatories not to attempt to obtain nuclear arms. The nuclear weapon state signatories to the NPT are the UK, the US, France, Russia and China. India, Pakistan, Cuba and Israel have not signed the NPT.

be in violation of the legal obligations of the UK, the US and France under the NPT. He suggested that such a policy was likely to damage non–proliferation efforts.[75] Ambassador Graham pointed out that under international law, responses must be proportionate and the provision under international law of belligerent response could apply under which international commitments are waived once there has been such an attack, thereby not negating the case for a declared policy of no first use of nuclear weapons.

39. However, the Secretary of State for Defence argued that a declaration of no first use—

> might actually be the opposite of encouraging or reassuring and might detract from the concept of deterrence. Deterrence is essentially based on the doubt that is in any potential aggressor's mind, which has to be kept as uncertain as possible. A declaration of "no first use" would simplify any potential aggressor's planning because the clear implication would be that that potential aggressor could mount a substantial conventional, or a chemical or biological assault, without any fear of a nuclear response. So to add that into it would, we believe, be more dangerous than to leave the uncertainties that basically underpin the deterrent posture at the present moment.[76]

We only note that this doctrine of 'mutual uncertainty' requires both potential aggressors and NATO to live with the uncertainties about a potential attack by weapons of mass destruction and a potential nuclear response. In our report last year on the Strategic Defence Review, we recommended that the government restated and brought up to date the UK's strategic *and* sub-strategic nuclear strategy.[77] In its response, the government agreed that it should take an early opportunity to do so.[78] **We look forward to this statement, particularly if it clarifies the sub-strategic role of Trident**. However, the Secretary of State told us that he believed that a 'no first use' policy—

> ... might actually be the opposite of encouraging or reassuring ... [and] would simplify any aggressor's planning ... It was something we ruled out. Most of our Allies have also ruled that out.[79]

But he told us that NATO's review of its nuclear posture was ongoing and that—

> ... the Alliance after Washington should look, as we do, at existing nuclear posture; and make adjustments to some aspects of that to take into account contemporary circumstances.[80]

It seems that the debate about NATO's use of nuclear weapons policy among Allied nations has been resolved for the time being,[81] and that the policy will remain unchanged in the new Strategic Concept. **While we recognise that nuclear weapons remain central to NATO's strategy, the Alliance's nuclear policy will continue to evolve, and we welcome open debate upon it.**

40. Sir Michael Alexander wrote that—

> NATO would do well to follow the example of the SDR and, alongside a continuing reduction in the number of nuclear warheads deployed and in their potency, pursue a policy of greater transparency about the numbers, capabilities and roles envisaged. In the long run ... even greater transparency offers the best hope of controlling the dangers posed by military nuclear technology ... NATO should make "greater nuclear transparency" one of its slogans.[82]

---

[75]Ev p 113
[76]17 February 1999, Q 308
[77]Eight Report, Session 1997–98, *op cit*, para 152
[78]Sixth Special Report, Session 1997–98, *Government Response to the Eighth Report of the Defence Committee*, HC 1198, para 28
[79]Q 308
[80]Q 308
[81]Q 308
[82]Ev p 122

We agree that greater nuclear transparency by NATO could only be beneficial.

The New Missions

PEACE SUPPORT OPERATIONS

41. Peacekeeping and peace support operations are currently the most pressing and immediate challenges faced within NATO, with the Alliance embarking on military intervention in Kosovo. As well as having force structure repercussions, as discussed above, such missions offer—

> ... a highly practical way of integrating former Warsaw Treaty Organisation countries into NATO structures or restructuring their armed forces so as to be compatible with NATO forces, and this in itself is a major confidence and security building measure. It holds particularly true for relations with Russia.[83]

Neither NATO's Implementation Force (IFOR) nor its Stabilisation Force (SFOR) in Bosnia and Herzegovina[84] involved exclusively NATO forces, but for a variety of political reasons accommodated non–NATO (and in some cases even non–PfP member) forces. These included not only Russia, for which special command and information arrangements had to be devised in theatre,[85] but also contingents from Egypt, Jordan, Malaysia and Morocco.

42. Yet, while NATO's available capacity for projecting stability contains remarkable, but highly specialised weapons, beyond its military capability its competences for peacekeeping may be more limited. Our witnesses stressed the importance of the organisation recognising the limitations of such operations—

> Peacekeeping forces cannot pursue war–fighting goals, ... cannot deliver just solutions, ... cannot punish aggressors, ... cannot defend territory, ... cannot enforce passage of convoys everywhere all the time, ... cannot stop ethnic cleansing.[86]

One might add that NATO is not a channel of economic aid; it cannot generate large–scale employment, help restructure non-defence industries, support democratisation through grants to democratic political parties, send out social workers, or build multi–ethnic communities. It cannot police all the villages of Bosnia and Herzegovina, protect all returning refugees, or help integrate other ethnic minorities throughout Eastern Europe. NATO is not capable of making Eastern Europeans rich, of preventing reactionary movements in Russia, or of converting peoples to democracy whose culture has never experienced it in the past.

43. As the Secretary General of NATO has said, the Alliance is not the only player in the peace support game. The international community has to be involved in the Balkans in those areas where NATO is *not* competent—

> ... without such a comprehensive approach we will never get beyond treating the symptoms only. We must do more than protect the peace ... We must create the conditions for reconstruction, the climate for reconciliation ... That is why the entire Euro–Atlantic community—its nations and institutions—must become engaged ... In short, what the Balkans need is a 'Partnership for Prosperity'.[87]

---

[83]Evidence, not published
[84]See First Report, Session 1997–98, *op cit*
[85]Q 240
[86]Q 189
[87]Speech at the Royal United Services Institute, 9 March 1999

44. NATO can contribute to this comprehensive approach by creating an environment of stability in which these other things can happen. As our witnesses told us, what NATO can do by its presence as a peace support force is—

> ... first of all alleviate suffering ... [and] ultimately create the conditions in which there can be some peaceful settlement of the problem.[88]

But, as the Secretary General stressed, this mission only makes sense in a much wider political context; and it demands feats of cooperation and coordination which will prove quite as demanding, in their different way, as the requirements for waging total war. General Sir Michael Rose told us that—

> ... the tragedy for Bosnia ... is that NATO did not see it as part of its role in 1991 when it wrote its new strategic guidelines to get involved in peace support operations beyond the border of its member states. Today of course the situation is very different ...[89]

We expect to see the new Strategic Concept clearly outline NATO's competences for peace support operations and its plans for cooperation with other organisations to pursue lasting peace and stability in the Euro–Atlantic area. We note the important work being done by NATO on Infrastructure, Logistics and Civil Emergency Planning in working with humanitarian aid agencies and relevant government agencies, and hope that this work will be pursued further.

COUNTER-PROLIFERATION

45. It is likely that NATO of the future will become more involved in measures to counter the proliferation of weapons of mass destruction. The security threat to the Allies of proliferation was formally acknowledged by NATO in January 1994, and a decision was taken to intensify and expand NATO's political and defence efforts against proliferation. Yet very little tangible results have so far been seen.[90] Counter–proliferation is likely to be one of the topics to be touched upon in the new Strategic Concept. The Minister of State at the Foreign and Commonwealth Office told us that—

> Britain would be very supportive of ... a weapons of mass destruction initiative within the context of NATO. That essentially is about information exchange. It is about pooling the knowledge that NATO members may have.[91]

But he also pointed out that—

> There is also considerable activity taking place in different international fora in this whole area ... a lot of the important roles that need to be pursued ... will not be directly NATO responsibility because they are better done elsewhere.[92]

The US Deputy Secretary of State has outlined those areas where NATO does have a role—

> We must find better, more efficient, more timely ways of sharing information and assessments so that our troops are properly protected from an enemy equipped with nuclear, chemical and biological arms, and we must improve our ability to deal with the consequences of a WMD attack against our civilian populations.[93]

The Pentagon has suggested, for example, that Allies cooperate in the creation of databases listing vaccine stocks, protection suits and medical centres.[94]

---

[88] Q 189
[89] Q 194
[90] *New Threats Await NATO,* Defense News, Vol 14 No 11, 22 March 1999
[91] Q 306
[92] Q 306
[93] Royal United Services Institute, 10 March 1999
[94] *New Threats Await NATO,* Defense News, Vol 14 No 11, 22 March 1999

46. There is a certain ambiguity inherent in the phrase "non–proliferation": in NATO's sphere it applies mainly to in–theatre defence together with, as John Roper of Chatham House told us—

... what is described in our Strategic Defence Review as defence diplomacy.[95]

There have been concerns in some areas that NATO's taking on of a counter–proliferation mission would lead to creeping globalisation, including perhaps punitive strikes against those thought to be proliferators. For our part, **we are aware of the high risks of proliferation of weapons of mass destruction, and would support NATO's adoption of a non–proliferation mission. But NATO must be aware of the limitations of its role in counter-proliferation: its principal objective in this area should remain the more even-handed prevention, or reversal, of proliferation through diplomatic means and the support, rather than duplication, of the work of other international organisations.**

THE MANDATE QUESTION

47. NATO's movement from its traditional self defence role has opened up the question of its mandate for non–Article 5 operations. The overarching framework of international law for such operations remains the United Nations Charter—formulated in the very different world of 1946. While Article 5, self–defence operations would be legal under Article 51 of the UN Charter, the legal authority for other types of operation is more debatable. Article 39 of the UN Charter states—

The Security Council shall determine the existence of any threat to the peace, breach of the peace, or act of aggression and shall make recommendations, or decide what measures shall be taken in accordance with Articles 41 and 42, to maintain or restore international peace and security.

Article 41 deals with non-military sanctions. Article 42 states—

Should the Security Council consider that measures provided for in Article 41 would be inadequate or have proved to be inadequate, it may take such action by air, sea or land forces as may be necessary to maintain or restore international peace and security. Such action may include demonstrations, blockade, and other operations by air, sea or land forces of Members of the United Nations.

Chapter VII of the Charter (in which the above Articles appear) is qualified to an extent by Chapter VIII, which deals with 'Regional Arrangements'. Paragraph 1 of Article 52 states—

Nothing in the present Charter precludes the existence of regional arrangements or agencies for dealing with such matters relating to the maintenance of international peace and security as are appropriate for regional action, provided that such arrangements or agencies and their activities are consistent with the Purposes and Principles of the United Nations.

Paragraph 3 of that Article states—

The Security Council shall encourage the development of pacific settlement of local disputes through such regional arrangements or by such regional agencies either on the initiative of the states concerned or by reference from the Security Council.

And paragraph 1 of Article 53 states—

The Security Council shall, where appropriate, utilize such regional arrangements or agencies for enforcement action under its authority. But no enforcement action shall be taken under regional arrangements or by regional agencies without the authorization of the Security Council, with the exception of measures against any enemy state, as defined in paragraph 2 of this Article, provided for pursuant to Article 107 or in regional arrangements directed against

[95] Q 112

renewal of aggressive policy on the part of any such state, until such time as the Organization may, on request of the Governments concerned, be charged with the responsibility for preventing further aggression by such a state.

In its response to the Committee's SDR Report, the government comments—

The Government recognises that in certain circumstances regional security and cooperation bodies can play an important role in maintaining international peace and security. In other cases, it may be more appropriate for the UN to exercise these responsibilities directly. The Government attaches high priority to developing both UN and regional capabilities, but to attempt to produce a blue-print for the use of regional organisations by the UN would not be feasible given the unique nature of each situation and mandate. However, the UK is working very closely with other members of the UN to improve liaison with regional organisations.[96]

48. The Washington Treaty neither provides the specific authority for, nor expressly prohibits, non-Article 5 operations,[97] but its signatories have pledged—

... to refrain in their international relations from the threat or use of force in any manner inconsistent with the purposes of the United Nations.[98]

A further complication has arisen from the 1975 Helsinki Final Act and the creation of a new regional security organisation, the Conference on Security and Cooperation in Europe. At Oslo in 1992, NATO also stated its readiness to act on behalf of the CSCE, now the Organisation for Security and Cooperation in Europe (OSCE), as a regional authority under the UN Charter.

49. The MoD notes the British government position which is that—

All NATO operations must have a basis in international law. The legal basis required in any particular case will depend on the particular circumstances. Article 51 of the UN Charter recognises the inherent right of self-defence, which includes the right to seek aid from elsewhere; friendly nations can give such aid individually and collectively. In other cases, a UN Security Council Resolution under Chapter VII of the UN Charter may be necessary to authorise the use of force.[99]

The Minister of State at the Foreign and Commonwealth Office reiterated that—

... it is inconceivable that NATO would operate outside international law,[100]

but that—

... we are not saying that every form of military action has to be underpinned by a direct Security Council mandate,[101]

although such a mandate, according to the Secretary of State for Defence, "would probably be the ideal".[102]

50. Some Allies, notably France and Germany, have seemed eager to see NATO commit to only acting out–of–area, or to non–Article 5 operations, with the express mandate of the UN or OSCE; however, strong elements within the US administration and Congress appear to resent any such restrictions on NATO's freedom to act.[103] While the French Foreign Affairs Minister

---

[96]Sixth Special Report, Session 1997–98, *op cit*, para 27
[97]QQ 70, 71
[98]Article 1 (see Appendix 1)
[99]Ev p 89
[100]Q 295
[101]Q 294
[102]Q 302
[103]Ev p 122

insisted last December that all NATO missions calling for the use of force be placed under the authority of the UN, his US equivalent was stating that the Alliance must continue to have the right to take action on a case-by-case basis without UN Security Council authorisation.[104] The Foreign Secretary told the North Atlantic Council that—

> I am not sure that it would be wise to limit ourselves by writing a legal base, rather than by making sure that as an organisation we have the flexibility to respond to problems in the real world.[105]

51. Since November of last year, NATO's threatened air strikes on the Federal Republic of Yugoslavia, which were eventually activated on 24th March, were *not* expressly mandated by the UN Security Council[106] because of the consistent opposition of the governments of the Russian Federation and China. However, we were told by the Minister of State at the Foreign and Commonwealth Office that—

> ... under international law we have absolutely no doubts that there would have been a justification ... for action designed to alleviate and resolve that humanitarian crisis.[107]

and the Secretary of State reiterated in his evidence to us on Kosovo on 24 March that—

> ... the objective here we are confident is inside international law[108]

While we have been told that the US would like to view this as a precedent for future NATO action, in practice other Allies are unlikely to accept this as a clear cut case. **We concur.**

52. The issue of the subordination of NATO non–Article 5 operations to the UN (or OSCE) remains hotly contested among the Allies, as the statements of US Secretary of Defence Cohen and of German Chancellor Schröder at the *Wehrkunde* conference in Munich showed.[109] However, as the Secretary of State stressed to us in his evidence on Kosovo,[110] NATO cannot act collectively, or its collective resources be used in any operation, without the express consent of *all* Allied nations. It seems likely that a reiteration in the new Strategic Concept of NATO's commitment to operate within international law (without a mention of the UN) will be acceptable to both sides of the argument. This may appear to be a fudge, but each non–Article 5 operation will continue to be decided by the Allies on a case–by–case basis in future.[111] While we agree that 'the widest involvement of the UN ... is clearly desirable',[112] in practice, accepting that NATO should not act except in self defence without a UN Security Council mandate would mean accepting a Russian veto on NATO action—this would not be tolerable. **That NATO cannot act without the consent and agreement of all 19 of its members, each of which belongs to the UN and respects that organisation's philosophy, ought to ensure that any operation is legitimate under international law.** As the Secretary of State for Defence told us—

> As the Chairman of the Defence Council ... I have to have a legal base before I can order the bombers in or I am personally liable, ... a fairly onerous responsibility.[113]

---

[104]*The NATO Summit and its Implications for Europe*, report by Tom Cox MP submitted to the Assembly of the WEU
[105]Speech to the NAC, 8 December 1998
[106]Ev p 93
[107]Q 294
[108]Q 377
[109]*Europäische Sicherheit* vol. 43 no. 3 (March 1999)
[110]Q 356, Q 366
[111]QQ 293, 300
[112]Ev p 94
[113]Q 302

After NATO had taken the decision to conduct air strikes against the Federal Republic of Yugoslavia's armed forces, he again reinforced this point—

> ... speaking as I do on behalf of the United Kingdom and as Chairman of the Defence Council, I have a particular personal responsibility in this regard which would turn into a legal one if it came to it.[114]

KOSOVO

53. NATO has taken the international lead on the worsening crisis in Kosovo, drawing up its own resolutions in support of UN resolutions previously adopted. The danger of a Russian veto in referring matters relating to the Kosovo crisis back to the United Nations Security Council has encouraged the NATO powers to act on their own authority for subsequent attempts to resolve, or ameliorate, the current crisis. In its statement on 8th December 1998 the North Atlantic Council's Foreign Ministers cited UN Security Council Resolutions 1160, 1199 and 1203 as authority for NATO's continuing endeavours over Kosovo—the air verification mission (Operation Eagle Eye) and the build-up of the NATO-led Extraction Force (Operation Joint Guarantor).[115] These resolutions were again cited in the North Atlantic Council Defence Ministers' session of 17 December 1998,[116] and by the Secretary of State in his evidence to us on 24th March.[117]

54. Whatever the outcome of the Kosovo crisis, several features of NATO's role in it are innovative. Firstly, the command arrangements for the NATO-led force now assembling in Macedonia may depart from previous practice. The NATO-led force will be commanded by the Commander of the ACE Rapid Reaction Corps (ARRC) who is ultimately answerable to SACEUR, an American. It looks likely that for the first six months of its deployment, the ARRC will, in the first instance, be answerable to the major subordinate commander CINCSOUTH—also an American. If confirmed, then the command arrangements will be similar to those that were adopted during the initial IFOR deployment in Bosnia. Nevertheless, on this occasion the United Kingdom will be the single biggest contributor to a force in Kosovo and the proportion of US troops within the whole force will be somewhat lower than was the case in Bosnia. In this case, however, the commander of the Kosovo force (KFOR) will be the commander of the ARRC, General Sir Mike Jackson. At the theatre level, therefore, US troops will be under a NATO command which is led by a British officer and dominated by British HQ staff officers. Though not historically unique, this arrangement is out of the ordinary for contemporary US military deployments and may represent something of a model for the future.

55. A second innovation concerns the way the NATO force in the former Yugoslav Republic of Macedonia (FYROM) has been developed flexibly. The initial deployments were to create an Extraction Force for the potential protection of the 1125 OSCE verifiers in Kosovo. This force, however, has been supplemented to be something more than an Extraction Force as originally envisaged and now stands as the leading elements of a KFOR should it be deployed in Kosovo. Whereas the IFOR deployment in Bosnia in January 1996 could draw upon the UN forces (UNPROFOR) that were already in place and which had used large elements of NATO infrastructure, in the case of a Kosovo operation no such existing framework exists on the ground. NATO has therefore had to develop its force elements as an exercise in "power projection". British, French, German and some Italian units are now in place in FYROM and provide a framework which can be supplemented up to higher operational levels. In the British case an Armoured Battle Group is now fully deployed. The battle group consists of a squadron of Challenger tanks, a company of Warrior armoured infantry vehicles, an AS90 artillery battery, the Fourth Armoured Brigade Tactical Headquarters and other supporting units.[118]

---

[114] Q 362

[115] 'Statement on Kosovo' Meeting of the NAC in Foreign Ministers' Session N-NAC-2 (98) 143, 8 December 1998, para 2

[116] 'Final Communique' Meeting of the NAC in Defence Ministers' Session M-NAC-D-2 (98) 152, 17 December 1998, para 8

[117] Q 362, Q 385

[118] Ministry of Defence Press Notices

56. The British contingent presently numbers some 4,500 in this force, and in the event that there is a full KFOR deployment in the province of Kosovo, will rise to some 8,000. The British contingent will be the largest single contribution in terms of numbers by virtue of the fact that Britain commands the ARRC which adds something over 2,000 personnel to the total deployed number.

57. **This Committee will monitor the developments carefully and we will ask the government to give us a considered view at the end of NATO offensive action and after the first six months of any peace enforcement deployment on how the arrangements have worked in practice. We will wish to take evidence, *inter alia*, on the military advice given to the North Atlantic Council, the military assessment provided to UK ministers and the coordination of political objectives and military strategy.**

NATO's Area of Action

58. The area covered by Article 5 of the North Atlantic Treaty is strictly circumscribed by Article 6 of that Treaty: it is—

> ... the territory of any of the member states in Europe or North America, the territory of Turkey and the islands under the jurisdiction of any of the Parties to the Treaty in the area north of the Tropic of Cancer.

Moreover, Article 5 applies to the forces, vessels, and aircraft of any of the member states—

> ... when in or over these territories or any other area in Europe in which occupation forces of any of the Parties were stationed [in 1949] or the Mediterranean Sea or the North Atlantic area north of the Tropic of Cancer.

There is however no restriction in the Treaty with regard to any other area in which its members can choose to co–operate in military or other operations, over and above the obligations of Article 5; the subject is simply not covered.

59. Two other parts of the Treaty lend themselves to wider interpretation. In the Treaty's preamble, the Allies have pledged to 'seek to promote stability and well-being in the North Atlantic area', which is not specified geographically. Article 4 stipulates that the member states—

> ... will consult together whenever, in the opinion of any of them, the territorial integrity, political independence or security of any of the Parties [to the Treaty] is threatened.

There is no word in the Treaty about the type of action that might ensue from such consultation.

60. In the past few years there has been an ongoing debate about whether or not NATO should assume a more global role, and the subject remains controversial, not least amongst the Allies themselves.[119] It is not entirely a new debate; for example, the 1991 Gulf War was not undertaken by NATO as it was clearly out-of-area. Nevertheless, many of the Allies were involved in the eventual *ad hoc* coalition that undertook the operation, which was undoubtedly made more effective by those nations' habits of cooperation through NATO. As John Roper wrote in his submission to the Committee, the formal adoption of a global role—

> ... may be considered by some to be a move too far, with overtones of great power neo–imperialism.[120]

---

[119]Ev p 98
[120]Ev p 99

And Dr Jonathan Eyal told us that—

> ... almost everyone within the Alliance, especially the Americans, is schizophrenic about this entire question of the geographical remit of the Alliance's operations.[121]

Many others share General Sir Michael Rose's opinion that—

> It is far better to use NATO in its own theatre ... than to try and say that NATO has some sort of magic which we can deploy anywhere in the world,[122]

and that operations outside the Euro–Atlantic area should be left to other regional bodies, such as the Organisation for African Unity. However, according to some witnesses, some groupings in the USA apparently see no need to limit future activities of NATO that are of a non–Article 5 type to any particular area.[123] However, the French[124] and German governments have been more circumspect, and we have heard that they are most unwilling to have NATO commit to a more global role without specific assurances on NATO's mandate for out–of–area operations, discussed above.[125]

61. The question now is to what extent any global limitations will be spelled out in the new Strategic Concept. We were told that—

> ... the British government's instinct will be to leave [the definition of NATO's area of operations] as it is at the moment, very flexible,[126]

but that the new Strategic Concept would, according to the MoD's Policy Director—

> ... give ... a clear flavour of where NATO sees its prime interests as being, which is in European security ... what it will not do is lay down precise limits ... for a number of very good reasons, one of which is [that] we want to avoid the slight mistake of the last Strategic Concept of writing down something which looks really quite sensible today but looks dated only two or three years later.[127]

The legitimacy of out-of-area operations by NATO as a whole, or by Allies in *ad hoc* coalitions, where there is no direct threat to NATO's interests, continues to be debated. The Secretary General of NATO has said[128] that the question of NATO's global reach will be addressed in a precise manner in the new Strategic Concept and we look forward to this clearer indication of NATO's view of its global role.

[121] Q 114
[122] Q 198
[123] Ev p 122
[124] Q 67
[125] See para 47
[126] Q 61
[127] Q 62
[128] Speech at the Royal United Services Institute, 9 March 1999

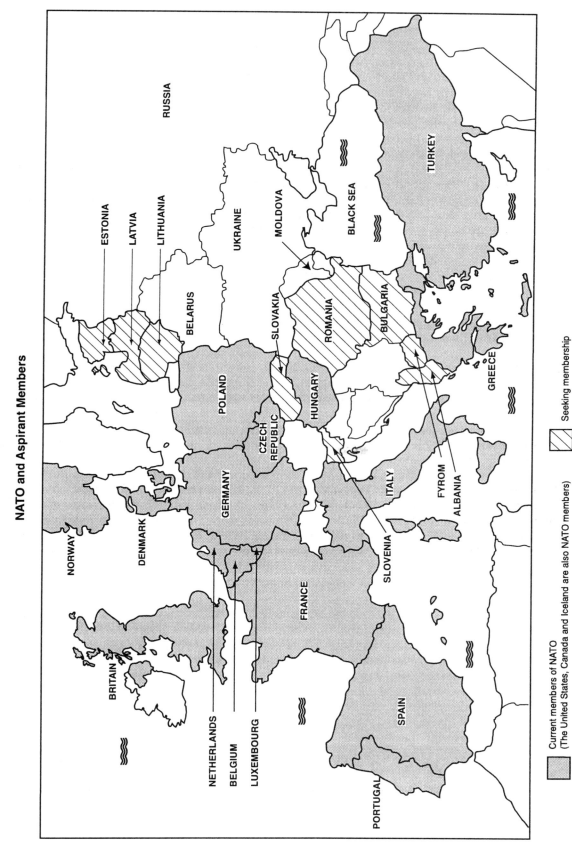

NATO and Aspirant Members

Current members of NATO
(The United States, Canada and Iceland are also NATO members)

Seeking membership

THE EUROPEAN SECURITY AND DEFENCE IDENTITY

NATO and the WEU

62. In this 50th anniversary year, NATO has continued to overshadow its older but much less well-known sibling, the Western European Union. This alliance, which celebrated its own 50th anniversary with much less razzamatazz last April, was founded on the Brussels Treaty of 1948.[129] It was rapidly displaced from the centre of attention in the family of western security organisations by the more assertive and potent new arrival, NATO. During the Cold War, the WEU almost disappeared from view and was widely believed to be defunct. In their Report of 1996, our predecessors commented that—

> ... the WEU's role in collective defence ... is of no continuing significance, provided that NATO membership continues to be a prerequisite for membership of the WEU.[130]

And the Secretary General of the WEU noted in a recent speech that—

> One of the many disobliging things that has been said about WEU is that it has a great future behind it.[131]

Had France remained in NATO's Integrated Military Structure, the WEU probably would have disappeared. There were a number of attempts to revitalise it (notably in the mid 1980s), but these were undertaken as often as a diversionary tactic as with a serious purpose of reform.

63. Since the end of the Cold War, attempts to reinvigorate the WEU have been more purposeful. [132] The European Union's 1991 Maastricht Treaty included agreement on the development of a Common Foreign and Security Policy (CFSP)—

> ... including the eventual framing of a common defence policy which might in time lead to a common defence.

It also included reference to the WEU as an integral part of the development of the European Union created by the Treaty and requested the WEU to elaborate and implement decisions and actions of the European Union which had defence implications. In 1992, the 'Petersberg tasks' of humanitarian and rescue missions, peacekeeping, peacemaking and crisis management were defined as appropriate missions for the WEU. In January 1994, NATO heads of state announced that they stood ready to make collective assets of the Alliance available, on the basis of consultations in the North Atlantic Council, for WEU operations undertaken by the European Allies in pursuit of their Common Foreign and Security Policy.[133] The Declaration of the 1996 Berlin NATO Summit[134] moved towards a consensus on the development of a European Security and Defence Identity (ESDI), defined by a concept of 'separable but not separate capabilities', which could be used by the European Allies in pursuit of the Petersberg tasks, using NATO assets under the political control of the WEU. However, although the EU's Common Foreign and Security Policy pillar had been established under the Maastricht Treaty in 1991, the UK continued to insist that the European *defence* capability, as embodied institutionally in the WEU, should not be formally incorporated into the EU, but should remain poised between NATO and the EU. At the Amsterdam Summit the European Union reaffirmed the formula first adopted at Maastricht but the Amsterdam Treaty revised the Maastricht Treaty to provide for the closer institutional relationship between the WEU and the EU. Reports of negotiations on the Amsterdam Treaty in 1997 emphasised the UK's resistance to the incorporation of a 'common defence'. The Prime Minister told the House in his statement on the Amsterdam Summit that—

---

[129]See Appendix 2

[130]Fourth Report, Session 1995–96, *Western European Union*, HC 105, para 11

[131]Dr José Cutilero, speaking at the RUSI, 10 March 1999

[132]*ibid*

[133]Declaration of the Brussels Summit

[134]See Appendix 3

... while retaining our veto, we have taken steps to improve the effectiveness of foreign policy co-operation with better planning and coordination. That is an important British interest, but getting Europe's voice heard more clearly in the world will not be achieved through merging the European Union and the Western European Union or developing an unrealistic common defence policy. We therefore resisted unacceptable proposals from others. Instead, we argued for—and won—the explicit recognition, written into the treaty for the first time, that NATO is the foundation of our and other allies' common defence...[135]

In the course of our enquiry into the government's Strategic Defence Review last year, Ministers told us—

... the Treaty of Amsterdam was a defining moment when it came to the Western European Union ... whilst it allows the European Union to engage in dialogue with the WEU, it certainly does not see it within the EU's capacity to make political decisions that would command the WEU ...[136]

and that—

A certain line was drawn under [the ESDI] at the Amsterdam Summit, largely at British instigation, by preventing the merger of the WEU and the EU.[137]

We ourselves noted in that Report that while the EU's Common Foreign and Security Policy had made limited but significant progress in the previous five years, the rate of development of ESDI within NATO had distinctly slowed,[138] and that we found that the SDR—

... had done nothing to clarify or advance the development of the European Security and Defence Identity.[139]

64. Until recently, therefore, ESDI was a generally ambiguous concept, representing for some the attempt to build a European defence capability separate from NATO, associated in ways still to be determined, with the European Union; for others, it was an attempt to increase the capabilities of the Europeans within NATO, precisely to strengthen the political and military fabric of the Alliance. In its response to the Committee's SDR report the government stated its belief that—

... in order to be effective, CFSP needs to be underpinned by a credible military capability which can act in circumstances when the United States chooses not to be fully engaged. We have no pre-conceived ideas about how best to achieve this ... It is partly a question of European political will and leadership, supported by better CFSP mechanisms, but also a matter of European countries taking the necessary practical steps to develop further the means to carry out a broad range of European-only operations, and having an effective mechanism for using them ... Improving European military capabilities and cooperation in this way will help to strengthen NATO. We do not want to do anything to undermine the Alliance or to attempt to duplicate its structures. Nor do we envisage in any way removing defence from the control of national governments or creating some form of standing European army. Our aim is to encourage our European Partners to continue the development of their armed forces to meet the kind of challenges which are likely in the future, and to consider with us ways in which European cooperation can be improved, so that a credible European defence identity can be created.[140]

[135]HC Deb, 18 June 1997, c314
[136]HC (1997–98) 138–III, Q 2881
[137]HC (1997–98) 138–III, Q 1630
[138]Eighth Report, Session 1997–98, *op cit*, para 137
[139]*ibid*, para 140
[140]Sixth Special Report, Session 1997–98, *op cit*, para 18

But in a speech in May 1998 the NATO Secretary General stated that the development of an ESDI within NATO would offer—

... the broadest possible menu of military options for managing future crises,

and would make—

... a major contribution to a more mature and balanced transatlantic relationship.[141]

There has also been a sudden and dramatic shift in the UK government's position since last summer. The Prime Minister took most observers by surprise by his initiative at the informal EU Summit at Portschäch in October 1998 to move the development of ESDI up the EU agenda. The government has made a number of statements on how it sees the role of the UK in addressing the Common Foreign and Security Policy of the European Union, and the attendant issue of the future role of the Western European Union, and it is clear that the role of the EU in defence and security issues is evolving at least as quickly as NATO itself. For example, in its memorandum to this inquiry, the MoD told us—

The Government believes that the European Union needs a more unified and influential voice in world affairs, articulated with greater speed and coherence through the Common Foreign and Security Policy (CFSP), and that the development of the security and defence dimension would reinforce its capacity and standing ... The Government believes that the capacity for Europeans to act together where the United States and the Alliance as a whole are not engaged should be enhanced, building on the existing European Security and Defence Identity arrangements.[142]

65. In evidence to this inquiry the Secretary of State told us that the government has "looked with a new focus at the way in which Europe handles itself" for two main reasons: first because the EU has decided[143] to appoint a High Representative for CFSP matters which will have the effect of "sharpening" and "personalising" the EU's impact on foreign and security policy (and perhaps providing an answer to Henry Kissinger's famous question, "If I want to talk to Europe, who do I call?"); secondly, because the present Kosovo crisis had brought us "face to face with [a] credibility gap and the Prime Minister believed it was right we should start focussing attention on that..."[144]

66. The unheralded St Malo agreement between France and the UK announced following a bilateral summit in December 1998[145] was characterised by former US NATO Ambassador Robert Hunter as 'short on substance but long on political significance';[146] but the Minister of State at the FCO told the Committee that—

... the process begun at St Malo has already led to considerable practical working together between the British and the French, but since then it has also engaged others, the Germans specifically, who are very important at the moment because of their joint chairmanship of both the WEU and ... the Presidency of the European Union,[147]

although Franco-British military cooperation, it should be noted, has long been underway and arguably was a precondition for the St Malo accord. It was a process, the Minister said, to deliver capacity at the sharp end rather than to engage in a debate about the future of institutions.[148] The Secretary General of the WEU, in his speech to the 50th Anniversary Conference, described the work that the WEU had been doing since the end of the Cold War to make the ESDI a reality, and noted this tone of impatience with institutional debate—

---

[141] Speech to the WEU Colloquy, Madrid, 4 May 1998
[142] Ev p 131
[143] At the Amsterdam Summit
[144] Q 318
[145] Ev p 132
[146] Quoted in *Jane's Defence Weekly*, 31(9) 3 March 1999, p. 22
[147] Q 317
[148] Q 323

Your Prime Minister and other European leaders have expressed their exasperation with the size of the European mouse that has come out of all these mountains. They want to know why Europe's political voice is still so slow to speak and so confused when it does, and why Europe's mailed fist is not stronger to strike after all the resources we have put into it.[149]

67. Though these attitudes are very clearly stated, they still leave open the question of the future of the WEU, and the Petersberg tasks that the WEU is mandated to perform. It is possible that the new Strategic Concept will outline similar tasks as core functions of NATO, and we would certainly expect it to do so. This would have the effect of undermining both the Petersberg Declaration and further sidelining the WEU itself. The Secretary of State for Defence acknowledged that, "there is a question mark as to what the role of the WEU should be".[150] Three alternatives were possible, he told us; to merge the WEU into the EU, to strengthen the WEU so that it is capable of performing properly the roles it has already taken on, or to devolve its political roles to the EU and its military roles to an ESDI component within NATO.[151] These are the three areas on which eventually decisions will have to be made.

68. In doing so, it will be vital to avoid three crucial problems that the US Secretary of State has pointed to, and which have been reiterated and reinforced by the WEU Secretary General.[152] **In formulating the arrangements for a strengthened ESDI, there must be no decoupling of the transatlantic alliance which would alienate our North American Allies. There must be no duplication of NATO resources. And there must be no discrimination amongst the European countries on the basis of their differing relationships with the EU and the Alliance.** We discuss these problems further below.

Transatlantic Attitudes

69. There appears, therefore, to be a growing consensus in European capitals that the European powers have to address the question of their deployable defence capabilities and the circumstances in which they might be used, and perhaps strike a new bargain with the USA. Within NATO, the European powers account for more than 60% of the Alliance's population and over 60% of its armed forces personnel. On paper, European–NATO countries collectively spend on defence the equivalent of around two thirds of the US defence budget (although proportionately probably more of the European spend is allocated to NATO).[153] President Clinton has sought approval from Congress for a 4.4% increase in the US defence budget for 1999–2000, the first real terms increase since 1991.[154] Yet it is generally agreed that the European Allies possess much less than the capability of the US, partly because of the duplication of capabilities between European states. The issue of equitable burden-sharing (not just of costs, but also of capabilities) within NATO has been politically sensitive between the US and the Europeans since the foundation of the Integrated Military Structure (IMS). There has never been a generally agreed way in which to gauge the relative contributions of the US and Europe, and the debate has been characterised as—

... dominated by myths, emotion and special pleading.[155]

However, in the present international environment, where the challenges to European security do not manifestly share the risks equally among NATO members in the way that was commonplace during the Cold War, it is perhaps inevitable that burden-sharing issues should take on renewed importance. In the US the debate can become very heated—

... a lot of it on false premises, certainly if you hear the debate about Bosnia,

---

[149]Speech at the Royal United Services Institute 10 March 1999
[150]Q 323
[151]In each of these cases, many special arrangements would be required to cater for the needs of non-EU NATO countries and European non-aligned states.
[152]Speech at the Royal United Services Institute, 9 March 1999
[153]Q 36
[154]*International Herald Tribune*, 4 January 1999
[155]*NATO Burden Sharing: Past and Future*, Professor Keith Hartley and Professor Todd Sandler, 1999

as one British official commented.[156] With the new emphasis on NATO's new missions, the calculation of burden-sharing will no longer revolve around the performance of a single major Alliance function, and it will be more difficult than ever to measure respective burdens inside an evolving Alliance that finds itself in such an uncertain security environment. But as the US Deputy Secretary of State recently said, it—

> ... is a fundamental and enduring truth: the well-being of the United States depends in large measure on what happens in Europe: the US will not prosper without an economically vibrant Europe; the US will not be safe without a secure and peaceful Europe. That said, most Americans recognize that the phenomenon of "Europe" is not static. Rather, it is organic. In the nature and composition of its institutions, even in its geographical scope, Europe is constantly reinventing itself; it is, in the vocabulary of Euro-speak, both deepening and broadening. As Americans watch the evolution of Europe, we have our own hopes, and sometimes our own apprehensions, about where the process will lead. We want to see Europe define its identity and pursue its interests in a way that not only preserves, but that strengthens, the ties that bind your security to ours, and, of course, ours to yours.

70. It is evident that there exists a growing consensus for the Europeans to increase their physical and organisational competence to respond to the growing security challenges they face. The MoD's policy director told the Committee that—

> ... the weight of the European military capability ... [contributed] to the Alliance is not commensurate with [Europe's] political weight ...[157]

And the Assembly of the WEU has said that—

> ... we now find ourselves in a situation of dependence and imbalance that is extremely disadvantageous to Europe and even to our American partners.[158]

An enhanced ESDI in some form—whether or not it is developed exclusively within NATO, or in some other arrangement involving more closely the EU—continues to have significant, potential, practical defence benefits.

71. In evidence to us, officials confirmed that the government agreed on the need to 're-balance' NATO—

> ... to actually help cement the Alliance because as anybody who visits Washington knows, whether there is a burden-sharing debate in the UK or in Europe, there is always one in Washington ...[159]

and as the US Deputy Secretary of State confirmed—
> We're in favor of ESDI. We want there to be a capability within the Alliance whereby the European members can address and solve problems without always requiring US combat involvement. That's in everyone's interest ... But as with every aspect of modernizing and adapting NATO, this particular innovation, ESDI, carries with it risks and costs; and it carries with it an obligation for the highest possible degree of transparency and consultation. If ESDI is misconceived, misunderstood or mishandled, it could create the impression—which could eventually lead to the reality— that a new, European-only alliance is being born out of the old, transatlantic one. If that were to happen, it would weaken, perhaps even break, those ties that I spoke of before—the ones that bind our security to yours.

We concur. Under no circumstances must the development of the ESDI, now or in the foreseeable future, be seen to be an attack on the transatlantic nature of the Alliance.

---

[156] Q 99
[157] Q 98
[158] Assembly of the WEU's Draft Plan for Action, *A Time for Defence*
[159] Q 99

72. Current preparations for the establishment of a KFOR taking place in FYROM represent a potentially significant step forward for ESDI initiatives. France and the UK were the leading players in establishing so promptly an Extraction Force in FYROM to act as the ultimate guarantee of the safety of OSCE monitors. Both countries were prepared to do this without the explicit military support on the ground of US forces and have taken the lead in planning for the transformation of this force into a potential KFOR. Though it is very unlikely that the Europeans would see a full KFOR operation as feasible without the involvement of US ground troops, it is clear that London and Paris both want to use this operation to send a message to the rest of NATO that tangible ESDI contributions are now appropriate. The Secretary General of NATO recognised this in his recent speech at the Royal United Services Institution when he said—

> The Kosovo Implementation Force should also be the start of yet another new feature of how we manage security today; it should be the start of a stronger European role in NATO. The Kosovo peace implementation mission, should it materialise, will have far greater European input, and will even be led by a European – a NATO first. ... Such a new bargain does not mean 'less America' it simply means 'more Europe'.[160]

73. The Kosovo crisis also demonstrates that the six nation Contact Group—consisting of the US, Russia, the UK, France, Germany and Italy—is rapidly emerging as a form of European security council, certainly on matters relating to current instabilities in the Balkans. NATO is drawing significant authority from discussions taking place in the Contact Group and has demonstrated that it is struggling to articulate a new relationship between itself and the United Nations. The authority under which NATO operates in Kosovo will crystallise the debate about the legal basis for future NATO operations in areas of Europe and its periphery, where Article 5 jurisdiction is not relevant.

European Approaches

74. The emergence of an enhanced ESDI, therefore, takes on a vital significance as a tangible symbol of Europe's greater willingness to 'rebalance' the Alliance—whatever form that may eventually take—and provides an essential building block to the conclusion of a 'new transatlantic bargain'—whether tacit or explicit—that the US is clearly seeking. The US appears to have been reassured that an enhanced ESDI will not undermine NATO and will not serve to exclude the US and other Allies from key decision–making. Current US policy–makers within the Executive (though perhaps not in Congress) appear to view the enhancement of the ESDI as a positive advantage in the transatlantic burden–sharing debate while for the Europeans, it represents the prospect of greater military competence in operations that may be deemed vital to their interests but in which US forces may only be involved indirectly in back-up, surveillance or logistical roles.

THE UNITED KINGDOM

75. The Committee was told that, from the UK's perspective, the most promising way forward, that commands the greatest degree of intra–allied consensus, seems to be in the development of a 'toolbox' of forces and equipment, maintained by NATO member states, to which the European Union or the WEU would have some degree of access; in which processes of consultation and decision-making would be clarified and streamlined. European forces could be more closely tied in to both NATO and WEU structures and genuine operational capabilities increased. In June 1998 NATO Defence ministers agreed, in the words of the MoD and the FCO—

> to direct work to ensure that the key elements of the implementation of the Berlin and Brussels decisions are in place by the time of the Washington Summit. The results of this work should be reflected in the updated Concept to enable the practical development of the ESDI to continue in support of the overall aims and evolution of NATO.[161]

---

[160]Speech at Royal United Services Institute, 9 March 1999
[161]Ev p 91

The St Malo Declaration of December 1998 between France and the United Kingdom—the two most important European military players in this debate—stated plainly that—

> Europe needs strengthened armed forces that can react rapidly to the new risks.[162]

While there may be some ambiguity between Paris and London as to what constitutes 'strengthened' armed forces—whether it implies the commitment of more defence resources, for example—and while there was some cynicism in the public reaction to St Malo that it did not go further, the direction of the final communiqué and the concentration on specific military capabilities is entirely consistent with the enhancement of the ESDI. However the St Malo declaration also included reference to—

> ... the European Union will also need to have recourse to suitable military means (European capabilities pre-designated within NATO's European pillar *or national or multinational European means outside the NATO framework)*.

We regard the reference to means outside the NATO framework with concern and believe that this element of the declaration may mean different things to each of the parties.

76. The Prime Minister himself told the recent NATO 50th Anniversary Conference at the RUSI that—

> The initiative I launched last autumn on European defence is aimed at giving greater credibility to Europe's Common Foreign and Security Policy. Far from weakening NATO this is an essential complement to the Transatlantic Alliance. We Europeans should not expect the United States to have to play a part in every disorder in our own back yard. The European Union should be able to take on some security tasks on our own, and we will do better through a common European effort than we can by individual countries acting on their own. Europe's military capabilities at this stage are modest. Too modest. Too few allies are transforming their armed forces to cope with the security problems of the 1990s and the 21st century.[163]

77. It seems therefore that the government is keen to investigate the possibilities for greater involvement among the members of the EU in defence questions as a way both of helping the Europeans to punch at their right weight in defence terms, and as an ingredient in a more balanced transatlantic relationship. In fact the United Kingdom has shown a marked reluctance to involve itself in the debate on the institutional arrangements regarding the ESDI, which the Secretary of State for Defence has called "narrow and sterile".[164] The Secretary of State stressed in his evidence to us that the accent was on practicalities—

> The fact is that we Europeans have spent an awful lot of time debating institutions, creating institutions, creating wiring diagrams which show you who would be involved, who would not be involved, where the decisions are taken. Well, the stark reality is, you cannot send a wiring diagram to deal with a crisis, and what we want to do, and what I believe our allies are now facing up to, is to address [the] capability gap.[165]

He also told the NATO 50th Anniversary Conference that—

> The trend in European defence budgets is downwards. Pressure on public spending suggests that this trend could continue ...Without effective military capability to back up European foreign policy goals, we are wasting our time. We risk being an economic giant, but a strategic midget ... Institutional re-engineering alone will solve little ...Our ultimate aim, therefore, is not so much a European Security and Defence Identity but something altogether more ambitious—namely a European Defence Capability.

---

[162]Ev p 131: Declaration on European Defence, St Malo, 3–4 December, para 4
[163]Speech at the Royal United Services Institute, 8 March 1999
[164]Speech to EU Ambassadors, 18 February 1999
[165]Q 315

78. On this basis, the government has pursued a number of initiatives. Within NATO, the Secretary of State told us, the UK has urged closer integration within some of the European multinational forces that already exist—such as the UK/Netherlands Amphibious Force, the Eurocorps, the ACE Rapid Reaction Corps, and among the other mixed forces at corps level and lower.[166] Further initiatives will flow, the government believes, from the implementation of the Strategic Defence Review and the interest that other European Allies have expressed in its process and outcome as they embark on similar reviews.[167]

79. In moving this process forward, therefore, the government has also been anxious to indicate what it should *not* involve. The Prime Minister stressed that—

> We decided that we should go beyond the Berlin arrangements agreed by NATO in 1996 to give Europe a genuine capacity to act, and act quickly, in cases where the Alliance as a whole is not militarily engaged. In any particular crisis, the European Union will develop a comprehensive policy. But within that, deployment of forces is a decision for Governments. I see no role for the European Parliament or the Court of Justice. Nor will the European Commission have a decision-making role on military matters.[168]

In evidence to this Committee, the Secretary of State for Defence stressed that both the British and French governments assumed that defence questions must remain "intergovernmental".[169] The Committee pressed the Minister of State at the FCO on the question of whether EU institutions will become more powerful in relation to defence questions. But Mr. Lloyd insisted that there was "no pressure" to move from the present level of the CFSP—

> It is intergovernmental, it is not within the competence of, for example, the Commission or some parallel organisation.[170]

The Secretary of State added that the government was "not interested in some single European army,"[171] and we endorse the government's determination to resist any increasing pressure to move in this direction.

FRANCE

80. A further element that will play in this debate will be France's role within an enlarged and reformulated NATO. French defence policy has been in the process of major reorientation since the end of the Gulf conflict in 1991. French politicians have long accepted the need to embrace a reformed NATO as a pre-requisite to effective security in contemporary Europe. Indeed, intense French concerns with security in the Mediterranean, and Southern European, theatres has increased its stake in a successful evolution of the Alliance to help France address those issues. In addition, Paris is keen to further develop its role in peacekeeping and humanitarian intervention, where the use of NATO assets is difficult to avoid.[172] If this suggests, however, that there is no objective reason why France should not re-enter the Integrated Military Structure and resume its place as a full Alliance member, then it underestimates the symbolic importance to Paris of making such a move. Prior to 1997, such re-integration was regarded as inevitable and French politicians actively fed such a perception. The dispute over command of NATO AFSOUTH in the autumn of 1996, however, proved to be a considerable setback and something of a humiliation to President Chirac. Its aftermath has effectively ruled out any early formal re-entry of France into the IMS or the Nuclear Planning Group.[173] Earlier French enthusiasm for a reformed NATO has cooled since the beginning of 1997 and a France that is 'in, but not integrated' into NATO, in the words of the French Defence Minister Alain Richard in 1997,

---

[166]Q 314
[167]Q 315, Q 331
[168]Speech at Royal United Services Institute, 8 March 1999
[169]Q 324
[170]Q 324, Q 327
[171]Q 329
[172]Ev p 117
[173]Meeting at IFRI, Paris, 19 January 1999

seems to be the limit of what Paris is now prepared to offer.[174] However, we would welcome France formally re-entering NATO's Integrated Military System whenever it feels it is prepared to do so.

81. In strictly military terms, however, this problem may be more apparent than real. The Committee was told in Paris and Brussels how keen French defence ministry officials were to set in place procedures and mechanisms that would improve its armed forces co-operation within the NATO structure, and France remains fully involved in the planning for Combined Joint Task Forces which almost certainly represent the most likely framework in which NATO forces will be deployed over the coming few years.[175] Not least, France has taken a leading role in deploying to FYROM to establish the extraction force for potential operations in Kosovo, and France promised what would be the second largest contingent, after that of the UK, in the force that would be drawn together to enforce any successful agreement in Kosovo. However, France may still be attached to a view that the development of the ESDI is more about separate development of European defence than reinforcement of the transatlantic Alliance. Political problems between French and American perceptions of NATO's future are likely to remain for some time to come, and have the potential to cause the Alliance major problems. In a military sense, however, the process of operational planning continues on a generally convergent course and France is of, if not in, the IMS; though the speed of progress may be affected by political disputes.

GERMANY

82. The prospect of an enhanced ESDI, in the context of the articulation of new military missions for NATO, is also likely to sharpen some key differences of emphasis as between the UK, France and Germany on the future orientation of the Alliance. One view, generally favoured within Germany and sometimes expressed by the new German government, is that NATO should remain firmly a regional organisation—capable of more effective, multilateral, military deployment and crisis management, but applied only within Europe. At the Munich Conference on security policy in February 1999, German leaders expressed considerable concern at what was perceived as the tendency of the US to seek unilateral military solutions to security problems that affected all Europeans. Gerhard Schröder, the German Chancellor commented that—

... there is a danger of unilateralism, not by just anybody but by the United States.

The German Foreign Minister, Joschka Fischer added that the "growing tendency to avoid multilateral solutions" should be seen by Europe as "a challenge to build up its own political authority".[176] However, in the four months in which the new government has been in office, its foreign and security policies have also emphasised continuity with the previous administration—despite the presence of the Greens in the coalition, membership of NATO has not been a debating point. The new government has also announced a Force Structure Commission to look at the structure of the Bundeswehr, but we were told that it will not be appointed until after the Washington Summit, and our impression was that there was not much sense of urgency about its work—by the time it was due to report the next election would be looming, and little concrete action can therefore be expected for at least four years.[177]

83. Our perception from our visit to Bonn in March was that the government supported the moves in the direction of a 'new' NATO, but were perhaps more conservative than the UK about the new missions. The main Green/SPD tensions were demonstrated in Foreign Minister Joschka Fischer's call for a 'no first use' of nuclear weapons policy to be adopted by NATO which we discuss elsewhere in this Report.[178] We also found that the change in attitudes towards overseas deployments of German troops had been slow but deep.[179] At the time of our visit, Germany had

---

[174]Ev p 118
[175]Meeting at MoD, Paris, 19 January 1999
[176]Quoted in *New York Times*, 15 Feb 1999
[177]Meeting in Bonn, 4 March 1999
[178]Paras 36–40
[179]Embassy Briefing, Bonn, 4 March 1999

1000 troops already deployed to the Kosovo region (in FYROM) and had assembled a further 4,500 (plus 500 reserves) ready to go if a peace deal was struck. While overseas deployment had been ruled by the Constitutional Court to require an authorising vote of the Bundestag, approval for the deployment to Macedonia had been by an overwhelming majority.[180]

84. Like the UK, the German government does not wish to see governments becoming over-involved in defence industry rationalisations and mergers. But at the same time they also saw a rationalised and competitive industry as a cornerstone of ESDI. For the German government, ESDI has three essential elements: the military; the political; and the industrial. They see the creation of a unified European defence industry as an essential third element of the ESDI (alongside the military and political integration). All our interlocutors whom we met on our visit to Bonn, whether from government or industry, emphasised this element.[181] While the German government accepts that in the end the institutional structure of the ESDI would have to be that on which all the participants could agree, and that the military redesign should take precedence, they made it clear that once that process had begun, and political control of European defence had moved to within the EU, the WEU will cease to be needed. The German Defence Minister made clear that they believe that this process of assimilation should be completed sooner rather than later, as he told the 50th Anniversary Conference—

> It is obvious that we Europeans must increase our foreign and security policy influence in international affairs. Europe should speak with one voice and should exercise its global responsibility ... It will therefore be very important to implement the decisions of Berlin at the summit in Washington. However, it is also important to realise as quickly as possible the concrete perspective of developing a European defence and security policy as stipulated in the Treaty of Amsterdam. This includes the appointment of a High Representative for the Common Foreign and Security Policy as well as instruments enabling the early detection of crises, including strategy planning and early warning structures. But it also includes integrating the WEU into the EU soon. Concrete ideas on how this could be done should be developed in the near future so that they can be implemented soon, which, means within a time frame of two years to a maximum of four years ... However, the military command structures and the armed forces structures must clearly remain elements of NATO. We do not want to have dual military structures ... These should supplement the corresponding US capabilities within the integrated NATO structure. The rapid merger of WEU and EU would provide a guarantee and would be an essential precondition for an effective and efficient European security and defence policy.[182]

85. Germany currently holds the presidencies of both the EU and the WEU, and it is clear that one of its aims is to use this dual mandate to produce a firm programme for the development of the ESDI at the WEU ministerial meeting at Bremen, to be followed-up at the Cologne EU Summit. Despite this vigorous support for the development of the ESDI, the Germans nonetheless appeared to have been taken by surprise by the UK initiative at Portschäch, as they had been disconcerted by the Austrian initiative in convening (under its EU Presidency) an informal summit of defence ministers at Vienna which followed-up the Portschäch initiative. However, while having obviously been caught on the back foot by Portschäch and St Malo, it is evident that the German government are determined to seize the initiative once more in the ESDI debate. They are pushing hard to have decisions made at the Cologne Summit which will spell out the end of the WEU and its absorption into the EU/CFSP. They have now become the pacemakers in the run up to institutional change, and for them the death of the WEU is foretold.

86. **There is a large measure of agreement on the aims of a strengthened ESDI though there are differences of emphasis between the main players. It will be necessary to reconcile the industrial, political and military elements whilst maintaining transatlantic cooperation. In addressing the industrial restructuring element, close attention will need to be paid to security of supply issues.**

---

[180]Meeting with Bundestag Defence Committee, 14 March 1999
[181]Meetings at MoD, Foreign Office, Bonn, 4 March 1999
[182]Speech at the Royal United Services Institute, 9 March 1999

THE NON-ALIGNED AND THE UNINCLUDED

87. A problem frequently raised in relation to the integration of the WEU and the EU is that of the role of the European members of NATO which are not members of the EU, and the members of the EU who are not members of NATO. There are now six countries in the former category (Czech Republic, Hungary, Iceland, Norway, Poland and Turkey) and four in the latter (Austria, Finland, Ireland and Sweden). Of these four, all except the Republic of Ireland have joined the PfP, and it has been recently reported that the Irish government intends to seek parliamentary approval for an application to become a Partner.[183]

88. Proponents of an enhanced ESDI tend, in their public pronouncements, rather to skate over the institutional problems of integrating the political and military capabilities of the ESDI with these non-concentric memberships, although all pay lip-service to the necessity of their inclusion. The Foreign Secretary has said that—

> ... we do not just seek the tolerance of NATO colleagues who are not members of the European Union; we want their enthusiastic support for the enterprise in which we are engaged and also their participation wherever it is appropriate.[184]

But while the WEU does, potentially, provide a political decision-making forum for controlling military deployments, it is not self-evident that it is inherently more efficient than the EAPC (or the OSCE for that matter). The Secretary General of the WEU told a recent conference that the WEU could have coordinated Operation ALBA, which was designed to protect the delivery of humanitarian aid in Albania in Spring 1997;[185] but this operation was eventually undertaken an *ad hoc* coalition led by Italy.

89. The institutional arrangements for political decision making within a reformed ESDI will require careful consideration, and must be so framed as to include and reassure our Allies who are not in the EU, and avoid the risk of impasse with the member States who are not in the Alliance. **If the EU is to be merged with the WEU, NATO together with Austria, Finland, Ireland and Sweden, will have to reconsider their relationship to take account of those nations' traditions of neutrality.**

The Future of the ESDI

90. On the basis of progress so far, a 'Berlin Plus' concept may emerge from the Washington Summit which would represent a significant step in the direction of more effective burden–sharing within the Alliance. Equally, work and expenditure on the Defence Capabilities Initiative—which is intended to identify key European weaknesses that need to be addressed—would demonstrate the determination of the Europeans to take ESDI initiatives seriously. The US Deputy Secretary of State expressed the hope that—

> Looking back over the calendar of 1996 through 1999, we will also see a map featuring a clear, straight, well-lit path leading from Berlin to St Malo to Washington to Bremen and to Cologne.

An Atlantic Alliance, enhanced by a greater ESDI, will, we believe, allow NATO to operate more effectively in a strategic partnership with the US both in and outside the European region as situations arise. As US Secretary of State Madeleine Albright put it in December 1998—

> Our interests are clear: we want a Europe that can act. We want a Europe with modern, flexible military forces that are capable of putting out fires in Europe's backyard and working with us through the alliance to defend our common interests. European efforts to do more for Europe's own defence make it easier, not harder, for us to remain engaged.[186]

---

[183]See eg *Financial Times*, 29 January 1999
[184]Speech to the North Atlantic Council, 8 December 1998
[185]Speech at the Royal United Services Institute, 10 March 1999
[186]Madeleine K. Albright, 'The right balance will secure NATO's future', *Financial Times*, 7 December 1998, p 22

The differences in emphasis which we have outlined above lie behind all current discussions of potential new missions for NATO, and although the Washington Summit will address them, it is unlikely that they will finally be resolved there. Officials have suggested that the new Strategic Concept should avoid being overly precise as to the contingencies for which NATO prepares.[187] **We recommend, however, that the UK should press for a clear statement of support for the development of the ESDI to be included in the new Strategic Concept.** As *The Economist* expressed it, fairly starkly—

> America's interest in transatlantic co-operation will be proportional to Europe's willingness to face future challenges: poison gas, germ warfare, rogue [states'] missiles, ethnic wars on—or a little beyond—NATO's periphery... The alliance will not survive, in any solid sense, unless Europeans and Americans do some hard, honest talking about their division of labour.[188]

91. In this difficult situation the United Kingdom has a potentially important role to play. In the wake of discussions in November and December 1998, the Prime Minister,[189] the Foreign Secretary[190] and the Secretary of State for Defence all went out of their way to incline towards Washington's emphasis. This still leaves a great deal to play for, since recent arguments have become considerably more heated in the run-up to the April Summit. However there is an implicit bargain in the decision to make a reality of the ESDI—and the UK should understand the significance of that bargain. We set out below some of the key outcomes required of the Washington Summit which we believe would demonstrate that this profound shift of policy was merited.

92. First, we support the UK government's emphasis on measures to reinforce Europe's military capability, and agree that these should be the priority in the development of the ESDI. As the Secretary of State for Defence has said—

> ... the key military assets required for the type of peace support operation that [the Europeans] may face, in particular air assets, are overwhelmingly American ... and we frequently neglect the vital logistical tail that would be required to sustain our armed forces over a long duration far from home.[191]

We hope that the Washington Summit will produce a convincing plan, based on the findings of the Defence Capabilities Initiative, to bring our European Allies' force structure into line with NATO's new missions. We believe that this will, inevitably, require some reconsideration of the thorny problem of role specialisation within the European forces. **We hope that the Washington Summit will lay the foundations for a mature reconsideration of measures to improve complementarity and interoperability amongst the European Allies' armed forces, and will embody a recognition that this will involve further pooling of national resources, with the trade-offs that such a development implies.** To underpin these changes, **we would see great advantage in the Washington Summit announcing the creation of a second, European-led, Allied Rapid Reaction Corps.**

93. Second, while the military dimension of the ESDI should, we believe, take precedence, the Summit should not simply fudge the institutional questions. It seems that the Allied governments have finally decided that the WEU has run its course, and has become an impediment to the development of the ESDI rather than an aid. Even the Assembly of the WEU seems set to suggest that procedures be set up to—

> ... give the European Council a real military operational capability by transferring to it WEU's decision-making and command capability,

---

[187]Q 62, Q 66

[188]Economist 12 December 1998, p. 20

[189]Tony Blair, 'Time to Repay the United States', *The New York Times*, 13 November 1998.

[190]*The Independent*, 9 December 1998, p.14

[191]Speech to the WEU Assembly, 1 December 1998

leading eventually to the setting of—

> ... a schedule for the gradual integration of the WEU into the EU.[192]

This should in part be seen as a tribute to the efforts of the WEU to reinvent itself since the Berlin Summit. But that said, **we would see advantage in the Washington Summit producing a clear statement of NATO's view on the proposed integration of the WEU and the EU.**

94. In our Seventh Report of last session, we noted that it was regrettable that for the last several years, while the US defence industry had significantly restructured, little had happened in Europe until very recently, and concluded that the imbalance between the industries of the US and Europe required urgent attention. We endorsed the government's view that it remains a matter for the industries whether and how they restructure. Only the industries concerned can determine what links—with firms in the US as well as in Europe and elsewhere—will generate business synergies. We also concluded that it would not be in the UK's national interest for Europe to give any hint of building some sort of 'fortress Europe' while industry in Europe is restructured, because that could create barriers in the US, and we urged the UK Government to use its influence in Europe to avoid any undue European-preference policy emerging. **We believe these conclusions hold good for any moves to bring industrial restructuring within the ambit of the ESDI.**[193]

95. **A stronger European Security and Defence Identity could strengthen the Alliance and reinforce its transatlantic dimension. We believe that by making Europe more capable of acting without the USA in defence of its own interests it will, paradoxically, make the USA more ready to remain within the Alliance and work with its European Allies. We would support any move which would have the effect of bringing closer transatlantic cooperation, and which might as a consequence make unilateral military action by the USA less likely. But the advantages of a strengthened ESDI do not lie only to the West. Russia finds the EU a much more natural partner in developing European security cooperation than it does NATO. The EU has a fundamental role to play in securing, through political and economic means, the stability of Europe.**

---

[192]Assembly of the WEU Draft Action Plan: *A Time For Defence*
[193]Seventh Report, Session 1997–98, *Aspects of Defence Procurement and Industrial Policy*, HC 675, p xxix

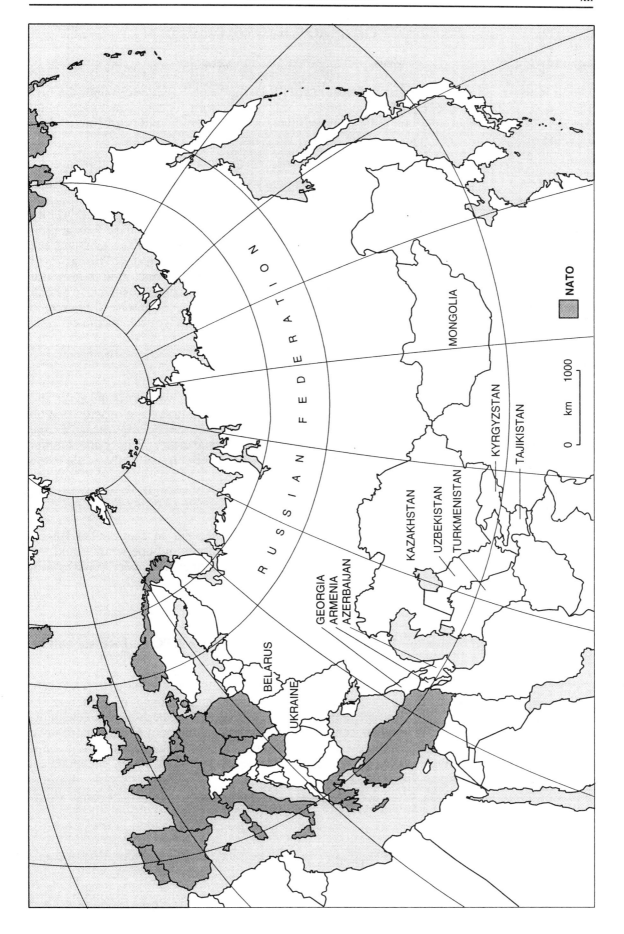

NATO AND THE FORMER SOVIET UNION

Introduction

96. It is now nearly ten years since the opening of the Berlin Wall,[194] nine years since the first Baltic state declared independence from the Soviet Union,[195] Boris Yeltsin's first election as President of the Russian Republic[196] and the reunification of Germany[197] and nearly eight years since the dissolution of the Warsaw Pact[198] and of the Soviet Union.[199]

97. Nonetheless, NATO's relationship with the former Soviet Union, and in particular the Russian Federation, still lies at the heart of its strategy to secure peace in the North Atlantic area. It is clear that NATO and Russia are in the same boat, rowing in the same direction, towards stability in Europe. However, despite Russia's membership of Partnership for Peace, this unity of purpose is far from apparent in the tone of relations between the two. The Washington Summit, and the new Strategic Concept, provide an opportunity for NATO to establish the formal framework of a clear, post-Cold War relationship with its old adversary. This task will be all the more difficult in the light of Russia's suspension of military cooperation in response to NATO's operations against the armed forces of the Federal Republic of Yugoslavia. In March of this year we visited Moscow and Kyiv to seek to get some measure of the state of opinion in Russia and Ukraine in the run-up to the 50th Anniversary Summit, and we seek to convey some of what we learned below.

Russia

98. The transforming relationship between NATO and Russia was formalised in the NATO–Russia Founding Act[200] of May 1997, which includes commitments to consultation on Euro–Atlantic security issues; promotion of transparency and confidence–building measures; the peaceful settlement of disputes; the strengthening of the OSCE; and closer military cooperation between the signatories. The Founding Act has been praised by the Russian Ambassador to the UK as—

... provid[ing] extensive opportunities for creating an atmosphere of trust in Europe.[201]

The Founding Act also included provisions for the establishment of the NATO–Russia Permanent Joint Council (PJC), which is a forum for consultation and cooperation and the development of joint initiatives. It will, in the words of Sir Michael Alexander, have to deal with—

... all the twists and turns which lie ahead in the NATO/Russia relationship.[202]

It was clear from our visit to Moscow that the road ahead for NATO and Russia will be neither straight nor smooth.

99. Our discussions in Moscow brought home to us the extent to which attitudes to NATO are as much a badge of political expediency as a product of reasoned analysis of the threats to Russia's interests. While the fissure between the liberal, democratic, western-oriented elements of the political elite and the nationalist, isolationist supporters of a distinctive Russian or Slavic course is one that runs through almost all other areas of policy, it seems there is only one set of attitudes towards NATO, hostility of a greater or lesser degree. However, the practical

---

[194]9–10 November 1989
[195]Lithuania, 11 March 1990
[196]30 May 1990
[197]3 October 1990
[198]1 July 1991
[199]25 December 1991
[200]Founding Act on Mutual Relations, Cooperation and Security between NATO and the Russian Federation, available on the Internet at www.mod.uk/policy/nato/enlargement/founding_act.htm
[201]Ev p 140
[202]Ev p 120

continuation of political and military cooperation in Bosnia and Herzegovina in support of the Dayton and Paris agreements and the efforts by NATO and Russia to maintain a joint approach to the crisis in Kosovo are encouraging in the light of concerns that Russia's objection to NATO's enlargement would lead to the breakdown of cooperation in practice.[203]   None of our interlocutors in Moscow were able to point to an area of NATO-Russia relations which would have been changed in practical terms if the accession of the Visegrad Three had not taken place.

100. Nevertheless, it was clear from our discussions that it is possible that the NATO–Russia relationship could become yet more problematic in future. Russia has in the past threatened to withdraw from or reduce cooperation in response to NATO's proposed enlargement, US/UK action in the Gulf in 1998 and NATO's involvement in Kosovo. This last factor was at the forefront during our visit in March, and was reinforced by Prime Minister Primakov's sudden aborting of his visit to the USA on 23rd March. Even those of our interlocutors who were relatively sympathetic to NATO's case predicted a dramatic slump in NATO-Russia relations if there were air strikes against Milosevic in Serbia. A statement by the Federation Council (the Upper House of the Federal Assembly) on 26 March expressed a widely-held Russian view that—

> This action is tantamount to an erosion of the basis of the contemporary international law order ... a most flagrant violation of the UN Charter, of the generally accepted norms and principles of international law. Attempts to justify the air raids by references to "the prevention of a humanitarian catastrophe" are absolutely groundless ... The North Atlantic Alliance has actually usurped the authority of the Security Council of the United Nations and violated its own Charter which allows the use of force by the Alliance in precise conformity with the UN Charter ... NATO's unilateral action runs counter to the whole complex of decisions and measures taken by the Contact Group, OSCE and the United Nations which served in the last months as a basis for active efforts aimed at achieving a settlement in Kosovo on the political track.[204]

The new Strategic Concept therefore has a role much greater than setting out the mission statement for NATO's military planners. It must provide the platform from which NATO can seek to explain itself to Russia—and it cannot begin to do that if it cannot explain itself to itself.

101. Representatives of the Russian government have themselves complained that it—

> ... is kept unaware of even the basic elements of the drafts [of the new Strategic Concept] discussed,[205]

and that the new Strategic Concept cannot be viewed as simply an internal Alliance matter,[206] although the Russian Deputy Defence Minister appeared to suggest that he *had* seen a draft. The key issue to be addressed in the new Strategic Concept as far as Russia is concerned will be NATO's move towards a more global role. Discussions on its mandate were a central concern of our interlocutors in Russia. Russia has expressed 'serious concerns' at the possibility of NATO extending its global reach 'without any constraint from the UN Security Council',[207] and the Russian Ambassador to the UK has stated that NATO's declaration of its willingness to use force in Kosovo in 1998 was a 'transgression' of 'the sanctity of international law'.[208] Discussions of this problem again revealed to us the extent to which foreign and security policy issues tend to be viewed through the prism of concerns about domestic policy. We were told by a high-ranking official at the Ministry of Foreign Affairs that "Russia cannot act as a proponent of separatists anywhere in the world". The reasons were made clear enough—the fear of secessionist insurrection among the republics of Central Asia and the North Caucasus is a constant preoccupation of Russian politicians, and the analogy with Kosovo's demands for

---

[203]Third Report, 1997–98, para 34

[204]Appeal by the Federation Council of the Federal Assembly of the Russian Federation to the Parliaments of the World, 26 March 1999 (unofficial translation)

[205]Ev p 139

[206]Statement by the Deputy Foreign Minister of the Russian Federation, Munich, February 1999

[207]Ev p 139

[208]Ev p 139

independence seem all too obvious to them.

102. We also found the political situation in Russia in a state of some flux. As the power of the President wanes, the power of the Duma (Parliament) is growing, and this is acting as a brake on reform. The present government is looking increasingly transitional as the country approaches parliamentary elections at the end of this year, and presidential elections no later than the middle of next year.[209]

103. The financial crisis of 1998 may also have weakened, if not discredited, many of those associated with a 'European course' in Russia and strengthened those who see Western models and values as inapplicable to Russian conditions and harmful to Russia's interests. Although some of these forces have supported the government of Prime Minister Primakov, we were encouraged by his representatives' evident recognition that consultation and cooperation with the West, along with observance of treaty commitments, remain the most practical means of advancing Russian interests in the current security environment. However it would be short-sighted to overlook the possibility that a less reasonable coalition of forces might gain power in future, and our meetings with members of the Duma made clear that the forces opposing *rapprochement* with NATO certainly predominate in that body.[210] We were also concerned by some evidence of increasing anti-semitisim and an at times irrational anxiety about Muslims. Although NATO appears to be viewed with indifference by the majority of the Russian people, opposition to its continued existence remains a potent rallying cry for the forces of reaction.[211]

104. NATO's fundamental interests are that Russia remains at peace with itself and its neighbours, that it remains committed to a democratic course and to internationally recognised standards of human rights, that it sustains its integrity as a coherent state able to implement arms control and other treaty commitments and that it continues to develop its relations with NATO on the basis of consultation, transparency, reciprocity and equality. Particularly at this critical time of internal difficulty, we think it important to stress that it is for Russia to decide how to realise these principles. The challenge for NATO is to persuade Russia, whatever its government, that it will gain more from respecting these principles than it will from contravening them.

105. Russian politicians are inclined to view the Washington Summit as a triumphalist celebration of a Cold War victory, and fear that the new Strategic Concept will mark a retreat from the development of NATO as a political organisation to an explicit prioritisation of military force as a legitimate instrument of diplomacy. Their fears should not be dismissed as groundless and **the drafters of the new Strategic Concept would be well-advised to consider very carefully how they can foreground the principles of cooperation and negotiation and make clear that the use of military force in support of political objectives (however worthy those objectives may be) is a last resort.**

106. Enlargement also featured prominently in the conversation of the politicians we met in Moscow, and in a generally unfavourable light.[212] However, our assessment of reactions to the actual accession of the three new Members (which took place on the very eve of our arrival) was that it was now accepted, however reluctantly, as a *fait accompli*. As one former military officer who is now a member of the Duma commented, "If a bride swaps one bridegroom for another, it isn't always clear which is the lucky one".[213] But all our interlocutors were agreed on two points—that the time at which Russia could be reconciled to the accession of a former constituent parts of the USSR to NATO was a long way distant, and that anxiety about the approach of NATO's borders to the western borders of Russia would be greatly increased by the stationing of foreign forces in the new members' territories. We have more to say on the first issue in our later section on enlargement. On the latter point, **NATO has already stated that it has no plan, no intention and no reason to station forces (either conventional or nuclear) in the new members' territories, and we see no reason why this commitment should not be**

---

[209]Embassy briefing, 14 and 15 March 1999

[210]Meetings with Defence and Foreign Affairs Committee, The Duma, 15 and 16 March 1999

[211]Briefing, NATO Documentation and Information Centre, Moscow, 16 March 1999

[212]Meetings at Ministry of Foreign Affairs, Ministry of Defence, 15 March 1999

[213]Meeting with Duma Defence Committee, 16 March 1999

embodied in the new Strategic Concept. However, enforced stationing of troops in Serbia would make it even more difficult to convince Russians of NATO's good intentions.

107. During and after the Washington Summit, NATO will therefore face four major challenges in its relationship with Russia. The first, in the words of the NATO–Russia Founding Act, will be to 'give concrete substance' to the Act's provisions and mechanisms. However, as we learned on our visit, and as is acknowledged by the Russian Ambassador to the UK—

> ... both sides approach almost diametrically the role and place of NATO in the construction of the system of European security.[214]

The Russian government has not disguised its view that NATO should evolve into a component of a comprehensive European security system—

> ... a united Europe free from dividing lines,[215]

which would give Russia a *de facto* veto over the way in which NATO interpreted and honoured its treaty commitments. Our interlocutors in Moscow repeatedly called for a strengthening of the prerogatives of the OSCE, whose leading members might form a European Security Council in all but name.[216] (As discussed above,[217] it can be argued that the Contact Group is beginning to take on this function.) In the longer term, the Russian position is that—

> ... there should be no closed élite club–type groups of countries in [the Euro–Atlantic] space.[218]

108. NATO has consistently supported collaboration with the OSCE, and we support further strengthening of this body, and it has also been open to measures which would enable that organisation to play a fuller part in crisis prevention and management, as well as in post-conflict conciliation. But in the Founding Act's own terms, which Russia has accepted, the Alliance has also consistently opposed steps that would 'provide NATO or Russia in any way with a right of veto over the actions of the other' or which would 'infringe upon or restrict the rights of NATO or Russia to independent decision making and action'.[219]   Russia cannot have it both ways on this question, however.   While it asserts its right to untrammelled freedom of action in establishing its security mechanisms on its southern and eastern borders,[220] it seeks to assert a predominant role in Europe's own security arrangements on its western borders. For its part the Alliance has never interposed itself in security mechanisms that Russia and its CIS[221] partners have established on a voluntary basis.

109. The most practical means of 'giving concrete substance' to the Founding Act lie in the mechanisms under the Permanent Joint Council which were beginning to function before Russia withdrew cooperation with NATO after the start of air strikes against the Federal Republic of Yugoslavia's armed forces on 24 March. Even so, it was still unclear how many of them were likely to fulfil their potential. Were these mechanisms to be brought fully to life following the Washington Summit, they could have three positive effects. First, they could provide the most effective means of breaking down stereotypes on both sides (stereotypes about which our own prejudices were certainly challenged by our visit) and expanding knowledge of NATO in Russia's security establishment. They could supplement high level consultation with working relationships between entities and individuals with 'hands on' responsibility in areas ranging from law enforcement to defence industry conversion. Moreover, as a first step to creating a common security culture, they could create institutional networks with an interest in ensuring that differences in policy did not lead to estrangement. NATO has developed a 'bottom-up' security

---

[214]Ev p 138
[215]Statement by the Deputy Foreign Minister of the Russian Federation, Munich, February 1999
[216]Ev p 139
[217]See para 73
[218]Statement by the Deputy Foreign Minister of the Russian Federation, Munich, February 1999
[219]NATO–Russia Founding Act, part II
[220]Meeting at HQ of CIS, 16 March 1999
[221]Commonwealth of Independent States

culture, which makes decisions not only by consensus but for the most part at committee level. Most of the Russian political élite has yet to appreciate this, let alone appreciate that the best way to influence NATO is to participate in it. Dr Irina Isakova writes that—

In some cases the Alliance was too slow to react to Russian proposals for cooperation,[222]

and this should not recur. **If NATO seeks to strengthen cooperation with Russia, not to say democracy and pluralism within Russia itself, it must invest as much effort in developing relationships with institutions as with high level officials.**

110. The second major challenge for NATO will be to exert a positive influence over the development of Russia's security policy and the direction of its military reform. The National Security Concept approved by President Yeltsin on 17th December 1997 is (from a NATO perspective) a broadly positive document which recognises that—

... the threat of large-scale aggression ... is virtually absent in the foreseeable future

and which notes significant opportunities to ensure Russia's national security by 'non-military means'.[223] But the characterisation of NATO enlargement as 'a threat to its national security' is one of many statements which suggest that there is still a disturbing gap between Western intentions and Russian perceptions of them. Although Russia's desire to preserve nuclear deterrence at a time of relative conventional military weakness is understandable, we are disturbed by a policy which assigns primacy to nuclear weapons in 'preventing both nuclear and conventional large-scale *or regional* wars'. Finally, we are concerned at the risks that the large number of Russian 'force ministries',[224] the deterioration in service conditions and training, and the partial degradation of command-and-control systems might pose to the management of conflicts.[225] **Russia's military doctrine, the condition of its armed forces, as well as their employment, will continue to remain important factors in European security. NATO has compelling reason to support policies designed to produce militarily effective and defensively structured armed forces that are firmly controlled by democratic, civilian authority.**

111. On our visit to Moscow we saw one concrete and small-scale example of the benefits of bilateral cooperation in this area. We were able to attend the graduation ceremony at a college outside Moscow[226] for a number of former military officers who had completed a retraining conversion course to prepare them for civilian employment. This was part of a joint German-UK funded initiative, currently funded by the UK to the tune of £1.2 million per year.[227] Our reception, and the reactions of the course participants, were a very vivid demonstration of the immense benefits such programmes bring in cementing relationships with the ordinary people of Russia, and demystifying the ogre of NATO as it is presented in much populist propaganda. **We recommend that this programme should continue to be funded and improved, for example by helping such former military officers to set up small businesses. It should serve as a model for other initiatives for practical, grass-roots cooperation with Russia in resolving the problems of the legacy of the Cold War.**

112. The third and related challenge in a less certain political climate will be to ensure Russia's continued adherence to arms limitation, verification and non-proliferation regimes. Apart from Russia's failure to ratify START II, which as we saw in Moscow largely reflects disagreement between the executive and parliament,[228] there are several areas of concern. First, Russia has taken only limited steps to implement US-Russian presidential undertakings to eliminate several categories of non-strategic nuclear weapons. A May 1998 meeting under the auspices of the PJC failed to provide any illumination on the disposition of 10,000 to 12,000 weapons in this

---

[222]*Relations with Russia: go slow, don't spoil the illusion*, RUSI Journal Feb/March 1999
[223]Russia's National Security Concept
[224]Ministries which control armed forces
[225]Meeting at Defence Ministry, 15 March 1999
[226]Scholkovo, 17 March 1999
[227]MoD briefing
[228]Meetings with Duma Defence Committee and Ministry of Defence, 15 March 1999

category. Second, if the interest expressed by some officials in developing 'third-generation nuclear weapons' with limited collateral effects were realised, it would not only raise questions about Russia's interpretation of the Comprehensive Test Ban Treaty, it might have reciprocal effects in the United States, which abandoned acquisition programmes for new nuclear delivery systems in 1991. Third, we are concerned by the influence of those inside official structures as well as outside them who believe that proliferation of missile technology offers a cost-effective means of expanding Russian influence and earning much needed foreign currency. We strongly favour early (albeit much belated) Russian unconditional ratification of the START II treaty and the early commencement of START III nuclear disarmament negotiations with the United States and NATO.

113. In turn, we believe that NATO should not minimise two areas of concern to Russia. The first is legitimate frustration at the pace of Treaty on Conventional Armed Forces in Europe (CFE) revision.[229] Again, this was a constant theme of our discussions in Moscow. Nobody contests the view that the 1991 Treaty has ceased to accord with military reality. The Founding Act rightly calls for adaptation 'as expeditiously as possible', bearing in mind that the new Treaty-Limited Equipment ceilings should ensure equal security not only for NATO and Russia, but for all States Parties, including newly independent states of the former Soviet Union. We favour early, re-negotiation of the CFE Treaty limits. The second area of concern is ballistic missile defence (BMD). The growth of interest in this area, particularly on the part of the United States, is driven by third–country missile programmes among potential 'rogue states' rather than by Russia's force posture. But no matter how often this point is made, we again heard frequently in Moscow that BMD programmes that appear to contravene the Anti Ballistic Missile Treaty run the risk of triggering dramatic changes in Russian policy, damaging as those might be to Russia's own long-term economic interests. **Pressures on NATO to acquire ballistic missile defences and on Russia to proceed down the path of nuclearisation are likely to grow rather than diminish. It will require imagination and restraint to respond to them in ways that do not damage fundamental mutual interests.**

114. The fourth challenge will be the maintenance of cooperation in the Balkans. Whatever agreements are ultimately reached on the ground, the likelihood is that the region will remain a zone of instability and of anxiety to both NATO and Russia. The risk of alienating Russia stems less from divergent geopolitical interests—although these were much discussed during our visit to Moscow—than from more internal factors, among the principal ones being a fear of insurrection within the borders of Russia. President Yeltsin and Prime Minister Primakov have therefore opposed the use of force by NATO against Serbia: not because it might fail to achieve its political end, but because it will appear to demonstrate to a wider Russian public that NATO's rhetorical commitment to equality of treatment is not borne out in practice. We recognise that NATO policy must be influenced by other considerations as well as these: not only the intrinsic humanitarian dimensions of the conflict, but the perils which this conflict poses to a region bordering a long–standing NATO member, Greece and a new NATO member, Hungary, as well as many of NATO's Partners.[230] **Forceful measures against the Federal Republic of Yugoslavia will provoke a strong public response from Russia, and NATO should be prepared to respond with rational argument. The challenge will be to preserve, behind the scenes, the mutual will to continue diplomatic cooperation in the Balkans, maintain the integrity of the Contact Group and continue military cooperation in Bosnia and Herzegovina.**

115. It must be remembered that, despite their differences, NATO and Russia have already made much progress together. As the Russian Ambassador to Britain told us, they have—

> ... together rid the world community of a heavy burden—the global confrontation between two opposing political systems which was the main driving force of the Cold War.[231]

---

[229]The CFE limits certain types of military equipment. It provides for information exchange and a rigorous inspection regime, with a Joint Consultative Group made up of state representatives conferring on any problems. The Treaty's objective is to reduce existing imbalances in the number of major conventional weapon systems in Europe so that capabilities for launching a surprise attack or large–scale offensive are limited.

[230]QQ 356–359

[231]Ev p 137

Michael MccGwire has described the dangers inherent in any breakdown of cooperation; such a breakdown—

> ... could negate Western attempts to contain conflicts such as those in the former Yugoslavia. It could bring to a halt the process of dismantling Russia's nuclear arsenals.[232]

The fundamental interest of both NATO and Russia—lasting security in the Euro–Atlantic area—remains the same; they are—

> ... two separate, balancing entities with a common interest in stability in Europe,[233]

NATO must ensure that its new Strategic Concept as well as its policy towards future NATO enlargement are as sensitive as possible to Russian concerns—

> ... NATO's policy will have to be formulated flexibly and with due regard for the evolving situation in Russia.[234]

116. **NATO's relations with Russia are constrained by Russia's internal mood and its attitude to sometimes unrelated global events. To maintain the maximum influence possible, NATO will need to give clarity to its policies and goals, especially when they diverge from Russia's, and develop relationships with individuals and institutions who see the value in practical, case–by–case cooperation. This has so far proved difficult in practice, but NATO must redouble its efforts.** NATO action to end the ethnic cleansing of Kosovo by Serbia will undoubtedly be portrayed by elements within Russia as a rehearsal for further NATO operations on the borders of the Russian Federation, or even within it. The diplomatic effort to persuade Russia that it is not the focus of an aggressive NATO strategy to further weaken its influence will become accordingly harder. Even after the air strikes had begun, however, the Russian government was making positive efforts to broker a peace deal in Kosovo. The first thing we could do is to re-emphasise to Russia that it is still welcome to attend the NATO Summit, and that debate about the Alliance's strategy in the Balkans is not closed. **We express the hope that Russia will attend the Washington Summit; this would be a powerful boost to future cooperation.** But even if Russia does not, we favour security cooperation between NATO and Russia being strengthened.

Ukraine

117. Ukraine became an independent state and member of the Commonwealth of Independent States in December 1991. Since March of this year, it now shares a border with two NATO members—Hungary and Poland. We visited Kyiv in the immediate aftermath of their formal accession, where we held discussions with representatives of the Defence and Foreign ministries, the National Security and Defence Council and of the Parliament, the Supreme Rada.

118. The Washington Summit is likely to underscore the view that Ukraine is a 'pivot' in European security. NATO not only has a stake in Ukraine's independence and friendship but, as with Russia, in its beneficial internal development. A secure and economically successful Ukraine will advance NATO's security objectives in several key respects.

119. First and foremost are the intrinsic benefits of stability in a country bordering two NATO members,[235] as well as two other Partnership countries who have applied for membership.[236] Second and almost as important, a Ukraine achieving its official goal of 'full integration' into Europe is likely to have a beneficial effect on Russia, strengthening those who believe in the feasibility of a European course. Furthermore, a Ukraine moving closer to NATO also has the potential to reinforce Turkey's role in NATO and the wider security of the region.

---

[232] Ev p 108
[233] Ev p 120
[234] *ibid*
[235] Poland and Hungary
[236] Romania and Slovakia

120. Perhaps the greatest contribution made by Ukraine to European security was the country's unilateral nuclear disarmament, codified by the US–Russia–Ukraine Tripartite Agreement of January 1994, which led to the removal of the last of over 500 tactical and 1,600 strategic nuclear warheads by June 1996.[237] Ukraine has acceded to the Nuclear Non–Proliferation Treaty as a non–nuclear state. It was the first country of the former Soviet Union to join Partnership for Peace,[238] and has conducted over 100 exercises under PfP and 'within the spirit of PfP'. Although the June 1996 Constitution enshrines the country's neutrality, the Ukraine government has been generally supportive of NATO's enlargement, and its November 1998 State Programme of Cooperation with NATO categorises NATO 'as the most effective structure of collective security in Europe'. Ukraine has also taken comprehensive steps to develop 'strategic partnerships'—and resolve border disputes and minority problems—with neighbours, most recently with Romania.[239] We pay warm tribute to Ukraine for all these significant actions.

121. On the front of civil reform within Ukraine, there has recently been some erosion of economic progress. There has been an increase in its indebtedness, and criminality and corruption in the economic sphere remains a problem. The government has yet to establish, let alone entrench, a civic and legal culture and degree of transparency conducive to effective state authority, open market relations and improved living conditions.[240] Ukraine's National Security Concept[241] expresses the view that these problems might, in combination, constitute a threat to Ukraine's security. While on our visit we discovered very positive attitudes towards NATO and Europe among representatives of the government,[242] there are those who express concern at the growing influence of those who perceive some kind of 'union' with Russia as the solution to Ukraine's problems. If their influence grows (and it was apparent amongst some of the parliamentarians we met), NATO may find that its policies carry less weight than they have in the past.

122. Ukraine's security and defence establishment is, as we discovered, vastly more pro–Western than its Russian counterpart, and has institutionalised cooperation in ways that will be difficult to reverse. The NATO–Ukraine Charter on a Distinctive Partnership,[243] signed in Madrid on 9 July 1997, builds upon a web of cooperation which already existed. This cooperation is strengthened by the bilateral UK–Ukraine MoD Programme of Cooperation, second in scale only to that maintained between Ukraine and the United States.[244] But NATO must ensure that its programmes address Ukraine's specific security needs and that they are seen to do so. Three areas are possibly in need of even greater attention than they have received.

123. First, more needs to be done in helping Ukraine rationalise its national security system. As the Deputy Defence Minister reminded us, in 1991 Ukraine did not inherit an army, but a force grouping—without a Defence Ministry, General Staff or central organs of command-and-control.[245] Since then, Ukraine has made enormous progress, not only in 'reforming' an army, but creating one. The National Security and Defence Council—that part of the Presidential administration that 'coordinates and controls the activity of executive bodies in the sphere of national security and defence' and whose Secretary we met in Kyiv—is staffed and led by individuals who understand the importance of creating not only a system of democratic, civilian control, but a transparent system of planning, programming and defence budgeting.[246] The Ministry of Defence and General Staff whom we met also appeared to recognise the need for further reform, if somewhat reluctant to surrender more control to civilians. These efforts, however, are still at a relatively rudimentary stage and have yet to be reinforced by consistent political direction, competent parliamentary oversight and in-depth civilian expertise. Moreover,

---

[237]Meeting at National Security and Defence Council, 18 March 1999
[238]on 8 February, 1994
[239]Meeting at Ministry of Foreign Affairs, 19 March 1999
[240]Meeting with Presidential Administration, Foreign Affairs Department, 18 March 1999
[241]January 1997
[242]Meeting with National Security and Defence Council, 18 March 1999
[243]Charter on a Distinctive Partnership between the North Atlantic Treaty Organization and Ukraine, available on the Internet at www.nato.int/docu/basictxt/ukrchrt.htm
[244]Embassy Briefings, 17 March 1999
[245]Meeting at Ministry of Defence, 19 March 1999
[246]Meeting with Mr Horbulin, 18 March 1999

in Ukraine as in Russia, there has been a worrying proliferation of 'force ministries' and insufficient coordination between them. As a Partner and sovereign state, it is of course up to Ukraine to define the form and level of cooperation that suits its interests. Nevertheless, we hope that the Working Group on Defence Reform established under the Distinctive Partnership will define clear objectives in this area.

124. Second, NATO has made only sporadic attempts to meet concerns about defence industry conversion and the retraining of retired and decommissioned servicemen. In this area as in the other two, we doubt whether high–level meetings and conferences will produce results on their own. Even if on a small scale and within modest budgetary outlays, cooperation should be continuous, conducted at working level and on site. What matters is to create models of success which Ukrainians can build upon, and the example which we experienced in Russia[247] serves as an excellent model to be pursued in Ukraine.

125. The third factor is Ukraine–NATO cooperation in Civil Emergency Planning first instituted in 1992. Since then cooperation has expanded to include a Memorandum Of Understanding on Civil Emergency Planning and Disaster Preparedness, the NATO–Ukraine Working Group on Civil Emergency Planning, the appointment of a representative from the Ministry of Emergency Situations to the Ukrainian Mission to NATO, the establishment of a Euro-Atlantic Disaster Response Coordination Centre and a number of crisis management exercises. To a country still suffering the effects of the Chernobyl catastrophe (and which devotes more resources to Chernobyl than to any single item in its state budget), the issue has profound psychological as well as practical importance. It is also of direct importance to national security. Ukraine's National Security Concept identifies ecological factors as one of six 'main potential threats' which individually or in combination could endanger the state. We believe there are other countries in Central and Eastern Europe which face similar problems and perceive that in this field Ukraine has at least as much to teach as it has to learn.

126. Finally, there is an area of development which lies somewhat outside the focus of this Report and of our area of concern, but which we believe deserves mention. All the valuable efforts which NATO has made to integrate Ukraine into stable European security arrangements could be vitiated if we fail to assist Ukraine to become a prosperous, free-enterprise economy. Our self-interest and our moral obligations coincide here. As we stated above, Chernobyl remains a massive drain on Ukraine's resources. That legacy is no fault of the present government or people of Ukraine, and we should not forget their heroic efforts to mitigate the potential world-wide effects of the disaster, or the terrible legacy with which they still have to deal. We heard on our visit their perception of the failure of the EU or other institutions to support their moves to close the other reactors at Chernobyl and build replacement power stations. We believe the failure to support this and other areas of Ukraine's economic development is unwise. NATO-Ukraine cooperation risks being vitiated by the widespread perception in Ukraine that international economic aid has been miserly.

127. We were told on our visit to Kyiv, several times in different words, that Ukraine does not share Russia's geopolitical and strategic interests.[248] Its government does not accept that Russia has a zone of interest distinct from NATO's, which must allow it to be the predominant power in the Baltics, Central and Eastern Europe and the Transcaucasus. A speech by the Secretary of the National Security and Defence Council to a NATO Conference which took place during our visit to Kyiv, sums up this position—

> ... the door of the Alliance should remain open for all countries that express the wish to join it ... In Washington we should receive a clear signal that the former Soviet Republics along with former Warsaw Pact members should not be left alone with the problems of providing for their own security ... Ukraine welcomes development of the dialogue between Russia and NATO ... At the same time, we are genuinely surprised that an influential part of the Russian political elite, while declaring their support for developing cooperation between the Russian Federation and NATO, is trying with all their might to obstruct developing relations of the Alliance with the other CIS countries, and primarily with Ukraine ... We

---

[247]See para 111
[248]Meetings in Kyiv, 18 and 19 March 1999

view such an approach as a glaring example of a 'double standard' policy towards Ukraine and NATO that is aimed not at cooperation but rather at confrontation ... Development of cooperation with the Alliance is based primarily on Ukraine's desire to ensure its independence, democratic development and territorial integrity, to strengthen external guarantees for national security, and to counteract the emergence of new threats to peace and stability in the Central and East European region, of which it is an inseparable part ... In this connection, it should be noted that there has been no instance on the part of NATO or its member states of a hint of any territorial claims on Ukraine. At the same time we are all witnesses to the recurrent claims on the part of some politicians from the fraternal Slavic nation and our strategic partner—the Russian Federation. Consequently, the leadership of Ukraine cannot but take these factors into account in formulating the country's foreign policy course ... Ukraine's cooperation with NATO is therefore in line with the strategic course of integration into European and Euro-Atlantic structures ... though Ukraine is not now raising the issue of joining NATO, it reserves the right ... to become a member of any military-political structure ... The decision to join any military-political structure, including NATO, is an inalienable right of any nation, and nobody can veto this sovereign right. Attempts to draw new 'red line' spheres of influence across the map of Europe ... are unacceptable.

But it is committed to working with Russia. Mr Horbulin went on to say in the same speech—

... It goes without saying that Ukraine's European and Euro-Atlantic integration can in no way can be conducted at the expense of narrowing mutually beneficial cooperation with the Russian Federation ... The Ukrainian-Russian relationship is an important component of European security architecture, and its status affects the stability of the entire European continent.

We believe that all of Europe would benefit from a close, growing relationship between the Russian Federation and a secure and independent Ukraine. But it is also clear from our visits to Moscow and Kyiv that this relationship is likely to remain problematic. The 1998 financial crisis has been exploited, even within parts of Russia's government, to raise hopes that a Slavic Union of Russia, Ukraine and Belarus is a realistic prospect. As we found in Kyiv, these views exist in Ukraine as well, but even a communist-led government might be cautious in advancing them too far, given the attachment of much of the population to Ukrainian sovereignty and the strength of national feeling in the country as a whole.[249] Russia's own internal problems have meant that, the last 12 months have been a time of retreat after a period of potential breakthroughs in relations, which culminated in the Inter-Governmental Accords on the Black Sea Fleet, the Interstate Treaty of Friendship and Partnership, the lifting of double taxation on Ukrainian goods and the respective visits of the two state Presidents. **NATO must approach the Ukraine–Russia relationship with subtlety and discretion. Nevertheless we should leave no doubt that Russia's respect for Ukrainian sovereignty and territorial integrity is not a bilateral matter, but a fundamental interest of the Alliance and a requirement of international law.**

128. NATO established close partnership relations with Ukraine not because of developments in Russia, but because Ukraine was ready for them; similarly the UK–Ukraine Bilateral Programme had reached a high level of activity well before a bilateral programme with Russia was established. Nonetheless, the Kosovo crisis may complicate the NATO-Ukraine relationship, although we hope its negative effects will persist only in the short term. A government which has loudly trumpeted the peacefulness and defensiveness of NATO is bound to feel vulnerable about expanding cooperation at a time when official opinion in Russia is outraged and public opinion in Ukraine is shaken. Ironically, it is pro-NATO opinion—understandably the most attached to the principles of sovereignty and territorial integrity, the most wary of those who might use 'human rights' as a justification to abridge them and the most conscious of a separatist challenge within Ukraine's own borders (Crimea)—who will be the most apprehensive about NATO's action, even if anti-NATO opinion will be the most angered by it. Nonetheless, NATO must not subsume its relations with Ukraine to considerations

---

[249]Meeting with Rada Defence and Foreign Affairs Committees, 18 March 1999

of Russia's position. **Any attempt to link progress in NATO's relationship with Ukraine to progress with Russia would insult Ukraine's independent status, diminish Western influence and undo much of what has been achieved.** If problems arise in this relationship, they should reflect the problems of the relationship, not the difficulties of a third country.

129. One of our interlocutors in Kyiv described 'Natoisation' of Ukraine as a prelude to membership of the EU. He told us that NATO had "changed in its essence" in the last decade, and placed its development firmly in the context of the PfP and the EAPC, the OSCE and the WEU (of which Ukraine is an associate, as well as being a member of the Council of Europe) as representing a growing European Security and Defence Identity.[250] It is in this context of the web of cooperation which underpins security and stability in the new Europe that NATO's relationship with Ukraine must be developed. **Ukraine is at present a contributor to security in the region, rather than a consumer. We must be prepared to ensure that it remains so, and improved NATO-Ukraine relations are essential for this to continue.**

Belarus

130. The government in Minsk appears, if anything, more intransigent in its public attitudes towards NATO than that of Russia. Its economy is in ruins. President Lukashenko's main policy appears to be to recreate a 'Greater Russia' by reuniting Belarus, Ukraine and Russia in something approaching the former Soviet Union.[251] There seems little enthusiasm for this project in either of his proposed partners outside the ranks of the incorrigible remnants of the old regime. There was also talk within Russia of 'rearming' Belarus, or even stationing nuclear weapons there. However, we understand that realists within the political élite, and even within the armed forces, recognise that such a move would be likely to backfire on Russia. But the prospects of any *rapprochement* between NATO and Belarus seem remote. The present government of Belarus will only be reconciled to the new European security order, it would seem, when Russia is and it has no other choice, or when President Lukachenko is replaced by a more democratic and modern-thinking leader.

Central Asia and the Transcaucasus

131. It is the security situation on Russia's southern borders which, as we discovered on our visit to Moscow, drives much of Russia's foreign and security policy.[252] The memory of the Chechen war is still raw. This is an additional driver of Russia's attitude to the situation in Kosovo. The region is certainly unstable—there is continued warfare and terrorist activity in the autonomous republics of the Russian north Caucasus, there is renewed ethnic conflict within and between the Transcaucasus states; there is growing competition over access to natural resources, particularly water, oil and gas; there is growing fear of a real or imagined increase in Islamic fundamentalist activity; and there are the widespread problems of poverty and the political turmoil which in most of these countries has followed the attempted transition to a market economy. There is also a legacy of weapons in the area left behind by the Soviet armed forces, and this contributes to instability in the region, although the withdrawal of nuclear weapons from Kazakhstan eased the threat.

132. Although the EU has sought to build up political and civil institutions and entrench human rights, progress in the region has not been rapid. Georgia is making progress, and is on track to be granted membership of the Council of Europe. Progress in Armenia and Azerbaijan is still retarded by the effects of the Nagorno-Karabakh war. Armenia is, however, displaying some signs of democratic development.[253] Azerbaijan's President Aliyev could not be described as a democrat, but has succeeded in unsettling Russia and his neighbours by threatening to invite NATO to establish a base in his country. This ludicrous and empty threat was a constant topic of discussion during our visit to Moscow, and was seized upon by several of our interlocutors there (whether cynically or credulously it was difficult to tell) as evidence of NATO's aggressive

---

[250]Meeting at National Security and Defence Council, 18 March 1999
[251]This proposal was referred to at several meetings in Moscow and Kyiv between 15 and 19 March 1999
[252]Meetings in Moscow, 15 to 17 March 1999
[253]See eg *The New Caucasus: Armenia, Azerbaijan and Georgia in the 1990s*, E Herzig, Chatham House, 1999

territorial ambitions. In contrast, the close military relationship between Russia and Armenia is well attested, and appears to have involved large scale transfers of weapons. There is scant progress towards democracy in Kazakhstan, Kyrgyzstan, Tajikistan, Turkmenistan or Uzbekistan.

133. However, all the nations in the region, with the exception of Tajikistan are members of PfP, and several have received funding from the UK's Military Training and Support programme (now replaced by the ASSIST scheme). Interestingly, a number of the states in the region manage to combine PfP membership with membership of the Treaty for Collective Security of the CIS. It is in this region that the interests of NATO and Russia in the establishment of stability most coincide, and if NATO can persuade Russia that stability in the Balkans and stability in Central Asia and the Transcaucasus are goals where they can develop mutually reinforcing policies, then this may do much to cement relations.

The Baltic States

134. We were unable to visit the Baltic States (Latvia, Lithuania and Estonia) during the course of this inquiry, an omission we hope to remedy at some stage. Their refusal to join the Commonwealth of Independent States symbolises their wholesale rejection of their Soviet past, and the refusal of their governments to acknowledge that they were ever legitimately parts of the USSR. They appear to regard membership of NATO as offering a far better guarantee of their independence than Russia might. The Russian government remains adamant that any invitation to them to join NATO would be seen, if not as an act of aggression, at the very least as a serious breach of trust. In any event, the date at which their accession to NATO is likely to be seriously contemplated is, in our view, some way in the future.

Membership of European Organisations

	OSCE	PFP	EAPC	WEU	EU	NATO
Belgium	■	■	■	■	■	■
Denmark	■	■	■	★	■	■
France	■	■	■	■	■	■
Germany	■	■	■	■	■	■
Greece	■	■	■	■	■	■
Italy	■	■	■	■	■	■
Luxembourg	■	■	■	■	■	■
Netherlands	■	■	■	■	■	■
Portugal	■	■	■	■	■	■
Spain	■	■	■	■	■	■
United Kingdom	■	■	■	■	■	■
Iceland	■	■	■	●		■
Norway	■	■	■	●		■
Turkey	■	■	■	●		■
Republic of Ireland	■			★	■	
Austria	■	■	■	★	■	
Finland	■	■	■	★	■	
Sweden	■	■	■	★	■	
Bulgaria	■	■	■	□		
Czech Republic	■	■	■	□		■
Estonia	■	■	■	□		
Hungary	■	■	■	□		■
Latvia	■	■	■	□		
Lithuania	■	■	■	□		
Poland	■	■	■	□		■
Romania	■	■	■	□		
Slovakia	■	■	■	□		
Canada	■	■	■			■
US	■	■	■			■
Albania	■	■	■			
Armenia	■	■	■			
Azerbaijan	■	■	■			
Belarus	■	■	■			
FYROM	■	■	■			
Georgia	■	■	■			
Kazakstan	■	■	■			
Kyrgyzstan	■	■	■			
Moldova	■	■	■			
Russia	■	■	■			
Slovenia	■	■	■			
Turkmenistan	■	■	■			
Ukraine	■	■	■			
Uzbekistan	■	■	■			
Malta	■					
Tajikistan	■	■	■			
Andorra	■					
Bosnia and Herzegovina	■					
Croatia	■					
Cyprus	■					
Holy See	■					
Liechtenstein	■					
Monaco	■					
San Marino	■					
Switzerland	■	■	■			
FRY	▽					

Legend:

- OSCE — Organisation for Security and Cooperation in Europe (OSCE)
- PFP — Partnership for Peace (PFP)
- EAPC — Euro-Atlantic Partnership Council (EAPC)
- WEU — Western European Union (WEU)
- EU — European Union (EU)
- NATO — North Atlantic Treaty Organisation (NATO)
- ★ Observer
- ● Associate Member
- □ Associate Partner
- ▽ Membership suspended

Source: The Military Balance 1997/98: The International Institute for Strategic Studies

NATO ENLARGEMENT

135. Last year the Committee undertook an inquiry into the enlargement of NATO announced at the Alliance's 1997 Madrid Summit. We looked at the context of enlargement; the possible effects on NATO as a whole; and the financial costs of the Alliance's invitations to the Czech Republic, Hungary and Poland. We took oral evidence from the Ministry of Defence, the Foreign and Commonwealth Office and, uniquely, members of the governments of Hungary and Poland; we also received written evidence from many and varied sources and visited NATO HQ in Brussels. It is not our intention to rehearse the arguments that we made in our Report[254] here, but to examine further developments in this area since we reported in March 1998 and to draw wider conclusions about the future of NATO.

136. This is not the Alliance's first enlargement: Greece and Turkey joined in 1952, the Federal Republic of Germany in 1955, and Spain in 1982. However, the current redrawing of NATO's boundaries to include former members of the Warsaw Treaty Organisation is of an entirely different order. As our previous Report outlined, there had been opposition to the current round of enlargement on several grounds: political (that invitations to Russia's former allies were several steps too far for that country), military (that the invitees' militaries were underdeveloped and underfunded) and economic (that the costs of enlargement to fall to current members were too high). However, at the Madrid Summit in 1997 those who were pro-enlargement prevailed, and NATO committed itself not only to this, but also to further rounds of enlargement. We were among those who welcomed this, concluding in our Report that the possibility of full membership of NATO had led to real improvements in the security of Europe—

... the incentive to improve the structure and control of the military, to enhance democracy and to resolve border disputes and internal problems with ethnic minorities ... would not have been as strong without the possibility of full membership of NATO;[255]

and, while recognising the misgivings that Russia had on enlargement, we endorsed the choice of invitees, stating that—

... none of the three countries invited to accede to NATO was an inappropriate choice.[256]

With regard to NATO's 'open door' policy, however, we judged that—

... we should approach any further enlargement with caution.[257]

NATO'S three new members

137. In the intervening period, between invitation and accession, both NATO and the three invited countries have been focussing their efforts on bringing the countries' military and political structures up to the required NATO standard. As previously discussed, the three invitees will not—as originally envisaged—formally accede to NATO during the Washington Summit itself, but have already completed the protocols and became full members of the Alliance on 12th March 1999. The efforts of NATO's three latest members to enter the Alliance as producers, rather than mere consumers, of security have been commendable and more substantial than we might have expected in the time available. The Czech Republic, Hungary and Poland have not only reduced the size of their military establishments (as mandated by the CFE Treaty), they have changed force postures and deployments, reformed systems of training and education and made substantial progress in producing the legislative framework required to make democratic, civilian control a reality. They are also contributing assets and facilities of direct importance to NATO's new, wider security and peace-support functions—especially in the case of Hungary which, at some risk to itself, has offered valuable host country transit, logistics and training support for IFOR and SFOR.

---

[254]Third Report, Session 1997–98, *NATO Enlargement*, HC 469
[255]*ibid*, para 33
[256]*ibid*, para 98
[257]*ibid*, para 108

138. We visited Hungary during the course of this inquiry and found that Hungary's achievements in its preparations for NATO membership have so far been impressive: a mostly civilian Defence Ministry has been created and the Army is being restructured. However, we heard that major problems remain with command and control and logistics. There is a serious equipment shortfall; the Army still relies on conscripts; and there may be a problem with IT interoperability of high–level systems. Pilots achieve well under the NATO standard of 200 hours' annual flying time. We were told that one of the major problems faced by the three invitees is lack of proficiency in speaking English among military and civilian personnel: in Hungary's case, perhaps 1000 of its 50,000–strong armed forces have reasonable English, with a further 300 fluent.

139. There is little doubt that there remain shortfalls in the capabilities of all three states (many of which will not have been resolved by the time of the Washington Summit in any case). As the Chairman of NATO's Military Committee has stated—

The three invitees have the double requirement to achieve interoperability with the rest of the Alliance and to upgrade their forces as necessary. These challenges are significant and will not be resolved prior to ratification ... I would anticipate it will take us a couple of years before the issue of interoperability is largely resolved, while equipment upgrades may take considerably longer.[258]

One of our witnesses suggested that it may take fifteen years or longer, rather than the ten envisaged by the 'general western view', to modernise the invitees' armed forces.[259] We were told at the Supreme Headquarters Allied Powers Europe that one of the lessons learned from this enlargement was that a two year preparation period was required to get a country in synch with the Alliance's Force Planning Process. This would suggest that the next round of enlargement should not take place before 2001 at the earliest. We outlined in our previous Report that this round of enlargement was based on political rather than military considerations,[260] and it remains the case, as stated in that Report, that NATO's military effectiveness can only, in the short term at least, be diluted by this enlargement.

140. **Yet there should be no doubt that the principal challenges are not those that have been faced, but those that lie ahead.** Only since the Madrid summit has it become thoroughly clear to the invited countries that NATO is not a substitute for national defence policy, but a framework for it and that far from removing pressure for change, membership will both intensify and institutionalise it. To date, none of the three new members possess armed forces and national security systems which are wholly NATO compatible. There have tended to be inconsistent, rather than coherent and sustained, efforts to connect the first principles of national defence with detailed programmes of force development and institutional reform. Military establishments have not felt at ease with themselves, confident of their place in the new democratic order or genuinely valued by it. Unsurprisingly, the armed forces have had difficulty recruiting and retaining talented officers and building up a corps of proficient NCOs.[261] Resource constraints, certain to continue,[262] have only exacerbated these problems, but they are secondary to the problems themselves. **Despite these deficiencies, we have been most impressed by the will shown by the Czech Republic, Hungary and Poland since the Madrid summit to address deficiencies and by the progress achieved. But it would be unrealistic to expect the integration of new members to be either rapid or straightforward.**

141. In our Report of last year, we conducted an analysis of the various studies that had been made on the costs of NATO enlargement, for the Alliance as a whole and for the individual invitees.[263] These estimated the total cost of enlargement at anything between $1.5 billion and

---

[258] *An Evolving NATO in an Evolving World—Revisited*, General Klaus Naumann, in NATO's 16 Nations Special Issue 1998
[259] Ev p 96
[260] Third Report, 1997–98, *op cit,* para 44
[261] Ev p 99
[262] *ibid*
[263] Third Report, 1997–98, paras 53–88

$125 billion, albeit with differing risk assessments, definitions of costs and timespans. NATO's official study of December 1997, written after the decision to take on the Czech Republic, Hungary and Poland was made, estimated the cost to Allies at $1.5 billion over ten years. This figure did not include the costs payable by new members for modernising their armed forces. According to the MoD—

A further assessment of the resource implications of accession was included in the report on the Alliance's medium–term resource plan, noted by Defence Ministers at their meeting in June 1998; this confirmed the Alliance's earlier assessment that Alliance costs associated with accession would be manageable.[264]

We note that the debate on the costs of enlargement has been somewhat subdued in recent months; however, we are pleased to see that NATO is continuing to update its analysis and hope that the implications of its studies and their correlation with reality will be taken into account as the Alliance contemplates further enlargement. **However, we remain disappointed that NATO has not made publicly available, as we have requested,[265] declassified versions of its studies on the financial and military implications of enlargement.[266]**

IMPLICATIONS FOR TRANS-ATLANTIC RELATIONS

142. The implications of enlargement for the future of NATO's transatlantic relations are difficult to determine at this stage. The three new members, particularly Poland, will add some military assets to the collective pool from which the European members of NATO can draw, and are all looking for opportunities to emphasise their commitment to the Alliance and to appropriate participation in NATO's contemporary peace support operations. In adding three Central European members to the Alliance, the Europeans have that much more weight within the 19, and the new members will be anxious to demonstrate their transatlantic credentials and will be pleased to constitute some of the new fabric that will help hold Europe and the US together in the future.

143. On the other hand, there are a number of ways in which the enlargement of NATO could make transatlantic relations more problematical, and create difficulties particularly for Europe's policy planners. The NATO consensus will be more difficult to achieve at 19, especially where issues may verge on the direct interests of the new members who have common borders with Ukraine, Belarus, Serbia and some of the unsuccessful NATO candidate countries. As members of the Committee learned on their recent visit, the best of intentions at this stage in Budapest do not disguise the fact that the problem of the 3.5 million Hungarian nationals living outside the country remains a prickly one for the Hungarian government and for its bilateral partners such as the UK.

144. A NATO of 19 will embody a more diffuse set of European interests and perspectives which, on some issues, may become a good deal more delicate. It might become more difficult to establish and maintain a firm strategic purpose for the Alliance, which involves setting its internal defence and management requirements in the context of a conscious external security strategy, of which further enlargement is now a part. The danger could be a NATO that was so intent on internal political compromise that it lost effective touch with a firm strategic purpose in relation to the rest of Europe.[267] All this could be more likely in the event that widespread crises in Russia, Belarus or Ukraine put immediate pressure on the security interests of the new members and exposed them to the ripple effects of any upheavals. The credibility of the Alliance, and its cohesion, will depend on its alertness to the needs of new members, as well as its ability to act with despatch and decisiveness to the challenges they face. In the immediate afterglow of the enlargement ceremonies, a honeymoon period with the new members may be anticipated. They can all prove themselves to be valuable allies in addressing the crisis in Former

[264]Ev p 91
[265]Third Special Report, Session 1997–98, *NATO Enlargement: The Draft Visiting Forces and International Headquarters (Application of Law) (Amendment) Order 1998*, HC 903, para 4
[266]Ev p 118
[267]Hans Binnendijk and Richard Kugler, 'NATO After the First Tranche' *Strategic Forum*, 149, Oct. 1998, p 2

Yugoslavia, where their principal interests are not directly threatened. But in more extreme circumstances, the new members are likely to regard the backing of the US as their only viable reassurance, and be sceptical about any subtle adjustments of a delicate Euro-American transatlanticism. They have been anxious to join NATO for a mixture of reasons, one of the most prominent of which has been to get as close as possible to the US in their own security environment. In a situation of real pressure they would not be likely to be sympathetic to the gradual, courtly dance of transatlantic diplomacy that has become so familiar to the core European members of the Alliance over the last 50 years.

145. The United Kingdom has a potentially important role to play in preventing dislocations of this sort in the future and helping to build on the positive aspects that a NATO of 19 will offer. It can do this through the influence it derives among the new members from its military prowess—especially in peace support missions where it has established the standard that other European-NATO members seek to emulate; through its ability to offer training and military education to the new members through the medium of English—which has become the essential pre–requisite for them to operate within NATO command structures; and through its natural transatlanticism—which has provided it with some acumen in anticipating how the US and other NATO members may react to events as they emerge.

Future Enlargement

THE IMMEDIATE PROSPECTS FOR ENLARGEMENT

146. After the 1994 Brussels Summit, at which NATO committed itself to accepting new members under Article 10 of the Washington Treaty, a study on the 'how and why' (rather than the 'who and when') questions surrounding enlargement was commissioned.[268] Following the study's publication, twelve countries entered into bilateral discussions with NATO. All twelve stated their wish to join NATO at the earliest opportunity. At the Madrid Summit in 1997, NATO not only invited the Czech Republic, Hungary and Poland to begin accession negotiations, but recommitted the Alliance to an 'open door' policy regarding further enlargement.

147. Since the Madrid Summit, the nine disappointed candidates—Albania, Bulgaria, Estonia, Former Yugoslav Republic of Macedonia (FYROM), Latvia, Lithuania, Romania, Slovakia and Slovenia—have continued their dialogue with NATO in the hope of being invited to join in a future round of enlargement. It now seems likely that there will not be a concrete demonstration of the 'open door' policy at the Washington Summit, and that no new invitations to join the Alliance will be issued; nor will there be—

... earmarking of any individual country or any particular time–frame for the next round of accessions.[269]

This is partly to ease the problems of 'digesting' the three new Allies, and partly to prevent any perception that the Summit is 'about enlargement'—which is also one of the reasons for the early accession of the three invitees. Such a perception could damage NATO–Russia relations, and would certainly make attendance at the Summit difficult for Russia.

148. There appears to be little internal consensus within the Alliance about the scope or timing of future enlargement beyond the acknowledgement that it will not occur at Washington; Dr Jonathan Eyal informed us that—

It is difficult to see how a new consensus could be created for another enlargement in a few years, how the US Congress could be persuaded to ratify another wave, and how the Russians could be persuaded that, yet again, this should not threaten their interests.[270]

---

[268] *The Study on NATO Enlargement*, available on the Internet at www.nato.int/docu/basictxt/enl-9502.htm
[269] Q 72
[270] Ev p 100

However, nine self–declared candidate countries continue to knock at NATO's door, and they will not remain satisfied indefinitely without proof that that door really is open.

149. The only criteria for candidacy for NATO are that countries must be European, and that they must declare themselves as candidates. So it is no surprise that among the nine remaining candidates, varying levels of suitability for membership can be seen. In terms of military capability and civilian control; stable democracy; progress towards a market economy; respect for human rights; resolution of border disputes and problems with minority groups—all unofficial preconditions for NATO membership—each candidate displays different degrees of attainment. It is, of course, also the case that existing members of NATO display some variation in their achievements against each of these standards, and we would do well to remind some of our Allies from time to time of the need to set the highest standards against these criteria if we are to justify NATO's moral right to pick and choose its members. Romania, Slovakia and Slovenia are regularly discussed as the three top candidates—despite those countries' desires for their aspirations to be decoupled. The Baltic states are similarly linked,[271] but dogged by Russia's declaration that—

It is an open secret that if any one of these states is enticed into NATO we shall have to reconsider our relations with the Alliance.[272]

Professor Michael MccGwire informed us that—

... while Moscow sees the inclusion of Warsaw Pact members in NATO as a breach of trust, these countries are in no way comparable to the former Republics of the Soviet Union.[273]

150. While not accepting that Russia should have a veto on NATO policy, we feel that the current *rapprochement* between NATO and Russia, which was shaken but not destroyed by the Madrid Declaration, should not be jeopardised at this juncture. One witness pointed out the 'almost universal Russian resentment' over NATO enlargement.[274] During our visit to Moscow we found that this resentment, in relation to the three new members, had become more muted, and was relatively relaxed in relation to other Central and Eastern European former Warsaw Pact countries. The 'line in the sand' that could not be crossed for most Russians was the accession of countries which had formerly been part of the USSR.

151. The UK government's position on further enlargement is that it—

... supports further enlargement when the Allies collectively judge that further invitations would strengthen European security and the Alliance itself.[275]

When considering candidates for NATO membership we stand by our statement that it is NATO's military effectiveness that makes the Alliance—

... unique and uniquely valuable as a guarantor of security.[276]

We would not wish to see the Alliance's military effectiveness jeopardised by future enlargements. Certainly it is the case that few, if any, of the candidate countries could add to NATO's military effectiveness at present. And few would deny that, for example, Albania and FYROM are further away from NATO membership than many of their rivals.[277] But without dismissing the importance of military capability, we also note that NATO has never been a partnership of equals,[278] and that political considerations can prevail over military ones in the overall quest for security in the Euro–Atlantic area. In our Report last year, we concluded that

---

[271]See Third Report, Session 1997–98, *op cit* para 93

[272]Ev p 138

[273]Ev p 112

[274]Ev p 112

[275]Ev p 91

[276]Third Report, Session 1997–98, *op cit*, para 43

[277]*ibid,* para 92

[278]Ev p 109

for NATO's previous enlargement—

... the benefits of increased stability in central and eastern Europe outweigh any potential military costs.[279]

152. We are still open to the idea of any enlargement that will increase security in the Euro–Atlantic area. However, NATO is not faced with the same situation now as it was at Madrid in 1997. At that time, there were three or four candidates who stood head and shoulders above the others, and, while debate on who to admit was "considerable",[280] the outcome was by no means a surprise. Today, NATO would face several problems if it were to embark upon a further round of enlargement straight away. Not least of those is that, as discussed above, a great deal of work has yet to be done with the Czech Republic, Hungary and Poland before they attain NATO standards in many areas, and further enlargement might disrupt this process.

153. A further consideration is that, were there to be further invitations issued at Washington, some candidate states would be in the unhappy position of having been rejected twice, which could have serious internal repercussions—particularly, perhaps, for those countries which are also experiencing rejection from the European Union.[281] For Romania, we were told, success with its NATO application was expected to alleviate the pain of economic reform,[282] and its 'failure' at Madrid created bitter disappointment and a rising cynicism about the West. NATO is certainly now aware of the need to manage expectations and stress that enlargement is a long–term process.[283]

154. We believe that the realities of the current round of enlargement must be taken into account when weighing up the complex issues connected with the further enlargement of the Alliance. To invite additional members into NATO at a time when its resources were already overstrained would not enhance the security of the Alliance or of Europe as a whole. Moreover, rushing the pace of integration could dangerously overstrain resources in the Czech Republic, Hungary and Poland themselves, possibly putting at risk the economic successes they have achieved. While NATO's future might still be seen to be in a state of flux, we stand by our comment that—

It is certainly appropriate that NATO's future Strategic Concept should be thoroughly debated and agreed *before* any further commitments to enlargement are made.[284]

For these reasons, **we believe that further enlargement in the near term should be approached with caution. Further enlargement should be based on an assessment of the benefits and costs for both existing and potential new members.** The benefits of enlargement could include increased stability and security, as well as the beneficial effects on burden–sharing created by the addition of new members; costs that could fall to either existing or new members, or both, include infrastructure and force modernisation costs as well as the difficulties of decision-taking in a larger Alliance.

155. But ruling it out altogether or delaying it indefinitely would have unsettling effects throughout the rest of Central and Eastern Europe, and would be seen as a serious political setback to democratic reformers in the candidate countries, for whom NATO membership is of immense symbolic importance. NATO must, therefore, come up with a 'Madrid plus' package to satisfy the candidate states. It is already working towards such a package; the final communiqué of the December 1998 ministerial[285] stated that the ministerial group had—

... tasked the Council in Permanent Session to develop for the Washington Summit a comprehensive package that will continue the enlargement process, operationalise our

---

[279]Third Report, Session 1997–98, *op cit*, para 52
[280]*ibid*, para 96
[281]Q 153
[282]Ev p 101
[283]Q 74
[284]Third Report, Session 1997–98, *op cit*, para 108
[285]Available on the Internet at www.nato.int/docu/pr/1998/p981208e.htm

commitment to the open door policy and underscore our willingness to assist aspiring countries in meeting NATO standards.

A 'MADRID PLUS' PACKAGE

156. We visited three of the candidate countries—Bulgaria, Romania and Slovenia—during the course of our inquiry.[286] In each case we were impressed by the strength of desire to become full Alliance members, the political commitment towards this aim, and the progress that had been made in areas such as reform of the military.

157. We learned in Bulgaria that its armed forces were still oversized and under- equipped. However, it appears to be politically stable and its government has embarked upon an ambitious reform programme, covering financial and military reform. The Bulgarians suggested to us that NATO should look less at the political or military aspects of inviting it to join, but should concentrate on strategic issues. Bulgaria's accession to NATO, it was argued, would represent a commitment from NATO to the stabilisation of south eastern Europe. While politicians seemed confident that full membership would eventually be bestowed on Bulgaria, they were not complacent; yet the military seemed to us somewhat less committed to, and realistic about, NATO.

158. Romania's military have been active PfP Partners, and have a track record of participation in multinational operations. Their level of cooperation with the UK military is considerable and appeared to us to have borne fruit. However, the political background gives somewhat less cause for confidence, with the possibility of future instability. Also, as a recent report by the European Commission[287] showed, the economy has gone into reverse in the last eighteen months, which must put pressure on Romania's ability to finance military reform.

159. Slovenia is half-way through its two year tenure on the UN Security Council. Its performance has been seen as competent, and as a result it has perhaps a stronger international reputation than any of the other candidates. Its army is small and mainly conscript, but it has undertaken many PfP exercises, including hosting one, and the government is in the process of drawing up a long-term defence plan, with the emphasis on interoperability and military restructuring. Slovenian politicians were keen to stress the strength of the Slovenian democracy and economy, and the strategic importance of their country both as a physical 'bridge' between NATO and Hungary and as having a unique insight into the crises in the former Yugoslavia.

160. While the Committee did not visit Slovakia, we took evidence from the Slovak Minister for Foreign Affairs.[288] The Chairman's separate visits to the country, which involved discussion of accession prospects with a number of politicians and officials, confirmed our impression of the conspicuous progress made there since the end of the Meciar government.

161. Each country seemed to have a realistic assessment of the likelihood of formal invitations to membership being forthcoming at Washington; but each stressed the importance of NATO's 'open door' policy being demonstrated to be more than simply words. They were similarly emphatic that the Summit should do more than simply reiterate the Madrid formula, which encouraged interested countries to increase their participation in the EAPC and PfP, committed NATO to continuing its intensified dialogue with candidates, and recognised and took account of—

> ... the positive developments towards democracy and the rule of law in a number of southeastern European countries,

---

[286]See Annexes A and B; the Chairman also visited Slovakia on two separate occasions to discuss enlargement issues with politicians and officials

[287]Composite Paper: *Reports on progress towards accession by each of the candidate countries*, 4.11.98. Available on the Internet at europa.eu.int/comm/dg1a/enlarge/report_11_98_en/index.htm

[288]QQ 157–187

singling out Romania and Slovenia for particular praise.[289] Ideally, it was suggested to us by the Romanian Deputy Minister of Defence, the 'open door' policy should be reaffirmed, but should be accompanied by practical as well as symbolic steps. The Summit, we were told, should set out a 'road map' for entry into NATO, define milestones along it and offer practical assistance in attaining those milestones; and that any criteria for membership should not be set higher than those for the Czech Republic, Hungary and Poland. These arguments were restated by many of our interlocutors in all three countries, as well as the Minister of Foreign Affairs of the Republic of Slovakia when he gave evidence to us.[290] The Bulgarian National Assembly Foreign Affairs Committee suggested that Washington should produce an invitation to start negotiations while possibly deferring the start to a date to be fixed. The Slovenian Foreign Minster hoped for, at the very least, a stronger statement on Slovenia's chances than that of Madrid. When we visited Hungary, then an invitee, the Hungarians (despite their privileged position) were also keen on NATO articulating the possibility of further membership at Washington; the Defence Minister told us that he hoped for a further round within the next three years. (One witness, Humphry Crum Ewing, suggested to us that the three new members would be much more vociferous advocates for further enlargement once they attained full membership.)[291]

162. The pressure from candidates leaves NATO with a rather uncomfortable problem to confront at the Washington Summit. As the US Defense Secretary has said, the—

> ... open door is at the top of a very steep flight of stairs.[292]

NATO is neither ready nor willing to invite further candidates this Spring. Some of the self–declared candidates are further up the staircase than others, yet any preferential treatment may cause friction where NATO most wishes to promote stability. However, to deny the progress that many candidates have made, and to rebuff their hopes of an early accession to the Alliance may cause just as many problems.

163. A further problem faced by NATO is that its Madrid Declaration singled out Romania and Slovenia for especial praise. Romania has now asked for the Washington Summit to produce a—

> ... differentiated listing of the eligible aspirants, starting with Romania and Slovenia.[293]

And the Slovakian Foreign Minister hoped for "some signal, some recognition" of Slovakia's chances, stating that the worst outcome would be if Slovakia was not mentioned at all.[294] Hence, as Sir Michael Alexander put it,

> ...the Alliance faces an awkward choice between disappointing Romania and Slovenia if it fails to indicate some kind of preference for their candidatures ... and disappointing eg. Bulgaria, Slovakia and Lithuania if it does do so.[295]

The Policy Director at the MoD told us that NATO was attempting to,

> ... produce a formula which does make it clear that there is a continuing process, a continuing expectation, but without making any rash promises or divisive language between one country and another.[296]

This will certainly be difficult. One thing that we are convinced of is that **there must be no champions—particular Allies unwilling to accept any enlargement that does not include their favoured candidates—and no 'beauty contest' among the aspirant members. NATO**

---

[289]*Madrid Declaration on Euro-Atlantic Security and Cooperation*, available on the Internet at www.nato.int/docu/pr/1997/p97-081e.htm
[290]Q 157
[291]Ev p 96
[292]*US, Germany iron out NATO nuclear differences*, Reuters, 8 February 1999
[293]Ev p 140
[294]Q 162
[295]Ev p 122
[296]Q 75

must make the criteria upon which membership will be offered clear and intelligible, without offering any guarantee of automatic membership, and offer candidates assistance in meeting those criteria where appropriate. Now is the time for practical measures rather than rhetoric.

164.   The Alliance is already trying to reduce the pressure for membership among the candidates and other non–members by offering them a variety of ways of cooperating with NATO, short of formally admitting them to the Alliance or of extending Article 5 guarantees to them. The measures are channelled particularly through the individual partnership agreements in the framework of PfP (enhanced PfP), which range from cooperation and advice on the restructuring of military industry, defence ministries and armed forces, budget management and defence planning in the widest sense to individually tailored joint exercises and the integration of Partnership staff elements into NATO's military structure. Partners are involved in many NATO exercises and are informed of NATO planning and decisions. While this is not expressly articulated, these measures are designed to blur the differences between full NATO membership and Partnership, so as to give many of the Partners the benefits of many forms of associations with NATO short of the coverage by Article 5.

165. Partnership for Peace and the Euro–Atlantic Partnership Council (EAPC)—which offers cooperation and dialogue between NATO and other states in areas such as peacekeeping training, the security aspects of economic development and regional security issues—have been two of NATO's greatest successes. They have extended stability outside the territory of NATO's members and provided valuable opportunities for cooperation between NATO and other European nations both within and outwith the defence arena. Without the work done under the auspices of these programmes, the three new members of NATO would not be able to contribute nearly as much as they can to the Alliance.

166. During the course of this inquiry, we visited the SHAPE Partnership Cooperation Cell, which coordinates Partners' interoperability with NATO structures and the initial planning of training and exercises, and were impressed by the obvious enthusiasm and professionalism of those working there. We were told during our visit that Partner nations do not necessarily take up all the assistance and cooperation that are offered to them, for a variety of reasons. Under PfP, each Partner nation has an Individual Partnership Programme, but we believe that further tailoring of PfP to individual Partners' requirements is required. Also important is 'tough love' for the Partners, with rigorous and credible external assessment of their achievements and shortfalls.

167. The effectiveness of the Alliance's 'Madrid plus' package must be one criterion on which the success of the Washington Summit is to be judged. As Dr Jonathan Eyal told us—

> ... how to phrase this promise in such a way that it offers concrete advantages to potential new members while not committing the West to any new obligations is now the biggest immediate problem.[297]

Suggestions for such a package apparently include increased feedback, advice and assistance, the promotion of transparency within the aspirant countries' militaries and attempts to maximise the impact of bilateral relations with Allied states. However, it seems that the Alliance will avoid giving any undertaking of automatic membership when any criteria set had been met.

168. The Romanian Ministry of Foreign Affairs has suggested that the 'Madrid plus' package should take the form of a 'Membership Action Plan', leading to an 'Upgraded Individual Dialogue' which would focus on—

- designing a specific accession–preparation strategy meant to cover all the dimensions of the process (political, economic, military etc.);
- establishing a well–defined mechanism for progress evaluation;

---

[297]Ev p 102

- singling out the areas where assistance and closer cooperation are needed for the attainment of the Membership Action Plan's goals;
- coordinating other tracks of the aspirant's relationship with the Alliance, such as PfP.[298]

We applaud many of Romania's points. However, **while we would encourage NATO to come up with a 'Madrid plus' package that will effectively aid aspirant members, NATO is not the appropriate forum for economic and political assistance. Other organisations exist for these purposes; NATO is however the only organisation which can encourage interoperability, civilian control of the military and the reform of the armed forces, all extremely important tasks for candidate states. A 'Madrid plus' package for membership candidates should include clear targets in those areas and strategies for achieving them in collaboration with the Alliance.**

169. **We are far from persuaded that membership will benefit the security of every state seeking to join the Alliance. But if doors are closed, the possibilities of finding constructive alternatives will be diminished, if not lost. On the other hand, we fear that 'waves' of enlargement or strict timetables will only exacerbate division, rivalry and insecurity. It is our belief that further enlargement should be limited, gradual and conducted on a case–by–case basis.**

170. **We also believe that the attitude of Russia—and the security of Ukraine—are factors that must be taken into account.** To accept that we must either give Russia a veto, or alternatively refuse to consider its interests and likely responses would demonstrate a deficiency of imagination and statesmanship. Although still opposing NATO's present enlargement, Russia has accepted it, and it has done so on terms which have not destroyed but, thanks to the Founding Act, have enhanced NATO–Russia cooperation.

171. Finally, we believe that NATO should be attentive to, and engaged in, the debate about EU enlargement.[299] **We perceive a serious prospect that the respective enlargements of NATO and the European Union could proceed at cross purposes.** In Partnership for Peace, NATO devised a mechanism that has been softening the distinction between members and partners. In contrast, the aim of the EU is not to lower barriers between members and non–members, but to deepen the integration of members. The Schengen agreement, binding upon any state that now accedes, has multiplied concerns in Central and Eastern Europe that an expanding EU could establish the dreaded 'new dividing lines' whose creation NATO has so studiously avoided. The risk is compounded by the tendency for officials with NATO and EU responsibilities to work in separate compartments. **It is time that the perennial NATO–WEU–EU dialogue about Collective Defence became a broader dialogue about the enlargement of the Western security community, and the security of the whole of Europe.**

---

[298]Ev p 140
[299]See also Foreign Affairs Committee, Third Report, Session 1998–99, *European Union Enlargement*, HC 86

CONCLUSIONS: THE CHALLENGES OF THE WASHINGTON SUMMIT

172. NATO, as it approaches its 50th anniversary Summit, has much to congratulate itself on. Despite the demise of its seeming *raison d'être* at the close of the Cold War, it has continued to be relevant, even increasingly so, in the 1990s, as demonstrated by the eagerness of many central and eastern European states to become members. It has taken on new roles and missions, and re-emphasised its diplomatic and political functions. These functions, as the US Deputy Secretary of State told a recent conference, are not wholly new—

> Our Alliance has always had broader political functions. During the 1950s, it provided the security umbrella under which reconciliation between France and Germany could take place, thus laying the foundation for the European Union. In the early '80s, NATO promoted the consolidation of civilian-led democracy in Spain and, thus, the full return of Spain to the European family. On several occasions, NATO has helped keep the peace between Greece and Turkey. More generally, throughout its existence, NATO's unified command and its collective approach to defence have largely eliminated military competition among West European powers.[300]

But NATO cannot rest on its laurels. The Secretary of State for Defence, addressing the same conference, said that—

> Organisations have two fundamental choices: they can adapt, or they can die. A state of irrelevance for a security organisation is no different than honest disbandment ... So, while of course we must allow ourselves a time for celebration, we dare not sit back for a second while the world continues to change around us.[301]

173. The Washington Summit provides a forum in which NATO must decide on the adaptations it needs to make to remain a viable and useful alliance in the next century. In its new Strategic Concept and its Washington Declaration, NATO will be expected to set out its response to the challenges ahead. In this Report we have asked a number of questions about NATO's future. This concluding section will recapitulate our conclusions.

174. We asked what priorities NATO should accord its new roles and missions as it formalises them in the new Strategic Concept. Despite the increasing possibilities of NATO's involvement in other types of operation, Article 5 must remain at the very core of the Alliance. Despite forty years of antagonism between NATO and the Warsaw Treaty Organisation, Article 5 has never been invoked. In these days of east-west *rapprochement*, we fervently hope that it never will be. Nevertheless, it remains the case that NATO's preparation for an Article 5-type threat remains the best way of ensuring that such a threat never arises. The Alliance's Article 5 mission of self-defence must remain its core, and its first priority.

175. The new strategic environment does require that NATO now do more than simply defend its own territory. We fully expect NATO to rise to the new challenges. But the new Strategic Concept must outline clearly NATO's image of itself and its capabilities. It must also state what challenges NATO will not take on, and how it expects to cooperate with other international organisations to address questions to which it cannot provide the whole answer. The new Strategic Concept must provide the reader with an explicit picture of NATO's competence and priorities.

176. We asked how NATO's non-Article 5 operations should be mandated, a subject upon which the new Strategic Concept is expected to declare. Insistence on a UN Security Council mandate for such operations would be unnecessary as well as covertly giving Russia a veto over Alliance action (a concept explicitly rejected in the NATO-Russia Founding Act). All 19 Allies act in accordance with the principles of international law and we are secure in our assertion that the necessity of unanimous agreement for any action will ensure its legality.

---

[300]Royal United Services Institute, 10 March 1999
[301]*ibid*

177. We asked what the implications of an increased European Security and Defence Identity would be. The development of ESDI was both timely and positive, but we consider that Madeline Albright's 'three ds'—no decoupling, no duplication and no discrimination— are of paramount importance. The work to create an enhanced European defence capability should not be sidetracked by debates over the institutional relationship of the WEU and the EU.

178. In our Report last year on NATO enlargement we concluded that—

> ... the main mission of NATO in the post-Cold War world is to seek to ensure peace in a world in which the risks we face are more unpredictable than at any period from the early stages of the Cold War to the fall of the Berlin Wall. We believe the key to achieving this aim is support for the emerging democracies, including Russia, and the projection of stability and democracy eastwards.

We have not changed our minds in the intervening period. While reaffirming our conclusions that NATO should approach further enlargement with caution, we encourage greater cooperation and communication between the Alliance and aspirant members. We hope that the Washington Summit will set out a strategy for achieving this that is more practical than rhetorical, and that the aspirant states will seize all opportunities to develop their relationship with NATO.

179. NATO, despite having experienced a diminution in the importance of its primary purpose during the Cold War, survived its identity crisis by putting increased emphasis on the political dimensions of the Alliance. This process must be judged a success, and invites optimism for its ability to meet future challenges in this area. But the process must be balanced against the need to retain NATO as an integrated military organisation, capable of rapid and decisive action. NATO remains the only international military organisation with an established and experienced command system able to take action either on its own behalf or at the behest of the UN or the OSCE, and this capability must not be jeopardised. But, NATO must do more than simply cooperate with aspirant members. Other states, including Russia and Ukraine, may be ambivalent, or even hostile, towards some of NATO's future directions. But it remains the case that their aspirations are the same as those of the Alliance: peace and stability in the Euro-Atlantic area. NATO must continue its dialogue with these countries, encourage them in their progress and empathise with their concerns. Much has already been done in this arena; more must be attempted.

180. The Washington Summit will be held in the shadow of the crisis in Kosovo. For the first time in its existence, the North Atlantic Council has authorised military action against an independent state. There could be no more dramatic illustration of the way in which the world in which NATO is operating has changed, as has NATO's role within it. The 'new missions' have shifted irreversibly from the realm of rhetoric to that of reality. The theological debate over NATO's 'mandate' has been overtaken by events. The new members of the Alliance have been put to the test within days of their accession. The capabilities of all the European Allies will also be put to the proof. And the challenge of maintaining cooperation with Russia has suddenly become an urgent and immediate diplomatic necessity. Many see this operation as the greatest test of NATO's credibility since the end of the Cold War. At the time at which we agreed this report, the outcome remained uncertain. But the Kosovo crisis should not be allowed to distract the Alliance from the many important tasks which face the Washington Summit. A new Strategic Concept needs to be agreed soon which explicitly declares that Article 5 remains the core task of the Alliance; which gives clear direction to Alliance force planners on the types and priorities of new missions, including peace support operations and non-proliferation efforts; which reasserts the North Atlantic Council's undoubted right to direct NATO's operations while making clear that the Alliance will continue to act in accordance with international law; and which gives a clearer idea of the strategic rationale which will underpin future operations for the Alliance. The Summit must also lay the foundations for a strengthened European defence and security capability, while reiterating the strength of the transatlantic alliance; and it must set out a timetable for the reform of the European Allies' armed forces. Equally importantly, it must define strategies and set out practical measures for continuing and reinforcing cooperation with Partners, including Russia and Ukraine. While the Allies at the Washington Summit should not announce any immediate further enlargement, they must clearly set out the criteria for any new

members to join the Alliance, and set out a package of measures for candidates for membership which will aid them, where appropriate, in attaining those criteria. The Washington Summit is not a preparation for war, however dangerous the international circumstances in which it takes place. Its prime aim is not to devise means to make NATO a more formidable fighting machine. The Allies must use the Summit once more to reinforce the message to the world that NATO's purpose is the export of peace and stability to all parts of the European-Atlantic area.

ANNEX A

ITINERARY OF VISIT TO ROMANIA AND BULGARIA
23-26 November 1998

ROMANIA

Tuesday 24 November

Meeting with the Deputy Defence Minister
Meeting with the Chief of Defence Staff
Visit to the Anglo-Romanian Regional Training Centre
Working lunch with Members of the Foreign Affairs Commissions
Visit to a Romanian Military Unit (Peacekeeping Battalion)
Working dinner with senior journalists

Wednesday 25 November

Meeting with representatives of Parliamentary Defence Commissions
Round Table Meeting organised by EURISC
Meeting at Foreign Affairs Ministry

BULGARIA

Audience with President Stoyanov
Dinner in Residence hosted by Ambassador

Thursday 26 November

Meeting with members of Parliamentary Committees for National Security and Foreign Affairs
Meeting with the Deputy Chief of General Staff
Meeting with the Deputy Minister of Defence
Meeting with the Chairman of Bulgarian Atlantic Association
Call on Vice President of the National Assembly
Meeting at the Ministry of Foreign Affairs
Dinner hosted by the Parliamentary Committee for National Security

Friday 27 November

Visit to the Romanian National Military Academy
Lunch with students and staff

ANNEX B

ITINERARY OF VISIT TO HUNGARY AND SLOVENIA

23-26 November 1998

HUNGARY

Tuesday 24 November

Meeting with the Defence and National Security Adviser, Prime Minister's Office

Meeting with the Political State Secretary, Ministry for Foreign Affairs

Meeting and lunch with Hungarian Defence Committee

Meeting with the Defence Minister

Meeting with the Deputy Chief of Defence staff

Meeting with 'No to NATO' group

Meeting with journalists

Wednesday 25 November

Forum with students at the Eötvös Loránd University on 'The Future of NATO'

Visit to a Hungarian Military Unit

SLOVENIA

Thursday 26 November

Meeting with the State Secretary, Ministry of Foreign Affairs

Visit to the Ministry of Defence

Meeting with the Chairmen of the Defence and Foreign Affairs Committees

Lunch hosted by the Ambassador

Round table discussion , chaired by Dr Anton Bebler, Slovenian Atlantic Council and attended by those in favour and those opposed to Slovenian membership of NATO

ANNEX C

ITINERARY OF VISIT TO PARIS AND BRUSSELS

19–21 January 1999

Tuesday 19 January

Meeting with the Institut Français des Relations Internationales

Meeting with the French Defence Committee, Assemblée Nationale

Working lunch with French Defence Committee, Assemblée Nationale

Discussion at the Ministère de Defence chaired by the Director of Strategic Affairs, Ministère de Defence and the Director of Strategic Affairs, Quai d'Orsay

Wednesday 20 January

Briefing from UK Delegation to NATO

Meeting with the Assistant Secretary General (Political Affairs)

Meeting with the Director of Defence Partnership and Cooperation

Working lunch with NATO Ambassadors

Meeting with the Chairman of the Military Committee

Meeting with the Assistant Secretary General (Defence Planning and Operations)

Round Table meeting with UK Delegation to NATO

Thursday 21 January

Meetings at NATO HQ

Meetings at Partnership Planning Cell and Supreme Headquarters Allied Powers Europe, Mons

ANNEX D

ITINERARY OF VISIT TO BONN
3–4 March 1999

Wednesday 3 March 1999

Embassy officials briefing

Meeting with the Director of International Cooperation, Rheinmettall

Meeting with the Director of Business Development, Daimler Chrysler Aerospaces AG

Thursday 4 March

Meeting with the State Secretary, Ministry of Defence

Meeting with the representatives of Federal Foreign Ministry

Working lunch hosted by Bundestag Defence Committee

Meeting with Bonn-based British Journalists

ANNEX E

ITINERARY OF VISIT TO RUSSIA AND UKRAINE
14–19 March 1999

MOSCOW

Monday 15 March

Meeting with the Deputy Minister for Defence
Meeting with the Head of European Cooperation Department, Ministry of Foreign Affairs
Meeting with the Deputy Chairman and members, Duma International Affairs Committee

Tuesday 16 March

Visit to NATO Information and Documentation Centre, Moscow
Working lunch with Central European Defence Attachés based in Moscow
Meeting with the Chairman of the Duma Defence Committee
Meeting with other members of the Duma Defence Committee
Meeting with the Secretary General of the CIS Treaty for Security Cooperation

Wednesday 17 March

Meeting with the Deputy Minister for the Interior
Working lunch at the Tschelkovskiy Uchyeniy Military Retraining College

KYIV

Thursday 18 March

Meeting with the Supreme Rada Committee for National Security and Defence
Meeting with the Supreme Rada Committee for Foreign and CIS Affairs
Meeting with the Presidential Administration Foreign Affairs Department
Visit to NATO Information and Documentation Centre
Meeting with the Secretary of the National Security and Defence Council
Chairman's speech to 'NATO at Fifty' Conference
Meetings with representatives of think tanks and institutes
Working dinner hosted by Supreme Rada Defence Committee

Friday 19 March

Meeting with the Minister of Foreign Affairs
Meeting with the Deputy Minister of Defence
Press Conference at British Embassy
Working lunch with Ambassadors of NATO countries

APPENDIX 1

The North Atlantic Treaty

Washington D.C. - 4 April 1949

The Parties to this Treaty reaffirm their faith in the purposes and principles of the Charter of the United Nations and their desire to live in peace with all peoples and all governments. They are determined to safeguard the freedom, common heritage and civilisation of their peoples, founded on the principles of democracy, individual liberty and the rule of law. They seek to promote stability and well-being in the North Atlantic area. They are resolved to unite their efforts for collective defence and for the preservation of peace and security. They therefore agree to this North Atlantic Treaty :

Article 1

The Parties undertake, as set forth in the Charter of the United Nations, to settle any international dispute in which they may be involved by peaceful means in such a manner that international peace and security and justice are not endangered, and to refrain in their international relations from the threat or use of force in any manner inconsistent with the purposes of the United Nations.

Article 2

The Parties will contribute toward the further development of peaceful and friendly international relations by strengthening their free institutions, by bringing about a better understanding of the principles upon which these institutions are founded, and by promoting conditions of stability and well-being. They will seek to eliminate conflict in their international economic policies and will encourage economic collaboration between any or all of them.

Article 3

In order more effectively to achieve the objectives of this Treaty, the Parties, separately and jointly, by means of continuous and effective self-help and mutual aid, will maintain and develop their individual and collective capacity to resist armed attack.

Article 4

The Parties will consult together whenever, in the opinion of any of them, the territorial integrity, political independence or security of any of the Parties is threatened.

Article 5

The Parties agree that an armed attack against one or more of them in Europe or North America shall be considered an attack against them all and consequently they agree that, if such an armed attack occurs, each of them, in exercise of the right of individual or collective self-defence recognised by Article 51 of the Charter of the United Nations, will assist the Party or Parties so attacked by taking forthwith, individually and in concert with the other Parties, such action as it deems necessary, including the use of armed force, to restore and maintain the security of the North Atlantic area.

Any such armed attack and all measures taken as a result thereof shall immediately be reported to the Security Council. Such measures shall be terminated when the Security Council has taken the measures necessary to restore and maintain international peace and security (1).

Article 6

For the purpose of Article 5, an armed attack on one or more of the Parties is deemed to include an armed attack:

on the territory of any of the Parties in Europe or North America, on the Algerian Departments of France, (2) on the territory of Turkey or on the Islands under the jurisdiction of any of the Parties in the North Atlantic area north of the Tropic of Cancer;

on the forces, vessels, or aircraft of any of the Parties, when in or over these territories or any other area in Europe in which occupation forces of any of the Parties were stationed on the date when the Treaty entered into force or the Mediterranean Sea or the North Atlantic area north of the Tropic of Cancer.

Article 7

This Treaty does not affect, and shall not be interpreted as affecting in any way the rights and obligations under the Charter of the Parties which are members of the United Nations, or the primary responsibility of the Security Council for the maintenance of international peace and security.

Article 8

Each Party declares that none of the international engagements now in force between it and any other of the Parties or any third State is in conflict with the provisions of this Treaty, and undertakes not to enter into any international engagement in conflict with this Treaty.

Article 9

The Parties hereby establish a Council, on which each of them shall be represented, to consider matters concerning the implementation of this Treaty. The Council shall be so organised as to be able to meet promptly at any time. The Council shall set up such subsidiary bodies as may be necessary; in particular it shall establish immediately a defence committee which shall recommend measures for the implementation of Articles 3 and 5.

Article 10

The Parties may, by unanimous agreement, invite any other European State in a position to further the principles of this Treaty and to contribute to the security of the North Atlantic area to accede to this Treaty. Any State so invited may become a Party to the Treaty by depositing its instrument of accession with the Government of the United States of America. The Government of the United States of America will inform each of the Parties of the deposit of each such instrument of accession.

Article 11

This Treaty shall be ratified and its provisions carried out by the Parties in accordance with their respective constitutional processes. The instruments of ratification shall be deposited as soon as possible with the Government of the United States of America, which will notify all the other signatories of each deposit. The Treaty shall enter into force between the States which have ratified it as soon as the ratifications of the majority of the signatories, including the ratifications of Belgium, Canada, France, Luxembourg, the Netherlands, the United Kingdom and the United States, have been deposited and shall come into effect with respect to other States on the date of the deposit of their ratifications.

Article 12

After the Treaty has been in force for ten years, or at any time thereafter, the Parties shall, if any of them so requests, consult together for the purpose of reviewing the Treaty, having regard for the factors then affecting peace and security in the North Atlantic area, including the development of universal as well as regional arrangements under the Charter of the United Nations for the maintenance of international peace and security.

Article 13

After the Treaty has been in force for twenty years, any Party may cease to be a Party one year after its notice of denunciation has been given to the Government of the United States of America, which will inform the Governments of the other Parties of the deposit of each notice of denunciation

Article 14

This Treaty, of which the English and French texts are equally authentic, shall be deposited in the archives of the Government of the United States of America. Duly certified copies will be transmitted by that Government to the Governments of other signatories.

Footnotes :

1.The definition of the territories to which Article 5 applies was revised by Article 2 of the Protocol to the North Atlantic Treaty on the accession of Greece and Turkey and by the Protocols signed on the accession of the Federal Republic of Germany and of Spain.

2.On January 16,1963, the North Atlantic Council heard a declaration by the French Representative who recalled that by the vote on self-determination on July 1, 1962, the Algerian people had pronounced itself in favour of the independence of Algeria in co-operation with France. In consequence, the President of the French Republic had on July 3, 1962, formally recognised the independence of Algeria. The result was that the "Algerian departments of France" no longer existed as such, and that at the same time the fact that they were mentioned in the North Atlantic Treaty had no longer any bearing. Following this statement the Council noted that insofar as the former Algerian Departments of France were concerned, the relevant clauses of this Treaty had become inapplicable as from July 3, 1962.

The Brussels Treaty

TREATY OF ECONOMIC, SOCIAL AND CULTURAL COLLABORATION AND COLLECTIVE SELF-DEFENCE

Signed at Brussels on March 17, 1948 between His Majesty in respect of the United Kingdom of Great Britain and Northern Ireland, His Royal Highness the Prince Regent of Belgium, the President of the French Republic, Her Royal Highness the Grand Duchess of Luxembourg, and Her Majesty the Queen of the Netherlands

... Resolved:

To reaffirm their faith in fundamental human rights, in the dignity and worth of the human person and in the other ideals proclaimed in the Charter of the United Nations;

To fortify and preserve the principles of democracy, personal freedom and political liberty, the constitutional traditions and the rule of law, which are their common heritage;

To strengthen, with these aims in view, the economic, social and cultural ties by which they are already united;

To co-operate loyally and to co-ordinate their efforts to create in Western Europe a firm basis for European economic recovery;

To afford assistance to each other, in accordance with the Charter of the United Nations, in maintaining international peace and security and in resisting any policy of aggression;

To take such steps as may be held to be necessary in the event of a renewal by Germany of a policy of aggression;

To associate progressively in the pursuance of these aims other States inspired by the same ideals and animated by the like determination;

...

ARTICLE I

Convinced of the close community of their interests and of the necessity of uniting in order to promote the economic recovery of Europe, the High Contracting Parties will so organize and co-ordinate their economic activities as to produce the best possible results, by the elimination of conflict in their economic policies, the co-ordination of production and the development of commercial exchanges.

The co-operation provided for in the preceding paragraph, which will be effected through the Consultative Council referred to in Article VII as well as through other bodies, shall not involve any duplication of, or prejudice to, the work of other economic organizations in which the High Contracting Parties are or may be represented but shall on the contrary assist the work of those organizations.

ARTICLE II

The High Contracting Parties will make every effort in common, both by direct consultation and in specialized agencies, to promote the attainment of a higher standard of living by their peoples and to develop on corresponding lines the social and other related services of their countries.

The High Contracting Parties will consult with the object of achieving the earliest possible application of recommendations of immediate practical interest, relating to social matters, adopted with their approval in the specialized agencies.

They will endeavour to conclude as soon as possible conventions with each other in the sphere of social security.

ARTICLE III

The High Contracting Parties will make every effort in common to lead their peoples towards a better understanding of the principles which form the basis of their common civilization and to promote cultural exchanges by conventions between themselves or by other means.

ARTICLE IV

If any of the High Contracting Parties should be the object of an armed attack in Europe, the other High Contracting Parties will, in accordance with the provisions of Article 51 of the Charter of the United Nations, afford the Party so attacked all the military and other aid and assistance in their power.

ARTICLE V

All measures taken as a result of the preceding Article shall be immediately reported to the Security Council. They shall be terminated as soon as the Security Council has taken the measures necessary to maintain or restore international peace and security.

The present Treaty does not prejudice in any way the obligations of the High Contracting Parties under the provisions of the Charter of the United Nations. It shall not be interpreted as affecting in any way the authority and responsibility of the Security Council under the Charter to take at any time such action as it deems necessary in order to maintain or restore international peace and security.

ARTICLE VI

The High Contracting Parties declare, each so far as he is concerned, that none of the international engagements now in force between him and any other of the High Contracting Parties or any third State is in conflict with the provisions of the present Treaty.

None of the High Contracting Parties will conclude any alliance or participate in any coalition directed against any other of the High Contracting Parties.

ARTICLE VII

For the purpose of consulting together on all the questions dealt with in the present Treaty, the High Contracting Parties will create a Consultative Council, which shall be so organized as to be able to exercise its functions continuously. The Council shall meet at such times as it shall deem fit.

At the request of any of the High Contracting Parties, the Council shall be immediately convened in order to permit the High Contracting Parties to consult with regard to any situation which may constitute a threat to peace, in whatever area this threat should arise; with regard to the attitude to be adopted and the steps to be taken in case of a renewal by Germany of an aggressive policy; or with regard to any situation constituting a danger to economic stability.

ARTICLE VIII

In pursuance of their determination to settle disputes only by peaceful means, the High Contracting Parties will apply to disputes between themselves the following provisions.

The High Contracting Parties will, while the present Treaty remains in force, settle all disputes falling within the scope of Article 36, paragraph 2, of the Statute of the International Court of Justice by referring them to the Court, subject only, in the case of each of them, to any reservation already made by that party when accepting this clause for compulsory jurisdiction to the extent that that Party may maintain the reservation.

In addition, the High Contracting Parties will submit to conciliation all disputes outside the scope of Article 36, paragraph 2, of the Statute of the International Court of Justice.

In the case of a mixed dispute involving both questions for which conciliation is appropriate and other questions for which judicial settlement is appropriate, any Party to the dispute shall have the right to insist that the judicial settlement of the legal questions shall precede conciliation.

The preceding provisions of this Article in no way affect the application of relevant provisions or agreements prescribing some other method of pacific settlement.

ARTICLE IX

The High Contracting Parties may, by agreement, invite any other State to accede to the present Treaty on conditions to be agreed between them and the State so invited.

Any State so invited may become a Party to the Treaty by depositing an instrument of accession with the Belgian Government.

The Belgian Government will inform each of the High Contracting Parties of the deposit of each instrument of accession.

ARTICLE X

The present Treaty shall be ratified and the instruments of ratification shall be deposited as soon as possible with the Belgian Government.

It shall enter into force on the date of the deposit of the last instrument of ratification and shall thereafter remain in force for fifty years.

After the expiry of the period of fifty years, each of the High Contracting Parties shall have the right to cease to be a party thereto provided that he shall have previously given one year's notice of denunciation to the Belgian Government.

The Belgian Government shall inform the Governments of the other High Contracting Parties of the deposit of each instrument of ratification and of each notice of denunciation.

APPENDIX 3

The Berlin Declaration

Extract from the Final Communiqué
of the Ministerial Meeting
of the North Atlantic Council
Berlin 3 June1996

1. We met today in Berlin, the capital of a united Germany and the city that stood for the success of Alliance policy and transatlantic cohesion for over four decades. Its unification is now a symbol of the new era of partnership and cooperation.

2. Here in Berlin, we have taken a major step forward in shaping the new NATO, a NATO taking on new missions such as IFOR. Today, we have taken decisions to carry further the ongoing adaptation of Alliance structures so that the Alliance can more effectively carry out the full range of its missions, based on a strong transatlantic partnership; build a European Security and Defence Identity within the Alliance; continue the process of opening the Alliance to new members; and develop further strong ties of cooperation with all Partner countries, including the further enhancement of our strong relationship with Ukraine, and the development of a strong, stable and enduring partnership with Russia.

3. This new NATO has become an integral part of the emerging, broadly based, cooperative European security structure. We are in Bosnia and Herzegovina, together with many of our new Partners and other countries, contributing through the Implementation Force (IFOR) to bringing an end to war and conflict in that country and assisting the building of peace in the region. This joint endeavour, the largest military operation in the Alliance's history, points the way to our future security cooperation throughout the Euro-Atlantic area.

4. We have today given new impetus to the process of the Alliances adaptation and reform, which began in 1990 at the NATO Summit meeting in London and was carried forward at the 1994 Brussels Summit. Taking into account the sweeping changes in the security environment in Europe as new democracies have taken root and following the adoption of our new Strategic Concept in 1991, we have reorganised and streamlined our political and military structures and procedures; reduced significantly our force and readiness levels; and reconfigured our forces to make them better able to carry out the new missions of crisis management, while preserving the capability for collective defence. In addition, we have been conducting an expanding array of outreach activities with our Partners. We want to make our adapted Alliance better able to fulfil its main purpose: peace and security in the Euro-Atlantic area.

5. Much has been achieved, but now is the moment to take a decisive step forward in making the Alliance increasingly flexible and effective to meet new challenges. Therefore we are determined to:

adapt Alliance structures. An essential part of this adaptation is to build a European Security and Defence Identity within NATO, which will enable all European Allies to make a more coherent and effective contribution to the missions and activities of the Alliance as an expression of our shared responsibilities; to act themselves as required; and to reinforce the transatlantic partnership;

develop further our ability to carry out new roles and missions relating to conflict prevention and crisis management and the Alliance's efforts against the proliferation of weapons of mass destruction and their means of delivery, while maintaining our capability for collective defence; and enhance our contribution to security and stability throughout the Euro-Atlantic area by broadening and deepening our dialogue and cooperation with Partners, notably through PfP and NACC, and by further developing our important relations with Russia and Ukraine, as we maintain our openness to new members through our established enlargement process and strengthen our links with other organisations which contribute to European security.

6. Today we welcome the progress achieved in the internal adaptation of our Alliance, building on the decisions taken at the 1994 Brussels Summit, in particular:

the completion of the CJTF concept. By permitting a more flexible and mobile deployment of forces, including for new missions, this concept will facilitate the mounting of NATO contingency operations, the use of separable but not separate military capabilities in operations led by the WEU, and the participation of nations outside the Alliance in operations such as IFOR. We now request the Military Committee to make recommendations to the Council for the implementation of this concept to the satisfaction of all Allies, taking into account ongoing work to adapt military structures and procedures;

the establishment of the Policy Coordination Group (PCG), which will meet the need, especially in NATO's new missions, for closer coordination of political and military viewpoints;

the first results of the Military Committee's Long-Term Study, which will result in recommendations for a military command structure better suited to current and future Euro-Atlantic security. We task the Military Committee to continue its work on the Long-Term Study, consistent with the decisions we have taken today;

completion of original work plans of the Senior Politico-Military Group on Proliferation (SGP) and the Senior Defence Group on Proliferation (DGP) to address the common security concern of proliferation;

the meeting later this month of the North Atlantic Council (Defence Ministers), in which all 16 NATO countries will take part.

7. In our adaptation efforts to improve the Alliance's capability to fulfil its roles and missions, with the participation of all Allies, we will be guided by three fundamental objectives.

The first objective is to ensure the Alliance's military effectiveness so that it is able, in the changing security environment facing Europe, to perform its traditional mission of collective defence and through flexible and agreed procedures to undertake new roles in changing circumstances, based on:

situation in Europe and enables all Allies to participate fully and which is able to undertake all missions through procedures to be defined in accordance with decisions by the Council;

HQ structures which are more deployable and forces which are more mobile, both capable of being sustained for extended periods;

the ability to provide for increased participation of Partner countries and to integrate new members into the Alliance's military structure;

the ability to mount NATO non-Article 5 operations, guided by the concept of one system capable of performing multiple functions. We will further develop flexible arrangements capable of undertaking a variety of missions and taking into account national decisions on participation in each operation, building upon the strength of NATO's existing arrangements. These operations may differ from one another in contributions by Allies and, as a result of Council decision on a case-by-case basis, aspects of military command and control. The CJTF concept is central to our approach for assembling forces for contingency operations and organising their command within the Alliance. Consistent with the goal of building the European Security and Defence Identity within NATO, these arrangements should permit all European Allies to play a larger role in NATO's military and command structures and, as appropriate, in contingency operations undertaken by the Alliance;

increased political-military cooperation in particular through the PCG, and effective exercise of political control by the North Atlantic Council through the Military Committee;

the need for cost-effectiveness.

The second objective is to preserve the transatlantic link, based on:

maintenance of the Alliance as the essential forum for consultation among its members and the venue for agreement on policies bearing on the security and defence commitments of Allies under the Washington Treaty;

further development of the strong partnership between North American and European Allies, both politically and militarily, and including a continued involvement of the North American Allies across the command and force structure;

readiness to pursue common security objectives through the Alliance, wherever possible;

full transparency between NATO and WEU in crisis management, including as necessary through joint consultations on how to address contingencies.

The third objective is the development of the European Security and Defence Identity within the Alliance. Taking full advantage of the approved CJTF concept, this identity will be grounded on sound military principles and supported by appropriate military planning and permit the creation of militarily coherent and effective forces capable of operating under the political control and strategic direction of the WEU.

As an essential element of the development of this identity, we will prepare, with the involvement of NATO and the WEU, for WEU-led operations (including planning and exercising of command elements and forces). Such preparations within the Alliance should take into account the participation, including in European command arrangements, of all European Allies if they were so to choose. It will be based on:

identification, within the Alliance, of the types of separable but not separate capabilities, assets and support assets, as well as, in order to prepare for WEU-led operations, separable but not separate HQs, HQ elements and command positions, that would be required to command and conduct WEU-led operations and which could be made available, subject to decision by the NAC;

elaboration of appropriate multinational European command arrangements within NATO, consistent with and taking full advantage of the CJTF concept, able to prepare, support, command and conduct the WEU-led operations. This implies double-hatting appropriate personnel within the NATO command structure to perform these functions. Such European command arrangements should be identifiable and the arrangements should be sufficiently well articulated to permit the rapid constitution of a militarily coherent and effective operational force.

Further, the Alliance will support the development of the ESDI within NATO by conducting at the request of and in coordination with the WEU, military planning and exercises for illustrative WEU missions identified by the WEU. On the basis of political guidance to be provided by the WEU Council and the NAC, such planning would, at a minimum:

prepare relevant information on objectives, scope and participation for illustrative WEU missions;

identify requirements for planning and exercising of command elements and forces for illustrative WEU-led operations;

develop appropriate plans for submission through the MC and NAC to the WEU for review and approval.

NATO and the WEU should agree on arrangements for implementing such plans. The NAC will approve the release of NATO assets and capabilities for WEU-led operations, keep itself informed on their use through monitoring with the advice of the NATO Military Authorities and through regular consultations with the WEU Council, and keep their use under review.

8. On the basis of the guidelines agreed today, we have tasked the Council in Permanent Session, with the advice of NATO's Military Authorities:

to provide guidance and develop specific proposals for further adapting the Alliance's structures and procedures;

to develop, with regard to the European Security and Defence Identity within the Alliance, appropriate measures and arrangements for implementing the provisions of paragraph 7. Among the arrangements which require detailed elaboration will be provisions for the identification and release for use by the WEU of NATO capabilities, assets, and HQs and HQ elements for missions to be performed by the WEU; any necessary supplement to existing information-sharing arrangements for the conduct of WEU operations; and how consultations will be conducted with the NAC on the use of NATO assets and capabilities, including the NATO monitoring of the use of these assets;

and to report to our December meeting with recommendations for decisions.

****

20. We are satisfied with the growing ties between NATO and the WEU, and are determined to broaden and deepen our cooperation with the WEU, on the basis of the agreed principles of complementarity and transparency. We welcome the conclusion of a security agreement between our organisations, and the framework it provides for the exchange of information critical to the pursuit of our common security objectives. We hope that this will open the way for more intensive cooperation. We are pleased that, in response to our mandate to the Council in Permanent Session, additional areas of focussed NATO-WEU cooperation (joint meetings on their respective Mediterranean dialogues and exchanges of information in the field of relations with Russia and Ukraine) have been identified. We will explore possibilities for enhanced cooperation in other areas as well. We attach importance to our consultations, including in joint NATO-WEU Council meetings, on issues of common concern. We welcome the resumption of meetings of the WEU Permanent Council with SACEUR.

We continue to support the WEU in its efforts to enhance the development of its operational capabilities and welcome the decisions taken in this regard last month at the WEU Ministerial Council in Birmingham.

21. The Organisation for Security and Cooperation in Europe (OSCE) has an essential role to play in European security and stability. We reaffirm our commitment to support the OSCE's comprehensive approach to security and the ongoing process of developing a security model for the 21st Century. We value the OSCE's effectiveness in the prevention, management and resolution of conflicts and the work of the High Commissioner for National Minorities. These are important contributions to regional stability which we will continue to support and

work to strengthen.

The OSCE is playing a vitally important role in Bosnia and Herzegovina contributing to implementing civil aspects of the Peace Agreement, particularly in supervising the preparation and conduct of the first elections, in promoting and monitoring human rights, and in overseeing implementation of confidence- and security-building measures and negotiation of arms limitations. These tasks are a major contribution to building a just and stable peace in the region. IFOR is supporting the OSCE's tasks, and in particular the preparation of the elections, by helping to create a secure environment and promoting freedom of movement. We are also pleased with the practical support that NATO has been able to provide through its Verification Coordination Section to the OSCE in helping establish measures to verify the arms control elements of the Peace Agreement. We support the continued development of such pragmatic cooperation between NATO and the OSCE.

We remain deeply concerned about developments in Chechnya which have caused so much suffering and so many casualties. We welcome the announcement of a ceasefire in Chechnya and look forward to its full and effective implementation. We call for continued meaningful negotiations leading to a peaceful settlement of the dispute, using the continuing good offices of the OSCE. We support the efforts of the Minsk Group to achieve a political settlement of the conflict in and around Nagorno-Karabakh.

We welcome the established contacts between the North Atlantic Council and the OSCE Chairman-in-Office. We will continue our efforts to strengthen dialogue between NATO and the OSCE on issues of common concern, including through senior representation at Ministerial meetings and, on a more routine basis, through the International Staff.

****

PROCEEDINGS OF THE COMMITTEE RELATING TO THE REPORT

WEDNESDAY 31 MARCH 1999

[MORNING SITTING]

Members present:

Mr Bruce George, in the Chair

Mr Crispin Blunt	Mr Michael Hancock
Mr Julian Brazier	Mr Jimmy Hood
Mr Jamie Cann	Mr John McWilliam
Mr Harry Cohen	Mrs Laura Moffatt
Mr Michael Colvin	

The Committee deliberated.

* * * *

Draft Report (The Future of NATO: the Washington Summit), proposed by the Chairman, brought up and read.

Ordered, That further consideration of the Chairman's draft Report be now adjourned.—(*The Chairman.*)

Report to be further considered this day.

[Adjourned till this day at half past Four o'clock.

WEDNESDAY 31 MARCH 1999

[AFTERNOON SITTING]

Members present:

Mr Bruce George, in the Chair

Mr Crispin Blunt	Mr Michael Colvin
Mr Julian Brazier	Mr Jimmy Hood
Mr Jamie Cann	Mr John McWilliam
Mr Harry Cohen	Mrs Laura Moffatt

Draft Report (The Future of NATO: The Washington Summit), proposed by the Chairman, again brought up and read.

Ordered, That the draft report be read a second time, paragraph by paragraph.

Paragraphs 1 to 180 read and agreed to.

Annexes agreed to.

Resolved, That the Report be the Third Report of the Committee to the House.

Ordered, That the Chairman do make the Report to the House.

Several papers were ordered to be appended to the Report.

Several papers were ordered to be appended to the Minutes of Evidence.

Ordered, That the Appendices to the Minutes of Evidence taken before the Committee be reported to the House.—(*The Chairman.*)

Ordered, That the provisions of Standing Order No 134 (Select committees (reports)) be applied to the Report.

[Adjourned till Wednesday 21 April at Ten o'clock.

LIST OF WITNESSES

LIST OF WRITTEN EVIDENCE

Page

MINUTES OF EVIDENCE

TAKEN BEFORE THE DEFENCE COMMITTEE

WEDNESDAY 18 NOVEMBER 1998

Members present:

Mr Bruce George, in the Chair

Mr Crispin Blunt	Mr Harry Cohen
Mr Julian Brazier	Mr Jimmy Hood
Mr Menzies Campbell	Ms Dari Taylor

Examination of witnesses

MR RICHARD HATFIELD, Policy Director, Ministry of Defence, and MR STEPHEN GOMERSALL, Director of International Security, FCO, were examined.

Chairman

1. Gentlemen, thank you very much for coming. This is the beginning of our inquiry into the future of NATO leading up to the Summit in April. We will be having a number of public sessions. We will be visiting eastern and central Europe. Next week we are going to Moscow and Kiev, Paris, Mons and Brussels, so it will be a very thorough inquiry. What I would like you to do at the beginning, Mr Hatfield and Mr Gomersall, is to give us as far as you can what the status is so far of any researches and preparations going on within foreign ministries and defence ministries. I understand there is a draft of the document in circulation and whilst we would like to know in greater detail I know you are slightly constrained in what you would be able to tell us. We would like to know what the current position is, the names to be done, what kind of work will be done, between now and the Summit.

(*Mr Hatfield*) On the Strategic Concept in particular or more generally?

2. The Strategic Concept in particular.

(*Mr Hatfield*) As you rightly say, there is a first working draft in Brussels, if you like in NATO circles, but this is very early days and it has been put together by the international staff. I suspect it will change quite a lot between now and the Washington Summit, not least because there are 16 nations engaged in the drafting process. We are both very happy to give you a feel of some of the issues and no doubt we will get into that. There is of course a wider package of initiatives being developed for the Washington Summit and although the Strategic Concept will be very much at the heart it will of course be either at the accession or immediately after the accession of the three new members, and there is a related set of force goal initiatives and so on being prepared.

3. Unfold as you wish then in what detail you are prepared to give us.

(*Mr Hatfield*) On the Strategic Concept quite clearly what NATO is trying to do is to produce a document which covers three things essentially. One is that it needs to state in what I hope will be a clear and intelligible way to the member of the public who is interested what the role of the Alliance is, what it sees its future as being. That cannot be utterly precise because it is evolving just as the strategic environment is evolving. It needs to give a clear sense of what NATO is about for the future. Secondly, it needs to provide a clear steer for the NATO planners on what the organisation is expected to do. It is the organisation's highest level planning document if you like and sets the basic parameters for detailed work, and of course it has also to update itself from the 1991 version which was written in a different strategic environment. Those are the three very broad objectives that are going on in the Strategic Concept.

(*Mr Gomersall*) In our view the support for the Alliance both in the United States and at home depends on keeping it up to date and relevant and the Strategic Concept is the means of preparing the Alliance for taking on possibly different challenges in the future. What we say in public will be very important in helping to build support for the Alliance. There will be no dilution, obviously, of the Article 5 element envisaged in the Strategic Concept, but there will be some discussion and paragraphs concerning the sort of actions outside Article 5 in which NATO might anticipate being involved in the future. It will try to encapsulate the idea of NATO as an all-purpose organisation for dealing with security challenges relevant to Europe.

4. How has the issue been dealt with in the UK with this first draft? Has a committee been formed of the MoD and the Foreign Office? Who is doing the drafting, who is doing the response?

(*Mr Hatfield*) The drafting at the moment on the Concept has been done by the NATO staff in Brussels. Back in London there is no special committee that has been established but there is a loose group which involves the Foreign Office as such, the MoD and indeed our NATO delegation to Brussels which is of course a combined MoD/FCO staffed delegation anyway. And of course there is bilateral and multilateral consultation between defence ministries in particular in various capitals.

Mr Campbell

5. You probably know because you will have heard the criticism that the 1991 Strategic Concept really was a rather timid response to what had been very significant changes and in particular the end of

[**Mr Campbell** *Cont*]

the Warsaw Pact, the bringing down of the Berlin Wall. How far do you think the document to be approved next year will be more radical than the document approved in 1991?

(*Mr Hatfield*)   I hope it will reflect what has been a transformation of the security environment. I am not sure I would say the 1991 document was timid if you think about exactly where we were at the time.

6.   It has been criticised as being timid.

(*Mr Hatfield*)   I certainly think it looks highly dated now, or most of it. I think it was not a bad response at that time because exactly how the world was going to develop was not entirely clear, but I take the basic point: we need to move on. There are some parts of it which I think, apart from the language, are more or less timeless, but other parts look definitely dated.

7.   Again without breaching confidences, do you expect any significant alteration in the role that nuclear weapons play in NATO's strategy to be reflected in the terms of the new Strategic Concept?

(*Mr Hatfield*)   That is one of the areas in which I think there will be least change because the Alliance does not, even in the 1991 concept, regard nuclear weapons as part of its war fighting strategy or anything like that. It is essentially a deterrent strategy and that remains at the heart of the Alliance. I think that section of the document will probably need little change if at all.

8.   Minimum deterrence, weapons of last resort?

(*Mr Hatfield*)   Very much so.

Chairman

9.   Although we will come on to enlargement later, could you give us an indication of current thinking within the British Government and within NATO as to when Hungary, the Czech Republic and Poland are going to accede? Will it take place at the Summit or will there be strenuous attempts to clear the decks before the Summit so that the issue of accession is resolved?

(*Mr Hatfield*)   I do not think there is a real issue over the access of the three members. In practical terms the political ratification processes are likely to be completed in all the 16 member countries probably by January. There are some more bureaucratic, military and NATO processes which also need to be completed. They will be completed shortly after that and essentially accession will take place between the early spring and the first day of the Summit. It has not been decided yet.

10.   It is just a matter of the choreography?

(*Mr Hatfield*)   Exactly. There is no real substantive issue here except that obviously the three are very keen to join and there is an argument that says it would be a very good symbolic step on the first day of the Summit. There is no real issue. It is just something to be sorted out in the choreography.

Chairman

11.   We spend quite a lot of time in our SDR response on the threat assessment. What are the current and foreseeable problems to which NATO is believed to be the solution and what do these imply for NATO's role and the strategic doctrine?

(*Mr Hatfield*)   I would start by the classic NATO Article 5 collective defence. I think that remains both the fundamental role and the fundamental core value of NATO. NATO has to be able to provide for that both now and into the future. Having said that, in terms of an immediate threat or even a foreseeable major threat to the Alliance of the conventional old-fashioned type, that does not form a major part of our day to day thinking. We have to provide the collective insurance that means first of all that such a threat is never likely to reappear and to be able to respond if necessary— the same thinking in a sense that underlay the SDR. In practice, clearly the Alliance is beginning to think much more, again rather like the SDR, about new risks to European security in general—and that is why the Alliance is involved in Bosnia for example—and it does have implications therefore about how we should develop our force structure and indeed also our ability to respond politically.

12.   Do you sense—and I suppose the recent crisis in Iraq might have given us a stronger indication— how countries are lining up on this? Is there any significant group of countries who say, "Hey, let us stick on our current Article 5 commitments and to hell with ranging more widely throughout the world"? Could there be any groupings that you can see?

(*Mr Hatfield*)   There is a quite animated theological debate going on about just how much emphasis is placed on which mission and what the practical consequences of that are. However, in practice there is certainly nobody saying that the only thing NATO is involved in is collective defence and it should not touch new missions with a barge pole. Indeed, this is demonstrated by what NATO has on an ad hoc basis essentially been doing even under the present Strategic Concept, responding to real events in Bosnia and Kosovo.

13.   The Government's memorandum states that "The UK believes that the 1949 Washington Treaty remains applicable, relevant and valid as a basis for our security and that of our Allies". Is it therefore the Government's view that territorial defence under Article 5 should remain the central plank of the Washington Treaty in unamended form?

(*Mr Hatfield*)   Yes.

14.   Do you see any tensions between the Article 5 focus of NATO and its newly developing missions?

(*Mr Hatfield*)   I think there is no real tension, but rather, as we concluded in our national debate in the Strategic Defence Review, for the foreseeable future the type of forces that we believe are necessary both for the sort of contingencies you could just about envisage for a collective defence scenario and for responding to crises on the periphery which may affect European security, whether as part of a UN operation or whatever, they are the same type of military forces essentially. Where there is a slight tension, and I think this goes back to what I was saying about the theological debate, is how you present the role of NATO, whether you are perceived as forgetting about the collective security, collective defence role, whether

[Chairman *Cont]*

you are perceived as NATO trying to become a world policeman and stepping beyond its role and, of course, in relation to both those angles, of course some of the outsiders, notably the Russians, have perceptions as well. It is much more about producing a coherent modern intellectual underpinning than a tension about the type of forces that NATO needs.

15.   Is the old Article 5 NATO ceasing to be a core around which other groupings (the PfP, the EAPC and the Russia/Ukraine Councils) revolve and becoming increasingly only one element in this web of security and defence groupings?

(Mr Hatfield)   I think where you ended up is right. It is one element but it is still, where you started, the core. The one thing that distinguishes a NATO member from a non-NATO member, whatever else it does, is the Article 5 commitment from the Alliance to that member and from the member collectively to the Alliance. Round that core you can build a lot and that is precisely what we are trying to do.

16.   Would it be fair to say that the attitude of the three invitees towards NATO's future direction is that NATO should focus on territorial defence and not branch out too far into becoming a security organisation?

(Mr Hatfield)   This is one where I might turn to my Foreign Office colleague for some advice, but I would have said that for very understandable reasons the three invitees show a very strong interest in the collective security dimension. They clearly also regard NATO as indicative that they are now as it were firmly part of what we used to call western democracy. I have not seen them avoiding the new missions and indeed they have all been very helpful, even though they are still invitees, in relation to potential planning for Kosovo.

(Mr Gomersall)   Given the psychological situation of the three, the acquisition of the territorial guarantee under Article 5 of NATO is a very important gain for them. They do accept all the obligations that go with membership of the Alliance and, as Mr Hatfield said, they are among the countries who volunteered for operations with NATO in Bosnia and with the United Nations elsewhere, so I do not see them as being purely introverted nations.

17.   How can the more traditional views of the invitees be reconciled with NATO's desire to justify its existence by finding new roles for itself?

(Mr Hatfield)   I am not sure I quite follow the question. Certainly I would not accept that NATO is trying to find new roles to justify itself. I rather think new roles have been finding NATO, in the last year or so anyway. As I say, I do not think there is a strong tension here. At the moment, understandably, the invitees are very focused on the immediate requirements for joining NATO and they recognise that in many ways the process does not end, it begins, when they join NATO, because they have got a long way to go to be a full operating part of the NATO Alliance. It just reflects a slightly different balance of focus; that is all.

18.   On the UK Government's position, does the Government recognise any conflict between NATO's role as a self-defence organisation and its role as a regional security forum?

(Mr Gomersall)   No. I think we have answered that question. The essence of Article 5 remains the core of NATO's commitment to its allies but NATO has a much wider role beyond that which has become not only increasingly accepted within the Alliance but also outside the Alliance and it is in that direction that we expect the Strategic Concept to edge NATO planning and strategic thinking.

19.   Do you see any anxiety about perhaps the concept of renationalisation of defence and, if there is this concern in NATO in relation to some countries, what can one do in the debate over the next few months to head this off or to justify NATO in such a way as to inhibit any move to a renationalisation?

(Mr Hatfield)   It is something that is of general concern inside NATO, not because anybody wants to do it—indeed, quite the contrary—but there is a natural pressure, such as pressure on defence budgets and so on, and not the same external pressure as there was during the Cold War not actively to renationalise defence but just to allow it to happen. Because that was seen as coming we are doing quite well in avoiding that. The development of the new NATO command structure has been specifically designed to avoid that. There are national elements in it, as there always have been, but at the major level it is definitely still organised militarily on a collective basis. We are seeing the development of the CJTFs, the combined joint task forces, and I think that despite the pressures we are resisting them.

Mr Campbell

20.   I think I understood you to say that if there is any tension in NATO at the moment it is in relation to the intellectual underpinnings of the organisation rather than the forces, but you have just made the entirely sensible point that when we look round there is pressure on defence budgets everywhere. Is there any risk that the pressure on budgets, which clearly has an effect on the quality and the range of forces may in turn inhibit a proper scrutiny of what the intellectual basis ought to be? It may be that the reduction in defence expenditure will inhibit proper theoretical analysis.

(Mr Hatfield)   To be honest, I fear that the real danger is not to the theoretical analysis but whether we actually produce the real underpinning to match the analysis when we have done it. For example, most Europeans would rapidly accept the principle that we need to have more deployable and flexible forces but that is one of the areas in which Europe is very weak at the moment.

21.   It would be pretty curious to embark upon a new Strategic Concept which was founded very heavily on those elements you have just described if at the time of doing so those responsible for creating this concept knew that there were not likely to be the resources to fulfil it.

(Mr Hatfield)   I would agree, though I think the problem is slightly less one of the total amount of resources, although more resources are always

[**Mr Campbell** *Cont*]

welcome in defence, but refocusing them on the newer type of capability and away from some of the more traditional areas of NATO individual nations' spending.

22. Take an example: you are talking about amphibiosty rather than heavy armour. Is this the sort of thing you mean?

(Mr Hatfield) Certainly I am talking about deployability, strategic lift, logistics, and the same sort of general ground we covered in the Strategic Defence Review. We identified some national weaknesses against this sort of pattern which we are now planning to remedy, and it will cost money and, as the Committee knows, having taken evidence, we will have to redirect some of our own expenditure to achieve that. In principle there is no reason why that should not be done more generally although clearly nations being of varying size they cannot all try and provide capabilities across the board, but that is what I mean. Europe has to collectively follow the Strategic Concept review by adapting its forces to match the missions it gives it.

23. Are we talking about things like interoperability?

(Mr Hatfield) Certainly.

24. Perhaps even, the most difficult of all to swallow for individual nations, force specialisation?

(Mr Hatfield) Yes, I think we are talking about both those: interoperability both in the equipment sense but perhaps even more in the current strategic environment, ensuring that command and control in particular is interoperable, not only within NATO but we have 14 partner nations in Bosnia at the moment. They are never going to have the same equipment as we do across the board. We are going to have to work interoperability in that way. Both points you raise are entirely fair.

(Mr Gomersall) We would hope to see all these things figuring very prominently in the Strategic Concept which is after all a statement of future intent. The language of the Strategic Concept will in itself influence the process of defence planning which will then be carried forward with the Alliance, so it will be an element of pressure upon the Allies to move in that direction.

25. Without asking you to conduct a textual analysis of what the Prime Minister said in Edinburgh on Friday, do I take it that from your standpoint you would see nothing inconsistent with what the Prime Minister said on Friday and what you expect to be in the Strategic Concept?

(Mr Hatfield) That is absolutely right. I never expected anything to be inconsistent.

26. That is an old principle of cross-examination: you should never ask a question to which you do not already know the answer. We have talked about command and control, Mr Hatfield. Do you think it may get to the stage at which we may then have to consider reconfiguration of command and control in order to take account of the crisis management and conflict prevention role rather than the collective defence role?

(Mr Hatfield) I think the answer to that is yes but we have already started down that route. The NATO command structure review moves in a direction which I think makes it easier to respond to the crisis management approach. The development of the combined joint task forces in particular is a response to that, both in the Article 5 context and in the non-Article 5 context, and includes for example provision for Partner Staff Elements at the NATO headquarters which are the parents of the CJTFs to make interoperability in a non-Article 5 operation with non-Allies much more feasible.

27. Generally the Secretary of State in the Strategic Defence Review talked about Britain being prepared to go to the crisis rather than the crisis coming to us. Do you think that is likely to be a principle which may drive the operations of NATO more in the future than ever before?

(Mr Hatfield) Yes. I think the answer is yes.

28. That therefore will require sophisticated crisis management procedures within NATO itself. If we expand from 16 to 19 that of course creates further inhibitions on the achievement of consensus and if we went from 19, say, to 23 or 24, which some argue, then consensus is more difficult to achieve and rapid response (not in the technical sense but quick response) becomes more difficult to achieve. What assessment have you made of these difficulties against your acceptance of the notion that NATO may have to deal more with crisis management?

(Mr Hatfield) You raise a very good point. At times the NATO machinery seems to be immensely bureaucratic even now and there is of course a fear that as you add more countries to it it will get worse. However, the experience of this year has been that despite the difficulties, and I would not underestimate the difficulties of getting consensus sometimes on some of the very difficult issues (difficult both in military terms and in political terms) working in really uncharted territory, NATO has actually proved able to do that. I do not see any real reason why that should not continue when it is at 19, or even if it goes beyond that. One thing I am sure of is that NATO will not have too much difficulty ever in reaching a consensus on an Article 5 issue. It is rapidly learning how to approach the wider crisis management issues that can arise on non-Article 5. It will learn as it goes along. As I say, I have been, if I can put it this way, pleasantly surprised that NATO has got its act together this year when it has mattered.

29. Article 5 of course is in a different category because there is an obligation. It is explicit and, as you have already accepted, both you and Mr Gomersall, one of the things which drives new members is admission to what one might describe as the Article 5 club. On this question of dealing with non-NATO countries, the operations in Bosnia are under the command of the RRC, the rapid reaction corps; yet we know that there are non-NATO countries involved, in particular most notably, the Russians who have a rather special relationship with the Americans. What has been the experience of that deployment as to how easily NATO's command and control, which after all

[Mr Campbell Cont]

lies behind the RRC, can be adapted to accommodate non-NATO countries?

(Mr Hatfield) First I should just say that the ARRC is not there at the moment, though of course it was. You are absolutely right on your basic point that it is a NATO operation and run under NATO procedures, although it is of course subject to a UN mandate. The experience is very positive. NATO has over the years developed procedures to allow it to operate with 16 rather divergent nations which at least in the circumstances in Bosnia have proved not too difficult for translation into wider use. It is known that from the 1990/91 Gulf War NATO procedures were actually quite useful in persuading the American Pacific fleet to work with the American Atlantic fleet.

30.   One of the major achievements.

(Mr Hatfield) So they have been designed for international co-operation of all sorts. They do not depend in interoperability in all equipment or anything like that. It would of course be different if we were conducting a major military campaign or an offensive operation or something like that, and that would be a different type of operation. Again, everybody concerned is learning from the experience. For example, the French, who are not members of the integrated military structure, have, through working in Bosnia, come much closer to adopting common procedures simply as a result of the practical lessons we have all learned.

31.   Of necessity.

(Mr Hatfield) Of necessity. I should not imply it is entirely a one-way process either.

Mr Cohen

32.   I would like to follow up one of the questions Mr Campbell asked earlier about force specialisation being a possibility, NATO countries concentrating on some functions and abandoning others and different countries doing different things. What assessment has the MoD made of this possibility at this stage? Is it just that the theory is acceptable at this stage or has any work been done or is proposed to be done on the limits of it, what we are prepared to give up or how the division would work?

(Mr Hatfield) To some extent it already happens in relation to some of the smaller nations. For example, the Dutch in particular have a contribution to make in amphibious forces and they work with us in a combined force, so that is one example. We have seen with the airborne early warning aircraft that NATO has developed a pool of such aircraft which nations have contributed essentially. You can see possible ways in which this could be developed in the future, particularly in responding to some of the collective weaknesses we have. Maybe there is a role here in relation to strategic lift for example. This is an area which is going to be worked forward gradually because everybody has to take account of their own national interest as well and their own national requirements. You cannot unilaterally decide that country X is going to make one contribution unless you are sure it is going to fit in with the other contributions and can be organised so that both bits

can go together when required. I do not think you are going to see radical change. What you are going to see is the development of much more co-ordinated responses to the future problems rather than somebody saying, "I am going to stop doing this suddenly and go and do something else." One of the things we would like to see in part of the Strategic Concept is the development of force goals, which NATO already has in the classic sense, but related to the areas in which we want to see particular improvements and perhaps some of those individual goals can be pointed towards some nations for some things and to other nations for others.

Mr Campbell

33.   I have a hint of what you say that you may be postulating something approaching a European defence review, certainly with regard to force goals and ensuring that there are resources to meet whatever the objectives are that are set out in the Strategic Concept.

(Mr Hatfield) I do not envisage a Strategic Defence Review of the type we have done on a grand European scale, not least because I do not think I could face the volume of work that would be involved.

34.   You would ensure the television cameras followed you again.

(Mr Hatfield) In that case I think I would just abandon the European defence review. What I do see, and I think the Strategic Concept is the start of this, is an attempt to start a much more long term process which goes in the same direction, and it will have some of the same consequences, although individual consequences will vary from nation to nation. Yes, I think it is a process though it is not a single event even of the length of the Strategic Defence Review.

35.   That was shorthand but I do detect in what you say the notion of trying to lay down political objectives and seeking, so long as one can keep the Treasuries of European countries at bay, to ensure that you provide sufficient military resources to meet these political objectives.

(Mr Hatfield) Very much so. I think that is the objective.

Mr Brazier

36.   Mr Hatfield, the Government's memorandum sets out in paragraph 10 the requirements of the Alliance in terms of military capabilities it must have to fulfil its new missions. In your view in which of these areas is the shortfall greatest at the moment, and what remedies are being proposed?

(Mr Hatfield) To be honest, I suppose what I would say is that to a large extent in some of these areas the Alliance has been carried by the Americans who do have capabilities across this range of spectrum. What we need to do is move the Alliance as a whole much more in that direction. In that respect I think this is one of the drivers behind the Prime Minister's recent comments about improving European defence capability. He is conscious that although Europe has quite substantial forces, its defence budget collectively

[Mr Brazier *Cont]*
(I am talking about the European numbers of the Alliance) is something like two-thirds of the American defence budget, but in some of the capabilities which are now critical to the new missions Europe as a whole is really quite weak. That is again going back to what I was saying earlier, where we want to try and refocus some of the defence spending and contributions from the Alliance.

37. Did I hear you correctly? Did you say that defence spending of the European members of the Alliance is now two-thirds of that of the Americans? Is that really right?
(Mr Hatfield) It is of that order, depending on exactly how you count it.
Chairman: But it is not spent as efficiently as the American budget.

Mr Brazier

38. To press you a little harder, Mr Hatfield, specific areas, some obviously come to mind: the American satellite capability, their heavy lift capability. Are there other specific areas?
(Mr Hatfield) More generally, logistics, particularly for deployed operations and sustained operations. To be honest, that was one of the weaknesses in our own forces because we are now facing a rather different set of tasks than in the past. That is one of the areas where probably every European country has a weakness.

39. Leaving aside aspirant members, of the existing European members of NATO who collectively have a gross domestic product slightly larger than the United States, are there any at all who are increasing defence spending rather than reducing it? France was for a bit but even they have turned round.
(Mr Hatfield) I am not sure of the answer to that, but what I would say is certainly the French in particular are reconfiguring their defence effort rather in the same way as we are trying to do with the same sort of motives. The Germans, as I am sure you know, are just about to start on a defence commission under their new government. Maybe that will lead in the same direction. As I have found from attempting to debate it with the Treasury, it is quite difficult to argue for increased defence spending in the current strategic environment. It is slightly less difficult to argue for redirecting it to be more effective.

40. We have a copy of the bid here this morning in fact. One is just left though with the feeling that however much we may talk about these things, at the end of the day NATO will always be an American organisation in which a number of European countries play a subsidiary role because we are not willing to spend the money they are. NATO member states are experiencing falling defence budgets and rising equipment costs. You have already said something about the implications of this for the structure of NATO's forces. Do you think there is a case for a NATO free trade area in defence equipment, rather in the way the EU has a mandatory purchasing policy for non-defence equipment? Governments place their major tenders out on the open market within the EU. Do you think there is a case for extending that sort of thinking to the defence equipment?
(Mr Hatfield) I have to say I had not quite thought about it in those terms, in the terms in which you phrased the question. I think it is very important that we do not end up with either or both a fortress USA or a fortress Europe syndrome in relation to the defence industry. As you have probably seen, the American defence industry has already gone through a major process of restructuring and concentration. There are signs, which the Government is encouraging, that British and European industry are going to do a similar process, though that should not be seen I think as just Europe and the US, because some of the industrial alliances ought to be transatlantic as well. Your general proposition, that we need to have healthy competition in defence industry across the Atlantic and purchasing in both ways across the Atlantic is sound. I am not sure that I see the particular institution of a free trade area as necessary, nor am I quite sure what it would involve, though it would be very important that we do not go the other way and see protectionist barriers being erected.

41. Could I pursue a little further as the official with the senior policy hat on the question that we pursued at some length with the Minister and official for defence procurement. Let us just try and put some flesh on to the answer you have given because in general terms I do not think anyone would argue with the view that we have got to have a two-way street and that there has to be some consolidation; indeed, much has already taken place on both sides of the Atlantic. When we come down to the real world starting from where we are now, the advice we were given on this Committee over in Washington I think my colleagues would agree was extremely clear. The Americans were very clear that at the moment they have this very special tie-up both at the research level between government research facilities in America and government research facilities in Britain, and at the next level up between American industry and British defence industry, although there are some much more limited ties with some of the European ones. The message we were given on three separate occasions was that that kind of tie-up simply would not be possible if British defence industry were submerged into a wider European one. I had better not quote the wording in the way it was put to us because I do not want to embarrass the official in question. Would you like to comment though on this difficulty, the special relationship?
(Mr Hatfield) There are two elements to that. First of all, as you started, there is a very close relationship between some parts of the defence scientific establishment in this country and its counterpart in the US. We remain very conscious of the need to protect those key interests in the interests of both countries. Similarly, in relation to industry, of course there are some very close ties between British and US industry but there are also plenty of other ties between British industry and other European industry already, which I do not think cut across that. I am not aware of the danger of the rest of European industry submerging

[Mr Brazier Cont]

our industry. I would have thought that in some countries they are probably worrying about British industry submerging theirs. The debate is rather false. Assuming it is done on a proper commercial and industrial basis, I do not think anybody will be submerging national interests. They will be advancing both commercial and national interests at the same time.

42. You put a caveat in just then: as long as it was done on a confidential and commercial basis. France's industry, and they are the most important industry in this context for us to look at, is not of course mostly on a commercial basis and the fact that they are not on a commercial basis presents serious problems for us, more serious ones than the Americans. At the same time the Americans are willing to share information with us not just in the scientific sector but in intelligence as well that they will not share with the French or our continental partners under their arrangements. Surely the issue is not one of submerging. The issue quite simply, at the security level and at the commercial level, is one of trust and the fact is that a degree of trust exists for a variety of historical reasons between America and this country which simply is not echoed with our continental partners.

(Mr Hatfield) Again you need to distinguish I think between bilateral intelligence relationships and wider commercially or technologically sensitive information and so on. There are perfectly good ways of safeguarding whatever tie-ups take place in industry and any such information. And it is not even entirely UK-US or US-UK. I imagine some of the other countries involved have some interests that they would wish to protect. That can be achieved. Going back to what you said about French industry, you are of course right, although I would add that the country with the biggest problem is the French as a result of that. It is a point we are making at every opportunity to the French. It is essentially their decision to make whether or not they are prepared, or how fast they are prepared, to see normal commercial pressures applied to their industry.

Mr Cohen

43. I would like to ask you about NATO's new force posture which actually downplays the role of stationed forces and stresses interoperability, integration and the capability for reinforcement. Can you give some indication of the implications of that? Presumably it also depended on this role specialisation which I asked a question about earlier. Is the necessary strategic lift capability and reinforcement infrastructure available for this new approach?

(Mr Hatfield) As you will have gathered, there are limitations in what we have at the moment, especially for non-Article 5 missions and in relation to the new members. This shows how there is a clear convergence now between the requirements of NATO's new missions if you like and the possible implications of having extended the security guarantee to three new nations. If there were to be some collective security problem affecting one of the three new nations, since we are not having permanently stationed forces on their territory we would have to respond by reinforcement and rapid deployment just as we do if we are going to, say, Bosnia or Kosovo. That is why you see a convergence. Equally, that is not just saying force majeure: we cannot afford to or it would upset the Russians or something like that if we stationed troops on the new nations' territory. We do not see a need in the current strategic environment to do so. We believe that as long as the strategic environment remains as it is now broadly we can fulfil that guarantee and be seen to be able to fulfil that guarantee through an ability to reinforce. This of course is also playing into the negotiations on modernising the Conventional Forces in Europe Treaty which was designed as a treaty between two blocs in very different circumstances, but one of the things we need to preserve in modifying the treaty is the ability to reinforce and indeed to exercise such reinforcement so that we know we can do it.

Mr Blunt

44. Can I move on to deal with the sensible relationship between NATO and the UN and what I would describe as peacekeeping in out of area operations. Do you expect the new Strategic Concept to clarify the circumstances in which the United Nations might make use of NATO forces? I think someone has suggested that one of the new missions identified for NATO might become the UN's military executive. What can we expect to see?

(Mr Gomersall) That is a pipe dream that some people have had from time to time. I certainly think that the Strategic Concept will reiterate the willingness of NATO to act on behalf and at the request of the United Nations in certain circumstances. That is not to say however that NATO would regard itself as having a right or being necessarily the instrument of first choice in dealing with the range of issues that the United Nations faces. What has proven to be the case, however, as a matter of practical experience is that the capabilities that NATO has and which by and large the United Nations does not have are very useful in the right circumstances. But NATO is only one of many security and political organisations that exist in the international arena and although the preparedness to do that will be there, we will not be looking to prescribe a particular role for NATO as the surrogate of the United Nations because the United Nations' ability to deploy its own peacekeeping forces in many parts of the world is still something which it is also our policy to encourage and support.

45. When the UN invites NATO to act on its behalf it has always been rather complicated as to who is going to pay. How will the financial backing for NATO taking part in UN missions be worked out in the future, do you think?

(Mr Gomersall) This is something which inevitably will depend on the circumstances of the case. It will depend on whether NATO is playing the central role in a UN operation or a partial role. It will depend on whether the Allies for whatever reason are doing more in support of the operation on a national

[**Mr Blunt** *Cont*]

basis than they are as it were contracted to do by the United Nations. There will therefore be a part, I would imagine, of any such operation which would be funded by the United Nations, but in experience we also find that there is a part which falls upon the Allies or the other contributing countries as a national cost.

46. So we cannot expect to see the new Strategic Concept deliver any clarity?

(Mr Gomersall) The new Strategic Concept will not get into this issue.

47. Obviously we are building on experience, particularly in Bosnia, and particularly in 1993 when we had a go at the UN and NATO working jointly. I wonder if you could tell us what problems you believe prevented that operation from working together and what lessons have been learned from that experience.

(Mr Hatfield) Could you be a little clearer about which particular operation and which particular problems you were thinking about?

48. Yes, in 1993 when NATO forces were postulated as coming under UN control and it never happened.

(Mr Hatfield) Is this the so-called "dual key" debate that you are talking about?

49. Yes, it is.

(Mr Hatfield) Because I would say that for a long period of the pre-IFOR operation of course there was a very effective UN operation in Bosnia delivering humanitarian aid and so on through UNPROFOR. I suspect you are on the more narrow point of the command and control of a military operation.

50. Yes.

(Mr Hatfield) And actually launching an active strike. The answer to that is yes, we have learned some lessons and that has been reflected in the way NATO has subsequently approached subsequent crises. It was not only a question about UN and NATO. It was also a question of how any multinational organisation is going to sort out political control and detailed military control once it has made the basic decision that it is engaged in operations. We have been having the same sort of debate for example around the possible operations in Kosovo. There is a level of decision to be taken by national governments through the NATO committee. Then there has to be—and this is what we have realised we have to be clear about—a clear set of parameters within which the military commander of the operation can operate. He cannot always refer for detailed decisions back to the political level. It just is not an effective way of running a military operation.

51. In 1993, if I remember correctly, what actually fouled up any prospects of the UN and NATO working effectively together was the fact that the Americans were not prepared to put their troops under UN command. To what extent is the development of an effective linkage between the UN and NATO going to navigate around this rock of the United States not being prepared to put its troops and blue berets under UN command? How much is that going to obstruct the creation of perhaps a more effective way of deploying nations on UN operations?

(Mr Hatfield) I do not think that is such a serious issue. You may have been more closely involved in 1993 than I was but I did not see that as being a major problem. Part of the problem was that it was not a NATO operation at that stage with the Americans involved. We now have a NATO operation in Bosnia with the Americans involved, yes, as a sub-contractor of the UN and that is a perfectly reasonable solution. There was a general reluctance once Bosnia started to move into what might be called a potentially heavy military operation to see the UN, which does not have the command and control machinery for that sort of operation trying to run the operation, and the ultimate solution was indeed to subcontract that to NATO.

52. But it has only really been subcontracted at the most political levels. In a sense it is a NATO operation under the cover of the United Nations Security Council resolution, is it not? There is not a sense of a linkage from any form of military headquarters in New York or the UN.

(Mr Gomersall) There is reporting from the head of SFOR to the Security Council on a regular basis. It is a monthly report which goes to the Secretary General and is presented to the Security Council, so the Security Council can raise questions about it and does from time to time.

(Mr Hatfield) And Dayton of course includes a very detailed annexe setting out what the roles of initially IFOR and subsequently S4 are required to be. When we move from IFOR to SFOR the Security Council had to review the mandate. There is a very clear set of parameters for NATO as a subcontractor to work within.

53. One of the effects of that contrast between the move from New York to NATO control in Bosnia in 1995 was the fact that in a sense it has reinforced the view in Bosnia and elsewhere in central and eastern Europe about how effective NATO is and how in a sense it is a panacea to sort out security problems. Mr Gomersall, I think you said earlier if I recall it correctly that part of the new Strategic Concept was to deliver a NATO that was going to be an all-purpose organisation to deal with security challenges in relation to Europe. Is that right?

(Mr Gomersall) What I meant was that the Strategic Concept should not artificially limit the situations to which NATO might be able to respond. I did not mean to imply that NATO would necessarily be the instrument that people would choose to deal with every kind of crisis.

54. Is there a risk, because NATO's high profile involves it in areas such as Bosnia and potentially Kosovo, of creating expectations which are going to be disappointed?

(Mr Gomersall) No, I do not think so, because I think NATO has been very clear about what it is doing and what it is not doing. What NATO has agreed to do basically is provide air verification for the Kosovo monitoring effort and it is establishing a small force in Macedonia which would be able in an emergency to extract members of the verification force. NATO has made it quite clear that we are not there to act as a shield for incidents by the UCK for example.

[**Mr Blunt** *Cont*]

55. How large is that force going to be in Macedonia?

(Mr Hatfield) I think it is still under debate.

(Mr Gomersall) The French are going to put in something like a headquarters and a company, and there are four other countries who are going to put in a company, so the overall force will be something in the region of about 1,200.

56. It is a sort of battalion group?

(Mr Hatfield) Yes, it will be a reinforced battalion I should think.

57. Are we expected to contribute to that?

(Mr Hatfield) We are expected to contribute.

58. At company level?

(Mr Hatfield) Yes.

59. You said, Mr Gomersall, that you did not want the Strategic Concept to unnecessarily limit NATO's involvement in European security, but how will the New Strategic Concept define the limits of NATO's role, or is it going to be unlimited, and how is it going to define its relationship and interaction with other international organisations promoting security by non-military means?

(Mr Gomersall) I think NATO will avoid, for example, any attempt to define a geographical area or a particular size or nature of conflict which will automatically call for or rule out a NATO response. I think it will include a lot of generic language about the sort of situations, challenges to regional security, threats to stability, humanitarian situations which could prompt a NATO response. Does that answer the question?

60. So it is not going to define it, so there will be no defined limits in the new Strategic Concept?

(Mr Gomersall) Well, we have not got into the textual negotiation yet of that, but I think our instinct——

61. But the British Government will seek to make it undefined and flexible?

(Mr Gomersall) The British Government's instinct will be to leave it as it is at the moment, very flexible.

Mr Campbell

62. Just how far does that flexibility go? It is a question I have asked before here and Mr Hatfield may even have heard me ask it. Does it include the Korean Peninsula?

(Mr Hatfield) Well, this is where I think it is quite difficult without having a document, but I think it is going to give you a clear flavour of where NATO sees its prime interests as being, which is in European security. I think it is going to give you a clear flavour of the sort of risks to which, in addition to the classic Article 5, NATO would be willing to respond if those contingencies arose. What it will not do is lay down precise limits or specify precise circumstances for a number of very good reasons, one of which is I think we want to avoid the slight mistake of the last Strategic Concept of writing down something which looks really quite sensible today, but looks dated only two or three years later. So we do not want to start writing down

specific threats or risks which, even if they are there, could be very transient and would give us another dated look in just a few years' time But it must give, and this is the difficulty, I think, in the drafting, that it has got to give a clear, I hate the word "vision", but a clear vision of what NATO is about. So I would be both surprised and disappointed if you read the Strategic Concept in a few months' time and thought, "This means NATO is going gallivanting around the Korean Peninsula".

63. But, as you know, you do not have to go very far in Washington to hear talk of what they sometimes describe as the "grand bargain", the effect of which is that the United States will stay engaged in Europe and there will still be 100,000 troops, "We will be part of NATO, we will assist Europe's security, but there is a price to be paid for that; we will expect NATO Allies to come with us on other operations out of area which we, the United States, conceive as being in our interests".

(Mr Hatfield) Yes, I have heard talk of that kind and I expect I will hear some more in the next 48 hours, but, first of all, I think that is a rather exaggerated view, although it is held by some Americans.

64. Yes, I may have put it in a rather exaggerated form, but I think you accept that it is an argument that you hear.

(Mr Hatfield) Indeed, and there is an element which I think is reasonable, although it should be focused not on NATO as NATO. But certainly I think the British Government, as reflected in everything we have said to the Committee in the course of the Strategic Defence Review, recognises that we have obligations and interests which extend beyond Europe and which in certain circumstances we might well contribute a military operation or military support to, but that does not necessarily imply that it would be as NATO. It was not NATO that went to the Gulf in 1990/91, although many NATO nations did so.

65. But do you understand the anxiety on the part of some people that we should not be seen to be the inevitable accompaniment to every United States operation? You are quite right that we have common interests and you might even argue, because of what some people, still want to call the special relationship, there is a presumption that we would be associated with the United States, but I think there are very good reasons why it should not become an assumption that we would be associated with the United States.

(Mr Hatfield) I think I would agree with that and the same is certainly true of NATO. NATO does need to remain focused on European security. That is what it is about and that does imply certain broad limits to what it does as an alliance, and I do not think that is inside the Alliance, including in the American Administration, in question and I think that is accepted.

Mr Cohen

66. Can I follow up on the out-of-area aspects. As far as you see the Strategic Concept going, could you envisage NATO taking part, for example, in

[**Mr Cohen** *Cont*]

peace-keeping operations outside of its present North Atlantic boundaries?

(Mr Hatfield) Well, in theory, the answer is yes. For example, I could see NATO being asked by the United Nations to conduct a military humanitarian operation in Africa. I am not sure that that would necessarily be a good idea to do it under a NATO badge, but, in principle, I would not see that ruled out. Much more likely, as indeed nearly happened, you might see a coalition essentially built around NATO members and maybe even NATO procedures as an effective way of mounting such an operation. But that is why I think the Strategic Concept has got to avoid being overly precise, but it does have to give the basic message about what NATO's fundamental role is, what its fundamental interests are, all of which are European. Exactly how you draw European boundaries is in a way, I think, irrelevant, not least because, as we all know, the Alliance is founded on the assumption that there is a fundamental involvement of the transatlantic members in European security. So, as long as that message is not blurred, I do not think we have to worry about absolute precision.

67. President Chirac said that he did not want "a holy Alliance with a sweeping mandate for intervention" and he said that that would be unacceptable to France if it just had total freedom to operate out of area in a military way. Is this argument very much tied up with having United Nations' authority, a United Nations' mandate for any NATO action to be taken outside?

(Mr Hatfield) In very broad terms, I think there is a connection, but one of the interesting things, I think, is that over the last year what started as a very theoretical debate about what the Strategic Concept would say on this, everybody's mind has been focused by having some real world examples to think about and I think in practice there is now a very large convergence. Quite clearly NATO, and indeed its individual members, whether they are acting as NATO or not, need to act in accordance with international law and, therefore, depending on the circumstances, there can be a range of possible bases for that, but I do not think there is a fundamental issue between any member of the Alliance.

(Mr Gomersall) Frankly, a holy Alliance is not anybody's agenda and, on the other hand, I think it is true to say that France has also recognised that there are situations which have occurred very close to NATO where NATO is by far the best military means of applying support to a diplomatic effort, so there has been some considerable evolution in a practical direction in French thinking.

68. It seems to me that we are moving towards these out-of-area operations, albeit limited, and there will have to be presumably tied up in the text what those limits are. That actually brings me to the point which is nearly preempted by the next question which was about international law: does there need to be a reassessment of what the international law is and how those sort of limited actions out of area could comply with international law? Does that need to come into that whole thinking of the Strategic Concept?

(Mr Hatfield) Well, there is obviously a linkage between international law and out of area, but there is not a direct linkage. Depending what you mean by "out of area", Bosnia is out of the NATO area in the sense that it is not within the boundaries of the NATO members, but clearly Bosnia has major implications for European security and what has happened in Bosnia has already had a direct impact on quite a lot of NATO members. The legal basis for operating in Bosnia is, however, nothing to do with its geographic place; it is to do with the circumstances of the crisis. The only linkage between the geographic limitations of NATO's area and law directly is in relation to collective defence where an attack across the NATO boundaries clearly gives you an automatic legal basis to respond whatever else is true about the circumstances, so you are certainly right to imply that there is almost a continuing review really of the appropriate international legal basis for all sorts of operations, but that is really responding to contingencies as they arise rather than being triggered by the Strategic Concept.

69. Will Article 6 be re-written—is that what you are saying—Article 6, which limits NATO's activities within the regions of Europe and North America, bounded by the Mediterranean and the North Atlantic area north of the Tropic of Cancer?

(Mr Hatfield) No, I do not think that Article 6 will need to be re-written.

Mr Cohen: You do not?

Mr Blunt

70. So what happens if you have got a NATO operation in Africa, which is the one you have postulated?

(Mr Hatfield) Article 6, I think from memory, is actually related to Article 5. So Article 5 clearly cannot take place in Africa, but I do not think the Washington Treaty, even as it stands, actually inhibits NATO activity, provided it is honest and lawful (as it were) elsewhere.

Mr Campbell

71. But it does not provide the specific authority for it.

(Mr Hatfield) No, I agree it does not.

Chairman: As I said earlier, the Defence Committee are off to Eastern and Central Europe. One group is going to Hungary and Slovenia and the other to Romania and Bulgaria, so we are going to have NATO enlargement up to our eyeballs for the next week, so we welcome any steer that you might give us. I hope we do not either over-enthuse or retard the aspirations of three countries who I am sure would be desperately anxious to join NATO and will be very enthusiastic about telling us so over the next week or so. I will ask Dari Taylor to lead on this, though I am sure there will be additional questions from the rest of the Committee.

Ms Taylor

72. As you hear, on NATO enlargement there is a collection of questions and we would really appreciate some steer and certainly your experience and your

[Ms Taylor *Cont]*

thoughts on it. Effectively we are hearing the Government's statement that NATO will remain committed to its 'open door' policy as long as we are talking about European democracies, and Article 10 is very clearly something the Government is actually defining as its stance and will continue to be. On that score, as the Chairman has already intimated, we are going to be speaking to people who are at the point of actually going to join and equally we are going to be speaking to people who feel quite clearly excluded. We are looking obviously at Bulgaria, Romania, Slovakia and Slovenia and these are feeling now when might it be their opportunity. Really I would like to ask you, to start us going, how are these new entrants to NATO going to affect other people's beliefs about their own opportunities and capabilities of joining? Perhaps you could just give us some idea of how you feel because they are obviously very clearly opening the door to that part of the world and others are waiting very keenly and believe frankly that they should actually already be embraced by NATO.

(Mr Gomersall) I think the first thing it would be good to convey to them is that they are taken very seriously as members of the European security fraternity and as aspirant countries to NATO membership and that we value very much the development of relations which has taken place with each of the countries that you are going to visit, both of a practical nature and of a more general political nature in the last six years, and perhaps Mr Hatfield could go into the details about specific co-operation that we have with individual countries, if you wish. At the same time I think it would be good also to intimate to them that the open door policy means exactly what it says; it means that NATO will not close the door to further enlargement after the Washington Summit, but that we do not expect that there will be either further invitations or, if you like, earmarking of any individual country or any particular time-frame for the next round of accessions. This debate is yet continuing in NATO, so I cannot say precisely what NATO will say beyond what it has said at Madrid. There is certainly a widely expressed desire to give countries like Romania, Slovenia and Bulgaria the impression that subject to their accepting and making progress towards the military and other preparations as are required, then it will not be an indefinite process, but these things are all rather subtle and, as I say, still under discussion, so it would not be wise to venture a guess as to how the Washington Summit will declare itself in precise terms. However, at the same time one can point out that through their membership of the Partnership for Peace programme and through all the other bilateral and multilateral programmes to which they have access, there is a natural process of convergence which has been going on, and that particularly their contributions to operations, peace-keeping operations, whether under the United Nations or under NATO auspices, which bring us into direct proximity and operating environment are exactly the sort of circumstances which will help to prepare them most adequately for eventual NATO membership.

73. Could I ask you a follow-on from that, which is that effectively Bulgaria, Romania, Slovenia and Slovakia are outside the Alliance, but to what extent do they influence then the military planning assumptions of the Alliance?

(Mr Hatfield) Well, while they are outside the Alliance, their influence on planning assumptions is very limited in the sense that the first part of NATO's obligations is to plan for the Article 5 commitment and they are not part of it, and, secondly, to the extent that they are not contributing directly to the Alliance, they can hardly expect to take part in its detailed planning. In relation to the three invitees, however, of course because we are now moving on a process which within a few months will have them in, we are on a convergent path which means both that the Alliance and the new members or candidate members are talking about what happens after they get in and how they fit into the structure, so for them it is slightly different. I think one of the things which is quite important is to try to convey to all the countries that whilst I can understand that from their point of view it is a great event "when we go through the open door", this is very much a process and it actually continues after you go through the door too, very importantly, and it is a process which involves three things: one, however you have judged the criteria, in whatever range they are, is country X ready; two, is the Alliance ready to absorb them and maybe others as well, and we have already discussed this and Mr Campbell pointed out the problems of consensus and so on getting greater; and, thirdly, how does it fit into the wider European security picture. All of those things have got to be managed simultaneously and it will take time and, if I can suck up to the Committee, I thought you did a very good report on this.

Mr Blunt

74. If I can ask a supplementary, at Madrid, Slovenia and Romania were mentioned in the Conclusions and we had the Romanian Defence Minister who came to talk to Members of the Committee and he made it pretty clear that if an invitation is not issued at Washington, the Romanians are going to be somewhat disappointed and they may have some difficulty explaining to their public exactly what has happened, and the point I think he made to us was sustaining the Romanian enthusiasm for NATO, so is there a danger of the parallel to what the European Union has managed to do to Turkey occurring with Romania and Slovenia, who clearly obviously see themselves as in pole position, having been mentioned in the Madrid Conclusions?

(Mr Hatfield) Yes, there is some danger, and there is some danger that they will come to see themselves, to use your words, excluded, which is wrong because they are not being excluded. It is still envisaged that they will end up in NATO if the process develops the way it is expected to develop, so there is a huge danger that expectations are created by whatever means and then disappointed and that is probably worse than the reality. I think there was certainly an element of that surrounding Madrid. Now, I suspect actually that this time round, despite what was said to you, and I have to say I have heard very similar things both from the Romanian Defence Minister and his entourage and

[**Mr Blunt** *Cont*]

only yesterday from the Romanian Ambassador, they are being more realistic about what is likely to happen this time. I hope that the Alliance too not only works out, which I think it will do, fairly clearly what it is going to do at the Washington Summit, but that it manages expectations in the lead-up to the Washington Summit so that nobody gets a surprise, and that this is seen as a long-term process. It is still, I think, largely lost sight of that what we are about to do with the three new members is the biggest enlargement NATO has ever attempted in terms of the number of countries at one go and coming from a very different background. So we are doing something radical and I hope that that will be seen as evidence of intent and we do not have to every time we have a meeting invite a new member through the door, because I think that way it will actually be bad news for everybody and for the long-term future of the Alliance.

Chairman

75.   I personally hope that France will be in the next wave of enlargement! There are a lot of silver-tongued diplomats in the Alliance and very smart people writing ambivalent phrases, but is there any serious discussion if, as is now pretty obvious, and I heard Alexander Vershbow speaking at Edinburgh and if I was a Romanian, I would not have left that meeting with any high expectation that they are going to be admitted, but is there not some grey area that is being explored by which you could say, "Well, the process of further enlargement will be re-examined in one year's time and the following are seriously considered?" Will there be some kind of seriously soft landing arranged that will give them an expectation that the process is not going to be 30 years, as with Turkey, but it is feasible and the ball is not simply being kicked into touch because those of us who visit countries in Eastern and Central Europe are aware of the fact that those forces in those countries that are not reconciled to either the Western approach or democracy would use this opportunity of saying, "There you are. You put your faith in those friends and they do not want you, so why don't you consider some other option than integration into the European Union, the Western world, NATO, et cetera?"?

   (Mr Hatfield)   And the short answer is yes, that is exactly what all these drafters in Brussels are trying to do, produce a formula which does make it clear that there is a continuing process, a continuing expectation, but without making any rash promises or divisive language between one country and another, so that is really exactly what the drafters have to do, to convey what is the genuine belief for everybody in NATO that this is a process which is going to continue, but without doing something which raises false expectation or adds to the problem.

Mr Campbell

76.   Part of the problem is that some of these countries have got powerful patrons within NATO. In the case of Romania, France was very anxious to promote Romania's cause almost irrespective of Romania having fulfilled the qualifications and that is

bound to create some kind of tension in Washington, is it not?

   (Mr Hatfield)   Yes, I think you are right and you could put it more widely, that different countries in different parts of the Alliance have particular concerns usually related to their own geographic area, so that is precisely the problem that these clever drafters are going to have to deal with.

77.   Was there not also a difficulty raised to some extent by Partnership for Peace where people thought that if you joined up for Partnership for Peace, that was, as it were, a bit like putting down your name for the MCC, I suppose, though I dare say it would not take quite as long, but your application was received and was lying on the desk, although you might not actually get membership? Partnership for Peace has changed and I detect that on the part of NATO there is a determination to make Partnership for Peace more effective in its own right. It is not a substitute for NATO membership, but might it, if it is more effectively used, provide some kind of comfort to some of these countries?

   (Mr Hatfield)   Yes, I think the answer to that is yes and I think anything that the Committee can do as it goes round to sell that idea would be helpful. Partnership for Peace, I think, has been in terms of the perceptions of people taking part in the programme outside the Alliance on the horns of a dilemma. Some people thought, "If we have gone into Partnership for Peace", as you say, "our application is on the table and it is only a matter of time", but of course from the point of view of the Russians, for example, that was an off-putting assumption about Partnership for Peace. The honest answer was that the programme was trying to have it both ways and, in principle, that was not unreasonable. It is not only about NATO membership, but clearly it is a way of working closer with NATO and if you are in the queue, it is a jolly good way of both getting closer to NATO and of advancing your cause, but it should not become seen as exclusively that, and if you can sell that to the people you visit, I think that would be a very helpful thing.

Ms Taylor

78.   All of that was really very valuable, but we are very interested also to hear how you imagine this new German Government is actually going to respond to further enlargement and particularly the notion of the drive to the east. It is looking at a recent election, new people, new ideas, so are they going to be wary or cautious?

   (Mr Gomersall)   To be honest, we have not any indication of the new German Government's position on this, but we have had no early intimation that they wish to be particularly aggressive as far as the further round of enlargement is concerned, so we will just have to see.

79.   But they are not new politicians, are they, but they are people with known opinions and known backgrounds?

   (Mr Gomersall)   Yes, but, to our knowledge, they have not put it high on their NATO agenda. We have had a number of discussions at various levels in the

[**Ms Taylor** *Cont*]

Alliance on which, as I say, a consensus is distilling itself that for the time being three is enough. You can reassure your hosts that the issue is not going to go off the agenda, no way. There is, if I am not mistaken, a provision for the ministerial meeting to review enlargement at regular intervals, I think it is every year, and I am sure that somewhere in the Washington outcome will be some language which tries to suggest the sort of steps by which countries, without naming names, can prepare themselves for the next round of enlargement and encourages countries to move along those steps.

Chairman: The trouble is that countries a year ago which were totally out of the frame are now seriously knocking on the door. I never thought that Bulgaria or Slovenia would be advancing a strong case and people espousing their cause in the light of the political progress that has been made, so that must clearly complicate the issue if one does not want too swift or too broad a further wave of enlargement.

Ms Taylor

80. Absolutely, and the add-on factor to that is how do we actually carefully organise or be seen to be supportive of a difference of opinion about the speed at which people can join or not join? How would you persuade us to handle it and how are you handling it?

(Mr Gomersall) I think that the important thing is to have some fairly clear criteria which are not related to particular countries, but which, applied to particular countries, can give them some clue in their own minds as to how fast and easily they are likely to be invited to join, so the democratic test, the military preparedness test, above all, are the key ones. NATO, it also seems to us, cannot just take countries individually and have them in, as it were, one by one. I think that would be difficult from a legislative point of view as well as from other points of view. Our sense is that there will be some time anyway between the Washington decision and the next invitations, but nobody will set any artificial deadline or pause in that context.

(Mr Hatfield) I think the Chairman's point actually helps to illustrate it. The apparent rapid rise of new candidates, and I do not know whether we will go through a phase where somebody starts to say, "One of the others appears to be dropping back", in a sense illustrates the point. Countries cannot change that fundamentally that quickly and coming into NATO is an irreversible step, or at least we certainly hope it is, and it should be a process of development and what has changed so spectacularly that transforms the situation in a year? I do not think anything has. What we have seen is the start of other countries moving further down a path which leads in the sensible direction, but the idea that somehow it is all different from when we looked at it in Madrid I think is just not true.

Chairman

81. Except that around that time there were governments in Slovakia and Romania which were seen to be vestiges of the old communist system and,

therefore, the transition to governments that were clearly democratic is more than a marginal change, whilst it would be premature to say just because a country is ruled by people inspired by democracy for one year that it is democratic, but I would slightly take issue——

(Mr Hatfield) I am sorry, but that is really what I meant, Chairman. There has been a very major step and a very welcome step on that side, but that was not the only thing that, as it were, meant that the time was not right to issue them invitations.

Ms Taylor

82. Again I am going to quote to you a Government memorandum and it talks about "the continuing risks, whatever their source, posed by...the existence of substantial military capabilities in the hands of non-NATO members". This is a statement which you see again and again in memoranda. Would it be right to conclude from this statement that the aim is to maximise military capabilities that lie in the hands of the Allies? It seems like a question for an obvious answer yes, but I would suggest Bosnia suggests to us that the obvious answer yes is actually not necessarily the answer that I am seeking here. Is there any geographic limit beyond the application of Article 10? We are looking here all the time and hearing the statement that NATO is so persuasive in so much of what it does, but what are the limits here, what are the geographic limits and what are the military limits?

(Mr Hatfield) Well, I certainly do not think we are trying to maximise military capability in NATO, I absolutely agree with that. I think we just have to come back again to focus on two things: one, that NATO is primarily, above all, concerned with European security; and, secondly, that actually NATO is in the end a military and security alliance and what it does depends on the political will of its member governments, 16, shortly to be 19, and it also depends on them doing that by consensus. Now, I think that sets quite large limits on what you can see NATO being prepared to do. Can we see 19 European countries agreeing to go and, to use the example earlier, mount a NATO operation in Korea? The answer I think in realistic terms is 'no' because it is not to do with European security, not to do with their fundamental collective interests, so I think that will set quite broad limits on it. But the ultimate limits are set by the 19 national governments, as they will be.

Mr Brazier

83. Could I just quickly chip in on that. You have said that several times, Mr Hatfield, it is to do with European security, but surely NATO's *raison d'être* is about North Atlantic security? The Americans, and the Canadians to a small extent too, but the Americans are providing 60 per cent of the total funding for NATO and the idea that some how or other it is only the end where the 40 per cent is being spent that actually matters for security seems to me to be rather extraordinary, and if a really serious threat were to arise to American interests, as the largest contributor

[**Mr Brazier** *Cont*]

is America, why should they not equally have a valid point?

(*Mr Hatfield*) I think that is a fair point and actually there is one sense in which we are beginning to think about that. I think actually there are two things there. First of all, the Americans actually regard European security as fundamental to their security and they are right.

84. Yes, we would agree with that.

(*Mr Hatfield*) Secondly, historically at least, the sort of direct threat to the United States was not a threat, except by being solid, as it were, in Europe– that the Europeans could contribute to very much. But one of the areas in fact the Americans are now talking about, indeed the Alliance is talking about, is the possible response the Alliance might make to, say, a terrorist incident——

85. Exactly.

(*Mr Hatfield*) ——and that is actually quite, quite true. It might well be that the Alliance European members could send some capabilities to help with an incident which occurred in the United States, so in that sense I think you are quite right to raise it and these are actually on the agenda.

86. A supplementary on that, the example of Korea has been mentioned several times, so we might as well stay with that, although it does not have to be North Korea, but supposing in the American view and backed up with good intelligence and so on the kind of serious terrorist threat by weapons of mass destruction which the Americans are now so very concerned about, the asymmetric threat to the American mainland, were to arise with, say, North Korea, to continue with the example, as the centre for that threat so that the Americans felt that their security of their country was closely bound up with dealing with North Korea or somewhere else, would it not be perfectly reasonable for American Congressmen to say, "If you people are really going to pass this one by and say that this has got nothing to do with NATO, why the hell should we continue to go on funding you?"?

(*Mr Hatfield*) I think I would draw the distinction, which I tried to draw earlier, between the members of NATO and some of them in particular from whom the Americans would expect support in a crisis of various sorts, depending on what the circumstances were, and expecting it to come from NATO as an organisation which is focused on European security. So I think the Americans would expect in a crisis, subject to the circumstances of course, to have political and maybe other support from NATO members, including this country, but that that would not be an Alliance response because the Alliance is not actually concerned with those areas of security, geographic areas of security.

Ms Taylor

87. I think you have answered my next question really in lots of ways, but let us do it again. Are there practical limits on enlargement in terms of working arrangements and in terms of Article 10 maybe?

(*Mr Hatfield*) Well, I cannot say there is any absolute limit, but clearly the further that process goes

in terms of numbers, the more the Alliance will have to adapt in all sorts of ways and that is one of the reasons why I think it needs to move forward at a measured pace because we simply do not even know quite how we are going to operate at 19, although we know in theory how we are going to operate at 19, so I think it would certainly have to adapt and if you concede that NATO could adapt to a position where it took in almost everybody in Europe, maybe everybody in Europe, if they met certain criteria, then it would have adapted to a completely different type of organisation on the way, but I think over a very long time and it may never happen.

Mr Blunt

88. On the Integrated Military Structure, in the same way as countries aspiring to join the EU probably will not be allowed to join unless they join the euro, is it British policy that new countries will not be able to join NATO unless the join the IMS?

(*Mr Hatfield*) Well, I certainly think we would be very surprised if a new country wanted to join NATO and did not want to join the Integrated Military Structure, and I always have hopes that the French will eventually rejoin the Integrated Military Structure.

Mr Campbell: You have not really answered Mr Blunt's question, have you?

Mr Blunt: It was probably deliberate.

Mr Campbell

89. What is the policy?

(*Mr Hatfield*) Nobody has laid down a specific condition. I think, to be honest, that if any aspiring candidate came along and said, "Oh, we would like to join and we would not like to join the Integrated Military Structure in the present circumstances", we would take that as an indication that they were not yet ready to take the full obligations on and it would not put them at the head of the queue.

Mr Blunt

90. So we would probably then veto their membership?

(*Mr Hatfield*) I do not think we would veto it. I think they would find that they were not at the head of the queue.

Chairman: Now that Mr Blunt has reached his anti-Europe quota for the day, we will move on to other things.

Mr Cohen

91. I have a very brief supplementary. I did a report for the North Atlantic Assembly on the costs of NATO expansion and you will know the history of that, that there were some very big figures quoted originally which came down to much more acceptable figures. Part of that was that the NATO common infrastructure was kept quite limited. Is there a risk that what happens in the Strategic Concept review would start rolling costs back on to the common infrastructure budget?

[Mr Cohen *Cont]*

(Mr Hatfield)   No, I think the answer is not. In the current circumstances in Europe and actually from what I know already of the drafting of the Strategic Concept, there is absolutely no question that that would change it. We are still in the costs equation very much where that the final NATO report ended up. Most of the earlier reports made some very different assumptions about how we would go about enlargement.

Mr Brazier

92.   As I know you are very pressed for time, Mr Hatfield, I will ask you several related questions together.

(Mr Hatfield)   You are very kind, Mr Brazier!

Chairman

93.   Where are you going, by the way, that we have to rush to finish? I hope it is worthwhile.

(Mr Hatfield)   I am going to Washington.

Chairman: Oh, you can go there.

Mr Brazier

94.   They all come under the heading of what is your assessment of the present attitude of Russia to further enlargement. In the early 1990s, the Allies implicitly led Russia to believe that enlargement would not occur. Now NATO tells Russia that it has no intention of stationing troops in the three new members' territory, but we have not actually made a treaty commitment. Has NATO actually given Russia enough evidence of its good faith to prevent Russia having good grounds for resenting enlargement and seeing it as threatening?

(Mr Hatfield)   This, I think, depends whether you are a Russian or a member of NATO how you answer the question. I would say, and I genuinely mean it, that I think that yes, we have. But I can quite understand actually if I was a Russian that I would not necessarily be convinced. I would want to see more things happening, a development of the relationship between NATO and Russia developing constructively. I would probably need to get over some of my psychological hang-ups about NATO, which are understandable given the history, so I do not think we are by any means out of the wood yet. It is going to be quite a difficult relationship to manage in a number of ways. Enlargement is part of that. Just to repeat old history or old doctrine, if you like, there is no Russian veto of NATO enlargement or individual areas of NATO enlargement, but managing a relationship with Russia is part of the same broad process of European security and that, I think, remains the case. I think the Russians have largely come to terms with the enlargement we are about to embark on. They remain sensitive about the possible future enlargement of NATO, particularly in some areas more than others. My own guess is that if enlargement goes forward steadily over time and the security environment develops in a way it looks like it might at the moment, this will become less and less of an issue, whereas if we try and hurry it or force it, it will become more of an issue.

95.   I have one specific quick follow-up on that. General Lebed, who of course halted the security machine by calling off the war in Chechnya and effectively virtually hauling up the white flag there, negotiating an agreement wholly suitable for Chechnyans, who also diffused the tension of the war in Moldavia and is somebody who is, by any standards, somebody who is not in favour of expansion of imperialism or anything, he has made very, very strong, as a potential presidential candidate the last time around, statements about NATO enlargement and he has also more recently made what one might call the sort of bitter underdog kind of statements which is, "This is something which we really can't stop, so maybe we should stop banging our heads against the wall at this stage", and these sort of things. As somebody who is pretty closely tuned into the moderate elements of the Soviet armed forces, this does not sound terribly promising.

(Mr Hatfield)   Well, I cannot speak for General Lebed, but certainly I was at a private seminar at the weekend where a number of senior Russians were present and I think that they did not feel threatened by what we had done. They would still argue that it was quite unnecessary and not a good thing for European security. There are still some areas which they clearly regard at least at the moment as being red lines, although it is not quite clear what consequences would follow from crossing the red lines, and they also, some of them, wonder what this means for the long-term future of the Alliance. They, ironically, argue that NATO should turn itself into a political security organisation away from the military organisation. Some of them then say, "Well, perhaps you are actually going to do that by enlarging", and then you get into a debate with some of them about, leaving aside what we in NATO might think about it, "Do you envisage that you could become a member of NATO?" and it produces some very interesting reactions. I think the whole point of this comes back to nobody knows where NATO is going in the very long term, although you can see the next steps and you can see the direction it is moving in, and nobody actually knows where Russia is going to end up in the long term. So it is not surprising that we are feeling our way, especially with the history of 40 years of confrontation.

96.   Where did you feel those red lines were?

(Mr Hatfield)   Clearly orange-ish lines start to appear the second you go into countries which they regard as being former states of the Soviet Union.

97.   The Baltic States and those sort of areas?

(Mr Hatfield)   Yes.

Mr Campbell

98.   I was just going to offer some advice, if I may, which would be that any country that did not want to join the Integrated Military Structure should not be admitted as a candidate for membership to NATO.

(Mr Hatfield)   I think I came quite as close as I could to saying that.

99.   But in preparation for your trip to Washington, you have no doubt been scanning the pages of the *New*

[**Mr Campbell** *Cont*]

York Times with some care and you will know that the Prime Minister wrote an article on the 13th November in which he developed some of the ideas which he has previously discussed about a greater degree of defence co-operation among the Europeans as a more effective contribution to NATO. Do I understand from that that there is an acceptance, or at least do you understand that there is an acceptance at least by the Prime Minister that the relationship between the European and the transatlantic dimensions of the Alliance needs rebalancing?

(Mr Hatfield)   Yes, I think so. Certainly I think the Prime Minister feels, as I mentioned earlier, that the weight of the European military capability, the actual European defence capability it contributes to the Alliance is not commensurate really with its political weight. The type of capabilities that Europe can bring at the moment are particularly deficient in the areas which we now have most need of and, yes, he does think that Europe should pull its weight more inside the Alliance for a number of reasons: one, to match its political weight; two, to actually help cement the Alliance because as anybody who visits Washington knows, whether there is a burden-sharing debate in the UK or in Europe, there is always a burden-sharing debate in Washington, and a lot of it is on false premises, certainly if you hear the debate about Bosnia, but in this area I think the Prime Minister thinks that there is a substantive point and it is in the long-term interests of the Alliance as a whole and the European members of it that we should contribute.

100.   I must say that I find myself in total sympathy with all of that. Can you just confirm for the avoidance of doubt that silly suggestions like Brussels determining the cap badges or there being a European army whose deployment would depend on resolutions of the European Parliament have no part, no intelligent part in this discussion?

(Mr Hatfield)   I can confirm that, although I find it rather odd being asked to confirm what I thought the Prime Minister had been very explicit about.

Chairman: I thought it was a Liberal Party policy actually!

Mr Campbell

101.   It certainly is not, but I think it is important that we get this debate off on a proper footing and that it is not bedeviled by the sort of the things which apparently get rounds of applause at the party conferences of some of the political parties.

(Mr Hatfield)   You could not expect me to comment on that.

Chairman: Well, thank you very much for coming. This dialogue will continue for some time and perhaps we will invite you back.

THURSDAY 3 DECEMBER 1998

Members present:

Mr Bruce George, in the Chair

Mr Crispin Blunt   Mr Harry Cohen
Mr Julian Brazier

Examination of Witnesses

Mr Humphry Crum Ewing, Research Fellow, Centre for Defence and International Security Studies, Lancaster University, Dr Jonathan Eyal, Director of Studies, Royal United Services Institute, Dr Beatrice Heuser, Senior Lecturer, Department of War Studies, King's College, London, and Mr John Roper, Associate Fellow, International Security Programme, Royal Institute of International Affairs, were examined.

Chairman: Thank you very much for coming. I am sorry for the slight delay, the latest reason was one of the lights went out. The lights are going out all over committee room 15. The work has been done and we now know the answer to the question "how many men does it take to change a light bulb?" In the House of Commons now only two and a supervisor. Thank you very much for coming. I am sorry our Members are rather depleted. We normally meet on a Wednesday but I understand that it was rather difficult for some of you to make the Wednesday, hence our miserable attendance for which I apologise profusely.

Mr Brazier: There is nothing miserable about the quality.

Chairman

102. The quality is usually quite high. We have worked out a number of questions. We know you are four, dare I say it, loquacious speakers. Please do not feel compelled to answer every question unless you are Welsh where there is a compulsion to answer every question. Thank you very much for your memoranda which clearly encapsulate much of your views. We appreciate you taking the time. The first group of questions will relate to NATO's mission and the New Strategic Concept. One of the witnesses from the Foreign Office was asked to "encapsulate the idea of NATO" and he said: "I think NATO will avoid, for example, any attempt to define a geographical area or a particular size or nature of a conflict which will automatically call for or rule out a NATO response. I think it will include a lot of generic language about the sort of situations, challenges to regional securities, threats to stability, humanitarian situations which could promote a NATO response." Could I ask you to sum up what you consider to be the current and foreseeable problems to which NATO sees itself as the solution and what these imply for NATO's role and strategic document after next spring?

(Dr Eyal) Perhaps I should say what NATO is perceived to be doing because the discussion is very often introspective in Western Europe or in the current Member States. What is it perceived to be doing for the other countries in Europe that are not members, both aspiring and those who do not officially aspire to membership? It is perceived by the former Communist countries to be the only guarantee that the results of the end of the Cold War are basically irreversible, namely that there will be no sliding back to a period of games, of spheres of influence. That is the biggest attraction as far as the former Communist countries are concerned. It is not an anti-Russian Alliance and I think even those who may be most visceral in their fears of Russia in Central Europe accept that it is not an Alliance positioned to deflect Russian military offensive. It is certainly one that would maintain the current *status quo* on the suspicion that the Russians are determined to reverse the present *status quo* which Moscow considers as temporary. That is their feeling. It is perceived also, and let us be frank about it, by some of the neutral countries usually considered in the West, such as Scandinavian ones, as being the only guarantee against tougher choices. Because it is there it prevents them or precludes them from having to think of new security arrangements. Ultimately it is a reassurance for its own Member States. The difficulty is that it is ultimately a military alliance but most of the benefits that are highlighted by governments, and indeed all politicians throughout Europe, are essentially political.

103. We will deploy your expertise towards the end more and in addition when we deal with NATO enlargement. Dr Heuser?

(Dr Heuser) I fully agree with the very last point in particular that Dr Eyal made. What is very important about NATO is that it is trying in my interpretation to go into two separate directions at once. It is very, very successful in the way in which it is presenting itself as the new NATO taking on completely different tasks, is serving the stabilisation process of Europe. What I am very concerned about is that although I fully admire all the efforts that have been made so far to combine these two different tasks, the task of the old NATO and the task of the new NATO, and to try to make them work side by side, the tensions between these two tasks at some stage can no longer be bridged by all the very ingenious ways in which the organisational problems and even the presentational problems have been overcome in many respects. The fact remains that there is a hard core of NATO which is the old NATO which people do not want to give up. On the other hand NATO, is paralleling in so many

[Chairman *Cont]*

ways the work of the OSCE. If you are going into the question of what sort of security problems NATO should be addressing in the future (a point that Dr Eyal made), it is strictly a military organisation. But it is now constantly taking on tasks which go so far beyond the military and taking on such a high profile, it is given such a high profile by the press in particular with which it has particularly good relationships, that there are far greater expectations of what NATO can do, change the hearts and minds of all people in Bosnia-Hercegovina for example, than NATO could ever fulfil. The discrepancy between what you can do with the military institution and what you can only do with a very, very large civil re-education programme, is ultimately there to make people claim that NATO has not done its business, has failed in many respects, that the last elections in Bosnia-Hercegovina was a great failure of NATO policy there which is unfair. NATO has manoeuvred itself into that position through its excellent relationship with the press and other media by basically simply presenting itself as being the solution to all of Europe's problems. What you have just said at the beginning about how the strategic concept is likely to present NATO, by simply saying: "Here are generic problems and NATO will be addressing all of them in all its many ways, dialogue, population, etc." glosses over the relative lack of substance in all the non military areas NATO has.

104. NATO has always been a political organisation as well as a military, political and security organisation. Are you being slightly unfair in saying it can largely chew and not walk simultaneously? I thought it had been very successful in doing a myriad of tasks. The committee structure shows it deals with science, defence co-operation, justice co-operation, it can do its peacekeeping, the political meetings it has may not be directly relevant to defence but maintain the transatlantic link. I thought NATO had been quite spectacular in its diversity. If it is capable of being diverse up to now would you have thought it would have the capability of being even more diverse in the future without losing its essential function of being a military alliance?

(Dr Heuser) NATO has been a political organisation only with regard to relations within NATO. New political relations are now obviously established with non members and trying to do this in a politically efficient way. The key observation I make is that in the committee meetings of NATO, particularly when you have the entire PfP group with Europe's Euro Atlantic Partnership Council, (EAPC) the very size of the group, dictates that the meetings are devoid of substance. That means that where political problems could be resolved in a relatively small circle of 16—even 16 is really a very unwieldy instrument—if you have 30 or 40 countries present, the problem immediately arises that you cannot actually thrash out problems to the very end. So I think the actual dynamics of the political relationship misrepresent themselves as being a very successful effort in co-operation for the simple reason that all the people who are present, all the delegations who are present, are of course diplomats whose very nature it is to try to find compromises and argue civilly with

other diplomats. I think this creates the illusion that everything is going very, very well, there is all this wonderful exchange once round the table, everybody is saying how happy they are to be working with NATO. But there is very, very little more. So the entire area of political co-operation that goes beyond NATO's current membership is the area which I think is lacking in substance and which is giving a false idea or false vision of everything going so well in Eastern Europe where this is just the very thin layer of ice on what could be very, very deep waters indeed.

105. Thank you, that is very helpful. We will wait for our questions on enlargement and the future enlargement question mark later on. Mr Roper?

(Mr Roper) Perhaps I could just come back in a moment to this question of the political versus the military role of NATO but let me just start by saying I believe that now NATO is a splendid instrument for military co-operation to undertake whichever tasks its members want to use it for. One of those is still the security of Europe but that is obviously a much smaller one now because the primary threat is fortunately one which is not immediately present. It can also be an instrument whereby its members can project security. It has a potential for this. It has a potential to constrain proliferators of weapons of mass destruction if it so chooses, it has a potential to punish perpetrators of genocide, it has a potential to bring humanitarian aid. Those are all potentials which it has if its members wish to use it for those tasks. I would like to come back to the question which you discussed with Dr Heuser which was the question of political versus military. Here there is a paradox. People say that NATO is now more political than it was. I would suggest it is in one sense because since the end of the Cold War its relations with non members have become much more political in a way that they were not during the Cold War, its relations to a significant extent with the members of PfP with the countries coming into NATO. Within NATO, and here I think I disagree to a little extent with Dr Heuser, among the 16 NATO has become less political with the end of the Cold War. During the Cold War it was the place where all 16 members had to determine their external policy. We had a common, foreign and security policy, it was called NATO—to quote Mr Major—and it was done within NATO. That was where we had to work out our policy towards the Warsaw Pact, towards Russia. That was the centre of our policy forming. With the end of the Cold War we very often form our policy on Bosnia, on Somalia, on other issues, on the Gulf elsewhere and then if we so wish come to NATO and use it not as an instrument for forming policy but as an instrument to apply military ends when we wish to do it. To that extent among the 16 members NATO, paradoxically, has become less political with the end of the Cold War which concentrated our policy concerns on one area.

106. Mr Crum Ewing?

(Mr Crum Ewing) I think it is wrong to think of NATO in the way that I felt the first two witnesses were doing, as if it is an autonomous organisation. I think it is right to think of it in the terms that John Roper expressed, thinking of it as an organisation of its members able to give effect to their policies. If I

[**Chairman** *Cont*]

could pick up a phrase that was used in the Defence Debate in the House of Lords last week——

107. We do not allow discussion of the House of Lords in this place, not under present circumstances!

(Mr Crum Ewing) It is a very good phrase, Chairman, with universal application. That is the remark that NATO is an alliance of allies, not an organisation of America's clients. I believe it is very important that the New Strategic Concept should recognise this. There are really two questions about the New Strategic Concept. One is to what extent does it extend NATO geographically, which is the question you are going to come on to later, and to what extent does it extend NATO's role? I was very concerned to read in the letter of George Robertson, the June letter, which you published in your Third Special Report, the Government's response, where he almost as a throw away phrase referred at the end to an even greater focus on new roles. I am very unhappy about the idea that there are all sorts of new roles that NATO can perform autonomously. I believe that our friends in the east are right to attach emphasis to its importance as a defence organisation. I think there are really difficult problems about the porousness of frontiers and to what extent NATO as such should take notice of these. There are arguments that have been eloquently phrased that NATO should concern itself with the southern frontier and what is going on in the SAHEL and the proportion of the population and so on. There are clearly very difficult problems about the porousness of the eastern frontier with the countries of the former Soviet Union and the Eastern Bloc. I do not know whether those are really NATO's job. I tend to think that they are not and that NATO should not cast itself in a role which engages in frontier security. So far as the area to which NATO should be responsible as distinct from extending its own area, yes, I believe it should concern itself with everything that happens in the Balkans, I think that is an extension of Europe. As you can see I am sceptical of how far it should go on the southern shore of the Mediterranean. I am hesitant about how far it should concern itself with events beyond Turkey's eastern frontier. Clearly it should not concern itself with Africa south of the Sahara and I believe that it should not, as an organisation, concern itself with what goes on in the Middle East. For its members to do so, yes, but for it to do so as an organisation, no.

108. Dr Eyal wants to come back.

(Dr Eyal) Chairman, I suspect this will be the last word on the distinction between the political and the military. I would submit that the distinction is probably less real. The bane of NATO up to now has been that it is seen as being one of the most successful organisations both in terms of conducting the Cold War and surviving the Cold War and therefore to a certain extent it has become a sort of dustbin, a place where people look both for any salvation but at the same time where all the inherently insoluble problems are placed. It is not the only institution which suffers from that. The European Union suffers from that to a certain extent as well, the OSCE, indeed the United Nations. The distinction between what it can do and what it may want to do is one that is faced every time

there is a new crisis. If we look at the latest crisis in Kosovo we have this rather unnerving ping-pong of institutions where basically the same Member States are present in most of them, the very same Member States make decisions in a critical way in all of them and very often the decision comes from Washington as to which organisation ultimately remains holding the baby. That certainly was the case in Kosovo. The distinction in academic terms between the political and the military is correct. In pure political terms I suspect that it is one that a Strategic Concept will not be able to resolve.

(Mr Roper) I quite agree the Strategic Concept will not be able to resolve it. What I am suggesting though is it becomes decreasingly a place where we make policy and in that sense it is less political.

(Dr Eyal) I agree.

109. I think one of the anxieties I would have is if NATO cannot perform these functions one wonders how well others can do so: OSCE with a near unanimity rule, paralysis often in the European Union. So I suppose in many ways in the absence of anybody else performing the task NATO has things thrust upon it not only for the reason that the United States is largely a powerful member of that organisation. Mr Crum Ewing started off by saying what NATO could not do but I wonder whether you could put absolute limits, as some of you have touched on it briefly, on things that are absolutely out of bounds and we should not raise any expectation that NATO could do these tasks after the NATO Summit, if you think there is going to be any realism and say: "Hey, this is not our field". Asymmetric warfare, if NATO does not do it, if NATO cannot get involved with boundaries and NATO is not very good at dealing with computer viruses, who is going to do these things and how is NATO going to co-ordinate? Somebody will have to co-ordinate dealing with asymmetric threats like terrorism.

(Dr Eyal) There are two distinctions that I will make. One is on the tasks. Clearly when it comes to the high age of technology and paradoxically to the low age of technology, when it comes to asymmetric responses, I do not see any other institution which could co-ordinate it at the European level. Sadly, what is happening is that the investment of the Europeans on the high end of technology is increasingly diminishing. The gap between the Americans and the Europeans is opening up to a point where if NATO takes on some of these obligations that would necessarily mean that the initiative would always be on the American side. I have no problem with it but some countries in the Alliance may. I think that where one should dampen down expectations is on the very excitable statements made in Washington about the geographic remit of NATO. Here I go quite a lot with Mr Crum Ewing on that one which is suggestions made in the US Congress that we can somehow as an Alliance help with Haiti but not with Latin America, help with Asia, counter-balance the American troops or help the American troops in Korea and all the rest; that is quite frankly fanciful and we have to be very careful. However, at the same time it would be very difficult to place the kinds of restrictions that are being

[**Chairman** *Cont*]

placed about our role in countries such as Algeria or indeed in the Middle East. I think that is where by necessity the issue will remain fudged.

(Dr Heuser) One of the key technical problems is how you can keep information separate, away from certain groupings you do not trust with the information and at the same time render an organisation effective by giving it the relevant information. One of the things that is very, very clear within NATO is that there are so many different levels of circulation of information, and particularly if you come to things like information warfare or dealing with terrorism, it is very clear that precisely because one is now dealing with so many different Partner States there is a tendency to keep certain things away from the group as a whole and to keep it out of NATO. It is particularly clear in that area that the American/British co-operation on intelligence and things like that is something that goes far beyond any information that would be given to the EAPC normally and the group as a whole is in a way too big to be trusted with a lot of that information. While it would be the most sensible place to be sharing information and bringing together, *de facto* what is happening is that information tends to come from only very few sources and because of that you have many peripheral players who almost should not be there, with due respect, because they are not contributing information in the same way and it is not clear what they are doing with the information they get. In a way there is this tendency and that is a very big theme in what is happening to NATO overall. Particularly in out of area questions I think over the next 5-10 years we will see the fracturing of NATO into groups using NATO assets in coalition of the willing. This is never mentioned in any NATO communications and statements. I think it will be a big subject in the future precisely because we are no longer facing a clear uniting threat that everybody is equally concerned about. Will there be any attempts to address this issue in the Strategic Concept and its formulation? I doubt it. And yet the issue will arise, and that means there is going to be continuing pressure on the structures of NATO to be able to cope with variable geometry, the use of NATO assets, by certain members only but not all.

Chairman: I think there will be an overlap in the questions we are going to ask so Harry Cohen has some questions he wants to ask now.

Mr Cohen

110. When we had Richard Hatfield here, the MoD Policy Director, he said that it was not a case of NATO finding new roles to justify itself, it was new roles coming to NATO, finding NATO. I would be interested in your comments on that. Clearly with Bosnia there are issues here and now on whether that has been the case but longer term I wonder. I would be interested to have your comments on that. What sorts of new roles do you think NATO should take on which should be perhaps specifically mentioned in the Strategic Concept and what should it discard?

(Dr Heuser) Shall I start with what is being discussed?

111. Please do.

(Dr Heuser) On the classic 'new roles' I think there is going to be a debate about whether the term 'new' will be used because by the time the Strategic Concept is adopted these roles will have a certain age as well and the Strategic Concept it is hoped will be relevant for about ten years or so, therefore by the year 2005 they will not be new. Much of what is now summarised under 'new roles' concerns outreach activity, projection of stability in Eastern Europe, projection of stability in the Mediterranean through dialogue with the Mediterranean partner countries. All these non fighting activities that may have a military component only in so far as there is a large involvement of NATO with re-education, re- forming, training, restructuring defence administration and armed force in East European countries and attempting to do likewise in the Middle East and Mediterranean areas with the partners. There is also the simple attempt to have more transparency by exchange of information. There are projects on helping defence industrial complexes in East European countries reform and go into civil production and things like that. Those are some of the key issues that are always listed as the 'new roles' but they already exist. The majority of them are things that NATO has actually volunteered to take on rather than having been imposed on NATO from outside. The outside pressure NATO is facing is that of all the East European countries who want to become members. All these outreach activities are part of the overall attempt by NATO to satisfy many of their needs without immediately accepting them as members.

112. What about no further reference to nuclear proliferation, the possibility of military action?

(Mr Roper) Counter-proliferation has already been considered within NATO so to that extent it is not a new role, it is one on which there has been a committee at work for three years and a number of reports have been developed. This is clearly an issue which is being discussed and is likely to continue to be discussed. If I could just come back to what Dr Heuser said, it does seem to me that one of the main functions is that what is taken at NATO level is what is described in our Strategic Defence Review as defence diplomacy. Those are the sorts of things of projections, education and so on and so forth. As far as NATO acting to deal outside its traditional area, I think one has to consider two things. One has to consider intentions and capabilities. First of all, are the European Members of NATO collectively yet ready to move in that direction and here the evidence is very mixed. Clearly there are what Francois Heisbourg once referred to as the extrovert members of NATO, namely the British and the French, and there are others who are rather less extrovert and less enthusiastic about moving into those sorts of directions. What is even more important is the question of capabilities. A lot of people have quoted recently the statistic about the European Members of NATO spending two- thirds of what the Americans do in their defence budget. Michael O'Hanlon of Brookings goes on in the way he says that to say: "But, in fact, despite spending two-thirds of what the United States does on defence, European NATO countries have less than 10 per cent

[Mr Cohen Cont]

of the transportable defence capability for prompt long range action". Therefore, a lot of these rather imaginative ideas about far range activities would mean very significant changes in the defence planning of a number of other European countries following basically in the direction which we are going in the SDR and which France begins to go but which the other countries are a very long way from doing. Therefore I think one has to be very careful about making suggestions that one is going to do things which one clearly does not have the capabilities to do at the moment.

(Dr Eyal) I just want to add to that. I could not agree with it more. I think it is absolutely the right issue. However, the way that the questions of the tasks of the Alliance or what the Alliance could do are usually posed in the real world, as it were, are after there is a decision that the Alliance will have a role in a particular crisis—if we look at the repeated crisis in the Balkans—the snag is that every time what is required is actually a package of measures and the package usually has to start with some credible military threat which only NATO could issue. Most of the package thereafter consists of humanitarian assistance, policing activities, law and order, recreation of a failed state, protection of NGOs that are supplying assistance, managing refugees and other humanitarian crises. The difficulty is that it is impossible for the Alliance which very often kicks off the package to divest itself completely from the other ingredients. Many other organisations who are then tasked with executing the other ingredients in the package often resent NATO's claim to be the superior organisation which decides on the distribution of labour. That is effectively the story of the Dayton Accord in Bosnia and it may yet turn out to be the story of the Kosovo effort. It is not a scientific explanation but that in a way is how the question of tasks impinges within the Alliance within the debate there.

113. Interesting.

(Mr Crum Ewing) Yes. Particularly in response to what Mr Cohen just said, I believe that one of the most important military tasks which NATO has to handle, and taking account of what Beatrice Heuser said about NATO's characteristic failure to disclose information as I believe it is failing to do, is really to assess what collective defence against missiles for Europe is required. NATO is the only agency that can deal with that. If we look for a moment at Russia, Russia sustains two key military threats, one is the work it is doing on its submarines (and that is clearly something NATO needs to watch) and the other is the frequent expressions by members of the Russian General Staff that Russia's claim to be regarded as a world power remains in its inter-continental ballistic missile power. I believe this is a matter which NATO should bring out into the open. I totally agree with what Beatrice Heuser said about the importance of publishing information. I even, if I may say so, Chairman, agree more strongly with what you wrote in your Special Report about the need for NATO to publish information and to open the debate. There is perceptibly a multi-tier dissemination of information and opinion about what is going on in NATO and it is

wrong that only the inner elite or the selective elite should really understand the way thinking is going and what the underlying factors are. It must be more opened up, just as it is absolutely essential the Ministry of Defence in this country opens up. One role that NATO is certainly performing is it has enabled the Ministry of Defence to shuffle information that it should be giving to us away to NATO and say: "Well, NATO is looking after that, I am afraid we cannot tell you".

114. I agree with that point. While I have the floor can I just bowl you a googly. You mentioned earlier about the geographical remit and its ability in out of area operations and we will come back to aspects of that later. Do you think that will be in the Strategic Concept? Do you think the Americans will try to push that into the Strategic Concept? If it does—and this is where the googly is—if out of area operations are written in in terms of something similar to Article 5, States' interests out of their area, what about something like Portugal and East Timor, how would that be written in and then us not have to go to war immediately or perhaps we should go to war immediately over East Timor?

(Dr Eyal) I think the answer at the moment is almost everyone within the Alliance, especially the Americans, is schizophrenic about this entire question of the geographic remit of the Alliance's operations. The Americans on the one hand are very doubtful about some of the discussions on, let us say, North African involvement and how they stumble over each on Mediterranean initiatives, the European Union and the Alliance, although the Alliance has been very reticent in what it actually claimed especially after Willy Claes was no longer Secretary-General. At the same time it was the same administration which encouraged speculation in Argentina, for instance, that it could have a special place within the Alliance, that one meant the Atlantic going from the north to the south of the globe. There is the temptation in almost any country member in the Alliance, Britain perhaps is an exception to that one, to claim that on the one hand the Alliance could do something in hot spots but at the same time it must not stretch itself too far. The Portuguese have, luckily for us, not raised the question of Indonesia within the context of the Alliance, although I must admit that it was raised frequently in the European Union CFSP process and very often it paralysed the CFSP process and indeed our policy in Britain towards Indonesia. I do not think it will be in any shape or form in the Strategic Concept, there will be no map with radiating arrows from it, of that I can give you a guarantee.

(Mr Crum Ewing) I think Jonathan is absolutely right to refer to American schizophrenia. It was made very clear to me when I was in Washington talking with very well informed observers of the political scene there that there is an implicit and almost an explicit bargain between the administration and the Congress that the administration will try to get NATO to take over some of the potential bodybag jobs and in return for that the Congress will continue to fund it. It is a schizophrenic situation.

Mr Blunt

115.   Can we move on to the issues concerning the three applicants. Richard Hatfield when he was here told us that it was going to be a good symbolic gesture for the countries to sign up in Washington. Nothing I have heard suggests that is not going to happen. When other colleagues on this Committee went to Hungary they heard that the Hungarians were anxious to formally get in early so they could influence the New Strategic Concept. To what extent do you think that the Hungarians, Czechs and Poles are going to be able to influence the New Strategic Concept?

(Mr Roper)   They are already sitting on a large number of the committees. In fact, as you were told in the last evidence, I think they have been given some pre-rights and so in many of the NATO committees they are now meeting as 19, therefore they are taking part. There is a question as to whether the actual date will take place on the first day of the Summit or before but in practice as I understand it in Brussels in almost every meeting these are now at 19 rather than at 16. Therefore there is a possibility for an input from the three new members as well as from the 16 existing members.

(Mr Crum Ewing)   The impression I have is a very clear one, that the three are determined to come in together. They may well decide that they are going to come in sooner than the Washington Conference for this reason but they do not expect that they will, they will come in together and they will come in. The important thing is they will come in together as a bloc with certain policies of their own which are significant to the discussions which will be crystallised in Washington.

(Dr Eyal)   I would strongly urge the Committee not to look at these three as a bloc, regardless of whether they come in together. The sooner we discard the idea that this is a bloc of countries with similar interests the better we will all be. To all intents and purposes the Czechs and the Hungarians are very nice but really are unlikely to change a great deal of the debate within the Alliance; the Poles are. Indeed, a great deal of the demands that Poland has made informally, including sadly for NATO the question of a regional command, are based partly on what is perceived by the Polish Government to be a specific Polish interest which is not addressed correctly in the Alliance and partly an attempt to make it very clear from the beginning that Poland is a big country and it should be treated as such. One has an element of psychology involved in it. I think the Poles will play a very strong role and a leading role in any security debate, in any concept debate within the Alliance. I have my doubts about the Czechs and the Hungarians, although I suspect to be brutally frank that they will make all the polite noises.

Chairman

116.   Dr Heuser, do you want to come in?

(Dr Heuser)   Not at the moment, thank you.

Mr Blunt

117.   —— for us you have talked about NATO trying to ride two horses and you have said that already this morning, two different directions. Mr Crum Ewing, you have commented on the fact that the three applicant countries have this particular interest in security guarantees and less of an interest in NATO branching out and becoming a security organisation. On the part of the Committee that went to Romania, the thing that struck me in Romania was the fact that whilst the Romanians had put significant importance on achieving NATO membership and achieving security guarantees, they had appreciated for some time that they were required to contribute military forces that were capable of going overseas and contributing to security operations which is why there was an enormous amount of effort going into teaching them English, they were forming peacekeeping battalions, they were deployed on almost every conceivable operation that they could and they had been to Albania and had a battalion in Angola. We contributed significantly less, none in Albania and less in Angola than they did. The Romanians seem to have accepted the fact that these two horses have got to be ridden and I wonder if that applies to the other three applicant countries who are about to come into NATO? Is my point about Romania correct?

(Mr Crum Ewing)   Jonathan is much better on Romania than I am but if I could just say I do not think they will be a bloc on a continuing basis. I think in response to Crispin Blunt's specific question about the entry, they are intending to operate as a bloc. Hungary, for instance, has a problem on sending troops abroad. If Hungary were asked to send fighting troops to Yugoslavia they believe they would find great difficulty because the Serbs would put together a battalion of native Hungarian ethnic Yugoslavs and put them up against them and the Hungarian Army would not fight them because they will not fight their fellow ethnic people. So there are limitations on what these countries can do. Okay, they certainly do recognise the need to contribute to NATO's external operations and I believe, as I have said in my paper, that there is actually a greater preparedness to take the rather less glamorous tasks of soldiering amongst them which is no longer acceptable to, say, the Belgians or the Luxembourgs or the Dutch. Yes, I think one has got to treat them to some extent as a case by case basis but one has also got to recognise that there are common interests there.

(Mr Roper)   I think there is a number of other examples. For example, in spite of what Humphry has said about the Hungarians being reticent, and I am not sure about this if we ever came to a combat role against Serbia, there has been an extremely useful Hungarian engineering battalion in Bosnia-Hercegovina doing a great deal of road building rather efficiently. The Poles, for example, in February of this year when we were talking about going into the Gulf were one of the very few countries who, apart from the British and the Americans, suggested that they would send some anti-CW people. There have been a number of offers and from almost any of these countries one can see that they have been trying to make sure that they are contributors

[**Mr Blunt** *Cont*]
to the new tasks as well as wanting to have the assurance about the traditional task of the Alliance.

Mr Brazier

118.   What did you say?
(*Mr Roper*) Anti-CW, anti-chemical warfare.
(*Dr Eyal*) You are absolutely correct about Romania but, of course, they have tried very, very hard to persuade us that they are serious about joining the Alliance and, to be frank, their security interests are very similar to those of the other Central European countries despite their geographic position, they have no particular interest further to the south. What I would say is that I think we must be brutally frank with the countries that are entering. Mr Crum Ewing mentioned the question of the Hungarian fears. There is actually a much worse situation in Hungary where the entire legal framework for them joining the Alliance is basically not in place. The approval that is required by parliament for the stationing of foreign troops has not been sorted out. They have rushed with the debate about ratification of membership and they have not done their homework so far as their own country's constitution. There was an outrageous episode two weeks ago when a
Romanian contigent——

Chairman

119.   We were there.
(*Dr Eyal*) —— was stopped at the frontier because there was not permission from the Hungarian Parliament to allow it to go through. All the specious arguments that followed thereafter are neither here nor there. Basically the truth remains that these countries do not take seriously the Strategic Concept debate that takes place in NATO. They think that the entire debate about a wider geographic remit for the Alliance is basically a frivolous exercise intended to keep France and Spain quiet and that nobody has any interest in it otherwise. They have absolutely no interest in diverting the Alliance's resources anywhere else from this but to keep it in the central region of Europe and they have scant knowledge of the pressures that may exist on western governments internally about how the Alliance should be presented to the population in our countries. The reality is that they are much more attracted to the notion of belonging to the club than being serious about understanding what the membership actually entails. We do ourselves no favours in not being very forthright and direct, especially since their membership now is completely guaranteed.
Chairman: I think we have the impression that life will be something of a shock for them after next April. I hope they are prepared for the shock they are about to experience.

Mr Blunt

120.   Do you think that applies to Romania or have they demonstrated sufficiently?
(*Dr Eyal*) It does not apply to the Romanians for a variety of reasons, basically because they are desperate. They are desperate because of a variety of reasons. The first one is that they have nowhere else to go, they have no alternative arrangements which could work. They know that this is realised in Brussels and therefore they could be postponed for much longer because they have nowhere else to go. They can always threaten to self-destruct but that is not a particularly persuasive threat. In other terms their difficulty is that they suspect that at the end, the Alliance will be locked into the position that we have in the European Union with Greece and Turkey. For whatever reasons the Hungarians would be able at the end to direct Alliance policies in a way that both simultaneously locks Romania out of realistic membership and at the same time pledges the Alliance to a policy of putting persistent pressure on the Romanians. It does not matter whether it is real or not, it does not matter whether they are fanciful in their fears, the truth of the matter is that is what drives it. Let us be frank, like any other Central European country they are also driven by this final seal of approval that they have made it into Europe. It is an imperceptible feeling but it is there in every one of them.

Chairman

121.   Dr Heuser?
(*Dr Heuser*) This is precisely one of those areas where you have this multiple-level approach of policy making, of understanding what is going on. This is precisely where dealings within the EAPC are very deceptive. One is dealing with a very large number of very, very educated, very sophisticated diplomats from all these countries who have learnt a long time ago that Russia must never, never be mentioned in the whole context of NATO enlargement.
(*Dr Heuser*) The obvious point is that public opinion is very much aware of the role of Russia in Europe but this is not part of the presentational packaging that governments now give to the whole project of enlargement and what new members are going to be doing in NATO. It is not surprising that what you find in any public pronouncements by governments or diplomatic enlargements is that the two different NATOs, old and new, are fully accepted by the invitees, that they totally understand that their future commitments are X, Y and Z, but this is something which is far, far away from what their publics at home think even after the educational campaigns in all three countries to make the public aware of what is going to go on. In that context, allow me a small comment on the question of force stationing, one of the things that again public opinion has not really quite woken up to which is another one of those dilemmas which NATO is trying to gloss over elegantly (because there is nothing else that they could possibly do) is this question of how you make enlargement palatable to the non members and particularly Russia. It affects precisely this question of Hungarian legislation with regard to the stationing of foreign troops: NATO still maintains that it has no intention, no reason and no plans to put forces on to the territory of its invitees. In that respect it does not matter if Hungary is behind schedule with sorting out

[Chairman *Cont]*

the legal issue, because for the time being there is no need for such stationing. Throughout history other Alliance members have insisted that being a member of NATO did not mean that foreign powers automatically have the right to station forces on their territory. Portugal has insisted on that since 1949. NATO has always had different deals with different members of the Alliance which means from that point of view we will have three new different deals. One of the problems of the Strategic Concept will be whether this is in any way going to be reflected in the actual text of the concept. I think it is unlikely. But one may wish to make some reassuring gesture towards Russia, which is the obvious paradoxical approach in the entire process;- how, I do not know.

Chairman: Jonathan, I was relieved the "R" word did not mean Romania, we were quite pleased about that, that it turned out to be something other than Romania.

Mr Blunt

122. Can I ask about the formulation of the concept itself, not least to help the Committee decide exactly what is the best point of influence when we publish our report and when we publish our report in order to try and influence the process, if we can, with our views. Richard Hatfield told us when he came to give evidence that a first working draft of the New Strategic Concept had been prepared in Brussels by NATO's international staff, and that substantial redrafting would be under way between now and the Washington Summit. Can you try and help us to understand the bureaucracy of the redrafting process, where it is now and what for us will be the sensible key points of influence to try and have some effect on the outcome, or indeed anybody?

(Dr Heuser) I would very much like to comment later.

(Mr Crum Ewing) I think that what we should be asking for is this. It needs to be divided into two parts: one, what are the subjects which the New Concept is going to address and, secondly, how precisely does it address them? I think there should be on the public record the issues which have been identified for the concept to address and those should be a matter for debate and discussion so that detailed comments can be focused on issues which the management have identified and then the detailed argument needs to be conducted, as in all diplomatic negotiations, around the table by the people involved at properly briefed meetings. We do need to know, I suggest you should ask, which Ministers are actually going to be directly involved in establishing those and how this is going to fall between the Foreign Office, the Ministry of Defence and indeed Downing Street and the Cabinet Office. I think the Government should explain quite clearly who is responsible and who is accountable to the House of Commons for getting the details right. I do not think you or anybody else can involve yourselves too far in the details.

(Mr Roper) In the answer which you quoted from Mr Hatfield he went on to say: "There is, of course, a wider package of initiatives being developed for the Washington Summit and although the Strategic Concept will be very much at the heart it will of course ... etcetera, etcetera." It is important not to get too fixed on a new Strategic Concept as such. My feeling is that it is being worked away among the bureaucracies of Brussels in a rather traditional way and may make some progress but I doubt how much. On the other hand, if we look at what has happened previously at summits, at the last moment there will be telephone calls from the President to the heads of government of major countries and there will be a series of initiatives put forward by Washington. Those are probably the things that are going to hit the headlines rather than a document which Nato's bureaucracy will produce called the New Strategic Concept. Therefore, it is this phrase about the "wider package of initiatives" to which Mr Hatfield referred in his evidence to you to which the Committee should address itself and not restrict itself just to the New Strategic Concept as such.

123. He did also say, if I remember rightly, that the New Strategic Concept was going to in a sense be the fundamental document from which NATO planners in the future are going to take the rules and when they come to any decision about anything it is going to have to be within the framework of the concept. Although the initiatives may be the headlines the day after the Washington Summit it will be the concept that is going to be guiding NATO over the next ten years.

(Mr Roper) Look at the Strategic Concept which was adopted in 1991 and look at what NATO has done since and you will see there is not too much correlation between the two.

124. That brings me on to my next question of whether the 1991 Strategic Concept is obsolescent which it clearly is given what NATO has got up to since then and will the new Strategic Concept be much more radical than the 1991 document or will it get compromised away by the bureaucracy and therefore not advance the position very much from the 1991 concept?

(Dr Heuser) As you rightly said, the Strategic Concept is the basis on which the military application is drawn up and that is the important thing. If the Strategic Concept says something about defining the NATO area that will immediately limit all military planning and that is very serious. Taken in isolation, any other statement by heads of state and government does not have the same institutional weight that the concept has. From that point of view it is crucial which compromises go into the concept. The question, however, is whether language will be found which is such a fudge that it will be impossible to translate it into a solid military application. That has actually happened in the past. From that point of view I think what is happening right now is of crucial importance and even in the 1991 Strategic Concept contained a whole series of crucial points from which policy flowed.

(Mr Roper) I think there is an important difference, and there has been really over the history of NATO significant differences, in different countries. For example, from the time Germany came into NATO there was nowhere else other than NATO's documents from which it was able to derive a basis for

[Mr Blunt *Cont*]

its own military developments. Other countries sign up to NATO declarations and then go on and do their own things, some outside the integrated command, namely France, others inside the military command like Britain and America but which do not feel the same constraints. On the other hand, what is the case is that it is quite difficult to get the NATO bureaucracy to go beyond things which have been set out or can be interpreted as having been set out in existing documents. The point I am talking about is this wider package of initiatives and these are not just presidential statements because there could well be other documents adopted by the NATO Summit as well as the Strategic Concept. One should not assume it is just the Strategic Concept which will be adopted. Some of these other documents may also have political importance subsequently although it is quite true that the Strategic Concept does have a centrality.

(Mr Crum Ewing) I would have thought documents leading to the development of things such as Armament Groups, leading to more common procurement, leading to more inter-operability are the other initiatives that might have been in mind and they are extremely important for determining the parameters. I personally think that there is a very great danger that we will hobble our military capacity in Europe by going in for some giant scale amalgamation for defence manufacturers which will reduce our ability to produce the right equipment but that seems to be one of the lines which is a received view within the Ministry of Defence and within the Ministries of Defence across Europe and I think it is a very worrying thing that there is a possibility that something like that can be written into the constitution in the margins of the Washington Conference.

(Dr Eyal) I do not think we should exaggerate in calling it a constitution. We should look at the exercise as essentially one of the renewing of marriage vows and as the number of partners increases and the marriage tends to get lengthier and lengthier there may be a need for a rather frequent renewal of the marriage vows. The idea that this is somehow going to settle the Alliance well into the 21st century is misconceived. I fully predict in a number of years we will have to return to this Strategic Concept yet again, and nor is that necessarily bad, but it does put the current exercise into a particular context. The idea that we can refashion the Alliance and we can find the correct answers, square all the circles, manage to get the French back in without annoying the Russians, project an image of stability throughout the world, at the lowest possible cost is, quite frankly, a bit misconceived. Clearly if we iron out a few of the immediate difficulties that is important. I would suggest in terms of the issues which the Committee may want to consider in greater depth, if it has not done so already, should include the subject of the fudge that will be obtained about the authority that could be given to the Alliance for assuming military roles (because this is what it will amount to) in particular conflicts, namely, are we going to say that the United Nations Security Council should grant authority, which is a nicer way of saying that the Russians will have a veto over the Alliance, or are we going to say that we can conceive of situations where

without UN Security Council authority we decide to act because the situation is either urgent or so inflammable rather like what our government suggested at the height of the latest Kosovo crisis. The fudge that is obtained there will be supremely important both in terms of the way the Alliance behaves internally in terms of the ability of countries such as France but increasingly Germany as well to question the activities of the Alliance in particular crises unless a mandate is obtained and in terms of the message it provides to countries such as Russia. In that respect I think it will be a supremely important point. I have a feeling that the other issues which Mr Roper was quite right to refer to are what are termed now privately in governments as "comfort packages", namely something more to the Romanians and Slovenes to tell them we have not forgotten what we said at Madrid but we do not like to repeat it too often, something more to those who were not mentioned at Madrid and something more of a nod towards the CJTF concept and towards whatever is being put together by the British and French Government as we speak at the moment. But I would not take it too seriously. It tends to pad up library shelves in universities rather than ultimately be the constitution of the Alliance.

Chairman

125. You have filled up a few shelves in your time and I hope you will continue to do so!

(Mr Roper) Are we returning later to this question of the United Nations or do you wish me to comment on it now?

126. I cannot wait. One question that you touched upon, have you noticed any deviant national attitudes on the Summit coming up? We will discuss nuclear strategy later on but have we seen anything cropping up from Spain or Denmark or are most of the traditional members or existing members of NATO moving more or less along the same lines?

(Mr Crum Ewing) I think there is a real possibility that Turkey will make a *démarche* in support of the opening of formal negotiations with Bulgaria and Romania and I think the three other newcomers will then be bound by the assurances that they have given to others of supporting extension and find themselves in the slightly embarrassing position of having to support that. The Turks may be diverted but that goes to the whole business of Turkey's relationship with Europe.

(Dr Eyal) I would only add to that, Chairman, apart from the known cases like the Germans who seem to be thinking of what actually should go into the wider debate and what should be taken as read, I think on the positive side there has been no public noisy championing of the Romanians and Slovenes by the French for instance for the reasons we know but I think it is a positive sign and therefore we are not going to approach the Washington Summit with this cacophony of jarring noises as we have done to the very last moment in Madrid. There has been some discrete lobbying, there have been some odd suggestions about offering an inclusion of Slovenia in

[**Chairman** *Cont*]

order to show the cart is still on the road but not actually to Romania. I think that is a fairly pointless exercise and I do not think it was picked up by a lot of other countries. When it comes to where the Alliance should go, on a positive note a lot of this debate was contained within Brussels or in the usual bureaucratic channels which is a good sign.

(*Mr Roper*) We have had of course the North Atlantic Assembly which may or may not be thought to be eccentric in advocating Slovenia's admission as an example so that one does have a major body of parliamentarians taking this view, Chairman, but I do not think very many other people have followed the Roth Report whatever the North Atlantic Assembly may have done. Nor do we have the Danes wishing to have the question of the Baltic states raised explicitly at this stage because they realise it is not right. What they want to see are patterns of co-operation in various ways developed so that perhaps the distinction between being a member and not being a member becomes less apparent. I think a number of people may be looking at ways that can be done. On wider issues I think there are people who have significant hesitation about some of the American initiatives for some new tasks and a feeling that we do not want to overload the organisation at this stage. This of course applies particularly to the point to which you said we will return—the question of a requirement for a United Nations mandate before NATO action.

127. Whilst we are on that would you like to expand slightly on the UN/OSCE mandate.

(*Mr Roper*) As you know, NATO itself has taken the view that it has required a UN or OSCE mandate in the past. Obviously, as we saw over the case of Kosovo, it was possible for a number of rather particular reasons for Act Ords to be adopted without there being an explicit NATO resolution. My own view—and here I think I differ from Jonathan—is that to get the Strategic Concept to give in a sense a blank cheque to say that NATO could auto-authorise itself for military action would be something you would not get the 16 members to agree to and therefore it is better for this subject not to be explicitly raised but to be treated on a case-by-case basis as occurred over Kosovo.

128. There are forms of words that could be used.

(*Mr Roper*) I believe it is better not to put in words because I suspect once you start putting in words you will start getting into some of these difficulties. As we have seen over Kosovo it was possible to get an activation order and I suspect that was better than raising the issue. There were some countries which deliberately wanted the thing put in explicitly saying it was necessary to have this and there were others who were saying it is better not to put it in. As I say, I think it is better to leave the whole thing out.

129. Are you saying that the current formula is sufficiently vague to allow NATO to proceed even if it does not have the preferred option of the legitimation by the UN or the OSCE?

(*Mr Roper*) I would draw the example of Kosovo to your attention.

(*Dr Eyal*) I tend to agree that if it had been possible to avoid this issue it would have been perfect.

Sadly, it is not. I would not like the issue raised at all in a Strategic Concept if we could have avoided it but the battle has been joined. Any omission of this would be interpreted by the media as essentially maintaining the deep division as it is seen in the media on such issues. Any omission like that would give rise to perhaps bigger debates especially in the Green/Socialist coalition in Germany on these issues and it could give rise to debates between governments in the member countries. More importantly, it would give a wrong signal to a country such as Russia. Essentially you mentioned the Kosovo example. The Kosovo example is right. We were prepared to act but we did not at the end. Basically the Kosovo example is six on the one hand and half a dozen on the other. We were prepared to ignore the Russian interpretation of our supposed mandate from the UN Security Council but at the end of the day we did not ignore it. We have stayed in our position but we have not done it. This is how it is interpreted by the Russians that at the end of the day they have managed to persuade us or through a set of threats to reach a situation where we basically blinked. The issue will return and it will return in almost every debate on almost any issue. I think it is a fundamental one. It would have been best if it was avoided, I agree with you, but it was not and cannot be.

(*Mr Roper*) Just on a point of fact, we did not blink; Milosevic blinked.

(*Dr Heuser*) Mr Roper is right.

(*Mr Crum Ewing*) Could I say something on the United Nations. I think that some weasel words are needed here. I think NATO should commit itself not to intervene until the particular case has been fully considered by the United Nations and authorise itself normally only to intervene in pursuance of United Nations resolutions, but it should certainly be prepared to intervene on the basis of general United Nations resolutions and it should not require specific detailed Security Council resolutions before it can intervene.

(*Dr Heuser*) Just for your consideration in making up your mind as to what you are going to put forward as your recommendations——

Chairman: I think we will have the same divisions that you have or NATO would have.

Mr Brazier: I have a feeling you are right.

Chairman

130. We must have clerks who will think up a very good form of words to encapsulate all of our views.

(*Dr Heuser*) The question you will want to ask yourselves, and I think you have fully grasped this, is whether you are going to wish NATO to be an instrument for vigilante action where the New Strategic Concept implies it can be used in such a way that it is completely divorced from the international order which you are simultaneously trying to sustain throughout the world. Even the suggestion that was just put forward by Mr Crum Ewing is such that you are divorcing NATO's action from a concept of international order which ultimately hinges on the UN Security Council being the supreme authority. If you want to do that basically you are going back to Charles

[Chairman *Cont*]

Bronson and the New York subway. If you are introducing that element which is clearly the wish of some governments then you are simply saying we think that force should be exercised where we think fit, never mind what the international system thinks, never mind what the Security Council says and we will be using it in our way like in the Wild West, you undermine conceptually the whole edifice of international order that NATO is trying to be part of.

Chairman: It is very easy to imagine situations not where the international community is critical but where Russia is and whatever administration emerges in Russia—and it could be a pretty nasty administration—would you seriously argue that the Russian national interest should be taken to act as a veto on any action that other nations wish to take? That is taking international law to a fairly absurd level.

Mr Brazier

131. North Korea's only major export industry is selling high tech armourments around the Middle East, as far as one can make out so supposing tomorrow the West had information that they were providing terrorists with nuclear weapons, would one seriously expect America and potential NATO allies under whatever umbrella to do nothing because the Chinese would as usual support the North Koreans?

(Dr Heuser) It is a different question. If I may just home in on that. It is not a question of asking whether one can imagine situations where we would want to act without the UN Security Council resolution: the Kosovo crisis was precisely such a situation in point. Certain countries which had been very steadfast in saying, 'we will not tolerate any out of area action or any redefinition of the role of NATO', found that they changed their views on the concrete example of the Kosovo crisis. What happened there was a very concrete case in point. There is a huge difference between saying the world is imperfect and making one off decisions *ad hoc* which may under-cut your overall stand of supporting international norms, or whether you make a general policy declaration in the Strategic Concept.

(Dr Eyal) At the end of the day you will face this problem one way or another whether it is in the Strategic Concept or not. This is the key problem we have got. Up to now certainly since the end of the Cold War we managed to finesse the issue by providing Delphic-style UN Security Council resolutions which the Russians were asked to subscribe to, the "all necessary means" kinds of resolutions which once they had been put on the books we said this is it and we can now interpret it in any way we want. That has been interpreted by the Russians and indeed some other governments as not having proper respect for international law either. Dr Heuser said the way we operated on the Kosovo issue is a concrete case, yes, but it is still the case that the Russians believed that despite the fact that the resolution on Kosovo mentioned Chapter 7 it did not authorise us to use force and we decided to interpret it in that way. Basically, Chairman, we face two options. One is we can conceive of situations when we will act without a United Nations Security Council resolution. I agree

with Dr Heuser that would be very difficult to justify. The other one is to say nothing but be clear in our minds that there may be situations where despite the UN Security Council resolution or perhaps because of a UN Security Council resolution we will take actions and defy what will very often be the Russian position.

(Mr Roper) I think we have to think about two things. We must be very careful not to create a precedent and it is very difficult for an international organisation which is part, as Dr Heuser has said, of the framework of strengthening international order itself to pass a resolution or adopt a document which is against the development of international order. Individual states can and have acted in such a way and in the case of Kosovo a group of states did, but to put it down in a Strategic Concept is something they should think about very carefully before they do so.

(Dr Heuser) We have no proper operational organisation elsewhere that has anything like the cachet, importance or functioning abilities of NATO. Imagine if the Organisation of African States said it would do the same and in future take action wherever it saw fit just because its members felt like it.

(Dr Eyal) That is exactly what has happened with Liberia and the Nigerian involvement without our blessing.

132. That is absolutely right. The idea that somehow the rest of the world is going to change because NATO sets a legalistic example here seems to me extra-ordinary. We have to make it clear that we will ——

(Mr Roper) —— break the law.

Mr Brazier: —— if you accept international law being on a par with domestic law, you can phrase it like that. Not all of us do.

Chairman

133. Before we come on to a series of questions on nuclear issues, if the whole of NATO at a level of 16 or 19 or 20 is not prepared to act then we will see what has happened in the past; coalitions of the willing. Would you care to comment on that generally about whether you see a Gulf model of yes, you can use NATO equipment, you can use NATO procedures, you can use a number of NATO allies but it not necessarily being a NATO action? Any comments on the likelihood of coalitions of the willing?

(Dr Heuser) I think NATO will be going in that direction. As I have already said, I am equally convinced that the Strategic Concept will not talk about it and the communiqués in the next few years will studiously try to avoid this question. This is a simple observation of the mechanisms of co-operation. I think it will become increasingly impossible to find consensus within NATO that will actually allow the Alliance as a whole to do certain things precisely because there happen to be some members who will wish to act, even without a UNSC mandate, and other members who will think it more important to stride to international norms so you will find there will be divisions within the Alliance which will prevent it taking collective action, other than adopting basic statements saying, "We condemn violence", and, "We

[Chairman *Cont*]

hope for peace". I think this is an area which is currently completely under-explored for the simple reason that everybody would be much happier if collective action were taken and if there were consensus among all NATO members. As long as any consensus can emerge people try to protect it, so much so that they do not want to explore possible ways of involving NATO collectively without every single member country sending a contingent. So, for example, a very likely interim scenario will be for the Alliance as a whole vaguely to say, "On the whole we are happy that NATO resources should be used in such a conflict", then a number of countries will not be contributing actively and will be refraining from participating in the process. So they will just give their approval in general without positively voting yes, and yet not stop the others from going ahead. That will create many new possibilities than all 16 and 19 getting involved to only three or four getting involved.

(Mr Roper) I think we will see something which is not quite like the coalitions of the willing. It will be a bit closer to what the European Union is doing through constructive abstention. People will not stop NATO being used for a political purpose but I think the way forward is to use this extremely valuable instrument for military co-operation by as many as possible of the members of NATO and the others would accept this. This is, of course, the difference between Article 5 missions to which we are all treaty bound and these other sorts of missions which for a variety of reasons countries will not take part in. Of course we have the example of the extraction force with the reinforced battalion which is going into Macedonia and which is going to only have five or perhaps six NATO countries involved. There may well be other examples where there is just a subset of NATO members and that is in a sense what the CJTF concept is about so that one can have a group of countries including perhaps some non-members of the Alliance also involved in such a package.

134. Can I ask for your views on the European Union dimension and the combined joint task force model. Will this have any relevance to extricating a set number of countries from military activity?

(Mr Roper) Yes, that is one way of seeing it. We see it primarily as the Europeans doing it collectively but I think one could see a combined joint task force bringing together another subset of NATO members and some countries from outside NATO. We see it as an excellent instrument for military co-operation being used sometimes by all its members and on other occasions, with the agreement of all the members, by a subset of members.

135. You mentioned this concept of constructive abstention. What about destructive abstention? If people say, "No, we are not having this. Not only are we not participating, we do not want any combination of NATO nations to do it"?

(Mr Roper) Of course that is one of the problems and this is one of the reasons there have been questions within Europe about the CJTF arrangements. What happens for example if Turkey says, "No, we do not want this to happen", or the United States says, "No, we don't want this to happen", should we not have

some back-up system of our own? The argument we have to go along with is because the members of NATO to such a large extent share the same interests there are occasions on which all members will not wish to take part but they will accept normally not to obstruct the others from doing something which they consider useful.

(Dr Eyal) I agree wholeheartedly with what has been said. Coalitions of the willing are utterly inevitable. It is built implicitly into most of the arrangements that we have got in place at the moment. I would not exaggerate the possibility of obstructive abstention. Kosovo has been mentioned a few times. I would not say the Greeks have been the most reasonable of people, nevertheless they had very serious doubts about air strikes against Yugoslav forces, they have accepted that their aircraft will not be involved in any air strikes that were being planned but they did not obstruct in the end what became a very strong American position and ultimately an Alliance position. So it is possible to overcome what appears to be very entrenched positions and they simply do not take part in these operations. What I think the challenge for NATO would be is what does it mean for formal political decision-making. It would require an enormous amount of very deft handling. The by-product of a coalition of the willing is also the Contact Group approach, namely a small group of countries, usually the same ones, for a variety of reasons getting together and making the decisions. It makes perfect sense but at the same time it could be destructive for countries that are not taking part and very often it would require very tender attention, namely, if there was a coalition of the willing there must be a formal way of reporting or keeping others informed because otherwise very soon you end up with a nucleus which is acting and usually it tends to be the same nucleus.

Chairman: We have a massive series of questions on nuclear policy in NATO. Because time is running out if we could ask a series of questions and then pick and choose which elements within them you would prefer to answer. Harry Cohen?

Mr Cohen

136. NATO declared in 1996 that it did not see any need to change any aspect of NATO's nuclear posture or nuclear policy and that it does not foresee any future need to do so. That rather puts the kibosh, if that is still the position, on any change at this particular round. Does it seem that they are putting the lid on this whole issue? What would you say are the options for possible change in NATO's nuclear posture. What is the implication of not changing on global non-proliferation efforts? Should NATO not adopt a "no first use" or "no first strike" policy? Would that not be an option for it to consider? Would that not be logical? What about the position of the United States? It seems to me that varying degrees of an umbrella still persist. Why would it not be possible for NATO to become non-nuclear for example? If the United States wanted to keep it as a nuclear state why could that not be separate from NATO? Surely that is an option that could be considered? Perhaps you could comment on

[Mr Cohen *Cont]*

that. How do you think the three new countries regard the nuclear policy? The last question is of course about the new German government and their attitudes to it.

(Mr Roper) Let me just answer one factual point. It is quite interesting that in the debate in the United Nations on the new agenda resolution three weeks ago at which this issue first came up, the three nuclear weapon states in NATO voted against this particular proposal which was put forward by the Australians, New Zealanders and Canadians, including the introduction of no first use of nuclear weapons and the three new candidate members voted with them. So there were three plus three and the other 13 members of NATO all abstained.

(Mr Crum Ewing) I feel that so long as we retain nuclear capabilities in our arsenal the greater sense of uncertainty we can generate amongst the potential enemies the better and to adopt a no first use policy would be to introduce precisely an element of rigidity that we do not want to do.

(Dr Heuser) May I home in on the uncertainty. I am now talking as an academic so I can let rip! All my knowledge here stems from public documents NATO has published itself. NATO strategy used to be to say that the adversary must not be uncertain at all that NATO will respond but the ways in which we respond we will not define in advance. That strategy has now been whittled down to simply saying we want to leave uncertainty in the minds of the adversary. Any historian of NATO knows that the last 30 years of the Alliance have seen great European fears been very afraid that the American nuclear guarantee might not be implemented in a war. The credibility of the American nuclear guarantee was a huge issue of uncertainty for NATO so, frankly, particular in a post-Cold War world, NATO does not exactly signal overwhelming certainty that it will definitely use nuclear weapons. The whole problem of NATO's strategy over decades was that people were afraid that America would not use nuclear weapons early enough which is why the British position was so incredibly crucial within this edifice because it was the British who would have been prepared much earlier than the Americans to use nuclear weapons. Frankly, we have an uncertainty problem of a very very large dimension. It is not a question of the adversary sitting there saying, sitting there saying, "How is NATO going to respond? Is it going to use these nuclear weapons or those?" Adversaries tend to sit there saying, "Is NATO going to respond at all?" It is precisely that sort of uncertainty we should be avoiding and which the Strategic Concept does not address properly because it underlines in its present form of 1991 the need for uncertainly. So I think the whole issue is very wrongly phrased. Instead of talking about uncertainty in the mind of adversaries we should say we will certainly punish any first use of any weapons of mass destruction in ways that will be so disagreeable, overwhelming and devastating for the adversary that the adversary will not want this. I do not see any reason why we should then go on and define that it will definitely be with nuclear weapons. There are ways by now in which we can devastate an adversary overwhelmingly that may or may not involve nuclear weapons. We do not have the chemical or biological options, thank goodness, but it does not necessarily mean if you want to really clobber somebody you have to say, "We will destroy Baghdad entirely with nuclear weapons." You can still threaten horrible things without spelling out precisely what and the uncertainty would be over the form of punishment rather than whether it will come, or whether it will be overwhelming and devastating. I think NATO should be going on to a strategy not of saying definitely that it will not use nuclear weapons first, but it should say 'we will definitely punish any first use of weapons of mass destruction'. This would also be a very interesting statement with regard to nuclear proliferation or B or C weapon, proliferation because it would basically mean rather than sitting back and saying, "Oh, a missile has fallen on Lampedusa. Oh, it contained a chemical warhead", NATO could muster up the force to say, "Lampedusa happens to be part of one of NATO territory, this falls under Article 5, we are going to punish the country that fired that missile", and be much more active on that score so the counter-proliferation side could be much developed. I know there is a small element of it in NATO but it has never been properly developed or enshrined in the Strategic Concept as an active option. I think counter-proliferation is an area in which all NATO allies should be completely clear that they have this interest very strongly in common and it is also an interest that is the basis of international law in the non-proliferation of chemical weapons and biological weapons treaties. So I have no problems with that. Challenging the first use commitment of NATO ——

(Mr Roper) The non no first use.

(Dr Heuser) Challenging NATO's option of first use which has been part of the old strategy coming from the Green Foreign Minister in Germany was to be expected given his party's past views on the issue. In a way it is still part of the old thinking parts of the Social Democratic Party and the Green Party being brought into the government and they are wrangling with it at the moment. What I think is absolutely brilliant about it is that it is forcing NATO to reconsider its nuclear paragraphs where, as you have rightly said, they declared that bar. It is completely silly that they declared them taboo in the first place because part of the nuclear paragraph was that NATO was in the process of reducing its tactical nuclear weapons da-di-da-di-da what has actually now been passed. There are whole sections in there which have to be updated anyway. To come back to the whole big question of what NATO is about. The whole issue of underlining the importance of nuclear weapons has changed so dramatically with the change in the international environment. I could very easily imagine another 'no' if we were really pushed to comment with regard to the question of first use. I am referring to the 'three nos', no plans, no intentions and no cause to station nuclear weapons or NATO forces in the new member states. You could also say there seems to be at the moment 'no cause' or 'no scenario' you can think of in which you would use nuclear weapons first. I would avoid any reference to the first use issue in a Strategic Concept and instead adopt a 'definite punishment' posture.

Chairman

137. What if your satellite communications or any other method you have recourse to use see a potential adversary stocking up ready for an attack? Are you going to be like a western gun fighter saying, "I am going to allow you to get your first shot in", because in order to have the legitimacy of saying you did not strike first you might have lost quite a lot of your cities. Is that not a rather Utopian view of legitimacy?

(Dr Heuser) There are two other options. One of them would be at that stage to use non-nuclear weapons against those weapons with the same missile technology.

138. How are you going to fly a B52 in 11 hours or whatever it is going to be? You are dead, you have lost Washington.

(Dr Heuser) On the other hand, we keep being told that the Tridents or Tomahawks are as good with conventional warheads as they would have been with nuclear charges.

Mr Brazier

139. Purely on the technical question, the penetrating power of conventional warheads even the ones we have got planned like CASOM (which is still some years down the road) against anything that is in a reinforced silo is a waste of rations. They are very powerful in other concepts but the idea you could use them to deter the use of properly found nuclear weapons seems to me to be technically impossible.

(Dr Heuser) You are talking about an old Soviet scenario in which you are talking about missiles in reinforced silos that are very well protected. What we would be talking about at the moment is potentially much more a scenario of a threat of a less sophisticated country possibly with bunkers and if they are really going to be prepared to fire why can we not at least close the bunkers with conventional means by making it difficult to open the bunkers. There are ways you can stop that on the surface with conventional means which would be preemptive but would not mean annihilating Baghdad at that stage. I have no problem with a preemptive strike that is 'active counter-proliferation' in the American jargon; i.e. going in with conventional weapons at that stage. The only scenario that has been explained to me where nuclear weapons, used very very carefully, would be the best solution, would be in dealing with the problem of a chemical weapons silo or biological weapons silo where you may be able with nuclear weapons to——

140. —— Sterilise it.

(Dr Heuser) —— Without spreading the contents all over the area. This has been explained to me by people who know it much better than I. The second way to react to this is I think an area which for years the British government has been sort of interested in but not quite going far enough mainly because France was always out of sync with Britain and whenever the French were interested, the British were not, and vice versa: that is the area of theatre missile defence.

(Mr Roper) I think that I am somewhat schizophrenic about this question and I admit it. First

of all, I had hoped that this was not going to be something which was significantly discussed because it does seem in terms of the Strategic Concept that there are other much higher priorities. I am rather sorry that instead of it being discussed within Alliance frameworks it broke in this particular way at a United Nations resolution, but the trouble is if there is a resolution where the government has adopted something in its policy statement it has to act in that way. That is almost inevitable. That having been said I do think that we do need to have a rather long, cool think about the position of those countries who are nuclear weapon states and therefore also the Alliance as far as nuclear weapons are concerned. The Indian and Pakistan tests this year have created a situation which at least means we have to go back and reevaluate what we have said in terms of our non-proliferation doctrine. I believe this takes some time. It is not something that is going to take place either within countries or within the Alliance between now and the Washington meeting but I do think it is something which we need to examine over a longer period.

Chairman: We have two quite substantial topics to talk about in 18 minutes, firstly NATO enlargement and then concluding with some questions on European and trans-Atlantic issues. I will call on Julian Brazier.

Mr Brazier: I thought I was doing European and trans-Atlantic dimensions.

Chairman: We are talking about uncertainty, and I am the archetypical inducer of total uncertainty and confusion!

Mr Brazier

141. I am going to go for the second batch first, as it is the most topical stuff. NATO's concept of a European Defence and Security Identity is obviously very much in the news as a result of the comments the Prime Minister made recently. Could I give you two questions together as time is quite short? Firstly, do you as a panel think that a more coherent role for the European Allies can and should be created? Secondly, what do you think the United States' attitude to that would be?

(Mr Crum Ewing) The United States' attitude to it would be schizophrenic. The answer to the first point is, possibly.

(Mr Roper) I think it is quite difficult to create a more coherent role among European countries. This is a long process but at least I think it is a good thing that the Prime Minister has recognised the need for these discussions to be carried forward. I also believe it is important, because of the risk of schizophrenia in Washington, that we make quite clear to the Americans that this is not a question of producing a rival to NATO but a method of using, as we have seen earlier, NATO's excellent mechanisms for military co-operation from time to time by Europeans for things for which they need to co-operate in a military way.

(Dr Eyal) All I have to add to that is that I think the debate is absolutely right, it was demanded by the Americans, although quite rightly, as was said, they are schizophrenic about it. They want the Europeans to do more but they want the Europeans to do what

[Mr Brazier Cont]

Washington decides to do at a particular moment. However, I think there is still going to be a big question mark—and there is always a question mark in my mind—about what kind of conflicts we are talking about. Let us be clear: what we are talking about is a conflict in which the Europeans feel strongly enough that they want to commit troops but the Americans do not feel strongly enough but they are quite happy to allow us to use their equipment in extremis and not tell us how to use the equipment. There is a lot of "ifs" in this one. If we look at Bosnia we can see that it is quite proper for a country like the United States not to be involved in the conflict for many years and still to have very definite views about what other countries' soldiers should do in upholding what America enunciates as principles. So in that respect there will always be that tension. The advantage of the Prime Minister's initiative in October is at two levels. First, it has turned the tables around in a rather miraculous way, it has deflected from the accusation heard in Europe that Britain is the laggard, Britain is the obstacle to any security discussions. That was always nonsense. There are many countries in Europe which have difficulties with a European defence identity, but it was easy to hide behind Britain. That shadow for countries to hide no longer exists. Secondly, it has made creative tension in the discussions between the Europeans and the Americans, and I doubt we will be any wiser when this discussion is over but perhaps we will be clearer about what the bones of contention are and what the channels of the discussion are.

Chairman

142. John, I am a bit surprised that you appear to think the process of a European defence identity is going to be more elongated than my perception of what you would have thought. I would have thought that you would be more optimistic about the ability of the European nations to get their acts together.

(Mr Roper) I cannot comment on your perceptions of me!

143. They are based on 25 years of observation!

(Mr Roper) All I can do is to say that one sometimes learns by experience!

Mr Brazier

144. A supplementary to that, do you see a big change in the role of the WEU, perhaps its replacement by a broader based organisation, both broader based geographically and in terms of role, or not?

(Mr Roper) Can I comment on this? I did give evidence to this Committee's predecessor in the last Parliament about the Western European Union, where I suggested that one really should not have unnecessary entities, that one should look very carefully as to whether this should be maintained. What one is now basically saying is that one wants to use the European Union for Europeans to work out common policies and then go and discuss them with the Americans within the North Atlantic Council as to whether to do something together or, where not, to use NATO and the CJTF procedures as the military

dimension of that policy. But it becomes more and more clear that having a third organisation does not facilitate effective decision-making, it complicates it, and therefore I think that if the WEU disappears there will be relatively few tears cast.

(Mr Crum Ewing) I entirely agree with that. I believe that a suitable end-use of WEU would be to return the military functions to NATO and to develop out of the political and administrative side of WEU a secretariat for the Common Foreign and Security Policy. The Europeans are setting about that in completely the wrong way. They are trying to appoint a high representative without determining his brief or his accountability or how he is going to be supported, so he will potter around the world like a loose cannon. I think the right way to do it is to give him a secretariat, determine his brief and then appoint a person.

145. Can I ask the obvious question then? Are you suggesting then that Ireland and any others, perhaps Austria, should be required to join NATO or not?

(Mr Roper) I am sorry, let me explain. The Amsterdam Treaty, which will amend the Treaty of the European Union, brings the Petersburg tasks within the function of the European Union already. So it would be perfectly possible for all these things, other than territorial defence, to be undertaken by the European Union using NATO as its military instrument. As for the question of Article 5 of the WEU Brussels Committee, I hope this can be brought into the EU but, in exactly the same way as Schengen where not everyone is in Schengen, like ourselves, it would be possible for those countries who were neutral not to be involved in that particular thing until they chose to be. It would be perfectly possible to use the military instruments or the other aspects in the same way as we are involved in a lot of justice and home affairs aspects of the European Union without being involved in the Schengen passport union.

146. I would love to pursue that further but we are almost out of time. Are there any views on the French and German attitude towards the Alliance? In particular, can you give us an assessment of the attitude of the new German Government to further enlargement? I am sorry, I am giving you a whole group of questions together. Are the French effectively back in the Alliance, in your view? The Chairman all the way round Eastern Europe was saying he was hoping they would rejoin. Or are there still problems with NATO's long-term strategies in France's view? Is there a cooling of French enthusiasm for NATO? So, in other words, French and German attitude and a battery of questions there. Any views?

(Mr Crum Ewing) Lafayette will be top of the pops in France and America every alternate month but not every month. So the French and the Americans are never going to agree permanently about anything, although they may have love-ins from time to time. So in that sense, France is not wholly back in.

Chairman

147. One must say that the Americans do not agree on very much either!

(Dr Eyal) I would point out that I think the French have learnt something from their rather unhappy experience last year before the Madrid Summit. They shot themselves in the foot, they miscalculated very badly, they had at least three options for a compromise over the demands they formerly had for returning to the military structure, they blew every single one of them. I think it is accepted by both the Elysée and by the Government that any approach that would be done now will be done incrementally while ignoring the formal framework which goes with it. If we look at the careful way in which in the latest Iraq crisis the French bent over backwards, at least formally, to appear not to be taking a different position from that of the United States, if we look at the way the French have accepted to lead the Extraction Force in the former Yugoslav Republic of Macedonia, we will see that they are thinking about functional integration. That indeed may go much further if the decisions on the European Union Defence Identity go any further, blurring the distinctions, preventing a big, monstrous debate in the Assembly in Paris as well on France's direction for a sort of functional integration. When it comes to enlargement, I think that clearly there is a waning, a tiredness, in Germany about the entire subject. They are much more concentrated on enlargement of the European Union to the countries of Central Europe for the obvious political reasons, but I do not think they want to rock the boat, and I think the argument from Bonn seems to be that NATO enlargement is something which clearly is not on the top of the agenda, it may not even be in the middle of the list, and certainly nothing should be done at this stage which can infuriate an unpredictable Moscow. I think the French position is different. The issue of further enlargement will come back, but what the French have realised is that it cannot come back by banging the table.

148. I think we will have to move on. I am sorry.

(Dr Eyal) The German question is not answered, which I think is important.

149. I will just whip through the last questions. I am sorry. Do you all assume that there is going to be no announcement in April that Slovenia or Romania are going to be admitted?

(Dr Heuser) I can only speak off the record.

150. I imagine, from the people we have spoken to outside Eastern Europe, that it is not really likely, but the argument which Jonathan mentioned is quite persuasive. Nobody would notice Slovenia, they are doing everything, it is incredible, not forgetting the role they are playing on the Security Council at the moment. They are not threatening to the Russians. The door will be kept open. I am sad that people do not think this is a runner because it seems a very plausible attitude that they are taking.

(Dr Eyal) There are some technical difficulties. You would have to get another set of ratifications and it gets, quite frankly, rather boring and cumbersome to inform Congress every single year that there is another

ratification on another enlargement of the Alliance. So, technically, one could keep the idea and the promise of further rounds of enlargement, but in practice with every one of them there is a law of diminishing returns, in a purely technical sense. If I believed the administration in Washington had the verve to push it yet again in a few years' time, I would be happy with that kind of arrangement, but I am not sure.

151. If we all agree that nothing is going to happen in Washington, can anybody realistically expect in the next five, seven years, that they are going to get the goal?

(Mr Roper) In the next five or seven years, it seems to me there could be a further enlargement.

152. Which ones do you think would have a fair chance?

(Mr Roper) Any of the ones which are under consideration. It depends very much more than anything else on what happens in Russia.

(Mr Crum Ewing) I think we must admit Slovenia and Slovakia very quickly. I do not think we should open negotiations with the Baltics to admit them. I feel very deeply sentimentally about the Baltics, but I think to try and bring them into NATO would be to fly in the face of Russia quite unnecessarily at this stage.

Mr Brazier

153. Absolutely right.

(Dr Eyal) I would say that the priorities should be to avoid double rejection. The two countries that are in the double rejection syndrome are Slovakia and Romania—and Bulgaria indeed. For practical reasons, when it comes to the enlargement, I would consider Romania at the top of the list, Slovakia number two, Slovenia further down because it will be in the European Union and it will therefore have not the same kind of degree of security in formal terms but in practice it will not make much difference.

Chairman

154. Dr Heuser, any league table?

(Dr Heuser) Romania and Slovenia.

(Mr Roper) I just should mention that the Turkish National Assembly in ratifying passed a law saying they would not ratify any further states unless they were Bulgaria and Romania.

155. What will the reaction be? The Romanians were very irritated, the Slovenians were very irritated they were off the list. There is a down-side to a further rejection in terms of domestic politics. Do you think that is a factor we should take into account?

(Dr Eyal) It is a factor we should be taking seriously. In the case of Romania it is internal politics. However, it was played very well, I must say, for once. The Romanians had been told privately that they should not raise any hopes or start again a propaganda campaign like they had done last time. They cannot afford, and neither can we afford, another rebuff on very public terms. So they have not raised hopes and they have already prepared the population for that. What they are demanding is what they call "Madrid

[**Chairman** *Cont*]

plus", ie another further indication that they are on the list and that they are at the top of the list. I doubt whether we can give them that because, sadly, the list composition changes every year, but there it is. I think the problem is going to be not the Washington Summit but when it becomes patently clear in about two years thereafter that the promise is a promise on a never never basis, namely that this is a situation where travelling is better than arriving. There is where you can have severe problems. I am very worried about Romania's internal situation. In the next few years I think that the NATO issue is secondary but only if the promise remains realistic of NATO.

156.   Are there any serious alternatives to NATO enlargement? Is there any scope for Partnership for Peace? Is there anything some clever diplomat may say, that this may not be full membership for them but it goes beyond what they have at the moment?

(Dr Eyal)   It is rather like being in the waiting room all the time. If you are being supplied with new magazines to read while you are in the waiting room and sandwiches and beer, it is all very nice, the first lot, the second lot, the third lot, but after the fourth lot you start asking yourself why you are in the waiting room and is it a waiting room at all. That is the problem. I think it could work in the first instance, it could certainly work with an enhanced PfP and the comfort packages that both NATO and the British

Government are considering. The Romanians are very pleased with the attention they are getting now from London, but there is a limit to how much this can continue.

(Mr Roper)   I think the now regular meetings of the South East European Defence Ministers and the activities which are taking place in this group on a regional chapter for Partnership for Peace has been a very sensible initiative. The fact that NATO Allies like Italy, Greece and Turkey along with the United States are playing a part with these other countries is something that we should encourage. This is a half-way house. It is not ideal but it is rather more than just straight PfP and therefore should be supported.

(Dr Heuser)   is yet another article on the commitment to the open door, and at the same time the NATO attempt to blur the line of distinction between the members and the non-members. So you have exercises which are conducted with members and non-members in various constellations.

Chairman: Thank you very much. We have had a very interesting time. I am conscious of the fact that we have managed to extract from you only a tiny, tiny percentage of what you could actually have said, and a number of you have been before. May I say on behalf of the four members of the Committee who are here that we have enjoyed what you said and we will digest what you have said and much of it we will incorporate into our report. Thank you very much.

WEDNESDAY 27 JANUARY 1999

Members present:

Mr Bruce George, in the Chair

Mr Crispin Blunt	Mr Harry Cohen
Mr Julian Brazier	Laura Moffatt
Mr Jamie Cann	Ms Dari Taylor

Examination of Witness

Dr EDUARD KUKAN, Minister of Foreign Affairs, Republic of Slovakia, examined.

Chairman

157. Dr Kukan, Ambassador, welcome to our House of Commons Defence Committee. It is always a pleasure welcoming a Foreign Minister to our midst. One day before I retire we might even have our own Foreign Minister appearing. We have only ever had two. One was László Kovács and Dr Horn, when our Hungarian colleagues visited Parliament last year. We are producing a report which will be published just before the Washington Summit and we are looking very closely at, amongst other things, the invitation to the three invitees and what happens afterwards. We were last week in NATO and SHAPE; we are going to Bonn; we are off to Moscow and Kiev; we were in Washington last year, so we are making a very serious appraisal of what is happening to NATO and what is going to happen in the future. Expressing a personal opinion, up until the mid-1990s, when everyone talked of NATO expansion then, Slovakia was always one of those names mentioned and then like a crash of an aircraft it disappeared from the radar screens and I am delighted that it has now re-appeared. I was in your country two weeks ago and I am going out on Sunday to take part next week in a seminar in your Parliament on parliamentary control. So there are so many questions we would like to ask you but initially would you care to make an introductory remark or two?

(Dr Kukan) Thank you very much, Mr Chairman. Yes, I feel honoured to be invited to your Committee and at the beginning I would like to read a prepared statement and then we can engage in the discussion, so that I can answer any questions you would like to ask. Mr Chairman, distinguished ladies and gentlemen, please allow me, first, to thank you for welcoming me to your Committee. I am very glad that you offered me the opportunity to meet with you and to deal with issues which we, for our part, consider very important since they relate to the security position of the Slovak Republic. I appreciate the possibility to address you the more as I know, as you have already mentioned, that your Committee is preparing already the fourth report on NATO enlargement. I am especially pleased that you, Mr Chairman, have only recently had the opportunity to visit my country and to see the real current situation. Ladies and gentlemen, I speak to you as a Minister of Foreign Affairs of the new Government of the Slovak Republic, which was created based on the results of the parliamentary elections in our country in September last year. Right

at the beginning I would like to emphasise that our new Government declared the attainment of Slovakia's membership in the North Atlantic Alliance as one of the primary goals of its foreign policy. This goal is not new; it was declared also by previous governments. In spite of that, it did happen that the Slovak Republic was not invited by the Madrid Summit of NATO to join the Alliance. I dare say that it was mainly a consequence of the way in which power was exercised by the previous government and their opaque and unclear policy, which did not reflect the warning signals from partners in NATO or in the European Union, but it did not respect the wish of the majority of the people of Slovak. The citizens of the Slovak Republic, however, seized the opportunity in September 1998 to express their opinion in the parliamentary elections. The very turnout in the election, that is, 84 per cent. of voters, proves that they are not indifferent about their future. The political parties which constituted our coalition government after the elections received enough votes to hold a constitutional three-fifths majority in Parliament. Is there any better proof that the people in Slovakia were not content with the style of government which left us behind Western integration structures? Is there any better proof that the Slovaks, quite on the contrary, wish to live in a state that will be a part of the North Atlantic Alliance and the European Union, sharing the democratic principles and values with these communities? Our citizens thus gave us a mandate in the parliamentary elections which our Government perceived in that way, that is, it has to do everything to lead the Slovak Republic into the integration group of democratic countries. We consider the North Atlantic Alliance the right choice as regards our policy on security. The substantiality of NATO's existence was proved also in recent years by events in Bosnia-Herzegovina or the current situation in Kosovo. These show again that NATO is the organisation which is able to get involved efficiently and successfully also in cases like those. As I have mentioned already, it is our goal to attain fully-fledged membership in NATO. We are very well aware that to attain membership we need preparation and fulfilment of all conditions. As regards political conditions which the Slovak Republic failed to meet and thus is not amongst the countries that soon will join NATO, I can say that some have been met already. Just to briefly mention a couple: the representation of the opposition

[**Chairman** *Cont*]

in Parliament or the attitude towards national minorities; representatives of the Hungarian minority are members of the Government. The remaining conditions will be met as soon as possible. From the professional point of view, our preparation concentrates on achieving interoperability of the Army of the Slovak Republic with the armies of the Alliance members, on enhancing the professional and language preparedness of the human resources in our Army—and in this respect we highly appreciate the help of the NATO member states and I would like to say thank you especially to your country for the study stays of our experts at the prestigious Royal College of Defence Studies. As you know, two of the highest positions in the Slovak Army are held by graduates of the Royal College; the Chief of Staff is a graduate of the Royal College and also the Secretary of State, who is the No. 2 person in the Ministry of Defence, graduated from the Royal College. Then the co-operation of Slovak and British aviation schools, military-political considerations and joint command staff exercises or the prepared use of training grounds on the territory of Slovakia by British armed forces, all these contribute not only to a consolidation of the Slovak/British bilateral relations but also to an acceleration of our preparation for membership in the Alliance. Within the effort to intensify our preparation the Ministry of Foreign Affairs and the Ministry of Defence of the Slovak Republic have only recently drafted a joint programme of activating the foreign and security policy of Slovakia in the run-up to the Washington Summit of NATO. To provide the financial resources necessary for meeting the criteria related to NATO membership, we intend to maintain and progressively increase the share of expenditures on defence in the GDP, which currently accounts for 2 per cent. of gross domestic product. In order to prepare herself for membership in the Alliance, the Slovak Republic has from the very beginning participated actively in practical co-operation with NATO member states within the Partnership for Peace and the Euro-Atlantic Partnership Council. It has been just a week since we organised in our capital a successful EAPC seminar focused on issues of regional security, which was attended by representatives of 33 countries, including your country. Distinguished ladies and gentlemen, the Slovak Republic is immensely interested in guaranteeing security and stability in Central European space but also on the entire European Continent, and we want actively to contribute to this effort, first of all by developing good relations with our neighbour states. Today I am pleased to say that the countries which soon will join NATO—the Czech Republic, Poland and Hungary—react positively to our interest in intensifying mutually beneficial co-operation in our region, so to speak, in reviving the Visegrad co-operation. I would like to emphasise that we welcome the accession of the aforementioned countries to NATO, since this will indirectly enhance the quality of the security situation also in our country. At the same time I would like to express my hope that the North Atlantic Alliance will continue to pursue the open door policy. I am convinced that when Slovakia, which is located in the

geographic centre of the aforementioned countries—we have frontiers with all those countries—joins NATO, this will be a gain not only for our country but also for the Central European region and NATO itself. Apart from strengthening neighbourly relations, the Slovak Republic also wants to contribute to the reinforcement of peace, stability and security in broader scope. Let me furnish you with a couple of examples to prove this. The National Council of the Slovak Republic, that is, the Parliament of Slovakia, approved the sending and active participation of the members of the Army of the Slovak Republic in the SFOR activities in the territory of Bosnia-Herzegovina; the Government of Slovakia approved the provision of the financial contribution to support the MAPE activities which are carried out in the territory of Albania; the Slovak Parliament approved also the sending of a combat unit of the Army of Slovakia and its participation in the contingent of peacekeeping forces of the United Nations, the UNDOF in the Golan Heights, the UN disengagement of the invasion force—that is what the aggravation is for. Distinguished ladies and gentlemen, I want to be frank and dare say that the objective of my meeting with you today is to convince you that the Slovak Republic is genuinely interested in attaining membership of NATO and that our Government is prepared to do everything necessary for our preparation for the accession and the commitment resulting from membership in the Alliance. We are aware that the Washington Summit most probably will not mention any country as candidate for the next phase of enlargement. Nevertheless, we appreciate it if you distinguished ladies and gentlemen, the member states of NATO and the Washington Summit itself, recognise the fundamental changes that, in our conviction, are obvious in the Slovak Republic after the parliamentary elections. I would like to ask you, representatives of the country which we regard as one of the most important members of the Alliance and as a special ally of the United States, for one thing: please do assess our country based on the same criteria as were used in the case of the Czech Republic, Poland and Hungary prior to the decision to invite them to join the Alliance and within the sense of a study on NATO enlargement from 1995. The message which the Slovak people sent in the parliamentary elections was not only a message for us, the Slovak politicians, but it was also a message for you. Mr Chairman, thank you very much. This is what I wanted to say at the beginning and to prove that the Government of Slovakia is really very serious about its future intentions of becoming a NATO member. We are very glad that you included Slovakia in your itinerary so that you could see the situation for yourselves. It is always much better to see directly and I will be pleased to answer your questions or to hear your comments or remarks, which I will take very seriously and I will bring them back home. Thank you.

158. Thank you very much. You have answered many of our questions, so when we do ask further questions it will be to amplify upon or make sense of your excellent introduction. I, Ambassador, need no convincing. I think it is truly remarkable what the

[**Chairman** *Cont*]

Coalition Government has achieved in a few short months and it seems such an immense sadness that your country made such spectacularly slow progress towards achieving its objectives in recent years. There is much catching-up to be done and I am sure the process has begun. May I ask this: coalitions are not particularly liked in this country. We have had one-party governments with one opposition party largely for most of the 20th century. Even the British Government with a majority of nearly 200 has to work quite hard at keeping the troops in line and different sectors of the party more or less in agreement with its objectives. Are you reasonably confident that the coalition of—is it four parties?—is going to be able to see out its mandate, because—forgive me for interfering in your internal politics—it seems to me as an outsider that the continuing progress of your country to achieve its genuine European objectives depends almost exclusively on your coalition holding together for a number of years to come?

(*Dr Kukan*) Thank you very much for your question. I do not take it as an interference in our internal affairs when I take into consideration what you said about the necessity for the Government Coalition to stay on and to pursue the measures which were introduced after the Government took office. Yes, you are right, coalitions are not exactly easy to lead and to co-exist but the coalition of four parties which formed the Government in Slovakia is united on the necessity to bring Slovakia back to the family of the democratic civilised states which are based on the democratic values shared by EU and NATO countries. To explain more, we used the four weeks that were between the elections and the actual forming of the Government to discuss very substantially all the important issues among ourselves so that these political, economic or whatever issues would not jeopardise the future co-operation or holding-together of this coalition after it takes office, and we even could manage to set out the political principles which we shall follow together. Of course, we had a lot of discussions but it was demonstrated throughout all the time they were conducted that there is a strong political will to stay together and to form a Government which will last the full term of four years. You are right that there are different parties in this coalition. I do not have to mention that there is also the party of the Hungarian national minority, who are participating in the Government; they have three cabinet posts. So it is a real participation, not just an ornamental one. They are really participating in the functioning of Government. So far the Government is really working very well. We agreed on everything we were discussing, which was on the table. We enjoy the 93 votes in the Parliament which, as I mentioned in my introductory remarks, is a constitutional majority, because to change or amend the constitution you need 90 votes, three-fifths of the parliamentarians. That was used only once when Parliament changed the constitution as far as the elections of the Head of State are concerned. Up until now he was elected by the Parliament; now we shall have the direct vote of the President, the Head of State, and these elections will take place probably in May. So returning to your question, yes, I am pretty confident that this coalition will stay together. It is guided not by the necessity to remove the former government, as the first step in the way to introduce a democratic society in Slovakia, but the foreign policy goals of bringing Slovakia into the European Union and NATO, OECD and other European and transatlantic structures and to change the situation in the country, to implement all the democratic principles, to introduce the rule of law, respect for human rights and all these things, this is the real glue which holds the coalition together. So we are a positive coalition, we are a constructive coalition which wants to change the situation in Slovakia. Concerning the foreign policy, I would like to emphasise that all four parties are completely united. Each of them is completely and categorically for Slovakia's NATO membership, for Slovakia's EU membership, so there are no differences on these two basic issues of the foreign policy and it also, I am sure, will result in following the united line while pursuing our foreign policy goals.

Chairman: Thank you very much. Julian Brazier?

Mr Brazier

159. Could I turn attention, Dr Kukan, to the Washington Summit and ask what expectations you have from the outcome of that Summit? Perhaps I could put the second half of my question with the first half. What would your reactions be if, as now looks increasingly likely, there are simply no further invitations issued at Washington?

(*Dr Kukan*) What do we expect from the Washington Summit? We expect that the Washington Summit will confirm the open door policy and we expect that it would indicate, at least in general terms, what should be done to enter that open door, because we consider ourselves as standing there before that open door. We would very much like to enter. The sooner the better. We understand that we have to fulfil all the criteria and we are not asking for any discounts. We want to be really 100 per cent. in this fulfilment of the criteria and what we would ask the Washington Summit to do is evaluate the situation in Slovakia or in each country based on really an individual approach, and to judge us objectively by how really we fulfil these criteria. I would combine the two parts of your question. From our negotiations or from our discussions that we have had with our partners abroad, it is clear to us that there will be no names of countries or no invitations sent from the Washington Summit. It will not discourage us, no. On the contrary, we shall take it as a challenge to prove that we are a really worthy candidate and we still shall intensify our road to the membership. Here again, and I touched upon it gently in my introduction, we would very much like the Washington Summit to take into consideration what really happened in Slovakia. I mentioned that the people of Slovakia appreciated that both NATO and the EU in their dealings with Slovakia showed that they are interested in having co-operation with the Slovak people, maybe not with the Government but with Slovakia as a country. In the elections the voters spoke up very clearly. They voted for the parties which are pro-NATO, pro-EU, and now the Government,

[**Mr Brazier** *Cont*]

which is in existence as a result of those elections, in order to prove that we are serious, responsible, about the future membership, would very much appreciate some kind of appreciation or encouragement to show the people that their vote was noticed by NATO members and by European Union members—but we shall speak about NATO now. So that is what we expect, a little bit more than confirmation of the open door policy, to get some signal, positive mention in the documents or some kind of expression of the appreciation of the new situation, of the new political reality in Slovakia, so that the population see that their vote was not in vain. This is what we are also looking for. I cannot define what kind of expression or what kind of language it should be, but we will definitely be very glad if this is really taken into consideration when the final documents of the Washington Summit are prepared.

Mr Brazier: There is an obvious supplementary to that but it has actually been allocated to someone else. Thank you very much.

Chairman

160. But in the last round or the last Summit, some countries had raised expectations. Our Romanian colleagues were led to believe their chances were quite high and when those aspirations were not met it was quite damaging internally. Your Government has not tried, I am sure, to inflate expectations so that if there is no offer of any further enlargement immediately public opinion will be disappointed, that people might say, "There you are. You put your faith in NATO and they have slammed the door in your face"? Do you think public opinion has been quite realistic about this, Foreign Minister?

(Dr Kukan) The Government is very much aware of the situation, that it would be wrong to raise the expectations of the population. In the previous Summit in Madrid three countries were invited. Some of the countries were evaluated positively; there was some criticism of certain countries. Slovakia was completely ignored. It was not mentioned, neither negatively nor positively. I think that is the worst thing. It is better if somebody is criticising you, better than that they ignore you completely, and we know what was the reason behind it. It was the policy of the previous government, and I am glad you mentioned, Mr Chairman, in your welcoming me, that some four years ago Slovakia was completely at the same level as the three countries which are being invited now, and it is, of course, Slovakia's fault that we dropped out. We do not want to raise expectations. In my talks with my partners I was told repeatedly that Slovakia's Government should be realistic. It is not possible to make up for four years by doing a good job in a couple of months. The partners need some time to see that Slovakia is firmly on the road to NATO. We are told that Slovakia is on the right track, that we should keep it up, but now I really understand that four years is a long time, although, to be fair, I have to mention that the situation in the Slovak Army was not stagnant. There were several positive things that were going on in the preparation of the Slovak Army: our participation in the Partnership for Peace; our soldiers

participating in manoeuvres abroad, in Europe, in the United States, in Western European countries, so it would be wrong to say that there was no progress in the preparedness of the Slovak Army. Unfortunately, the most important things were not fulfilling the political criteria, because we understand that NATO is not only a military or security organisation, it is a family of countries or nations who share the same values concerning democracy and all these kinds of things, and that was where Slovakia completely failed to show its readiness. That is why my point is that this Government has taken a completely different approach. All that criticism—and I showed it in my introduction—concerning the shortcomings in the political field, in the field of democratisation of the country, have either been removed or we are tackling them now, and I am confident that in the first half of this year, by the end of June, let us say, or even earlier, it will be possible to say that Slovakia has fulfilled or is fulfilling the political criteria for NATO membership. I can say it with the utmost responsibility, and that is why we are asking for the recognition of this fact. We know that it would be wrong to prepare the population to expect too much of the Washington Summit but we still expect something, as I mentioned, some signal, some recognition, because if the situation is—I do not want to predict anything but if the situation is the same as in Madrid, that Slovakia is completely ignored, then I would take it as unfair dealing with my country and with my Government.

161. Would you like no country mentioned? Would you like just those countries that have a realistic prospect within the next thee, four or five years, of everybody in PfP who has expressed an interest in joining NATO? There will be some tactical problems of deciding how to encourage people without being so unrealistic as to assume that—I hope I am not offending Albanian friends but it is not an immediate prospect that Albania is going to meet the requirements of NATO. Should they get everybody in, nobody in, some in, in alphabetical order, in order of likelihood? Maybe you could offer some advice?

(Dr Kukan) I do not want to interfere in the decision-making process of NATO——

162. Everybody else does!

(Dr Kukan) But to return to your first remark, last week I was in Washington. I had the possibility of discussions with Secretary Albright and with some other officials from the State Department and the White House and they were asking me the same question and I found out that this question is being considered now, what would be the best way; what kind of language or what kind of information should be included in the documents of the Washington Summit. I definitely would not prefer the list in alphabetical order because Albania would be the first one. Capitals would be good to use.

163. In reverse order!

(Dr Kukan) Bratislava! But seriously, I do not want to elaborate too much really but I think it would not be absolutely fair if no mention of any country were the result of your considerations. I think it would

[**Chairman** *Cont*]

be really fair maybe to mention countries and put them into groups according to the state of preparedness for NATO membership. I think that would be much more encouraging.

Laura Moffatt

164.   Dr Kukan, it is good to speak to you, to spend some time with you. I would like to pursue the issue that my colleague Julian Brazier was taking forward of how you connect people with the decisions that governments are making. You quite clearly said that people voted for pro-NATO, pro-EU parties, so the statement was there that that is what they were looking for, and you very clearly said that it was important not to raise expectations, to go gently forward. I would really like a few words from you about the expectations of people within the country, and if it were true that they are very much pro-NATO, perhaps you could say a little something about the referendum that was held in May 1997 and your analysis of that, please?

   (Dr Kukan) Yes, you are right, our voters expressed their opinion about the political parties they would like to see in the Government, and these parties are pro-NATO, pro-EU, as you mentioned, and, of course, they expect that the Government they voted for would lead Slovakia, would push Slovakia, towards membership of NATO and the European Union. In accordance with the opinion polls which were conducted recently, the majority of the population of Slovakia support NATO membership, yet the Government has a plan to launch the information campaign, what it means to be a member of NATO, to explain everything to people in more detail as to what it would mean to be part of the North Atlantic Alliance. In May 1997 there was to be a referendum but practically it was thwarted by the Government and we say that the referendum was null and void because only 10 per cent. of the people participated and the way it was prepared by the Government was against the law. I think that this Government is going to investigate all the legal aspects of the referendum so that we have a clear answer as to what actually happened at that time. I am sure that provided the referendum was held in a correct way it would have brought a clear answer that a clear majority of the population of Slovakia would have been voting yes, that they are for NATO membership, but frankly, the way the questions were formed in that referendum I do not think that it was correct because they were leading questions and they were questions which we should not have asked the people because they were dealing with issues on which NATO countries had a clear position: the deployment of foreign troops on the territories, of nuclear arms in the territory of the country and so on and so forth. Frankly, the constitution of Slovakia does not require a referendum on NATO, so my political party held the position that it was enough if Parliament voted on it, that we did not need the referendum, but once it was passed in the Parliament that the referendum should be held, then we of course participated. We launched a very active campaign to persuade the people to go and vote yes, but then, unfortunately, by the action of the former

Government, the Minister of the Interior personally, who was responsible for that, practically it was not possible to hold this referendum in a correct way, in a correct form. So that result we cannot take as a serious answer or a serious expression of the will of the people that took place in that referendum. So I wish to say that the Government is explaining. The Government decided on very transparent foreign policy, especially in this issue of NATO and the European Union, so that the people have a clear picture of what it would mean to become NATO members, because there are a lot of questions asked: how expensive it is going to be to become a NATO member. People are concerned about the things which can affect their everyday life and we have to explain and to give objective information. I only say "objective" because it would be wrong to paint the picture in bright colours because I am sure it could backfire if we raised the expectation or if we explained only all the things positively. So we want to tell, and we are telling, the people the truth and it is better to know exactly what situation we are going to face and we are really confident that people understand that, for the future development of Slovakia, we have to be a part of the organisation that can secure our security for the future.

Mr Blunt

165.   Dr Kukan, the British Foreign Ministry have expressed to us their view on the New Strategic Concept of NATO in saying that it should "encapsulate the idea of NATO as an all-purpose organisation for dealing with security challenges relevant to Europe". Some would see that as being a tension in a sense between that and the traditional Article 5 centre of NATO and some people would go further and say that, indeed, the only priority for the aspirant member countries is to get hold of that Article 5 guarantee, that that is the sole focus of their interest. They would not want to see the New Strategic Concept changed in any way to water down the Article 5 guarantee or to see a change of emphasis to other missions. What is the view of Slovakia on the New Strategic Concept and where it should go?

   (Dr Kukan) We are sure (as I maybe mentioned) that Slovakia sees its future NATO membership not only as a one-way street, meaning that we are going to get the security umbrella for Slovakia, but we really want to contribute also to the effectiveness of NATO as a whole as the organisation as such. We think that the region of Central Europe is very sensitive and its stability or instability is really of interest and of importance for NATO and we want to play a constructive role in securing the stability of this region. So the New Strategic Concept we foresee as giving the role to NATO or accepting the new member states, that it is not going to affect negatively the overall performance of NATO as an organisation, and that the acceptance of new member states would actually increase the region of stability in Europe for the territory of the newly admitted countries and that that would definitely be in the interests of the Alliance.

166.   May I also come in with a supplementary to that because in a sense what you are putting there is a

[Mr Blunt *Cont]*

geo-strategic or geo-political argument as to why there is a benefit to NATO from Slovakian accession, amongst others, but what would Slovakia be able to contribute, and what would it want to contribute, to NATO's new missions? I understand you have a brigade being formed on a trinational or quadrinational basis, but would that be the extent of the contribution of forces available to contribute to NATO's missions outside of Article 5 operations or would you want to go beyond that?

(Dr Kukan) Yes, we are preparing in the Army of the Slovak Republic the units which would be used in cases of emergency situations—I do not know, rapid deployment or something like that. We are ready to participate in it and we are preparing our soldiers to be ready for that. That can be seen as a contribution, or future contribution, of Slovakia, and also, as I mentioned, we are going to send a contingent of soldiers to SFOR, which is run by NATO. Our soldiers have participated already in the peacekeeping operation in Eastern Slavonia and we have actual experience of working together. There we were working together with the Belgian Army but it was under the auspices of the United Nations peacekeeping. Now we are going to participate in the NATO-run operations. So in this we would be ready to contribute to the operations of NATO in any conflict areas by the participation of our units of soldiers in them.

Chairman: Thank you. Is there any follow-up to that question? We spent a good deal of time when we were in NATO looking at whether NATO should, in the Summit, restrict its area of competence in the future, particularly whether it should be constrained by authorisation to act from the UN Security Council and the OSCE or anybody else, and I think that is going to be the most contentious issue that is going to be decided in addition to whether there will be further membership. Could I ask my colleague Dari Taylor to ask the next question.

Ms Taylor

167. You have mentioned this morning—and we mention these words all the time—"defence", "security", "stability". It is the language of NATO and it is the language we all speak so convincingly today. You also mentioned in your introduction Partnership for Peace, which I see as one of the most positive, very definite, moves and developments in NATO, and we all know from our briefings with you and with other people that the PfP exercise in 1998 took place in Slovakia, and again we were persuaded by your desire to be interoperable with other forces. This is all very persuasive stuff and we realise just how keen you are to be part of NATO, but I would like to ask what lessons did Slovakia learn from its participation in Partnership for Peace and also, of course, its Euro-Atlantic Partnership Council? Could you start me off by talking about it? What has the Army learned, what have you learned as a governing force, from that involvement?

(Dr Kukan) By participating in many events organised within this programme of Partnership for Peace there are many lessons which our Army has

learned, mainly that, in order to be more interoperable with other armies, we have to increase the communications, the ways or instruments of communication. We learnt the lesson that we have really to increase the language training. It is really necessary. Without it you cannot work. We learnt that it is very sensible and rational to send more officers to the courses organised by NATO in NATO countries and we also learnt the lesson that our soldiers are in completely equal partnership with the soldiers of other armies. We also learnt that we really need to increase the level of the armaments used in the Slovak Army and in some cases we learnt that the arms which Slovak soldiers are equipped with can be used effectively, but there is a need to modernise the Army and by participating we got the idea of how far we have to go and what will be the necessary financial resources to support this modernisation. The lesson is that while participating in these events, exercises, manoeuvres, it is important, because it brings the attitude of belonging together to the same family and to the same group of nations and is also brought the lesson that Slovakia can be a partner and it is very important to be a partner in this organisation, which can provide the security for our future development as an independent state. As you know, Slovakia is a very young state and when it was formed back on 1 January 1993 many people were happy that at last we had an independent state and some of them tried to argue, "We are going to join NATO or EU. Is it right or is it not?" Now the answer is clear that even that independence of Slovakia can be secured only by being a member and part of these organisations. That is a very important lesson which we gained for our future in these terms.

168. We hear all your sense of commitment and determination to be part of NATO. What else could NATO do? You are obviously very involved in Partnership for Peace but what else could NATO do to encourage you that at some stage in the hoped-for near future you will be a member?

(Dr Kukan) I think that NATO and its member states should continue the co-operation that we have had so far. We want to be assured that all these projects will be going on and I do not see any particular grand schemes. I think that as the co-operation has been developing so far, we really want to have assurances that it will go on. The discussion, for example, which I had today with the Minister of Defence of Great Britain, Mr Robertson, and the discussion I am having here with you are already a very great contribution to our desire and to our commitment. So I would not say that we expect something spectacular. We expect the same treatment as we were getting before. We just want to stay on track.

169. More of the same?
(Dr Kukan) More of the same.

Chairman

170. Could I add to this and say I would like to inflate your expectations and demands in that if there is going to be no further immediate round of offers, I

think it is very important that NATO shows that it is not disappointing genuinely aspirant and competent nations and that it has to do more than it offered at Madrid, otherwise the perception will be, "Well, it is more of the same." So I think personally, and I think most of the Committee would agree, that NATO has to put its thinking hat on and say, "We have to provide more to those who are genuinely interested and genuinely capable and who will be very serious candidates at some stage in the not-too-distant future." So I would hope—and I do not want to advise you, Minister—that you push them really hard, please, on putting together a package that will give people the encouragement that we in NATO are serious about an open door. I think that is crucially important.

(Dr Kukan)   Thank you, sir, I will.

Ms Taylor

171.   My second question, or even third question, to you, Minister, is actually quite a difficult one. I am going to ask you about budgets and I say this from a position where the British defence budget has been slashed over a number of years. It is always looked at by other ministries as potential spend if they can get their hands on it. For most people defence, when there are no wars, presents us with a fairly complacent approach sometimes to the way in which we spend money. I am assuming the Slovakia Government does not feel complacent to be quite honest with you but I am going to ask you the commitment in NATO, the financial commitment, is actually quite a serious commitment. You already say you are spending two per cent of your gross domestic product which is a considerable size. You have already intimated that you can increase that two per cent by 0.1 per cent annually.

(Dr Kukan)   Yes.

172.   Are you absolutely confident that this year on year increase in budget is actually going to take place because I think it sadly really needs to take place?

(Dr Kukan)   Yes. We are absolutely sure that the increase is going to take place. Judging from the statements of my colleague in the government, the minister of defence, that is the minimum which has to take place. We take it as a minimum increase which would give the possibility to fulfil all of our obligations in a responsible way. The financial costs of modernising the army will be high, we understand it, we appreciate it. We know that it will be necessary to spend this money anyhow and if this money is spent while bringing us to NATO we think that it will be spent much more wisely and much more rationally than to do it simply on an individual basis. You are right, it is a lot of money. Many people during peace time, as you mentioned, when there are no wars tend to put questions as to whether it is necessary but now, unfortunately, due to many bad things happening in different regions of the world they understand that it is necessary to keep NATO or to keep the army. Although we said we do not have any enemies abroad there are not only enemies like states there are enemies like organised crime, Mafia, migration, all these kinds of things. Unfortunately there are many occurrences when you have to deploy the army or armed forces.

The latest development in the Balkans showed that. We in the government are really very serious. There was a long discussion before it was decided that we were going to follow this line which you have mentioned about the increase of the finances. Yes, we know about it but it is the only way to do it.

173.   I think to be very real is very appropriate. Is there any thought at all or belief, Minister, that NATO will actually take a resource or place a resource in Slovakia? Is there that belief, because I have heard that in other countries we have visited that there is a sense that a regional command centre may be taken there which would obviously be very important to the country's economy? Is there a belief that could well happen in Slovakia should membership come along?

(Dr Kukan)   We would welcome it and it would be very good but in that sense we do not have very big expectations.

Ms Taylor: I think that is appropriate.

Chairman: May I say, Minister, that if there are any additional commands to go I think I would like to put in a bid for the UK because we have actually lost a couple in the last few years. In terms of expenditure two per cent by the standards of a number of our NATO partners is quite high. On that subject, Mr Cann.

Mr Cann

174.   Sir, may I congratulate you on your command of English, it is at least better than nine out of ten of my countrymen. Before I touch on the main questions that I am to ask you, could I ask you about Ruthenia. Is there a problem with what we call Ruthenia, which is the piece of Slovakia which was transferred to the Ukraine? Is there a boundary dispute there at all?

(Dr Kukan)   No, that is not a problem. Several years ago I remember that the government, I think it was still Czechoslovakia, received some appeals from the Ruthenians living in Ukraine that they were mentioning the possibility of interest to be transferred to the territory of Czechoslovakia but that was not taken up by the government and I think that issue faded away. In the present time it does not create any problem or any issue and we are glad that it is like that because we really think that moving the borders or people beyond borders is a very sensitive issue and we want to keep the regional arrangement or stability as it is now.

175.   Could I ask you, secondly, are you sorry now that you are not still part of Czechoslovakia because if so you would be in NATO?

(Dr Kukan)   No, we are not sorry for that. As the time passes by people do not think much about the past, about Czechoslovakia, although there are some groups with nostalgic reminiscences about the old country. Forming of the independent Slovakia brought about a completely different situation in our country. All of a sudden people understood that they are the masters in their own house and they realised that it is not that easy to form the government, to run the country, to take all the responsibilities. It was a great challenge for Slovakia. The Slovaks perform best

[**Mr Cann** *Cont*]

when they are under difficult situations, solving difficult issues, to prove to the world that they can do well, because frankly they were looked upon as the weaker partner in the former Czechoslovakia. I have had many people in the United States who did not believe that we could make it to be on our own, so it was a challenge that took the best out of us. I think it has resulted in achieving good results for Slovakia. We persuaded those who did not believe that we could be a viable participant in international co-operation. The fact that we are not in NATO now does not discourage us and that is why I was saying we are not asking for any discounts, we want to prove that we can fulfil all the criteria that we can fulfil. All the commitments we took on and we want to be judged by our own merits. We think that each country should be judged by its own merits and we think that we can really make it. There was a time when the Czech Republic was looked upon as the one which was doing very well. I want to repeat what I said in my introduction. I am sure that the situation in Slovakia, be it economic, political, democratic, is completely comparable to the situation which exists now in the Czech Republic. We are going to prove that soon we shall be at the same level as them again. We appreciate that they are helping us, they are assisting us, all of the three countries—Hungary, Poland, the Czech Republic. It is not only political statements, they mean it. We are glad that the Visegrad group is going to act together again. We want to be equal partners in the activities of that group. It will be a different arrangement because there will be three NATO member states and one aspiring NATO member state. We think that Slovakia's role will result in a situation where it will be beneficial for them as well as to us, not only to us. That would be my answer to your question.

176. You are putting together the Austro-Hungarian empire again, are you?

(Dr Kukan) Not completely. You should not return to history, history is history, what is done is done. We should look to the future. We should remember some lessons from history but we are living in the real world today and we should work for the future. I do not want to sound too philosophical.

177. No problem, so am I. Slovakia has got no territorial disputes with anybody?

(Dr Kukan) No. We do not have any territorial disputes with anybody.

Mr Cann: Fine. Could I then come on to what I am supposed to be talking about.

Chairman: Yes, you may.

Mr Cann

178. Thank you, Chairman. In which areas do you think you can best help NATO militarily?

(Dr Kukan) We think that the areas in which we can best help NATO militarily is the situation in the conflict region of the Balkans, in Bosnia Herzegovina, in Kosovo maybe, because we think that Slovaks are perceived as friends in those countries, in those regions, and if it is necessary to use soldiers or the armies I think that Slovakia can be very useful in these operations.

Mr Cohen

179. I have a couple of questions. Firstly, can I just come back on this issue of no territorial disputes, which is what you said. Perhaps you could just say a little bit more about your relations with your neighbours, particularly Hungary I am thinking of because there is a large ethnic minority of Hungarians in Slovakia and that from time to time has caused problems. I would be very interested in your views about that. You also made a comment in relation to the Ukraine if I could pick that up as well. You said that at the present time this passport dispute does not create any problems.

(Dr Kukan) Yes.

180. It is sort of fading away. That does not necessarily mean that it is resolved. Is there any prospect of actually closing the file on it by getting an agreement in relation to any long standing border dispute which may not be a problem now but which could possibly flare in the future?

(Dr Kukan) Concerning the relations with our neighbours, yes, you are right that there are ten per cent or 11 per cent of Hungarians living in Slovakia and there were some problems around this issue. I am happy to say that the current situation in Slovakia with representatives of the Hungarian national minority participating in the government, in the leading positions in the parliament, has changed already. There were several issues which it was necessary to take up, like bilingual school certificates for pupils who attend the schools that teach the language of national minorities because the former government cancelled those although they were in existence in Slovakia for many, many years. That has been solved already. In the half term the pupils will get the bilingual certificates again. We are preparing the law on the use of languages of the national minorities. Again, it will be presented to the parliament and it will be passed in April or May of this year. There were some problems with funding or financing the cultural institutions of the Hungarian national minority, the theatres, the newspapers and the core ensemble. This government, with the participation of representatives of the Hungarian national minority, has solved or is going to solve these issues. That is the situation in Slovakia. With Hungary I think that we have a new atmosphere in our relations, it is not only changing barometric conditions but also substantially. There are no emotions. The relations are business-like. I think it will result in much stronger co-operation between the two countries in many fields. There is one question that we cannot agree upon and I am realistic that it will be very difficult to reach agreement and that is on the dam on the Danube which was built. This case was sent jointly by Slovakia and Hungary to the International Court of Justice which announced its decision but it has to be implemented by agreement of the two sides and we cannot reach an agreement so far. We are negotiating. You need patience, you need a cool head to reach agreement but so far there is no progress. The difference of opinion is too wide, the gap is too wide, but the encouraging news is that we have both agreed to consider it as a legal issue, not a political issue. The fact that we cannot agree on that

[Mr Cohen *Cont]*

has meant that it was decided that we shall put it aside and it is not going to negatively influence the co-operation in all other spheres, so we can live with it. Tomorrow there is another meeting of experts in Budapest concerning this issue. We are negotiating hoping that a miracle can happen but it will be very difficult. Otherwise we really enjoy good relations. My partner, Mr Martonyi, visited Bratislava and he signed the protocol which the former government could not sign for four years. On 12 February the Prime Minister is coming on an official visit to Slovakia. As you know, the day before yesterday there was a meeting of the Prime Ministers of Slovakia, Austria and Hungary again. We really enjoy good relations. The same applies to the Czech Republic. There is only one issue which is not finished yet which is the division of property. In any divorce it is very difficult, the most difficult issue, be it family or state. There was a delegation of the Prime Minister of the Czech Republic and he brought a group of ministers of his government and we signed the agreement that we are going to solve it during this year and by the end of the year it will be resolved. Then we could have some preferential kinds of relations because we were living together for 70 years and countries like those should enjoy some privileged relationship. That is what we are going to do. With Poland we do not have any problems. Now I think co-operation is going to be even more intensive. Concerning the Ukraine, yes, we have a 98 kilometre border with the Ukraine and we consider it a very important player in international relations with a lot of potential and after solving its economic issues and putting its act together could be even more important. We enjoy good neighbouring relations with them. You mentioned that it is better to close some issues which may not pose any threat now but which could be the case in the future. I really do not see the Ruthenia or any other issues to be of that nature or of that character that they can turn into a problem which can outgrow their importance in the future. Nobody mentions this issue and we do not get any references to it, so we prefer to leave it as it is because it really does not pose any serious issues looking at it from my side.

Mr Cann

181. In NATO terms it might. In NATO terms it is the only piece of what used to be COMICON or the Warsaw Pact, etc., that is within the lines of the Carpathian mountains.

(Dr Kukan) I think that everybody accepts the situation as it is now. If you had not reminded me I would never have thought about it. Okay, maybe we should pay some attention to it if you take it that seriously but for us it really does not represent a problem. Okay, I will take a lesson from this discussion that maybe we have to think about it again. So far it really is not a problem.

Chairman

182. It is not an official request from the Committee.

(Dr Kukan) Okay.

Mr Cohen

183. I am just raising it as a potential problem.

(Dr Kukan) I have noted what you said.

184. NATO does want countries in without problems with their neighbours, with settled borders. Can I change tack now and ask you a couple of questions on a different aspect in relation to your armed forces. One of my colleagues mentioned about your English, which is of course excellent, but is the English of your leading commanders in the armed forces good enough to go on with inter-operability with NATO forces? Another very important factor for countries in NATO is that their armed forces are under civilian control. Are you satisfied that there is sufficiently strong civilian control of the armed forces?

(Dr Kukan) Of course army officers use different language, command language. There are many high ranking officers who do speak English. Many of them underwent a course in the NATO countries but still it is not enough. That is why I mentioned that by building that training accord one of the main tasks is to increase the language training, the language preparation, because that is the basic requirement for inter-operability and compatibility of the Slovak army with NATO armies. It is being improved but we still have to go some distance to be completely satisfied. We know about it and we are paying a lot of attention to it now. The civilian control of the army, I think we are satisfied with that. The minister himself is a civilian and when there are visits from the NATO headquarters coming to Slovakia this question is evaluated in a positive way. Civilian control of the army has achieved the required level to be in accordance with the requirements of NATO. We know that it is one of the prerequisites for membership and we are keeping a close watch on it.

Chairman

185. Thank you very much. Perhaps one day your general staff will be located a little closer to the Ministry of Defence, that is the best method of establishing civilian control. How many kilometres away is your general staff?

(Dr Kukan) Around 100 kilometres.

186. Ideal for the military.

(Dr Kukan) 116 kilometres.

187. Could I, on behalf of the Committee, thank you very much for coming. We appreciate you putting the effort in to come and talk to us. We thank you, Ambassador, for all of the work that you are doing and I can tell you, Minister, that you are very well represented here by your ambassador and your embassy. May I thank the gentleman at the back, our Ambassador to Slovakia, who is indeed doing a sterling job with the defence attaché, which I can testify to personally. Good luck with the rest of your visit.

WEDNESDAY 3 FEBRUARY 1999

Members present:

Mr Bruce George, in the Chair

Mr Crispin Blunt	Mr Mike Hancock
Mr Julian Brazier	Mr Jimmy Hood
Mr Jamie Cann	Mr John McWilliam
Mr Harry Cohen	Laura Moffatt
Mr Michael Colvin	Ms Dari Taylor

Examination of witnesses

LT GENERAL SIR RODERICK CORDY-SIMPSON KBE CB, GENERAL SIR MICHAEL ROSE KCB CBE DSO QGM and PROFESSOR CEDRIC THORNBERRY, were examined.

Chairman

188. Gentlemen, welcome. We are honoured that you have found time to visit us. Sir Michael, I hope your left arm is not an indication that the MoD have been trying to dissuade you from giving evidence to us.
(General Sir Michael Rose) A sports injury!

189. As you know, we are at a fairly advanced stage of producing a report which will be published prior to the Washington Summit and, because you all have had very extensive experience throughout the world in recent years in the former Yugoslavia, we thought it would be particularly appropriate for you to give us your expertise. One of the many issues being discussed in the NATO capitals and in Brussels and Mons is Article 5 of the Washington Treaty and whether that will survive in that form, whether NATO can operate more outside Article 5 conditions, and that is something on which we would seek to elicit information from you. Again, because of your experience in the former Yugoslavia, we would welcome your comments on what is happening in Kosovo and whether one can extrapolate the experience you have gained in Bosnia to the crisis in Kosovo. There are some questions which it will not be incumbent upon you all to answer if you do not wish to answer, so please do not think we are expecting everyone to answer every question. What do you believe are the particular challenges of peace support operations from, first, a military and, secondly, a political perspective?
(General Sir Michael Rose) I think the challenges are to ensure that the mandate that originally gets given to the organisation, whether it be a regional power like NATO or whether it be the United Nations "come-as-you-are" party, which is what I call it, spells out the limitations of a peace support operation as well as the aspirations of the international community for that particular operation. The limitations in my view are very clear. Peacekeeping forces cannot act in the same way that an army of occupation can act. It cannot pursue war-fighting goals, it cannot deliver just solutions, it cannot punish aggressors, it cannot defend territory, it cannot enforce passage of convoys everywhere all the time, it cannot stop ethnic cleansing. What it can do by its presence is first of all

alleviate the suffering because of course it will inevitably be involved in humanitarian aid in the sort of situation one finds in Bosnia or in Rwanda or in Kosovo. It will also by its presence ultimately create the conditions in which there can be some peaceful settlement of the problem. The difficulty that I see with some of NATO's utterances over Kosovo is that they are confusing what can be done by a war-fighting force with what can be done by a peacekeeping force, and there are great dangers in that. We cross the Mogadishu line and we end up in the situation in which we found ourselves in Somalia.

190. What difficulties would you have encountered with your experience in Bosnia in terms of the mandate you were given?
(General Sir Michael Rose) The mandate is bound to change all the time. The United Nations responds to crises as they develop. The United Nations Security Council resolutions relating to Bosnia started at about 740 I think it was. By the time I got there we were up in the 900s and many of them were conflicting. My predecessor resigned from the job because he said he could not get a clear idea as to what the mission was supposed to be. I had a different view in that, having culled through all those United Nations Security Council resolutions, it was quite clear to me that the primary role of the United Nations' protection force in Bosnia, not in Croatia but in Bosnia, was to facilitate the delivery of humanitarian aid. The secondary role was to try and create those conditions in which there could be a peaceful resolution to the conflict, and the underwritten third element within the mission was to prevent the conflict from spreading. It was ensuring that we never moved outside those three elements of the mission that proved the greatest challenge because of course NATO, largely driven by American politics, was pursuing another mandate, which was not impartial; it was pursuing war fighting goals and trying to get the United Nations to do it for them on the ground, although they provided the air power. It was to stop that happening, which of course would have caused a collapse of the UN mission, which was the great challenge I faced, and in the end we succeeded. We persuaded the Americans that had they forced the United Nations into using higher levels of force than were appropriate or pursuing war fighting goals, then

[Chairman *Cont*]

half the troop-providing nations would have withdrawn their troops because they would have been put at risk by that. The state of Bosnia would have been severely threatened because of course people forget that the Serb army were extremely powerful in 1993 or 1994 and were within a hundred metres or so of the presidential palace, and "lift and strike" would not have helped the state of Bosnia or the people of Bosnia, and the American troops would ultimately have had to come on the ground to secure the state and we would have got into a terrible situation of confrontation. In the end we succeeded in persuading them, mainly Richard Holbrooke, of the logic.

(Professor Thornberry) I agree what Sir Michael Rose has said. I think I would also, in looking at the question of the especial challenge of peace support operations from a political standpoint, look on the one hand at UN supported operations or the UN created operations in NATO and other regional organisational operations. I think there are a number of factors which can be significantly different. If I can address first of all the question of UN operations, about which perhaps I know more than about NATO operations, I agree with General Rose in his reference to the need for an agreement at the mandating level, in other words at the Security Council level. Although agreement has been easier to acquire in the Security Council over the last five or six years than it was in the previous 45 or so, that agreement has not always been capable of being translated into operations on the ground. I think there has to be a clear mandate and again, to refer to the incident involving General Briquemont, the Belgian general who preceded Sir Michael, he actually said to a press briefing, which was a fairly strong thing for a general to do, that he did not even bother to read Security Council resolutions any longer because they were so frequent, so inconsistent and so lengthy, which tends to be a sign of lack of agreement in any event. In Yugoslavia we rarely had a clear mandate and there were various other problems as well about those mandates which one could go into later if the Committee so sought. Another point I would like to emphasise is the absolute necessity for a peacekeeping or peace support force to have the continuing backing of the mandating authority. If I may give an example of that, I was in Namibia which was regarded at the time and since I think as having been one of the most successful of UN operations. It was not only successful because of the enormous virtue and ability of those running it, but it was very successful because we had continuous backing from the governments in question. My boss, Marti Abtasari, and I habitually would find on a Monday morning for example that we had the de facto ambassadors of the UK and the US and possibly the then USSR waiting on our doorstep saying, "We hear you have been having nasty trouble with the South Africans. Is there any little thing you would like us to do about it?" We would say, "Yes, please go to Pretoria and put on your boots." That was standard practice. We had continuous backing when something went wrong. The governments which had brought about the operation gave us their support because the UN on its own is not an effective channel for pressure unless it has that backing. In contrast, during the two years that I was in Yugoslavia, I cannot really remember any such instance in which I was visited by the ambassadors, whether of the European Union or of the United States, other than to complain perhaps about some of our troops having got drunk the previous night. It was a dramatic contrast in these two specific missions. I will leave that at this point, except for this, if I may. I would like to plug at this point the necessity for co-ordination on the ground, and I think this is a political issue, it is also an operational issue, and I am sure we will come back to it. I know that Sir Michael has written extensively about this and I personally, having done four or five operations in different parts of the world, am quite obsessive about it, but it does have a political base.

191. Please do not feel constrained, Sir Michael, from mentioning your truly excellent book, publisher and price, and we will happily hold up a copy to the television camera if you take me out for lunch afterwards! General Cordy-Simpson?

(General Sir Roderick Cordy-Simpson) I have not got much to add. We must start at the mandate. When I went into Bosnia in 1992 we had a very woolly mandate. From that inevitably one of two things happen. You either get into mission creep, which politically will cause problems elsewhere, or you get into mission paralysis, which is the other danger. No one will do anything because they are terrified of stepping over a very imprecise mandate because it has not been clearly spelt out. Politicians in the various nations of the contributing forces will interpret the mandate in different ways. That is what definitely happened in the very earliest days when I was there and Cedric was up in Zagreb. We were getting different directives from our national capitals which meant that Philippe Morrillon, the commander on the ground, was getting each nation interpreting it their own way on how he should employ their forces. There was a series of alternative chains of command. Some wanted mission creep; some wanted mission paralysis as much as they could. From a straight military point of view I think that the mandate should if possible identify what could be called a measure of success, and therefore what is your exit strategy and what are you trying to get to. Again I know it was not there in those early days. From that you can get your force structure right because again you do not just send troops in. I do not know but I have always been confused as to how the forces that arrived in 1992 with me ended up with one Orthodox battalion, one Roman Catholic battalion and one Muslim battalion. I do not know what went on in New York but it was clearly not the right force structure for what we were trying to achieve there. The final point I would make, because there are many that will come up in subsequent questions, is that the political/military interface is of great importance and, to be honest with you, it was not there in the early days. I say this with Cedric sitting on my right. We were getting so many different directives coming out of New York when they happened to be at work, because of course in

3 February 1999]

Lᴛ Gᴇɴᴇʀᴀʟ Sɪʀ Rᴏᴅᴇʀɪᴄᴋ Cᴏʀᴅʏ-Sɪᴍᴘsᴏɴ ᴋʙᴇ ᴄʙ,
Gᴇɴᴇʀᴀʟ Sɪʀ Mɪᴄʜᴀᴇʟ Rᴏsᴇ ᴋᴄʙ ᴄʙᴇ ᴅsᴏ ǫɢᴍ
and Pʀᴏғᴇssᴏʀ Cᴇᴅʀɪᴄ Tʜᴏʀɴʙᴇʀʀʏ

[Continued

[**Chairman** *Cont*]

those days they did not even man the duty desk 24 hours a day. I remember classically the safe areas issue. We had not been consulted in any form, shape or size about the safe areas when we were told that five towns were to become safe areas. When I managed to get a fax back saying, "What do you mean by a safe area? Does it mean out of artillery range or out of rifle range?", because it does make a difference of about 30 kilometres in distance, I could not get an answer because of course you could then determine the size of force structures. The political/military interface has got to be fully there so you do not get things that are unimplementable on the ground.

192. Was the confusion that made your task difficult the result of too many organisations involved, naivety, stupidity? Were there any ways in which it was feasible for you to have been given more precise instructions?

(General Sir Michael Rose) I think it was more than just confusion, naivety, stupidity. There were very firm political agendas being pursued by different elements within the international community and it did make it very difficult for the United Nations who, after all, are only the servants of the international community, to come up with a clear definition. If you take the example of the safe areas, 836 was originally designed to defend and protect and the United Nations Secretariat spent a lot of time with the sponsors of that resolution explaining to them that peacekeeping forces cannot protect or defend. The best they can do is by their presence deter attacks against and report when there are attacks, and a safe area depends on respect for that area from both sides in the conflict. They did finally get that through and the wording in 836 is very specific. But no-one ever reads 836. The propaganda machines of different elements around the world went into action to persuade the world that the United Nations' troops had a duty to defend or protect, which they never did. Today we still get criticisms of the Dutch for not standing and fighting when the Bosnian Army turned and ran.

193. Yesterday I met a Dutch politician who said their Defence Committee has been obsessed for the last couple of years with the whole issue of Srebrenica. Any topic somehow turns to that issue.

(General Sir Michael Rose) They were traumatised.

(Professor Thornberry) Might I add this. I think that Roddy Cordy-Simpson had a very bad experience in those early months in 1992 when UNPROFOR, which had been created initially to deal with Croatia, began getting mandates of a humanitarian kind in regard to Bosnia. What happened then was in my experience quite unprecedented in UN practice. It was arranged that a detachment from NATO, a unit with I think a NATO headquarters, should be moved bodily from western Europe and placed in Bosnia to support, as I remember, the Canadians, Lou Mackenzie and his guys, who were implementing the agreement on Sarajevo airport, the humanitarian mandate. There was a great deal of confusion in regard to this and there was even a certain amount of disagreement between the western governments and the Secretary-General of the United Nations as to how that detachment should be put together, what level of consultation there should be, how it should be financially and logistically supported, and so on. The outcome of this was, and I remember quite vividly such an incident taking place, that round about September 1992 at the end of the afternoon I was sitting with my force commander, who was an Indian three star from Namibia, and our chief of operations, a Danish brigadier-general, watching CNN, which was carrying live film of landings which the commentator asserted were by NATO forces on the coast of Croatia and these battalions who were coming in and who were apparently making unopposed amphibious landings, were coming in to be placed under the mandate of the UN's force commander and UNPROFOR. The thing was, we knew nothing about this. I remember my force commander saying, "Cedric, did anybody write to you about this?" I had to say, "Not really." Roddy Cordy-Simpson may remember that during the first six months of the UNPROFOR in Bosnia, it was not a force under UN command. It was a very delicate process of melding these two forces which, for one reason or another, at high level outside the country, had not been co-ordinated in the first instance. It was quite unique in my experience.

(General Sir Roderick Cordy-Simpson) I think though that we will have to acknowledge the fact that had we not taken a NATO headquarters, (it was the Northern Army Group Headquarters), I do not think we would ever have managed to get into Sarajevo and Bosnia at all. I was lucky. I was the chief operations commander in the army group at the time and I was told to pick up the headquarters and move it down there because after the demise of the Warsaw Pact we were available. We were therefore able to pick up headquarters, we were able to move it straight in at very short notice, and all I had to do was effectively leave behind my Germans who could not come with me, but all the rest, my Belgians, Dutch and Brits, came with me. I have to say even my four Americans came with me although the Americans never knew that I had four Americans in Sarajevo at the time. Then I filled it up with Spanish and French and Canadians when I got down there. If we had not had a structure I think we would never have achieved that, because it was on 18 September that I was warned and we were there by the 5 October; it was an ad hoc business.

(Professor Thornberry) I do not doubt that all.

(General Sir Roderick Cordy-Simpson) I think there are some great advantages in taking a formed NATO headquarters.

(Professor Thornberry) I agree.

(General Sir Roderick Cordy-Simpson) Of course we were still getting orders from two different directions. I was not aware that those two different directions were coming. After we were on the ground I never got a single order from NATO subsequently. I only got them from the UN. I never ever got NATO interference at any stage in those six months that I was there.

3 February 1999]   Lt General Sir Roderick Cordy-Simpson kbe cb,
General Sir Michael Rose kcb cbe dso qgm
and Professor Cedric Thornberry   *[Continued*

Mr Hancock

194. I am interested in what lessons have been learned because obviously you yourself, General, have written to suggest that when you have two mandates it can be a problem, but if you have a dual key and somebody takes control of it, it can be overcome. There were obviously pretty significant problems there, where the mandates were conflicting, where the soldiers on the ground were put in pretty difficult positions, as the Dutch were and as the Belgians obviously were. What lessons have been learned and is part of the problem the lack of real military knowledge in New York when the mandate is put together, because when we visited from the NAA to New York last year, one of the criticisms that came back to us was the lack of real support at the top in the UN of a military nature. They had one general there, a Dutch marine, who was extremely good at presenting his case, but I think he would have been the first to admit that he was a failure in the sense that it was he alone who was giving military advice to people who were then producing political mandates which could not be delivered on the ground.

(General Sir Michael Rose) The lesson that comes out of it is very clear, and that is that if you are dealing with complex emergency situations under Chapter VII arrangements, it is far better to use a coherent military organisation such as NATO to deploy into that theatre of operations, and the United Nations is far better suited for the old style Chapter VI, where it can deal better with civilian communities and civil reconstruction. The tragedy for Bosnia of course is that NATO did not see it as part of its role in 1991 when it wrote its new strategic guidelines to get involved in peace support operations beyond the border of its member states. Today of course the situation is very different, so I think that lesson has been learned. I think if one had a similar situation, and one may find it in Kosovo, it is obviously far better to deploy NATO with its common doctrine, common command and control, high technology capability, into that theatre of operations with all the limitations of any peacekeeping. Because it is militarily strong it does not mean to say it can use higher levels of force necessarily than UNPROFOR do, but nevertheless it is far more effective in a Chapter VII situation than the UN would be.

195. In administrative terms are the UN prepared to give up their involvement to NATO in those situations?

(General Sir Michael Rose) Tacitly I think that has happened.

(Professor Thornberry) I am not quite sure that it necessarily follows from the Bosnian experience that the UN is not capable of carrying out a Chapter VII operation. I think that there are indeed a number of lessons to be drawn from the Bosnian experience and I believe that the UN has actually learned a number of these. Certainly NATO has learned them. One of these is the danger that both my distinguished colleagues have referred to of the peacekeeping force on the ground being given an enforcement role when they have neither the resources nor the deployment, nor the political backing to conduct such an operation. I believe that IFOR and SFOR have certainly learned that lesson and I think the UN has learned it as well. May I also add that in looking at the United Nations effectiveness under today's conditions one has to remember that the UN is really walking on the very edge of bankruptcy on a continuous basis at the moment because of the withholding of contributions, mainly though not exclusively by the United States. It is virtually impossible for the Secretary-General to plan or to run any kind of operation at the moment. Governments are beginning to be very reluctant to commit soldiers to UN command because they know that at the moment there are no funds with which to pay it. The UN is having to raid its peacekeeping budget in order to manage to maintain the utilities. I think there are quite special circumstances at the moment which inhibit the UN as well.

Ms Taylor

196. What we are talking about is very serious. All three of you have made a statement that in different ways there is a disjuncture between governments and governing forces and possibly even the will to define appropriate military action. That is a very serious statement for all of us to try and get our heads around. None of you has actually identified something which I thought was quite crucial in Yugoslavia and Bosnia, and that was the nature of the conflict. Most people were unprepared to know whether they were defining the nature of the conflict appropriately or accurately, and certainly soon enough. There was very clearly in Britain a sense of disbelief that this was happening on our doorstep and people were actually trying to get their minds around what extent of conflict, how great a conflict, how quickly could we in any way cope with peacekeeping. Surely it is not just that we are talking about deployment of forces or appropriateness. It is actually having the intelligence to define what is the nature of this conflict and how long? Your statement there, and it was a very quick one about defining exit strategies, was such an appropriate statement because once we have defined how we get out we know why we are going in. Surely that is very much more than the most profound way of approaching any conflict. Most particularly we look back on our own. This is not going to be the last, sadly. This is going to be one of many more, I am convinced about that. I would appreciate it if you would look at the way in which intelligence informs government but informs governments in ways which they understand, not in ways the military understand. There is a very clear need here to communicate very much more effectively.

(General Sir Roderick Cordy-Simpson) I agree with you totally in what you have just said, but the facts are that we were totally unprepared, and we should not have been, for what happened in the Balkans. We did not understand the nature of the conflict when we went in. We went in, dare I say it, in reaction to some of those ITN pictures of the concentration camp and "something must be done"

3 February 1999] Lᴛ Gᴇɴᴇʀᴀʟ Sɪʀ Rᴏᴅᴇʀɪᴄᴋ Cᴏʀᴅʏ-Sɪᴍᴘꜱᴏɴ ᴋʙᴇ ᴄʙ,
Gᴇɴᴇʀᴀʟ Sɪʀ Mɪᴄʜᴀᴇʟ Rᴏꜱᴇ ᴋᴄʙ ᴄʙᴇ ᴅꜱᴏ ꞯɢᴍ *[Continued*
and Pʀᴏꜰᴇꜱꜱᴏʀ Cᴇᴅʀɪᴄ Tʜᴏʀɴʙᴇʀʀʏ

[Ms Taylor *Cont*]

attitude. I remember one of the briefing packs that I was sent by the Foreign Office in those three weeks as I went up to headquarters, which did tell me while I was in Yugoslavia—I can remember it quite clearly—what flora and fauna I would find, that lead-free petrol would be difficult to find (there was not a single petrol station that had not been blown up by the time we got there), what type of money would be used not that there was a bank because they had all been raided by then. To be honest, we were living in the Dark Ages. We had militarily no intelligence virtually, and certainly at the strategic level I do not think the nation had much true understanding of the nature of the conflict. I do not know at what stage we should have begun to understand it, probably in the early stages of the Croatian/Serb war that started at Vukovar or subsequently, I do not know, but we did not understand the conflict when we deployed. Certainly bigger players on the scene did not understand it because to most there were just good guys and bad guys, particularly in America, and that is why I do not think we ever had a consensus of clear reason for going in and therefore what we defined as success for an exit strategy.

Mr Colvin

197. It is interesting that all three witnesses, in answer to your original question, have homed in on the question of the mandate. I wondered if they would reflect on the UN Charter and say whether they feel that we ought to revisit the Charter in the light of events post-1989, or whether it is always reasonable to have the fallback of a United Nations Security Council resolution. You can take military action with the authority of the Charter without having to have a resolution. Should we revisit the Charter in the light perhaps of Boutros Boutros-Ghali's Agenda for Peace? Does it need to be rewritten?

(Professor Thornberry) Might I add something to my colleague's previous answer, and perhaps I might briefly attempt to address your question. I am really not sure that the problem with defining our purposes in Bosnia or indeed in any other mission that I have participated in relates to a failure of intelligence. I think that either before we have gone in or while we are there and are beginning to report back there has tended to be fairly high quality analysis and the situation which has been described I have found, going in usually as the chief political representative of the UN, is fairly accurate. I do not think that the problem has been that. Habitually again, in Yugoslavia, and in this case it was in Croatia in regard to the Krajina situation which we have not alluded to yet, although we repeatedly informed the people back home what was going on, the situation and what we saw as the dangers, that information was being fed into the Security Council in its private consultations, but was not being taken into consideration because at that stage there was a demonisation of the Serbs and it was impossible for the Security Council to look at any broader aspect. My feeling is that it has very often been not a lack of intelligence, whether military or

political intelligence, going back to those who create or shape or change or develop the mandate. Rather it has been other political factors which sometimes, dare I say it, relate to the desire of the Security Council to take a particular posture with regard to governments in that location. The other point, if I may make an attempt to answer your question, sir, is that I think there are a number of aspects of Charter revision which should be looked at, in particular for example the membership of the Security Council, which is an undertaking that has been going on for some time without too much success. I personally feel that the principle of the Charter of the United Nations, which is that there shall be no resort to force other than in self-defence and other than in implementation of a Security Council mandate with, I might add, the explicit authority of the Security Council, is a good foundation upon which we can go into the next millennium. I feel that if anything one needs to revisit and refresh those provisions rather than revise them.

(General Sir Michael Rose) I would absolutely agree with that point of view. Just picking up one point about exit strategies, although you can define a conflict, and I think there was a lot of understanding as to what was going to happen in the Balkans, I mean, President Izetbegovic in 1992 predicted what would happen and asked for preventative deployment by NATO, and I think had they deployed that would have allowed the JMA to withdraw without creating civil war in Bosnia, but of course his request was turned down. In these situations where deep-rooted rivalries and nationalism, ethnic differences and so on emerge, the talk of an exit strategy is unwise. When people ask me what would happen after SFOR, I say S5, S6, S7, keep counting. You cannot solve in a thousand days things which have taken a thousand years in gestation. The idea of an exit strategy is tremendous for something like the expulsion of the Iraqi troops from Kuwait, but in these complex situations it has no meaning at all, and I think the Americans have come to understand that.

198. In the light of NATO's new strategic concept, which is going to be debated in Washington, do you think there are any broad parameters which ought to be set? Could one say that there are certain sorts of crisis that NATO should never become involved in and there are others where NATO very much should be involved? In answering that question perhaps you could also comment on the suggestion that, given the inefficiencies of multinational operating, the problems of having no clear enemy, and the absence of clear military goals, which can obviously result from UN Security Council resolutions, that we should be very cautious about deploying the military to resolve political crises in places like Kosovo? You can answer that one obviously with the benefit of hindsight. To pick up on Namibia, we did not do anything about Namibia because everybody knew what the political outcome was going to be, so it was a great deal easier. In the Balkans it is far from clear.

(General Sir Michael Rose) There obviously is a limit to what NATO can do. It cannot be the world's

3 February 1999]

Lt General Sir Roderick Cordy-Simpson kbe cb,
General Sir Michael Rose kcb cbe dso qgm
and Professor Cedric Thornberry

[Continued

[Mr Colvin *Cont]*

policeman. There are some situations which do not lend themselves to a resolution peacekeeping means. We should not try to do that. There are better places to invest your peacekeeping efforts. I do think that the current programme for example of giving the OAU, which is being run by the Americans, the Danes and ourselves, their own peacekeeping capability and understanding the doctrines, the limitations, the technology that is required and so on, and the training, is a very useful thing indeed. It is far better to use NATO in its own theatre if you like in Europe and use the Africans in Africa than to try and say that NATO has some sort of magic which we can deploy anywhere in the world. The difficulty is that we are in an imbalance at the moment, that NATO really is the only organisation which has the capability and when one is faced with these horrendous situations in Africa one gets the urge to do something. Going to Kosovo, I think NATO has made a very prudent and sensible start which indeed reflects many of the lessons we have been talking about: the appointment of verifiers to see exactly what is going on with some loose political agreement is a start. My own view is that the next step if the war does break out again or there is more ethnic cleansing by the Serbs is to deploy NATO in a preventative role along the borders of Kosovo and Albania. People forget that there was preventative deployment of troops into Macedonia in 1993 and the war never spread into Macedonia. The Serbs once tried to cross the line into Macedonia but were seen off by those UN troops and it has been highly successful. The deployment of troops along the border between Albania and Kosovo, which is only just over a hundred kilometres long, would have two effects in my view. Political signals first of all would be sent to the KLA that we were going to exercise some control over them, and secondly, it would send a message to Milosevic saying, "If you do not abide by the agreements that we are about to achieve then we will do a train and equip programme for the KLA in the same way that we did for the Croatian Army and look what happened to your Krajinas." I would not stick them in straight away. I think you would be a hostage to fortune. Kosovo would be the next step beyond that.

Chairman

199. Especially where one or two of the parties resented the intrusion.

(General Sir Michael Rose) Peacekeepers always end up getting shot at by all sides. The next step in the escalator would be a preventative deployment on the border and then only after that would there be any air strikes and possibly deployment on the ground, but then you are talking about an army of occupation and a war.

Mr Brazier

200. So then we are talking about an army of occupation and a war, and an occupation that would go on for a very long time?

(General Sir Michael Rose) Sure. You are imposing then a political settlement which can only be done by force of arms. That is not a peacekeeping mission. That is a war.

(General Sir Roderick Cordy-Simpson) The question though is surely timing. If you leave it too late and the thing goes into a raging war such as we had in Bosnia. You are not into a preventative deployment at that stage. You are automatically in war fighting the moment you cross the frontier and you are dragged into it. If your preventative deployment is to be accurate and successful I believe it has got to go in before the thing explodes. That is a very difficult decision to make and a very difficult one of timing. We have all known that Kosovo was, in the American jargon, going to go south on us since 1992. It was just when it was going to go south, and it is now going very fast. If we do not get something in to support some form of political settlement there, I think it could drag us in in a very nasty way with it being very difficult to define success, very difficult to define exit strategies, and so I do not totally agree with General Rose. I think we could go back and we could look at Dayton. At Dayton's time I believe we were right to have gone in with a small monitoring force into Kosovo because Milosevic was on the ropes and I think he would probably have signed up if he had been pressurised to a monitoring force going in. I am sure that preventative deployment should be sooner rather than too late, although it is a difficult judgement.

(Professor Thornberry) On the question of preventative deployment, this has been a favourite subject of many non-governmental organisations and many writers for a long time, but one should not underestimate the practical and political problems about talking of a preventative deployment. I had something to do with setting up the Macedonian operation at the end of 1992, beginning of 1993. The reason that we were able to do that was that the authorities in Macedonia were so overwhelmingly enthusiastic that we should do this that they more or less for example gave us free run of their broadcasting system in order to tell the people about what we were doing and so on. It was an absolutely extraordinary rolling out of the red carpet for the United Nations. If one can think of many other instances, and Chairman you will forgive for example the residue of my Ulster accent, I wonder how the British Government might have reacted for example in 1966 had there been a well-intentioned suggestion by the United States that perhaps there were problems in Northern Ireland and it might be an idea to have a little international presence there to go and look at it. How would a British Government have reacted and how difficult would it have been, even for our cousins across the Atlantic, to have made such a well-intentioned suggestion. I do think that there are a lot of problems about this and one has to prepare the ground and be very cautious about using the concept. In the case of Kosovo it was my job at one stage informally to take up the question of Kosovo with Mr Milosevic in 1992, and I never ran into such a resoundingly thick, solid,

3 February 1999]

Lt General Sir Roderick Cordy-Simpson kbe cb,
General Sir Michael Rose kcb cbe dso qgm
and Professor Cedric Thornberry

[Continued

[Mr Brazier *Cont*]

negative wall: absolute refusal even to discuss the matter on an informal basis.

(General Sir Roderick Cordy-Simpson) It is the heart of his nationalist aspirations. On the 28 June 1989 he made his speech that set the Balkans on fire, so to him at that stage, in 1992, you could not have expected him to say, "I would be very happy to have a little monitoring force in there." I think though when we came to 1995 and Dayton he was on the ropes. That might have been the time to have forced the issue, but it is history now.

Mr Cann

201. What on earth interests NATO to have got into places like Kosovo and Bosnia and why are we involved in any case? Are we just the United Nations mercenary force? Secondly, I have heard newspaper reports at least that if we do go into Kosovo in land force terms, then it would be mainly British troops in there, certainly not Americans. Are we not paying a price for the fact that we have got the headquarters of the Allied Rapid Reaction Corps under our control and that the only fully functioning division that it has got under its control is British?

(General Sir Roderick Cordy-Simpson) In answer to the second part of your question, because it is the easier one to answer, is that we have command of the ARCC, as we have committed both of our major divisions to it. It gives the ARRC a very strong war fighting capability and that gives us considerable influence in military spheres and in NATO. That is really worth remembering. We have terrific influence as a result of command of the ARRC. I do not think for one minute though that it automatically follows that the ARRC has to be (and I see no reason why it should be) the headquarters capable of going into Kosovo.

202. It has been reported that that was the case.

(General Sir Roderick Cordy-Simpson) Maybe, but I am just talking as someone who is now a civilian. I do not see that it has to be the ARRC in any way at all, because the ARRC cannot be committed every time to every crisis that NATO faces. As to why it is in NATO's interest, I think it is exactly the same interest as it is throughout the Balkans. We have got a potentially explosive situation that could rapidly go over the boundaries into Albania, down into Macedonia, and all the rest of it that will follow. That is someone else's decision, not mine, but I would have thought there were some very good reasons to stop that happening. It is a pretty frightening thought to me anyway.

203. I rather thought that NATO was set up as a security organisation for the members of it. I was not aware that Bosnia or Kosovo or Macedonia or anybody else were actually members.

(General Sir Roderick Cordy-Simpson) I think the world has moved on since those days in 1992. That is my feeling.

(General Sir Michael Rose) What you are saying is that they should not deploy it to Bosnia as IFOR and SFOR, in which case the war would not have ended.

204. That is not what I am saying, General. I am asking for your view on that postulation, which is different.

(General Sir Michael Rose) I very much support what Roddy is saying, that the British command and the provision of some sizeable forces to the ARRC has been a very strong influence in giving NATO a wider view than it previously had. I think that is extremely good. The alternative at the time was that it was going to go under German command and we would have had a very different response from NATO to a place like Bosnia had the Germans been in command at that time. I think it has been a tremendously positive step, good for NATO, good for the British people. In terms of the ARRC commanding in Kosovo, of course it could never be there anyway ad infinitum. There would have to be rotations and if it was not one of the first lot to be in there, for sure it would be the second or the third lot. Normally they rotate every six months or a year at the worst, so it is bound to have a presence there at some point.

Chairman: I think the General's brief from the Foreign Office did point that Yugoslavia is in Europe. I think mr Cann was just asking a provocative question.

Mr Blunt

205. I would like to develop the theme that Mr Cann started, which was a remark he made about the changing nature of NATO, how up until 1989 effectively a consensus decision would be taken as to whether to launch a defensive war, and that was about the only political decision in a sense that the North Atlantic Council would take, and then it would be into what was regarded as a third world war largely under NATO military control but would in effect be under the command of the United States, an armed control system largely. On Monday, when the Foreign Secretary made his statement on Kosovo in the House, he said that the North Atlantic Council had delegated authority to the NATO Secretary-General to respond militarily, depending on the reaction of the various parties in Kosovo to the contact group's statement. When I asked him about that, whether that actually meant that the Secretary-General then had authority to put forces into action and, if so, what British forces were then at his disposal, he then hastily said, well of course the British Government would be expecting consultation back on exactly what was going to be done and all the rest of it and there would be a process of consultation, which suggests that we are now moving from having had a very clear single political decision to take to a rather cumbersome, consensus based, political structure above the military in NATO. Whilst the military structure is being reformed and we are for example moving towards a more expeditionary force-based capability, do you think that the political and decision making structure of NATO needs to be reformed? Is NATO capable of setting realistic military goals today for new missions, or do you believe that the consensus model of decision making is going to be sustainable into the future? Are we going

[**Mr Blunt** *Cont*]

to have to move to change the nature of how we take decisions in the North Atlantic Council?

(General Sir Michael Rose) I think there is a period of time that has elapsed between the Article 5 limitation if you like of NATO with the end of the Cold War and what has happened since. Surely the NAC over the intervening years has evolved as an organisation and has taken some very sensible, some very realistic, some very positive steps first of all in Bosnia and now subsequently in discussing Kosovo. I think the mechanisms are there. Whether they need improving or not is not for a military man, who lives at the bottom of a trench and has a narrow view of the world, to say. I do believe that the goals that are achievable by NATO are well within the capabilities of the NAC to define. I cannot see any great problem at all. If you enlarge NATO too much then of course you are getting an increasing number of competing national agendas and you may end up in the same position as the United Nations where there are 185 nations and it is very hard to get them to concur.

206. Would you all say that you are content with how the NAC operates as a political director of military operations today?

(General Sir Roderick Cordy-Simpson) I found the NAC extremely responsive, I have to say. I do understand that consensus is going to get harder as NATO enlarges, but it is the reality of the world. I did not find any bitter infighting that presented to me on the ground in the NAC if there was infighting going on, and I am sure there was infighting, but by the time it came to us the Military Committee had briefed it, they had been briefed back, and what came down to us from SACEUR was quite clear, which I have to say was, in comparison to those muddled early days, from a soldier's point of view much easier to deal with.

Mr Hood

207. I wonder if I could address my question to Professor Thornberry on the urgent need—your words, Professor—to create a new European civilian/military structure to deal with new missions. We were in Brussels a week or so ago talking to NATO people and were talking to one particular colleague from the WEU who was already writing their obituary, seeing no use for the WEU in the move to reforming foreign security policy. How do you see the structure reforming in this new climate you are talking about?

(Professor Thornberry) I am not sure how I see it changing. I do feel that if NATO is to develop as a regional security organisation, which is how, I must say, I would like to see it go, and I do think it has already managed to launch some very impressive operations and that its work with the PfP countries has also been very promising, it seems to me that the concept of NATO will have to be revised and I think that whether at a headquarters level or in the field there will have to be a more closely co-ordinated political/military role. I do not quite see how that is brought about, given the existence of a number of organisations in Europe at the moment which have

security as one of their concepts, including the WEU, but of course more specifically, the Organisation for Security and Co-operation in Europe, whose mandate is increasing and which again, as a matter of observation, I have noticed on a number of occasions seems to have been working very well. I do not know whether there is any possibility of a future for a closer co-operation between OSCE, which does represent all the nations of Europe but goes beyond them, and NATO. I find it difficult to look at the idea of NATO developing a new strategic concept which will have it operating what I call out of area at the moment without there being a political representation for areas beyond western Europe. I do not see at the moment how this will happen, and I am not experienced enough in this field or I am not clear-sighted enough; I do not know, but I think that we should really be looking at a more radical redisposition of the political and military structures of our region than we are up till now.

Mr Hancock

208. Is not a consequence of that happening the fact that NATO will be seen very much as the arm only of Europe? That the UN will have to look elsewhere for military support. Those countries who signed up for NATO will be extremely reluctant to get involved out of theatre where they would have limited themselves to get involved in a greater integrated Europe. Politically it would be a very difficult time for the UN ever to get a mandate which would put soldiers on the ground who were not from Europe.

(Professor Thornberry) I fully appreciate that, Mr Chairman, but I could think of scenarios in which there have been—it is almost unthinkable nowadays but let us think it in any event—an international conflict between two powers in Europe in which, in order to fulfil an effective peacekeeping or even a peace enforcement role with the requisite degree of objectivity or impartiality, so that the legitimacy of the force remained, I could imagine that a UN force might, in theory, be deployed. But, of course, it is correct to say that if NATO becomes a more effective regional body, then the danger (if that is the word) that the United Nations may be incapable of fulfilling a role in Europe, might become more real. This is not logical but this is how the world is. However, I am not sure about this because if you look at the way, for example, there are at the moment regrettably a number of appalling conflicts going on in Africa, in which there is little peacekeeping or peace implementation work going on, would you also say—if I may return the question to you—that if OAU or SACEUR or one of the other regional bodies within Africa were to develop an effective regional role, that would be good for the United Nations or bad for international peace and security? I do not know. There are a number of very large questions here of a strategic nature.

Mr Hancock: I was thinking that it has taken 50 years for NATO to get the sort of credibility in that, and for 40 of those years they did nothing effectively on the ground other than the threatening pose of a deterrent. It is only over the last ten years that NATO's

3 February 1999]   Lt General Sir Roderick Cordy-Simpson kbe cb,
                            General Sir Michael Rose kcb cbe dso qgm   *[Continued*
                            and Professor Cedric Thornberry

[Mr Hancock *Cont*]

physical strength has been deployed in different roles. My fear is that the confusion over the enlargement of NATO and the enlargement of Europe to take in the emerging democracies in Eastern Europe (and maybe the not so democratic countries which will be emerging) will, in fact, give a lot of pressure to make NATO very much an exclusively European thing for the future; and countries like the United States and Canada will be reluctant to be drawn physically on the ground elsewhere in places like Africa. It will take an awful long time for a credible force similar to NATO to emerge anywhere else. Even if you were the most optimistic of people, in realistic terms I believe that the opportunities in Africa for that to happen are pretty remote.

Mr Hood: I do not wish to be provocative, nor do I wish to invite you to be provocative. I went to NATO a week ago and I came away with a distinct impression that the problems there were not with the military; the problems were with the politicians. I can remember General Smuts saying to a Committee that we have to understand what our end game is before we do anything. He talked about the triangle of the ways and means and the end. It is the politicians who are noted as having the ways and the means but we cannot agree what the ends are. That seems to be the problem. Because of this there is a great frustration about the lack of resolve or attempts to resolve it. It seems to me to be the politicians who are vacillating and causing the problems now. I was speaking to a colleague (without mentioning any names) who was less than supportive of what happened in Iraq at the back end of the year. Having said that, we are very supportive of having to do something in Kosovo. You may find that the general public out there are more supportive of the need to take action in Kosovo than maybe they were in what happened in Iraq. I do not think the politicians are catching on to this.

Ms Taylor

209. My question is about mutual understanding. I am sure you will understand that I am very warm to that phrase, having such an awful Chairman! I am aware, General Rose, that you made a comment about mutual understanding and you have used a particular phrase, "dual key". In the quote from the brief it says: "Where two organisations with different mandates are involved in a single theatre of operations, it will be essential to have a 'dual key' arrangement similar to the one that operated in Bosnia." Equally, in the brief, and another obvious military expert, Lord Hurd of Westhill, is making the statement: "The dual key held in Bosnia by the UN and by NATO opened a door into disagreement and frustration." Listening here today, we are hearing both sides of those two statements and the reality of them. My question is about how we promote—and that is monstrously hard—greater mutual understanding between military and civilian operators: examples such as the United Nations and the NGOs. In answering that, you must have some examples of where best practice has actually worked. You may have actually seen the promotion of mutual

understanding and achieving goals which we all want to see.

(General Sir Michael Rose) In replying to that, in any of these situations you have three major elements, which have to be co-ordinated: the political action, the security action, and the humanitarian action. The difficulty with Bosnia was that never were all three properly co-ordinated. I think by 1993/1994 the humanitarian aid action and the security action were being very well co-ordinated. The headquarters were co-located. The security elements, the peacekeepers were saying to the UNHCR, who were the leaders of the entire humanitarian aid mission, including the NGOs: "We see our presence on the ground as only having one justification, which is the support of your efforts. We do not have another agenda." So the product in terms of aid delivered started to rise immediately we started to co-locate. So that if war lords were trying to hijack—and, of course, if you are delivering aid to a city under seige, you are operating against the strategic interests of those setting those sieges, so you will always have difficulties—there is no such thing as non-political aid. Therefore, if you can co-ordinate your response to hijackers by orderly convoys, if you refuse to allow yourself to be engaged in trade-offs and deals, your products will go up. That can be sharply demonstrated by the UNHCR graphs and statistics they produced each month. It was to do with the better understanding and the co-location between the aid organisations and the security of UNPROFOR. ICRC had a difficulty because of their constitution. They did not want to get involved but at the end of the day because of the such brutal circumstances they could not operate—although they did not pay public tribute to them—but they could not operate without using UNPROFOR. The political action was much more difficult because, of course, the UN was pursuing its own agenda. Along came the contact group thinking that the UN might do particularly well; ran its own agenda; and then, of course, in a way, NATO and America had another agenda; so we never really got our political act together. That was the cause of the problem.

Mr McWilliam

210. General Cordy-Simpson, I remember you used a very telling phrase when we last met in Sarajevo and that was that the previous structure—not the one you were operating—the flash to bang thing was far too long. Now if we are looking for a political military structure to operate in the kind of situation that is arising in the world today, how do we organise one where the flash to bang time does not take so long, where either soldiers' or civilians' lives are put at risk?

(General Sir Roderick Cordy-Simpson) I think we are getting there. Unlike the situation General Rose has described now, particularly when I first went back to Bosnia with Karl Bildt as the high representative and Michael Steiner as his deputy, the twice weekly meetings between those two, the military commanders, the UNHCR, the OSCE, the UN special envoy: frankly, if we all sang from the same song sheet we

[**Mr McWilliam** *Cont*]

had a fairly clear idea of what we were doing and how we were going to do it, and we achieved it. The facts are, of course, that the high rep did not have that authority to do that because it was not given to him under Dayton. It just happened to be the extraordinary personality of Karl Bildt who was able to achieve this and achieve consensus. In my opinion, in the ideal world we would have had that written into Dayton, that there was a high representative who was overall in charge. It was actually the personality of Karl Bildt that achieved the consensus. I believe this answers your question that on the ground by meeting together—at least, twice a week—we could achieve that. We could be called together, (we often were) at short notice, and solved the problem. We would all agree a policy which would go out and was achievable. This was a huge step forward in the areas where General Rose was and I before that: a completely different way where everything was very fluid and the best we could hope to achieve was the humanitarian and the military co-ordination. Even that was extremely difficult. So I think we have taken huge steps forward, but the fact is that the high representative does not officially have the authority down there to give the orders to the military. It just happens to be the way that Karl managed to achieve it.

(*Professor Thornberry*) I quite agree. The post-Dayton structure should have produced disaster. I think it speaks enormously highly not only of Karl Bildt but of others as well, that it has worked as well as it has. It reversed almost all the lessons which the UN had learnt about co-ordinating peacekeeping action, wherein we had an integrated plan in military and political command at almost all levels. Provided the personalities worked, on the whole this kind of unified structure was successful. I want to mention just one or two instances where it has been particularly good. I was thinking of the operation in Eastern Slavonia, UNTAES(?), in which for the two years in which UNTAES was on the ground and trying to carry out an enormously difficult mandate of adjusting the return of Croats to a territory which the Serbs had seized by extreme violence, and which was really conducted with considerable success and a lot of imagination by a commander who was both a diplomat and also a military man, that is one very good case in point. There have been others in which the situation did not work at all. In my opinion, for example, one of the reasons why we had a disaster in Somalia was the failure of the military and political personnel to work together. That is a spotty record in my experience but I think there has been enough experience gleaned to be able to draw up, as it were, good blueprints for the future.

Mr Colvin

211. In answer to the question to Mr Hood about the future architecture in Europe, I do not think we got a clear reply on the OSCE. Our report is going to have to address the security architecture of Europe. We know the civil, economic, politico-architecture of Europe is on the agenda, being discussed at the

moment—the future of the Council of Europe and things like that—but the OSCE only came into being in 1975, with a role to undermine the Soviet Bloc. It has done a very good job. It now seems to have new jobs extending outside Europe, encompassing membership from Northern African states, for instance. I did not get a clear idea as to how you saw that changing, if at all. Should we, for instance, merge the OSCE with the Council of Europe? Both have an enormous degree of overlap. NATO operations in Bosnia, at the moment, are said to be done with the authority of the OSCE, but the OSCE has no mandate to instruct NATO to take such operations, so how do you see its future specifically?

(*Professor Thornberry*) I am not at all sure about this, Chairman. In my own head I ventured this as one idea, but the purpose of it in my written evidence was to breathe extra air on to what I hoped was already a burning fire in regard to this, because of what I perceived to be the need to achieve greater integration. The OSCE is fulfilling an increasing range of tasks. I have seen it in the very difficult role of election monitor or supervisor in a number of countries and different focuses.

212. For example, in the Council of Europe.

(*Professor Thornberry*) Yes, indeed, and in the European Union actually. In Azerbaijan all three, in fact, were working together at the same time. The difficulty I have now on this is that I have been told by many people who are very much more "insightful" than myself that this is a non-starter—"forget it," they say. That it will not be feasible to combine the roles of NATO and of the OSCE, but I simply cannot understand why not. I appreciate that OSCE with 50 members is an unwieldy body, and a body which has to work on the basis of unanimity. However, let us face it. At the moment NATO, if it does not have American support, will not probably be very effective in any concrete situation either. It would seem possible——

213. But America is a member of the OSCE.

(*Professor Thornberry*) Nevertheless it would seem possible that in regard to OSCE a group of identified countries could, in respect of a particular operation, assume a level of political leadership—or at least a level of political input—to leaven the otherwise rather limited political support which NATO's Council itself might have. This is simply one idea. I believe that the principle should be looked at further of how one broadens the basis of political support and political input for NATO, both at the strategic and the operational levels.

Chairman: I think we shall probably have to let NATO and the Council of Europe and the OSCE survive. I do not think we are going to be able to solve that. Mr Blunt, please. Remember that General Rose has to leave in about ten minutes.

Mr Blunt

214. I have a question directed to him. General Rose, in your book you are quite critical of how NATO and the UN interacted in the early stages of Bosnia.

3 February 1999]
Lt General Sir Roderick Cordy-Simpson kbe cb,
General Sir Michael Rose kcb cbe dso qgm
and Professor Cedric Thornberry
[Continued

[Mr Blunt *Cont]*

You then, towards the end, are quite hopeful in the sense of your conclusion about lessons learnt: that NATO will have a continuing relevance for the future because it appears to be learning lessons. As you look at the Kosovo crisis development and NATO's reaction to that, are you concerned that the necessity for NATO to maintain its credibility is going to draw us into policy in Kosovo which would not otherwise be necessarily wise? The need for NATO to sustain its credibility and overtake the decisions which have otherwise been taken?

(General Sir Michael Rose) The short answer is yes. However, the words "maintaining credibility of NATO" is a convenient expression for actually indulging in the use of military force. That is what it actually means, and has usually been driven by the Americans and very often by the air powers. Of course, NATO is a consensus organisation as you, yourself, say. The surprise to me when I was in Bosnia was that there were some members of NATO, whose troops were on the ground as UN, and the military and political chiefs of those countries, when they were in New York would caution against the extended use of force and would point out the limitations of a peacekeeping mission; but the very same people would stand up on the night and say, "We must sustain the credibility of NATO," usually with an American hand on their back, and, "We need to use more force." They perfectly well knew that could collapse the mission. I never understood why the chiefs of staff of those seven countries did not put their hands up and say, "Hang on, we have the guys on the ground. This is a consensus alliance. The new Americans cannot drive the agenda the way you are trying to do it." I think we need to take a very firm action over Kosovo if we do deploy that; not to allow these seven voices to lead us into a war.

215. Did you actually see a risk of that happening?

(General Sir Michael Rose) Yes. There are many people out there who think you solve these problems by the use of force.

Mr Hancock

216. So what sort of organisation do you have to have which prevents that being the object?

(General Sir Michael Rose) The organisation already said: "All you need is the political and military leaders to put their hands up and say 'stop!'"

Mr Hancock: Does it not go back to what the Professor says? You will end up with a bigger NATO but a smaller group. You will elect an inner core of countries who will be exercising all the powers. You will have the UN and Security Council scenario all over again.

Mr Cohen

217. We are back to the point about credibility. We are back to this current issue of Kosovo. Is the threat of force behind the current situation a real one or not? That is the credibility.

(General Sir Michael Rose) If they do, would it achieve the goals that are spelt out or do you put troops on the ground to back it, etcetera? We know who is not going to put troops on the ground.

Mr Hancock: When we were in the room in Brussels a week or so, with all the NATO ambassadors sitting there and the Secretary General, there was not one of them, including the American ambassador, who had a long-term plan for Kosovo. The fact that that lunchtime they ordered the two generals to Belgrade was the extent of their involvement. They had no thought past that. And when asked: what is the next step when they return? (because there was a suggestion that Mulosevic should not even meet them) there was no fall-back scenario to expose to us. It appeared, talking to them after the meeting individually, that they had not been able to get their heads round where they went from there. That is the problem at the moment. When there is a problem we send people there to see the problem, without ever discussing the end game and what we are hoping to achieve. I think what you have told us today is a very pessimistic picture about the expansion of NATO and the future of NATO.

Mr Blunt

218. Do you believe that the real problem is the fact that the American political process seems a hostage to American media coverage? Does that explain why it is so inconsistent and short-term?

(General Sir Michael Rose) That is absolutely true but the debate goes on, of course, in each of the capitals of the member states of Nato: those who feel that force will achieve things and those who do not. That debate is bound to be reflected in the lack of decision.

Chairman

219. To what extent do current initiatives such as Partnership for Peace prepare NATO and other nations for co-operation within realistic operational scenarios?

(General Sir Roderick Cordy-Simpson) I have seen one Partnership for Peace exercise. I would have to say I saw it about two years ago. I think it was probably the first one. It was definitely the lowest common denominator with the levels which were trying to be achieved. Therefore, for well-trained NATO armies I would suggest to you that there was not a tremendous amount in it. Of course, there was for those who were applying it for the first time. The level of expertise which was required was very low. Also, I have to say, understandably the language problems were enormous. I think it has progressed a long way since then but what I would say is that within Partnership for Peace, while I was in Bosnia, I think we had 36 different nations under command. They, themselves, learnt in a fairly (by then) benign situation an enormous amount about NATO. I remember they learnt our procedures. The language problems were very much overcome but they had learnt our procedures and that is what they wanted. I remember the Rumanians saying to me—they were an engineer

[Chairman *Cont]*

battalion—"We can build bridges anywhere you like. That is not our problem. Why we are here is to work with you Brits, Americans, (etcetera), to learn how your NATO procedures operate. That is really why our Government has sent us here and we are frightfully keen to do it." So I look at that as an essential Partnership for Peace and I found that this was probably the best training of all. The actual NATO Partnership for Peace exercises, Cedric has seen them more recently than I have and is in a better position probably to speak about them.

(Professor Thornberry) I would only add that clearly a number of countries which are participating in the PfP exercises, which are mostly in a peacekeeping format, as you know, an implementation format, are wrestling with enormous problems of resources and of language. There is a tremendous difficulty. This is the overriding problem: language. But it seems to me that from rather a layman's point of view, that they are approaching the inter-operability question in a very workmanlike way. I would just say that although there are other factors involved about the quality of these exercises, the level of harmony has perceptibly increased over the last five years. I have done about five or six of these. I think they are progressing. But everyone has latched on to the language question.

Mr Cohen

220. May I ask General Rose if he would comment on the "fur caps" affair. I know he was in the SAS in Oman.

(General Sir Michael Rose) Which affair?

221. Fur caps. Where members of the SAS in Oman effectively sold guns to non-existing tribesmen and then pocketed the proceeds. That has been reported in recent reports. Indeed, you made a mention of it or an allusion to it in one of your books. I would be interested to hear if you had any knowledge of it or a brief explanation about it.

(General Sir Michael Rose) Absolutely not. I cannot help you at all.

Mr Cohen: Okay. That cleared that up anyway.

Chairman

222. General Rose, thank you very much for coming. I hope your book signing is not affected by your injury to your arm.

(General Sir Michael Rose) Not at all. Thank you very much for inviting me.

223. How can non-Article 5 operations be exploited to the benefit of NATO's relationships with non-NATO nations?

(General Sir Roderick Cordy-Simpson) I think it is evolving. The more I see of it the more it is, by definition, just getting better and better. They are learning our procedures. They are operating with us comfortably. I think one has to understand that some are more capable than others. Therefore, the principal structure is one of the things on which probably we

need to look towards the future. I am not making myself completely clear but I do not think the force structure necessarily always reflects what we are trying to achieve on the ground. Some nations are very capable of producing good transport, or good logistics, but some are not so capable of producing good war fighting troops on the ground. That is the area which possibly we ought to try and develop and exploit, so that when we press the button we know we will have a first-class aviation battalion company from X country with helicopters which are compatible, for example.

Laura Moffatt

224. We have been talking this morning about the enormous political difficulties involved in any operation. We have talked about the military difficulties. May I add another dimension and that is the influence of the media on operations undertaken by NATO. I know Sir General Rose spoke about how we did not really win the battle. We lost that long ago. Most of us can remember, if we shut our eyes, the hideous picture of the thin man standing behind the roads. I still see him regularly in my mind's eye and how it influenced our thinking. Can I ask both of you, have we learned any lessons from the way in which we conduct our business in NATO operations, under what is constant scrutiny? Have we adjusted the way in which we work, to work with the media? What influence does it have? Does it make decisions, perhaps back home, that are not correct?

(General Sir Roderick Cordy-Simpson) I think there are two sides to that. First of all, the media. The information war of a country that one is in, which I do not think we addressed properly at the beginning because there was so much else going on—in other words, getting the message across to warring factions as to what the UN and then subsequently NATO were doing and, why they were there—I do not think they understood in any form, shape or size. We failed badly there. We have learnt that lesson now. It is being seriously addressed. Certainly it was when I was there subsequently. I am now talking about the international press. I think I only had one bad experience with the press in 1992/1993. Other than that I found them thoroughly supportive, wise and fair. Yes, they would give you a seriously hard time if they thought we were not getting the message across to them. One of the lessons we have learnt from them is that we now probably almost brief them to death. First thing every morning when I was in Sarajevo we were getting all the people who had been on duty in the last 24 hours— not all, but a handful—and we would talk about what was likely to come up, and how we would approach it. "You can't duck it, it is bound to come up, let's go on the front foot with it and give them their briefing." So the quality of briefing we give to the press, we have learnt to give it upfront to them. That does not mean that we do not regularly get a hard time from them, but we have learnt to get on the front foot with them rather than wait for them to come to us. So, in answer, the two types of media: the first is to make sure that

[Laura Moffatt *Cont]*
the in-theatre word needs to be got out, the Information Campaign. I am not talking psy-ops, to be honest with you. I am talking straightforward honest getting a media message across to the people: why we are there and what we are trying to achieve. Frankly, the hatred that was there in Yugoslavia was so great that without a proper information campaign you could not solve the problem. The second, the role of the media themselves, I found has been supportive. If you are honest with them, by and large, they are almost totally honest with you and will not let you down. They have reported very fairly in Bosnia throughout the time, certainly both times I have been there. I do not have a criticism but it does mean from our point of view that we have to be absolutely upfront with them.

225. What about if the operation was not particularly supported at home though and it was used as a way of sending messages back? Let me talk about Iraq then, a very different type of report and which had a different effect back home. Was it difficult to manage while you were there, if you were there?
(General Sir Roderick Cordy-Simpson) Yes. I accept the fact that this is the case. I accept the fact that to a certain degree we ended up in the Balkans because of the press pressure that came on our nations. You almost infer that the press would be reporting inaccurately.

226. No.
(General Sir Roderick Cordy-Simpson) I do not think necessarily that everyone in this country was thoroughly supportive of our nation's commitment subsequently in the Balkans but they still went on reporting it. It got bored in some areas and certainly you hardly see very much about Bosnia these days. The only area I found very difficult the second time— and I will be quite open with you—was on the subject of war criminals. This is because there I was being given a very strong clear direction by NATO as to what should happen. It went against the principles of human nature to know that war criminals were running around that country, and yet our rules (I would not call them rules but you know what I mean, Chairman) we were quite clear what our rules were, down the military chain of command there. The press, quite rightfully, went for us pretty hard, to be honest with you. It was quite a difficult thing to defend oneself in that position.

Chairman

227. But they did not ask any questions on reincarnation, General. That might have caused you real difficulties!
(General Sir Roderick Cordy-Simpson) I am not particularly after that other job, Chairman!

228. Media adviser to the FA has got to be a job worth going for!
(Professor Thornberry) May I say that as regards public information and UN operations, I think the UN has learned (or should have learned) an enormous amount in the last seven or eight years. Until the operation in Namibia in 1989/1990, the UN did nothing virtually in regard to public information and in regard to informing the people amongst whom they worked about what it was trying to do, never mind the outside world. Since that time, UN operations have had rather spotty public information support. In the UN, public information has not really been a major priority. I suppose that in an organisation in which there was not an overwhelming majority of democratic countries, the idea of freedom of expression inevitably had a certain question mark over it. I often asked myself why this should have been. In some of the operations that the UN has done there has been a very effective relationship. Here I would support what Roddy Cordy-Simpson has said. I also had very little difficulty with the press in Bosnia in 1993. It was after that time fundamentally that many of the press, the liberal press in particular, had a particular agenda. It wanted war in Bosnia. It scourged us daily because we were not fighting a war. As we were there we were blamed. But I think it is absolutely crucial. I am sure that it is worth at least a battalion or even a brigade to have a good, effective public information outreach programme working alongside of these people in the operation. I am not just talking about psy-ops either.

Mr Brazier

229. Just moving on to the actual full structures, two questions together if I may. How do you believe NATO forces need to be restructured to overcome the differing demands of peacekeeping and peace support as opposed to the more traditional ones of war fighting? More specifically, how well do you think our allies within NATO have adapted to the demands of peacekeeping? How well suited are they to combined and joined operations?
(General Sir Roderick Cordy-Simpson) It is quite difficult for me to answer the first question: how should NATO's forces be restructured? Our military restructuring has effectively been done. I think there is an understanding that we will still require a war fighting capability and that if you have a war fighting capability you can always train downwards to a peace support type operation. What you cannot do is gear yourself in the opposite direction from a full structure, which is purely designed to do peace support, peace enforcement operations, straight up to war fighting because your procurement is all wrong for war fighting weaponry, etcetera. I think most nations understand that. Therefore, most nations have made their minds up as to whether they are going to go down that line. Speaking as an ex-British officer, I am quite convinced that we need to retain our war fighting capability. It is not an easy capability to maintain. One, is that it is expensive. Two, it needs a lot of time for training. All our other types of operations take people away from that central training which is so needed. Certainly as you get operations with troops going into Bosnia, going to Northern Ireland, and then coming back, trying to find time to train for their primary role is quite difficult. What was the second part of your question?

3 February 1999]   Lt General Sir Roderick Cordy-Simpson kbe cb,
General Sir Michael Rose kcb cbe dso qgm
and Professor Cedric Thornberry   *[Continued*

[Mr Brazier *Cont]*

230. This was on allies. How well are they measuring up to it?

(General Sir Roderick Cordy-Simpson) I think they all, in different ways, are measuring up. The ones I came across in Bosnia, one knew their capabilities and one knew whether they were outside their capabilities. I would like an opportunity to come in and say one thing. In NATO, we have slightly in this room and, particularly Michael, slightly had a go at the United States. My personal view is that any type of difficult operation simply cannot, at the moment, be undertaken without the United States' support. I say that because of, if for no other reason, their immense fighting power. They have also got something which is irreplaceable and that is their intelligence capabilities. When I was in Bosnia there were 35 different nations providing intelligence to us. I would have to say that I do not know the exact figure, but I would have thought that somewhere around 70 per cent of the intelligence came from two nations, ourselves and the Americans. The rest of the nations, frankly, put very little into the pool. They took quite a lot out but they put very little in to what we were getting. If we had not had the Americans with their amazing capabilities, I think I for one would simply not have survived. When I consider some of the things that we were able to find out because the Americans had the capability which no-one else had, we would have been in dead trouble in any operation without them.

Mr Brazier: In fact, you have anticipated my next question. Could I ask you just to expand that last answer a little. Intelligence obviously is top of the list. In what other areas do you think you could not go it alone without the Americans?

Mr Cann

231. For example, heavy lift.

(General Sir Roderick Cordy-Simpson) Heavy lift is the obvious one. I am just trying to think. Their sheer size and what they can commit on the ground. They were by far the biggest force contributor there. Without them there you lose that integrated command. We must remember that not only is the theatre commander an American but also the supreme commander is an American. That may be a good or a bad thing, but the fact is that this opened doors to us which I do not think would have otherwise been opened. I would re-emphasise time and time again that the intelligence which the Americans brought with all their capabilities was something that I know that as a commander on the ground I simply would not have survived without. UK plc gave me a great deal but there were masses of things I could not even have got from them.

(Professor Thornberry) It is also my experience on the political side of peacekeeping that without United States' active support it would be very difficult indeed to achieve most of the goals that the UN has achieved. I think obviously of heavy lift and support in that regard. But also I would talk about the political support. The fact that one could constantly count on active American backing in regard to particular

problems. Their ability to smooth one's way. On the intelligence side also, it has to be said that certainly again in south west Africa in Namibia without American backing at that level, working in the joint commission on the intelligence side in south western Africa, we would have been in very, very serious trouble.

Mr Brazier

232. One final question on that. Just at the technical level, the revolution in military affairs. Are we confident that the European element of NATO will continue to be able to work so closely with the Americans as their integrated systems get more and more integrated—not perhaps quite so much ourselves—but as most of their European colleagues get left further and further behind.

(General Sir Roderick Cordy-Simpson) Yes, I think so. Take communications, for instance. When I was first out there in Bosnia, I have never known a nightmare like it was in 1992. It was quicker for me to drive the 12 miles to Phillip Morrillon's separate headquarters than it would be to chance getting through to a telephone, which I would guarantee was being listened to by all three sides. So it was much quicker to drive and talk to him face to face. Subsequently, when I went back with the Americans, they took over from the ARRC. We removed the British system and the Americans adjusted it, they threw the system at it. They took it down to all their NATO allies and instructed them how to use it, how to use secure communications, and really brought them on side in a very big way. I cannot see any major operation of that size and complexity, unless there is a big shift in European thought processes and huge consensus that would be wise to undertake, without a great deal of support from the Americans. I am not saying every bit of support but a great deal of support.[1]

Chairman

233. I suppose the argument there is this: our Committee has been four or five times to the area. When the Americans have committed themselves you know the Americans would be prepared—perhaps it would be unfair to say play dirty pool—but you knew that if you pushed them they would get as mad as hell. The idea of Malaysia and Belgium and Canada, with due respect to them, would not have frightened the

---

[1] The US will soon (maybe within 5 years) be so technnically superior with their integrated systems that it will not be possible to be on the same "battlefield" unless we possess systems that will integrate with theirs. This will be hugely expensive and well beyond most of the Allies' Defence budgets. It may even be beyond our defence budget. I believe that this should be limited to warfighting. It could therefore mean that in any future warfighting conflict, a coalition with the US may be difficult to form, the implications for NATO could be serious. However coalitions for peace support operations should not be faced with these problems as this type of operation will not be so dependent on these integrated systems.

Lt General Sir Roderick Cordy-Simpson kbe cb,
General Sir Michael Rose kcb cbe dso qgm
and Professor Cedric Thornberry

3 February 1999] *[Continued*

[Chairman *Cont]*
warring party into doing things that otherwise they would not have wished to have done.

(General Sir Roderick Cordy-Simpson) We go back to mission creep and mission paralysis, Chairman. Americans will go beyond mission creep if they have to, without thinking twice if that resolves the problem. Most others, when they are given the options, will probably go towards mission paralysis as an easy way out.

234. In a place like Bosnia you really need to show the sword.

(General Sir Roderick Cordy-Simpson) If there is a problem you have to be prepared to use it and be understood that the sword will be used rather than just waving it around in the air.

Chairman: Sure. Thank you. Mr Hancock.

Mr Hancock

235. Going back but avoiding talking too much about Bosnia or those situations, it is just about the way in which NATO can survive, taking Julian's point about the quality of the countries who will be involved and others who still aspire to be involved. Indeed, some of those are already there. But with their defence budget diminishing and so much of the defence budget in these countries just being taken up by paying wages and pensions, some of the big countries in NATO currently are spending very little on procurement and research and development. Most of it is going on personnel. What is the future for these countries? How can an organisation like NATO survive unless it is by the likes of the United States, the United Kingdom, and possibly Germany, helping to subsidise the improvements which will be needed to get countries on side in all of the issues that they need to be involved in, not only on communication but just getting the kit that their men are using up to a scale, which is usable over a long period of time in a theatre situation.

(General Sir Roderick Cordy-Simpson) In terms of personnel and their use, we will have to accept the fact that some of them will come to the party in the best form they can. In other words, in a peace operation such as in Bosnia, they will come with adequately provided troops which they know will never be war fighting troops. They will probably never go into that level of genuine war fighting because they cannot and they will not, they do not have the time, and they do not have the wherewithal to do it. This means probably that we are looking at the first and second events ultimately. That is what I fear will be the way it comes to, because technology and the cost of technology is so astronomical now that not everyone will be able to keep up. So what you do is you look at nations and ask them to take on blocks, or modules in areas where you can support the operation; understanding that some of the modules are beyond their capabilities because of defence budgets alone.

(Professor Thornberry) That is true also in the case of UN operations. Although most contingents (even from third world countries) can pretty well afford it, there were quite a few notorious instances in which other countries had to step in and buy kit. But even in regard to PfP exercises, there are some countries where one knows that their participation means that Germany or one of the other well-off and benevolent uncles will have to pay their fares and probably their hotel bills as well.

Mr Cann

236. But is it not the case, General, going back to Bosnia, at this stage of the operation something was required which we have not got. This is the *gendarmerie* types of forces. That is needed now in some of the places and not the kinds of forces which we have put in.

(General Sir Roderick Cordy-Simpson) I do not argue that as we downsize, as normality is reached, that we probably do not want these highly sophisticated forces. There comes a moment when you are actually back to a pure peacekeeping operation. In that case you can downsize your forces. We are quite capable of going downwards in scale and other nations can also come in at that stage. It is when it goes above that level that you need these better trained, better equipped forces. As it comes down I do not think there is a problem because other people can take it on and everyone can meet it, and we can come down to that level if we want to. If we wanted to one day, if the situation is such in Bosnia to reduce the amount of heavy weaponry that we have in there, this is easy for us to do. It would also reduce the constant pressure on the same men going back again and again and again into Bosnia.

237. The only point I was making is that forces like the French *gendarme*, the *carabiniere*, people like that, are actually in some of the villages and areas. They are settled there where is a policing problem because they are far better equipped to do that job than somebody who is not trained, and someone makes an attack on a defended police.

(General Sir Roderick Cordy-Simpson) But we would then move to an international police task force. I have forgotten how many bobbies there are on the beat out there, but not a great number in comparison to the French and the *carabiniere* and the Americans. I have forgotten the number we now have.

Mr Hancock

238. 100.

(General Sir Roderick Cordy-Simpson) At that stage you have definitely moved into something we soldiers are not good at.

(Professor Thornberry) I am very glad this point has been raised. Increasingly, in the last ten years, the UN have found that civilian policemen, well trained policemen doing community policing, have been absolutely invaluable in what we tend to call complex operations. Because they live among the people, they work among the people, they are really enormously supportive. They are also an incredible source of information.

3 February 1999]   Lt General Sir Roderick Cordy-Simpson kbe cb,   *[Continued*
                          General Sir Michael Rose kcb cbe dso qgm
                              and Professor Cedric Thornberry

Chairman

239. I have seen the West Midlands police in riot training. They are certainly impressive. I would not like to tangle with them. What effect do you expect NATO enlargement to have on the Alliance's military effectiveness? Now we touched upon that. Will military planning procedures and the ability to mount operations be weakened? Could you perhaps enlarge upon what was said earlier?

(General Sir Roderick Cordy-Simpson) Like everything else, as you expand NATO, it is inevitably going to become slightly more, because of consensus, it is going to be less responsive, I would suggest. The knack is already quite well removed, still reasonably well briefed but I think it is quite well removed from the realities on the ground. Actually what you have got now, as it expands, at the moment you have got operational command, up to SACEUR, across the military committee and then to the NAC. The danger of all this is that as NATO expands it gets harder and harder on the ground because each nation on the ground has its national commander who is not reporting to the NATO commander on the ground. It is quite staggering the number of people who will ingratiate themselves back to their nation knowing something full well before they will tell the NATO commander on the ground, because I suppose they think they will get a tick in the right box and all the rest of it. This makes actual command for the man on the ground much harder. I think Cedric will have seen it a thousand times, probably more than I have, it is very difficult. As NATO expands what are we going to have? First of all, we have to tackle NATO procedures. That sounds easy but takes a long time and we must remember that we got our procedures the way we did by sitting for years facing the Third Shock Army coming and because it did not attack we had time to get our procedures right. T bring in a new army that has based itself on a completely different ethos, the way it trains, the way its procedures are, does take time. That said, they have all got a very good grounding now already on the ground, because they have all taken part in this operation in Bosnia so they have seen NATO, we have seen them. I do not think that the expansion, therefore, of NATO will ultimately present big problems from an operating point of view. I think the expansion of NATO has a much bigger political problem and that is outside my sphere of remit. I think the expansion of NATO will create some big political question marks.

240. I know the Russians were most at war with the US but did you have any impression that they were able to fit into the kind of operations they had signed up for?

(General Sir Roderick Cordy-Simpson) I would have to say that the Russians were completely different from anyone else in Bosnia. First of all, even as Director of Operations, I was not permitted ever to visit the Russian troops because their chain of command—which they had written, and they were the only ones who had written them—was completely different. Their's went up to their man who was sitting in SHAPE, sideways into SACEUR, downwards into the American divisional commander on the ground and then back to the Russian brigade. Therefore, for us in Sarajevo, they were the one organisation we had no direction over whatsoever. Now that of course is done for understandable reasons and it was a remarkable achievement to bring them on side at all but quite clearly they were not going to go under NATO command. All the rest came firmly under command. You only had to look at the British sector, you had the Czech battalion sitting firmly under command, its helicopters operating quite naturally for us and all the rest of it. No problems at all. All the rest of the nations involved were firmly under command. The Ukrainians under command of the French. It worked. It was just this one, I will not say "funny" but it was a remarkable achievement to get the Russian brigade there on the ground at all but its command and control was very carefully crafted to ensure that no NATO orders, (they were American orders but not NATO orders) had come from us.

Chairman: Thank you. Are there any more questions before we draw stumps?

Mr Cann

241. Just a quick one from me, Chairman. The United Nations went to war in Korea in the 1950s, and has never been able to do so as far as I can see since, being an organisation of 185 states or whatever it is, paralysed, in other words. How much larger can NATO get without becoming paralysed to the same extent?

(General Sir Roderick Cordy-Simpson) In fairness, the bigger any organisation gets the less efficient it is going to be, that is inevitable. I am not going to try and put a judgment on how much it can expand further or otherwise. Sorry, to go back to it, sometimes even in Bosnia there were operations which we did not share with all the nations taking part. I will give you an example. The first operation against two indicted war criminals, only ten of us knew that operation was going to go ahead and planned that operation. Only two nations were involved in the planning in any form, shape or size and we always met in a separate building which had been carefully debugged before we even met.

Chairman: You are not going to tell us who those who were excluded were?

Mr McWilliam

242. Obviously we know who one of them was because one of our troops got shot.

(General Sir Roderick Cordy-Simpson) The bottom line was that was the only way we could guarantee operational security. I got into the most appalling flack which I received from the European ambassadors in Sarajevo because we had not told them. We had not even told the Higher

3 February 1999]

Lt General Sir Roderick Cordy-Simpson kbe cb,
General Sir Michael Rose kcb cbe dso qgm
and Professor Cedric Thornberry

[Continued

[**Mr McWilliam** *Cont*]

Representative but for very good reasons, we were affecting the lives of our soldiers. Going back to your question, therefore, the wider NATO is going to be the more people and operational security is one area, it becomes more inefficient. Everyone wants to report back to their nations because they all get a ticks on their confidential report that he is doing a good job but that jeopardises security and there are operations where this simply cannot be. I gave it as an example but I think it is quite a good example of how the bigger an organisation becomes the more you have to account for these problems.

Chairman: There were instances in both Iraq and the former Yugoslavia in the last six months where one or two nations were seen to have been less than helpful in terms of the final operations. Look, I think we will draw stumps there. Thank you both. It has been very interesting.

TUESDAY 16 FEBRUARY 1999

Members present:

Mr Bruce George, in the Chair

Mr Crispin Blunt	Mr Jimmy Hood
Mr Jamie Cann	Mr John McWilliam
Mr Michael Colvin	Laura Moffatt
Mr Mike Hancock	

Examination of Witness

MR ASEN YORDANOV AGOV, Chairman of the Foreign Policy Committee of the Bulgarian National Assembly, was examined.

Chairman

243. Well, welcome. It is a great pleasure seeing you here and thank you for coming and talking to us. I am sorry that some of us were not able to go to your country; we were in Slovenia. As you realise, we are producing a report to be published a week or so before the Washington Summit. I went to a meeting of the North Atlantic Assembly yesterday and we were told that there is still jockeying going on and fighting going on, that the position is not absolutely fixed in stone even in connection with whether further invitations will be extended, but the overwhelming impression I have, as I am sure you have, is that the current state of thinking is that there will be no announcement in Washington of any further enlargement at the moment for reasons you will be familiar with, although Slovenia is putting up a strong struggle and Slovenia has very strong supporters, particularly in Washington. The first question I would really like to ask you is what Bulgaria's expectations are from the Washington Summit because I am sure that you will be pretty well apprised of realistically what might happen. If you are offered membership immediately, fine, but will your country be angry, disappointed if there will be no immediate offer at Washington of membership of NATO?

(Mr Agov) Well, Mr Chairman, ladies and gentlemen, first of all, let me thank you for this opportunity to speak before this very distinguished committee. I am even more glad to see so many friends here, having met all of them on other occasions, and I am really delighted to have the opportunity just a month and a half probably or seven weeks before the Washington Summit to discuss this issue with you. As some of my colleagues who have visited Bulgaria in late November might have noticed, Bulgaria has a very pragmatic approach towards the enlargement process. We do not see the enlargement as a beauty contest in which we have to compete with, let us say, Romania or Slovenia. We do see it as a very important preparation process for Bulgaria to meet its commitments as a fully-fledged ally of the NATO countries, so we are very well aware of all the arguments of the allies as to why they should not go towards an immediate second wave of enlargement in Washington. We are clear about that. We have been consulting constantly our allies and we understand very well their arguments.

We understand very well that the alliance has to digest the first group of three and we know very well that the alliance has to keep its reliability as a political and monetary union, a group of people which has to remain efficient, and we understand very well, and I am not putting any critical note on this, that although Poland, Hungary and the Czech Republic will be adopted as new members on the 12th March, still they have to do a lot of work to meet the full criteria to become allies, fully-fledged allies of NATO. So understanding all of these arguments, I would like to point out that our view is clearly stated. There has been a vote in my committee and we clearly supported a position which goes in favour of making a significant step forward after Madrid. This will mean, for us at least, that Bulgaria has to be mentioned as a potential ally, first of all. I myself, and this is shared by most of my colleagues, am a firm supporter of the clear mentioning of the potential allies.

244. In what order—alphabetically?
(Mr Agov) I remember the argument in Edinburgh, but still I would say that for us it does not matter. Of course we will be in a very good position starting with a "B" to be at first place, but——

245. Well, Albania will be first if it works like that.
(Mr Agov) Yes, what I would insist is that of course expressing our solidarity with Romania and Slovenia, of course we cannot see why Bulgaria with all the problems that it met lately should not be mentioned first of all and in what sequence, it does not matter very much. Second, there should be a clear distinction, Mr Chairman, between the countries who are partners within the PfP, and the countries who are potential allies. That is our strong point because, otherwise, this will be detrimental to our political position back home and this is part of the answer to your question. We are very sensitive on this issue, politically sensitive. As you might very well know, we were elected on a platform on which joining the NATO alliance is very high on our agenda and this will be a setback for a government which has been successful in so many areas, as is well known. I would like to mention one more thing. Each of the nations which is aspiring to join the alliance is preparing itself and is going through a very important and very deep reform of the military, and is setting a lot of resource

[**Chairman** *Cont*]

to this reform and this for Bulgaria, for instance, means that it is allocating 2 per cent of its GDP for the time being and for the time coming to defence in order to support the effort of restructuring the military. I would like to add also that there are going to be even more resources because the GDP is rising, it is on the rise, and we have a rise of about 3.5 per cent and this will mean that there will be an increase in the spending on military reform. Finally, if this reform is not recognised as a very important part of the common security of all of us, then this will discourage the military and, as you might understand, this is a very difficult process. We will have about 3,000 officers redundant in the next several months and there will be a complete change of military command structure which will mean that we will have about 70 or 75 per cent of junior officers and then we will have only 25 per cent of senior officers or general officers, and all these people who come up have to be involved in outsourcing through other methods in the reform. So I would not risk discouraging all those people. We have political discouragement and we have military discouragement. Finally, we would like to see coming out of Washington not only recognition of all those efforts but recognition of a clear set of criteria because obviously we cannot expect to be called before 2001 a new wave of enlargement. On the other hand, we think that we should all utilize this policy in order to prepare Bulgaria, Slovenia and Romania and possibly the Balks (of which I am a great supporter) in order to meet the criteria and become a reliable ally within the North Atlantic Treaty Organisation. I am a great proponent of mentioning not only Bulgaria, Romania and Slovenia but also mentioning the Balks. I know how difficult and how politically sensitive this might be vis-à-vis Russia, but I do not think there is a more suitable time, reflecting on the Russian situation at the moment, to mention them. I think the Balks deserve it and they have to be mentioned together with Bulgaria, Romania, Slovenia and Slovakia. I would insist on what the Americans call a membership action plan, but there should be a clear set of steps to be taken and the Washington final document, declaration or whatever it is should be committed to that.

246. Public opinion is fairly much in favour, is it not, of membership?

(Mr Agov) Yes, it is.

247. What about the former Communists or the Communists, would they try to exploit the situation if you do not get membership or a good promise of membership at the next round, whenever that should take place?

(Mr Agov) Mr Chairman, the ex-Communists in Bulgaria are generally against enlargement and against Bulgaria taking part in enlargement. There are clear policies in place, although they have been showing signs lately that they are split on this because they understand that they cannot integrate the political life not only of Bulgaria but of Europe if they do not have a clear position on this issue. We can expect some leering in the political circumstances of Bulgaria.

Mr Blunt

248. You expect some?

(Mr Agov) Leering. They will enjoy not having an invitation or anything encouraging for Bulgaria. Of course, they can declare "this is the wrong policy", they can declare that we are seeking allies in places where we do not find any and we should go back to seeking allies at quarters where there used to be some, to the east and this will definitely build a bridge in terms of our relations with Turkey which are excellent at the moment.

Chairman

249. Every year I have to get a resolution through the Assembly attacking Bulgaria for its policy on the Moslem minority and it is quite gratifying to see relations with Turkey so very much better now.

(Mr Agov) Actually, Turkey voted a law which recommends that the Government works for Bulgaria's membership to NATO and this is the only country that has voted a law like it. So it is a complete change. There has been a major development in our relations with Macedonia. Next Monday we are expecting to have the Prime Minister of Macedonia and the Prime Minister of Bulgaria sign a declaration for the future development of relations between the two nations. This was another stone in the shoe, but I think this issue has now been resolved. We will be able to support Macedonia fully now that we have that support there and obviously Macedonia is going to play a very big role in securing peace in Kosovo.

Mr McWilliam

250. Mr Agov, may I apologise as I have to chair quite a complicated meeting in the House in ten minutes' time.

(Mr Agov) That is normal Parliamentary life!

251. Can I also say thank you on behalf of myself and my colleagues who were with me in Bulgaria fairly recently. We were certainly impressed by the progress that Bulgaria has made, in particular the political progress and Bulgaria should not see itself without allies in the sense of wanting Bulgaria to progress towards membership of NATO and that is not something we want to see. What is your analysis of public opinion on NATO membership of Bulgaria? How strong is the public debate on defence and security issues in general in Bulgaria?

(Mr Agov) Public opinion is in the majority favourable to Bulgaria joining NATO. At last we have a clear-cut view amongst the public who see membership of NATO as part of the general development of Bulgaria. It is interesting to note that the most educated part of the population, which forms about 35 per cent of the opinion poll entries, are very strong supporters of us joining NATO. The public debate is now at a very intense stage since the public has to make a choice between allocating resources to restructuring the military and then cutting the military or continuing to spend even more in not reforming the military. In this economic and financially orientated debate that we are having in my country defence starts

[**Mr McWilliam** *Cont*]

to play a very key role. I spoke about outsourcing which is going to be, thanks to some British advice, a very serious segment of the restructuring of the military. All those people who come out of the military will be involved in the economy and involved in creating new jobs. This is due to a change in attitude. Whereas the military were perceived in the past as something very secretive, as something which is happening behind the public's eyes, now it is fully exposed to the public eye and the debate is, I would say, quite enthusiastic in Parliament, in my committee, and the National Security Committee, and you would find in the press a lot of articles which are definitely part of this debate and yes, it is a vivid debate.

Mr Cann

252. The question I was going to ask, Mr Chairman, was what progress is being made to the implementation of defence planning and budgeting required by the National Assembly in view of the fact that you agreed to up your expenditure on GDP to 2.24 per cent, I understand?

(Mr Agov)   Let me say first that some three or four years ago defence planning was *terra incognita* for most of the MoD people. Defence planning was something which was introduced in the MoD and Parliament quite recently, I would say, in the last two or three years, but all the efforts there are, first of all, structurally to establish a defence planning unit within the MoD which then sends all the requests to the Cabinet and then the Cabinet includes all of this in the republican budget and then the republican budget goes, when it concerns defence, to the National Security Committee, and since my committee is overviewing the procedure and the process of integrating within the North Atlantic alliance, we are looking at this part of the budget which is politically linked to the North Atlantic alliance adhesion. So there is a due process of debating defence planning. The important thing about the present-day situation is that defence planning is done along a new military doctrine which is critically linked to the accession to the North Atlantic alliance, so is there any opposition to the 2.24 increase of defence spending? Very surprisingly, there is not any, and very surprisingly, I must say, because obviously everybody is convinced that there should be a reform within the military, that they should feel more dignified, to have new tasks, to work better in better conditions, so nobody practically is touching this issue, so there is a general consensus on this issue in Bulgaria.

Chairman

253. Could I just say that 2.24 is quite formidable. We are getting down to 2.3, although our GDP is higher than yours, so we are going in the opposite direction.

(Mr Agov)   But you have fulfilled a lot of tasks that we have not fulfilled yet, so you have a very well trained military, as you very well know, and we are restructuring part of our military force going into a volunteer force and this is something which you have already done, and then procurement is something which has to be done in Bulgaria, whereas I think the British military are much better equipped than ours are.

254. Can your committee or the National Security Committee, the Budget Committee, can they recommend an increase or a decrease in defence expenditure?

(Mr Agov)   Yes, they can. For instance, I myself, as Chairman of one of these three committees, would be very careful in that if I want an increase, I should be very specific as to in what area should I insist on this increase because if I am not well prepared, and this is the case also for the National Security Committee, it will be only a populist and demagogic move and just to be allowed by the military itself, it has to be a very responsible suggestion.

Mr Cann

255.   If I may just follow on then, it is all very well to have these plans, but how sure are you that your National Assembly has got the will behind it to actually produce the necessary amount of money for the necessary amount of years to actually deliver?

(Mr Agov)   It has already a good record in this direction. For the last two years we have been voting the necessary resources and I do not think there will be any problem until the end of the mandate, and there are two more years of this National Assembly which are the most important years. We are expecting the second phase of military reform to end by 2001 and the mandate of this Assembly is ending on the 4th May 2001, so what we expect is not to have any problems and to have many more votes behind these kind of resources than the mere majority that my party has in Parliament.

Chairman

256.   I know that in the case of Hungary, our Ministry of Defence produced a report for the Hungarian Government on civilian-military relations, the reform process, and I know when I was in Bulgaria ten years ago the Americans were offering very considerable advice. In this whole complex set of issues of defence planning and budgeting and resource accounting and budgeting, very American-style methodologies, do you think your Defence Ministry has been receiving advice on ways in which they can improve finance accounting and budgeting and resource allocation?

(Mr Agov)   Mr Chairman, we had already an extensive mission and extensive research done by the MoD of the United Kingdom and it provided a very profound report for which we were very grateful because it was a report which was not simply recommending along the lines which the Americans normally do, but it was clearly setting out the sore points in the military-civilian relationship of ratios of the military and civilians in the MoD and the general staff and finally how we should intensify civilian control over the military, including parliamentary control, so it was a very useful report for all of us. However, the more important thing which this report

[Chairman *Cont]*

produced was a very basic, I would say, and very profound relationship between the MoD of the UK and of Bulgaria. We are having now a two-pronged action towards reforming the military. Once we had an American mission which was led by an American general, General Kavanagh(?), who provided the same kind of report for the Hungarians and I think the Poles, and then we are having another prominent military man who is General MacKenzie who is the Deputy Supreme Allied Commander of Europe who is becoming more and more active in providing very practical advice on how to continue with the reform and we are hopeful that General MacKenzie when he returns from his present-day position——

Mr Blunt

257.   He has.

(Mr Agov)   Has he? We are expecting him on the 3rd March to Sofia and we are expecting him to say yes to a request to become the chief consultant of the Ministry of Defence on promoting the reform, so we will be glad to have General MacKenzie and I have met him already twice and I am hopeful that I will meet him when he comes to Sofia and to contribute more to the conviction that he should come and help us.

258.   Is that just on the civil-military relationship?

(Mr Agov)   No, it is a general consultancy, I would say, and it goes much deeper than the civilian-military relationship. Practically, if I put it in a framework, this would mean that having all the methodological advice coming both from the Americans and the British, practically the man who will be putting that in place will be General MacKenzie.

259.   Can I ask you what chance of success you think he has got because what has impressed itself upon me and I think other colleagues who went to Bulgaria was this extraordinary disconnect between the political process and the vision of the politicians from the President downwards to yourself, whom we met in the Parliament, and to the young Defence Minister who had been in office about 24 hours when we met him, and I am afraid I cannot recall his name, but you will know who I am talking about, who were keen to push things forward and the whole attitude of the military that seemed well rooted in a previous era, if I can put it like that. With the enormous number of senior officers left depending on remaining in the Bulgarian armed forces, just how easy is it going to be for General MacKenzie to deliver the Bulgarian Army to actually change into something that will be of more utility to NATO?

(Mr Agov)   I am very glad that you have raised this issue because it has always been difficult, especially with senior officers who are entrenched in the old system. You cannot expect these men to change their minds and it would be absolutely unnatural to push them to change their minds. We would be breaching their human right. So I would not go for that. There was a crucial meeting between the Prime Minister and the Minister for Defence on Friday on what has to be done. As a result of this meeting an article was published in the Bulgarian press on Monday which

said that 800 of these senior officers, Lieutenant Colonels, Colonels and general officers will have to leave in order to ease up the reform of Bulgaria. Of course, they would not be pushed too hard, they would not be thrown onto the street. There would have to be some compensation paid. One of the conclusions of the meeting was that it is much cheaper to compensate these officers than to continue to spend on their salaries and practically stalling the reform of Bulgaria. So I think the task of General MacKenzie would be much easier with this process in hand. I do not think General MacKenzie will meet any resistance from the major rank officers or Lieutenants or even younger ranks because they are very enthusiastic about the work that has to be done.

260.   How many?

(Mr Agov)   800 senior officers.

261.   You said 3,000, did you not?

(Mr Agov)   3,000 as a whole, that is senior officers, some junior officers and some NCOs also.

262.   So it is only anticipated to make 3,000 redundant?

(Mr Agov)   I think it is perfectly realistic to have this number.

263.   What sort of size of armed force do you envisage Bulgaria having in ten years' time?

(Mr Agov)   First of all, we are expecting by 2001 to have a force of 75,000, that is down from 120,000 and the final goal by 2010 is to have a force of 45,000, which is comparable to the Belgian military or to the Dutch military. We are receiving a lot of advice from the Belgians and the Dutch because they have populations of a similar size. So we are very grateful to the Dutch and the Belgians.

264.   Thank you. That is very interesting. What I want to do now is to move back to the questions that John McWilliam was starting off with about NATO's new strategic concept. We went to see Mr Sterk after we had seen you and he told us that he thought that the major strategic choice for NATO was going to be to commit itself to stabilisation of the Balkans. What is your view of the future direction NATO should take as outlined in the strategic concept?

(Mr Agov)   I cannot omit the Balkans from any view I give because I live there. For instance, Kosovo is just 100 kilometres from us and you cannot expect me to view any strategic development in the area without looking at the issues from a Balkan point of view. There could be two approaches towards the enlargement of NATO: firstly, staying away from the Balkans, because they are too dangerous and too problematic to get involved in; secondly, getting involved with the Balkans to seek solutions in the Balkans. I would definitely opt for the second approach, not because I am selfish but because I think if the Balkans are not stabilised through a very clear set of alliances and very close links between the Western nations and the nations who are existing on the Balkans then that will continue to pose serious problems for all of Europe. For instance, I have always been cockish on how to seek solutions. I have always supported the military option much earlier than

[Mr Blunt *Cont]*

military options for the Balkans because obviously when we had post-Communist nationalism flourishing in a country like Yugoslavia it turned out to be a very important part of the transition of Communist nations as then people cannot be convinced through political means or through normal political talk to go along the normal route of defending human rights and so on. I have always been a great supporter of the military option myself and hopefully a lot of people support me on this issue. The military option should be clearly supported by all the nations which surround Yugoslavia, otherwise any single nation which stays away from this solidarity approach could provide Milosevic or other brutes like him with a way to build bridges in our bid to find a solution.

265. So would you be prepared for Bulgaria to commit troops to support the peace process in Kosovo?
(Mr Agov) Yes, I would. I do not only think Bulgaria but also Romania should. I wonder if my Rumanian friends would speak so forcefully of Bulgaria, but I would definitely speak in favour of the Rumanians and the Slovenians. I do not know what the case is with the Slovenians. I know that some Senate members are very strong supporters of Slovenia being invited, but we support Slovenia. We think that Macedonia should also be involved and should receive further guarantees that it will be involved in the process.

266. What is the motivation underlying that willingness? I remember when we met in Bulgaria you told us about an occasion in which Bulgaria had had to use the PfP process because there had been some Serbian threat to the power station on the border. Presumably that situation still exists and the nuclear power station is still there. Is this anxiety to contribute troops to Kosovo or whatever actually driven by the fact that what is important about it is demonstrating your credentials for NATO membership because it is the Article 5 guarantee that is of central importance given the fact that you have a neighbour like Serbia?
(Mr Agov) One of the deficiencies of partnership for peace is that countries get involved and their military get involved in inter-operability activities with NATO while they do not get any support on major security issues like, for instance, the nuclear power station of Bulgaria which is very close to the Serbian border and if there was a military solution to the Kosovo issue then we could imagine some Serbian planes blackmailing the whole of Europe because a nuclear power station exploding does not only affect Bulgaria, it would affect all of us. How do we proceed? We have suggested to the North Atlantic Council that the Kosovo issue should teach us how important it is to upgrade our relations and we should wait until the second wave of enlargement to apply our legal relationship and to create a network of small agreements that will provide us with more guarantees which will make it absolutely automatic to move troops around or to move defences or to provide defences. So that is how we see the upgrading of our relationship with NATO and this will make all the nations much more prepared to meet their full commitments under Article 5 of the Washington Treaty once they become members of the alliance.

267. Some commentators see a tension between the Article 5 focus of NATO and its newly-developing missions of peacekeeping and peace support. How enthusiastic are you? You have spoken about Kosovo and that you would be willing to support troops there, but do you think it is more important for Bulgaria to get itself in shape to be able to defend its own territory under Article 5 or should it be contributing to the newly-developing missions of peacekeeping and peace support?
(Mr Agov) At least we do understand the accession to the alliance as a contribution not only to our common defence, but also a contribution to this part of the common defence which is called peacekeeping missions. We do not look at Article 5 defences only in terms of security, but we also look at Article 5 as a very crucial basis providing force to any peacekeeping operation of the alliance. That would mean that if we do not have the power of Article 5 that will initially guarantee our security, then we will feel much more insecure to go on missions beyond the territories of Article 5 countries, so if I can make it clear, we need the backing of Article 5. This makes your decision-making process much easier and then when we see a threat in Kosovo or anywhere, it will be much easier for us to say, "Okay, we feel secure here, but because our security is jeopardised somewhere outside the Article 5 territories, then we have to go there". That is our attitude. For instance, I spoke this morning to our Ambassador to NATO——

268. But that was an attitude we met in the military who were saying, "We can't change the structure of the armed forces until we have a guarantee because our armed forces are structured in order to defend the territory of Bulgaria".
(Mr Agov) This is a small argument we are constantly having with the military, between the politicians and the military. They would prefer of course to have first the cart and then the horse and we would like to have the horse and then the cart, putting the right thing first. We tell them, "Okay, you have to prepare yourselves to meet your commitments as military people. We are making the political decisions and you do not stop the political decisions by just setting the cart before the horse", so that is our attitude. I do not think that the military would continue to resist this; no, they are looking forward and I am sure some——

269. But you were saying earlier, and sorry to interrupt you, that you would be much more willing to assist in peace support operations, and you have mentioned Iraq and Kosovo or wherever, if you had the Article 5 guarantee because you would then have the security, but in a sense what NATO is looking for is for you to restructure your armed forces in advance of NATO membership before you get the Article 5 guarantee, rather like in the example of Romania who in a sense is following this particular strategy of contributing to every conceivable peace support operation it can humanly send troops to in order to demonstrate that its armed forces are changing and are becoming useful in a new NATO setting. Do you think you will be able to carry that debate in Bulgaria?

[Mr Blunt *Cont]*

(Mr Agov) Well, probably I was generalising on peacekeeping missions before and probably I was not very clear on this and it is my fault, but definitely I would like to mention that the resolve to go into a peacekeeping mission does not necessarily go hand in hand with full membership of NATO, which means Article 5. I started to say that I spoke this morning to our Ambassador to NATO and the North Atlantic Council demanded of Bulgaria that we participate in a new peacekeeping mission in Kosovo and I spoke to Sofia and I was told that we are ready to provide not only logistical and all kinds of support for a combined mission to Kosovo, but also to contribute troops as we did within the IFOR or the SFOR in Bosnia, so this is our case. We are fully committed to the peacekeeping mission in Kosovo and hopefully there will be an agreement and then we will participate fully. Article 5 or not Article 5, this is our commitment to the regional stability and we do that without any hesitation.

Chairman

270. Has the Government made a formal acceptance of the kind offer by NATO requesting——

(Mr Agov) It was extended only yesterday. Only yesterday the North Atlantic Council decided to extend to the PfP nations of the area the invitation to participate in this force and I know that now this morning in Brussels, in SHAPE, we have a very, very intensive final period of preparing the plans for deploying the force in Kosovo and hopefully all of this will involve Bulgaria.

Mr Colvin

271. If I were you, I would not be too worried about your ability to fulfil Article 5 commitments because at the moment Britain cannot fulfil all of ours. It remains to be seen just what NATO's new Strategic Concept is, but if it involves out-of-area operations, we cannot get there. With Operation Sea Adriatic, in the Balkans, we had to hitchhike with the Americans on both boats and aircraft. Most of the flights out there have been done in Ukrainian Antonovs and in fact most of the movements of the Minister of Defence last year were in Antonovs, so I think it remains to be seen just what the new Strategic Concept has to say about out-of-area operations before you can tell precisely what is going to be required. You have already been very active both in Partnership for Peace and also in the Euro-Atlantic Partnership Council. Now, I know that politicians by nature are meant to be optimistic, but can I just for a moment be pessimistic and assume that you do not get into NATO in the next wave. How do you see PfP and EAPC being developed to enable you to participate more in joint security not just in Europe, but in those areas that affect Europe, like the Maghreb, like the Middle East and so on? Perhaps you could also say what you have learned from your existing involvement that would enable you to look ahead.

(Mr Agov) Well, we do not even discuss this fall-back option of remaining in PfP and not being upgraded along the road to full membership, and this is not because of the politicians' optimism. We think

that there is a vested common interest in integrating South-Eastern Europe, closing the circle there and having Greece, if you can just imagine the map, Turkey, Bulgaria, Romania, Slovenia, Macedonia, everybody involved in this. Of course the Yugoslav issue will continue to create problems. We were last week in Ankara meeting the South-East European Chairmen of the Foreign Affairs Committees and it was a very small format on the initiative of our Turkish friends and we were all together there. When I spoke to the Croats, they were very concerned about the fact that Bosnia is still too fragmented. They are very concerned that if there are no new economic developments there people will continue to flee the area and go elsewhere seeking jobs. PfP taught us that we can work together. It was a very important psychological exercise. It pointed clearly to the points where we have to work to create the inter-operability networks that will involve the militaries of Central and Eastern Europe within the alliance. Initially the Chairman asked me what we expected from Washington. I insisted on having an upgrading for those nations who are potential members of the alliance. I do not see how the PfP, with all its major achievements in practically melting the remnants of the Berlin Wall in the minds of the military, can remain in its present form without discouraging the aspiring nations. I think this is crucially important. Of course there is always an if, i.e. if you are not invited, if you are not accepted as new members of the alliance. I would not opt for that. It is in our joint interest to go along the enlargement route when we are ready to enforce this enlargement to make it a very vivid alliance. I am sure that this alliance, with its new strategic concept, would provide a means for transporting our special missions to places where we are interested in being sent as a mission.

Mr Hood

272. How do the people of Bulgaria perceive what is happening and what do they expect the Government to deliver, because I see the aspirations of countries like Bulgaria to want to join NATO, to want to join the European Union as part of that aim to fit into the European scene both in economic and defensive terms? In order to accomplish both countries like Bulgaria will have to make substantial economic and politic reforms in their country. Is there not a danger of raising the expectations above the realistic achievable aims? One of the problems for us who are in the European Union and for us who are in NATO is to be very careful that we do not have a reverse reaction, i.e. an expectations clause, especially in the economic field where people are making sacrifices and suffering to achieve something. How do you feel about the dangers in your own country if the expectations and the perceptions of the public of what they have had to go through in the way of accepting reform is not seen by them to be deliverable in a quicker time than what is envisaged?

(Mr Agov) I can remember very clearly when we had our COSAC meeting in Luxembourg during the last Luxembourg Presidency we were discussing the same issue, i.e. what would bring a rejection in

[**Mr Hood** *Cont*]

Luxembourg for nations like Bulgaria and others. I think all these arguments are absolutely valid when we discuss the enlargement of the North Atlantic Alliance. Rejection is something which might be extremely discouraging to the people who are making a lot of sacrifices. Bulgarians never go to a party without being prepared for the party, it is part of their psychology. They would not go to a marriage celebration without being prepared for the celebration. This was the case, as you will remember, in Luxembourg. They should involve us in the process and let us do our homework. We are not insisting on being accepted as new members tomorrow. We want to prepare ourselves for when we become new members and to contribute to this European Union and to this alliance. I want to make it very clear that rejection would have some unpredictable consequences in political life in Bulgaria, not for me because I am committed to this process, not for my Prime Minister who is also committed, not to the party that I am committed to, but these people would find this a clear sign that we were going along a road where at the end of it nobody expects us to be. On the one hand people in Bulgaria are making their sacrifices and on the other hand they know their deficiencies. The public criticises some of the politicians for raising too high expectations on the European Union or NATO when they say, "Okay, we are there. We had to do a lot of work in order to get there." Visas are a major issue for Bulgaria and we have discussed it on several occasions, through the COSAC format and now Bulgarians are saying, "Okay, let's put our house in order and then ask for free access to Europe." It is a matter of how we face things and how we understand things. We are very careful not to raise expectations too high. There is another nation which is also striving for full membership and it is a little more noisy in presenting its case. Sometimes I wonder if we should not be doing the same, that is pushing and knocking on each door and saying, "Okay, if you do not accept us as new members this will be a catastrophe for all of us." I do not see the abolishment of Communism as the only necessary reason to become a member of NATO. We have to contribute there. I think that is the basic philosophy with my government.

Chairman: What has been quite startling is that two countries who a couple of years ago were not even remotely going to be considered for membership (Bulgaria and Slovakia have made quite startling progress. Now you are a contender and it will take some time before political elites in NATO countries, European Union countries are aware of what has been happening. I suppose it is a delayed action and it will take a little time before it penetrates their brains that Bulgaria is not the Bulgaria of two or three years ago or ten years ago, it is making quite spectacular progress and maybe it will not be a catastrophe if you do not get offered a place this time because, like Romania, Slovakia and Bulgaria, it will give you a little more time to make the necessary preparations across a variety of fronts, civil/military relations, your economy, dealing with crime, which will make you really serious contenders in two or three years from now. I hope, even if you do not get all you wish out of Washington, at least the expectations will be fairly realistic, that you will be in the next wave. Could I ask my colleague Laura Moffatt to put a question.

Laura Moffatt

273. I wonder if we could take this process forward on modernisation. We were very impressed when we visited Bulgaria to look at the process, particularly the politicians. Sometimes that was not quite matched with the military that we spoke to and I do not underestimate the difficulties of modernising forces and I see what that must bring, in particular, to conscription of course, and I know that Bulgaria does not need to have a change in law because it is not part of the constitution.

(*Mr Agov*) No, it is not.

274. So, therefore, presumably that makes it somewhat easier, though that does not make it politically easier when people rely on it of course for employment and income and, therefore, I recognise those difficulties. Perhaps firstly you could just tell me about that process because I know that phase 2 will be complete in 2001 and phase 3 has not been started on yet, so how do we expect to get much of this done in that timescale?

(*Mr Agov*) We have dwelt a little bit on this issue in our previous discussions and I clearly understand your impression. From time to time I get frustrated——

275. Don't we all!

(*Mr Agov*) —— at the slow pace of all of this since I am not driven by my wish to be re-elected necessarily, but by my wish to see things going much faster, but on conscription and compulsory service, the volunteer service is gathering momentum and we have already 171 registered volunteer soldiers and just several months ago we did not have even any interest in a volunteer service, so the process is going well. We are expecting this mechanised battalion or rapid-reaction force, the first battalion, to be of 700 people just in a year's time and to have a fully-fledged volunteer force and it will be the most modern one in the Bulgarian military. Then, as you know very well from your visit to Bulgaria, we have a diminished term of compulsory service which is twelve months and then we have the alternative service, so I do not think conscription is any more a problem. I am sure that reform, the second stage of reform, cutting the military and streamlining the military command structure, will end by 2001. Furthermore, I expect the pyramid, which now is upside-down in the military, you have a full field of colonels who are sitting on the turned-around bottom of the pyramid, the MoD and the general staff, and we expect all of this to turn around in 2001, so that is how we see the reform. The third phase, once you get all these young officers involved in the reform, I think they will become the driving force behind the third stage of the reform, so that is what we think. It is a self-generating process. Once you have the young military, they have their stake in their career in this kind of military and not in the previous type of military that we used to have, so that is how we see things.

[Laura Moffatt *Cont]*

276. I think you are absolutely right and it will develop a momentum on its own, but does that mean looking very closely at the workings of military colleges and the expansion of non-commissioned officers—surely that is part of that process?

(Mr Agov) Well, I was provided before coming here with some notes on these issues, but I would strongly recommend a website so that you can get all these details and not make me read all these notes that have been prepared by the MoD. I would only say that I know clearly, since I went through all these notes this morning, that there is a clear set of new defence college programmes which are in language training, new command structures, all the needed compatibility with the military practices of NATO nations and we are and hopeful that the aid we are getting from military officers from NATO nations like Holland, Belgium and the UK will provide us with a lot of opportunities to train our young people to be fully compatible practically, so that when you give an order, this would mean the same order for both a Dutch soldier and a Bulgarian soldier, and this is the important thing. Then of course, with non-commissioned officers, we are at the start of establishing a volunteer force where they will start to understand that this is a career, that once you get through a soldier status, you can receive your promotion and become an NCO and so on. This is the process and you cannot expect to have NCOs immediately, just all of a sudden or——

277. You cannot plant them, can you?

(Mr Agov) It just cannot happen and I think, as the Chairman was saying, we need this time to prepare ourselves, but it should be a stimulating time and we should know clearly where we are going, where we are heading for. Of course we are doing it mostly for ourselves, but once we have the solidarity in a clear decision in Washington, then these people will be even more motivated to go along this road.

Mr Hood

278. I wonder if I could ask you about your relations with your neighbouring countries like Romania, Slovenia and Macedonia. How do you see your influence in the Federal Republic of Yugoslavia, for instance, *vis-à-vis* your relationships with those countries?

(Mr Agov) Let me start with the most difficult part which is the Federal Republic of Yugoslavia. I will not be using any diplomatic language in this and I will share my beliefs and the beliefs of my colleagues. Until the Federal Republic of Yugoslavia is a democracy, until it becomes a free country with the rule of law and respect of human rights, until this moment, Yugoslavia will be the sore point of Europe. I do not expect this Government in Yugoslavia to bring any solution through goodwill. It will be producing solutions only through pressure put on this Government because they understand only pressure and we are very clear on this. Unfortunately enough, the whole Western community or European community, including of course Bulgaria very modestly, we never paid enough attention to

alternatives in Yugoslavia and we never cared to develop political alternatives to support, to encourage political alternatives in Yugoslavia, so I do believe that only if Yugoslavia goes through the process that all the other Central European nations went through, only then will Yugoslavia be a reliable and good partner and it is absolutely valid for its relations with Bulgaria. We do not see a chance up to now, and that is why we are insisting so much on participating in all the efforts to bring peace in Kosovo because we know that because we have a NATO force which is enforcing peace in Kosovo, this will start a brewing process, seeking democracy, seeking alternatives in Yugoslavia, and we think this is encouraging. We keep our relations with the Yugoslavs because the Serbs are not only Milosevic, but there are very nice and very good people living there and we are going to live with them in another 1,000 years, so it is important to have all these venues of contact with people who might be alternative to the rule of nationalists like Milosevic. Romania is a crucial partner. We share the same priorities, we share the same strategic goals and we are working quite closely together in different areas. We support strongly Romania, although it is going unfortunately through a difficult time right now, but we think that that is the time when Romania needs support, not at a time when it is flourishing and blossoming, but they need support right now and that is why we think we should show solidarity. Finally, I have already mentioned Turkey and our excellent relationship with Turkey. Greece is a traditional partner and the most natural partner of Bulgaria, being a member of both the European Union and the Atlantic Alliance. I would stress once more the major breakthrough in our relations with Macedonia. This is confirmation of what I was trying to say about Yugoslavia. While we had in Macedonia a government which was more or less a product of the Yugoslav era or Tito era because most people were linked to this regime, we had the problem of establishing a normal relationship. Once we had the change, through a democratic election and due democratic process, we could see a new opening for our relations and this is absolutely valid when we view Yugoslavia as a potential future partner along with Bulgaria. I think Macedonia should be strongly supported now that it is hoping the extraction force is going to play a crucial role in our efforts to bring peace to Kosovo. So it is important to have Macedonia as a robust country in the area. That is how we see our relationship.

279. The Ukraine?

(Mr Agov) The Ukraine is just across the sea. We think that the Ukraine is a major strategic factor vis-à-vis Russia. We have a very special relationship with the Ukraine and it is different from the relationship with any other country from the former Soviet Union. We see the Ukraine as a counter-balance to the Russian presence especially in the Black Sea basin and as a potential ally in its way of thinking and considering the world. We have put a lot of strength on our relations with the Ukraine.

280. Does Bulgaria have any outstanding border disputes at present?

[**Mr Hood** *Cont*]

(Mr Agov) No, we do not have any. We do not have any ethnic minority problems. Fortunately enough, having probably the same mixture or cocktail of nationalities or ethnic minorities that Kosovo has, we are doing just the opposite, we are living together and we are not fighting each other.

Mr Cann

281. You used to have border disputes with Macedonia which has got a Bulgarian minority. Southern Romania, the Dobruja region and parts of Greece up against Turkey, have you no ambitions in that area whatsoever any more?
(Mr Agov) We did not discuss Greece at all. We are involved, together with the Greeks, in a plan to have at least five openings in the border between Bulgaria and Greece because we believe strongly in original development. The minorities have their families on both sides of the border. Our belief is that whilst we are opening up the border, having more contact between families, this issue is not on the agenda any more. We have agreed it and it is solved. Macedonia is going to sign with Bulgaria a declaration on the basis of relations between the two countries. The draft document includes respect for the constitutions of both countries and it also includes the rejection of both countries to resolve the minority issues between themselves. So it is a very strong goodwill document that we think will regulate the relationships that we are going to have with Macedonia. Macedonia is a very special case for the Bulgarians. During the Ottoman Empire this used to be the same territory and the same people. My grandmother comes from this area. Some of my relatives come from it. One-third of Bulgarians have their relatives in territory which is now in Macedonia. The vast majority of Bulgarians see Macedonia as a separate nation and we respect this and we say okay, romantically we might have been linked in the past, but now if they wish the Macedonians to go on their own way, let them go.

Mr Hancock

282. That could easily change, could it not, if the situation in Kosovo deteriorated to such an extent that the KLA decided they would not be satisfied with Kosovo, that they would turn their attention first to Albania and then to Macedonia? Some people in that area feel that the long-term scenario ends up with a greater Albania, greater Serbia and a greater Bulgaria. I can remember speaking to Bulgarians in Macedonia who would be only too keen to see that scenario develop and they had no loyalty whatsoever to the Macedonian government.
(Mr Agov) The coherence of a Macedonian government, which includes the Albanians, is something which is crucially important to all of us. This is the worst case scenario, of course. We had Arbenger Verry (?), the leader of the democratic party of the Albanians in Macedonia, in Sofia two weeks ago and I was impressed by the commitment of this man to the integrity of Macedonia and to full participation in the government of Macedonia, which

sounded very encouraging to me because I had the same disturbances as probably many of the people you have met in Macedonia. I do not think there will be a spill over from Kosovo to Macedonia. The Albanians in Macedonia are not eager to joint their brethren in Albania proper.

283. Not in Albania, no, certainly not.
(Mr Agov) And the Kosovo Albanians are also not eager to join the Albanian Albanians because in Macedonia and Kosovo there are higher standards of living. The Albanians themselves would not go as far as saying that they would accept territories together with the minorities that are living on these territories. I do not expect this worst case scenario to happen now that we have these positive developments in Macedonia, now that we have the extraction force in Macedonia and a strong NATO presence in Macedonia.

Mr Hancock: Can I just take you back a couple of questions because I was very interested in your reply about the price to pay for NATO membership and the political goodwill that would be lost, the fear factor of not really considering rejection. The expense to the nation of Bulgaria of getting themselves into a position to make Bulgaria an acceptable political force and military force in NATO is going to be a very high price to pay. I sensed when I was last there that it had been suggested that this price was worth paying, as it has been in Romania and other places, as a stepping stone to EU membership and the payback would come not through membership of NATO, but that would give you the credibility which would strengthen your bid for EU membership. I would be interested to know how you are going to pay as a nation to get your armed forces into a good enough state so that you bring a commodity to the table that would be readily welcomed and one that would mean the burden would not be so great on the economy of Bulgaria that people would believe it was a price worth paying?

Chairman

284. You can be fairly brief because if Mr Hancock reads the transcript he will have two-thirds of the answer. Maybe you can just remind him of what you said.
(Mr Agov) I think there is an important issue to be raised about the link between EU enlargement and NATO enlargement. We are starting to realise the link and it is not necessarily ESDI, although it is a very important issue, ESDI, what we do as Europeans to build up our own identity, all of this, but I would not raise this issue because I know you have had a lot of debate on this issue, but we would not substitute NATO with the European Union or the European Union with NATO. We think that unlike friends who say that these are separate procedures and separate tracks, we see a lot of intertwining movements or movements which wrap those tracks in one single package. What would it mean? Once you try to join the European Union, you have to reach certain standards of living or a certain growth of GDP and once you reach a certain growth of GDP and when you dedicate two percentage points of your GDP to

[**Chairman** *Cont*]

military restructuring, then it will mean that the movement towards the European Union naturally will bring more money and it would not be too much of a sacrifice to the population, too much of a sacrifice, no, you can spend this money on other issues. Then as to how NATO accession or earlier NATO accession might influence the EU accession, first of all, once you are rejected both from the European Union, and let us say that Bulgaria is in the second group, then NATO, second wave, whenever it happens, as a worst-case scenario, then it is only natural for foreign direct investors to stay away from countries like Bulgaria and Romania, thus keeping growth lower and thus opening more the breach between the Central European nations like the Czech Republic, Poland and Hungary and the South-Eastern Europeans like Romania and Bulgaria, so once you have, for instance, a clear commitment by NATO not necessarily to invite Bulgaria, Romania or Slovenia now in Washington, but when you have a clear commitment and a clear prospect, then foreign direct investors, who are very sensitive about where you are, how they feel and how they smell the stability of a country, would start to come and this will help finally to increase GDP, and increasing GDP will bring Bulgaria closer, first of all, to meeting her economic criteria to become an EU member and then of course spending more on the military restructuring without putting so much pain on the population. So it is a process which is definitely wrapped in the same package, although people would like to separate it and to compensate some countries with EU membership instead of NATO membership.

285. You have mentioned Russia three or four times, but almost tangentially. Russia historically has had a long interest in Balkan politics and in the era of the Warsaw Pact, Bulgaria and the Soviet Union were umbilically linked. Do you suspect that Russia wishes to retain an, albeit weakened, influence in the Balkans? Might they seek to exploit any rejection of Romania and Bulgaria from NATO? Do you sense that they do hanker after that influence to an extent that they had for much of the last 100 years or even longer?

(Mr Agov) When the NATO membership prospect for Bulgaria and Romania was not so clear on the horizon, then we had the venue for the Russians to interfere much more energetically in the Bosnian conflict, providing illegally, and breaking the embargo,

arms and ammunition to the Serbs. Now that we have this prospect, you can see the change. The Russians now do not see a bridge they can build towards the Serbs, so now they contribute through the contact group efforts to bring peace to Kosovo. Will it happen in the reverse if Bulgaria and Romania are not invited? Yes, it will happen, it will happen. This is a perennial Russian interest in the area and this is another reason why we should think very seriously that Russia should not be encouraged to promote or to dream about this policy any more. Russia has to be forced because it is always a Russian dream to reach the warm seas through the Bosporus and the Dardanelles and so on and it has been the reason for so many wars in the area. The Russians should know that and Russia should be involved through the peace-making process, through co-operation and through solidarity with the Western democracies and European democracy into bringing peace in the area, not through promoting its power or projecting its power in the area. Yes, Mr Chairman, I do expect the Russians to become much more versatile in the area once they feel that there is rejection in the air coming out of Washington. I would like to thank you all very much for listening to me talking passionately about my country. I am sorry that I was sometimes passionate, but we live there and we know all the problems there.

Chairman: We read too much about passion in legislatures, Mr Agov. Having spent much of the eighties anticipating what the Bulgarian and the Soviet order of battle was, the routes both of your armies would take heading towards Turkey, the capacity of your ports to receive reinforcement from the Soviet Union, battling with your government over its appalling record on minority rights, it is quite exhilarating for me to see Bulgaria as a democratising country with its economy improving, developing closer and closer links with Europe and re-entering normal European world politics. I hope that even if your aspirations are not immediately satisfied in April, it will not mean you coming too often to our House of Commons arguing passionately for your country's inclusion in NATO. I hope the time will come in the not too distant future where you will simply slip into membership quite naturally and we would offer you all the encouragement we can. Thank you very much to you and your colleagues for coming and I am sure we shall see you soon. Thank you very much.

WEDNESDAY 17 FEBRUARY 1999

Members present:

Mr Bruce George, in the Chair

Mr Crispin Blunt	Mr Michael Hancock
Mr Julian Brazier	Mr Jimmy Hood
Mr Jamie Cann	Mr John McWilliam
Mr Harry Cohen	Laura Moffatt
Mr Michael Colvin	Ms Dari Taylor

Examination of witnesses

MR GEORGE ROBERTSON, a Member of the House, Secretary of State for Defence, MR TONY LLOYD, a Member of the House, Minister of State, Foreign and Commonwealth Office, MR RICHARD HATFIELD, Policy Director, Ministry of Defence, and MR STEPHEN GOMERSALL, Director of International Security, Foreign and Commonwealth Office, were examined.

Chairman

286. Secretary of State, Minister of State, Mr Gomersall and Mr Hatfield, a happy recess. I hope you realise we are on time and a half now so the longer we can go the happier we will be. Secretary of State, when you responded to my Rock and Spain statement last week you said that you looked forward to meeting all the Members of the Defence Committee. We have provided ten. I am sure Mr McWilliam will roll up in due course.
(Mr Robertson) It is very flattering that the Committee have decided to break into the recess in order to be here and interrogate us. I will be more cautious about making these debating points when I reply to you in future.

287. I was thinking that we have seen you both so often in the last twelve months that we ought to be including your names on the attendance list of the Committee. It would be very impressive. We thought it was about time for us meet. What I thought, gentlemen, was that all of our questions until plus or minus 12 o'clock would be on the NATO Strategic Concept; and then after that, 12 to 12.30, if that is okay, we would move into Kosovo. Otherwise, Kosovo will get mixed up with the Strategic Concept. One of the main reasons we asked you to come along is that we will be finalising our report publication just before the Washington Summit. Therefore, what you say will be very important in our final report. In a way, it was gratuitous that Kosovo blew up, (if I may say that politically incorrectly), because it gave us an opportunity in the recess to talk to you on something which is of great immediate importance. I suspect we will be having meetings like this for the next 50 years. We will start off then with the general NATO Strategic Concept. I am not sure whether you feel it is necessary for you both to answer. If there are any profound disagreements between the MoD and the Foreign Office we will be more than pleased to listen to them. We will be most intent.
(Mr Lloyd) I guarantee there are none.
(Mr Robertson) Indeed, it is inconceivable.

288. Firstly, a question on NATO missions and the new Strategic Concept. When we were in NATO a couple of weeks ago, the impression we had informally was that the United States was not putting the same amount of effort into the Strategic Concept that one might have expected. Their position is a little fuzzy and the French may not have produced anything prickly or worthwhile either. Two questions. Firstly, have you detected any fuzziness or lack of far-sightedness in either the American or French position? Having said that, perhaps you can give us some clues as to what are the British principal goals in the redrafting of this Strategic Concept.
(Mr Robertson) I think I detect no great fuzziness. I detect what is probably quite a common NATO phenomenon. That people do not concentrate their minds until very close to the event. I participated shortly after the election in the last NATO Summit in Madrid. In terms of planning and preparation we are much better off than before Madrid. A lot of loose ends were tied up on the floor of the Summit itself, so we are far further down the road on that. The engagement of all of the allies has been close. I think that we are probably reaching the basis of an agreement—give or take some of the details—on what the Strategic Concept is likely to be. I do not detect a fuzziness in the American side or even on the French side about where we are going. This takes one on to where it should be going. In a way, that defines the problems—if there are problems. This Strategic Concept has got to be updated from 1991, when it was looked at immediately after what would be regarded as the end of the Cold War. Since then NATO has not changed her character. In terms of Article 5, common security guarantees are still there and will still be the core of this Strategic Concept. Clearly the activities over Kosovo, non-Article 5 missions, have led to some lessons being learned, which should be incorporated into the Concept itself. They will be, and they have to be, because NATO in many ways will find itself, as we are at the present moment in Kosovo, having to deal more with non-Article 5 problems than with Article 5 itself, the self-defence part of the Treaty. It is interesting in this week, where you actually make the point that Kosovo is a live crisis which we have to deal with, that when the Deputy Prime Minister of Iraq

THE DEFENCE COMMITTEE

71

17 February 1999]   Mr GEORGE ROBERTSON, MP, Mr TONY LLOYD, MP, Mr RICHARD HATFIELD and Mr STEPHEN GOMERSALL   *[Continued*

[**Chairman** *Cont*]

visited Turkey last week, he left a veiled threat of an attack on Turkey if they want to continue to be part of the coalition that was engaged in Iraq, in containing Iraq at the present time. So it is remarkable that in NATO's 50th year we actually have what might be a veiled threat of an attack on one NATO country, which would have dramatic ramifications given the nature of Article 5.

289. Perhaps we should send Mr Aziz a copy of the NATO Treaty that the warning attack of a NATO country entails. I do not even think our colleague, Mr Benn, would be able to say there was not a constitutional legal justification for military action. Mr Lloyd, have you anything to add?

(Mr Lloyd) No, I think that is a complete statement. There is only one point I would make. There has actually been a lot of work done already at a direct level within NATO. That work is moving to make sure that the relatively minor areas of uncertainty will be ironed out before the Washington Summit, but there is broad agreement on the basic philosophy of NATO as outlined by the Defence Secretary.

290. In terms of the final run-in and the British position, how is this well-oiled machine of Government being activated? What would be the structure, formal and informal, that the Foreign Office and the Ministry of Defence and the Cabinet Office would be taking to get our position final? And to comment on the earlier drafts, have things differed from what has been happening hitherto in preparation?

(Mr Robertson) The Concept was last revised in 1991 when I was outside the system. But maybe Mr Hatfield, who was inside the system, might like to tell us of that.

(Mr Hatfield) Unfortunately in 1991 I was not dealing with NATO. I have no reason to believe it adopted a different approach. It is essentially through day-to-day informal co-operation meetings and so on. From time to time clearly submissions go to Ministers, or from Ministers jointly, on the next phase of work. It is perhaps worth mentioning why you might have a slightly fuzzy picture of NATO recently. NATO bureaucracy has had its eye on other balls in the last few weeks and this has slowed down some of the simple bureaucratic handling. I do not think there is anything to add to the Secretary of State's main answer.

291. Will the British position have to be approved by anybody above the level of Secretaries of State?

(Mr Robertson) The Prime Minister will be at the NATO Summit so the ultimate imprimatur on the final document would be that of the Prime Minister. As you know, it is done on a very collegiate basis. Elements are put together. The documentation we are seeing just now is huge because each section has been taken in turn. That will have to be refined and distilled and digested before the end. Among NATO allies, although there are some debates going on, the bigger issues—the balance between Article 5, the collective security guarantee, and non-Article 5 e.g. intervention outside of a NATO area—that has largely been resolved by agreement between all of the individual parties there.

292. Will there be agreement because we have decided on lowest common denominator? Will it be a serious paragraph or will it just be a compromise to allow everyone to carry on in the way they wish to?

(Mr Robertson) I think it is fair to say that some of the allies were stuck very much on Article 5 as being the absolute. Beyond that very little needed to be said. Our view has always been that we need to deal with non-Article 5 issues here because, as Bosnia has shown, as Kosovo is increasingly showing, we have to have procedures to deal with that. Therefore, they must be in the Concept. As I say, that was one of the discussions. It was not an argument. It was a debate which went on. We are coming now to a sensible balance between the two, which is based on the pragmatic role that NATO will have. There was another debate about the whole question of the legal mandates. That is an issue which I think has been reconciled as well, as the discussion has gone on.

Mr Colvin

293. This leads directly on to the question of the mandate. With Article 5 operations there is no difficulty but with non-Article 5 operations there is. It also raises the subject of NATO's region and out-of-region operations. The air strikes, for instance, in the former Yugoslavia, took place without any authority from the United Nations Security Council. How do you see out-of-area operations being authorised in future? Should we always have to go back to the United Nations Security Council for resolutions, or do you think a precedent has already been set for operations without a special United Nations Security Council mandate?

(Mr Lloyd) If I can begin. One thing which is obvious is that NATO already is, of today, acting out-of-area in Bosnia. We are considering the possibility of operating out-of-area in the context of Kosovo. Within that I do not think it is possible to say to the Committee that we can do anything other than on literally a case-by-case basis at the time when any form of military action is being contemplated. What is certainly the case is that under Article 51 of the UN Charter, there is an inherent right of international fora for self-defence and collective self-defence. Obviously once we go out-of-area we are looking at a different series of issues. For example, we have made it very clear that in the Kosovo context, that any commitment of ground forces would only take place if that were done with the willingness of the parties on the ground: in other words, both the Belgrade authorities and the Kosovar Albanians. So by invitation that clearly is well understood within the international law. Mr Colvin did raise, I think you said about air strikes which had taken place. I may be wrong about that, but in any case the point at issue is your referring to the possibility of air strikes in the autumn of last year.

294. Yes.

(Mr Lloyd) It was clear at the time—and if I can remind the Committee simply so that the point is fairly established on the record—at that time some 50,000 Kosovar Albanians in the mountains faced death through cold or through exposure. At that time there

72   MINUTES OF EVIDENCE TAKEN BEFORE

17 February 1999]   Mr George Robertson, MP, Mr Tony Lloyd, MP,   *[Continued*
                          Mr Richard Hatfield and Mr Stephen Gomersall

[Mr Colvin *Cont]*

was no doubt that the level of humanitarian need was enormous, was recognised, and under international law we have absolutely no doubts that there would have been a justification at that time for action designed to alleviate and resolve that humanitarian crisis. I do not think it is possible to anticipate every future circumstances except simply to say this. Therefore, we are not saying that every form of military action has to be underpinned by a direct Security Council mandate. That was not the case in the autumn.

295. That explains how the authority was arrived at. But the fact is that Article 51 is about collective or individual country's defence and not offensive action. I guess that the humanitarian issue that you have just raised with regard to Kosovo had its fall-back in the Universal Declaration of Human Rights rather than the UN Charter. The Charter was written in the early 1940s. Is there a case for revisiting the UN Charter in the light of what has happened since 1989, and agreeing amendments that would give authority to countries to take offensive action outside their region. Is the UN Charter not a bit outdated, now that we have a different world order? There are going to be different problems arising which will need addressing without necessarily always having to go back for the United Nations Security Council authority.

(Mr Lloyd) Again, I must say this. It is inconceivable that NATO would operate outside international law. That is the first leg on which we must stand. There has to be a legal base for any action. Mr Colvin then asks whether it is possible to consider redefining the United Nations Charter. In practice, the prospect of that is so daunting that I would ask the Committee to quickly throw it out of their sights, if you would. But in practical effect the Charter, of course, does allow for the kind of actions that we would legitimately anticipate. That NATO, neither in terms of its own legal framework nor in terms of its international law, is constrained to operations within the NATO area.

296. What is the NATO area precisely? What is in-region and what is out-of-region?
(Mr Lloyd) There is no definition.

297. North coast of Africa?
(Mr Lloyd) There is no definition.

298. There is none?
(Mr Robertson) It is defined by NATO. Your decision in NATO is one of its great strengths because they are taken by consensus. It would be up to NATO members to make the decision as to what the NATO interest is.
(Mr Lloyd) There is no predefined area of operation. Therefore, the concept of inside area and outside area is a verbal convenience at any point in time. It has no prior existence in terms of a legal base for action.

299. It is not a line on a map.
(Mr Robertson) Nor a Treaty. That is not there.

Mr Blunt

300. May I ask a supplementary about the legal base for action. You quoted the humanitarian situation as some formal of legal potential basis for action in

October. What would be the legal basis of action to enforce the attendance of Serb party at Rambouillet. There was no Security Council Resolution as such, as I understand.

(Mr Lloyd) Let me repeat. Any action taken would have to have a legal base, but that legal base would have to be determined quite literally at the time action was being contemplated.

301. But the problem with this is that it depends which lawyer you talk to. Over Sierra Leone, with which you are of course all familiar, the UN lawyers had a different opinion from the Foreign Office lawyers, about what the UN Security Council Resolution meant in terms of the embargo.

(Mr Lloyd) With respect, this is not qualitative of the same nature.

302. Except that you are drawing, as I understand it, on a rather vague understanding of the position on a humanitarian crisis to justify the air strikes. That is what you said to us. What I am trying to identify is whether in the Strategic Concept we are actually going to see a rather firmer definition. There was talk of the Germans, and perhaps one or two other parties, who were looking for a Security Council Resolution as being the vehicle for NATO to act. If that is not going to be the case (and you suggest it is not), what is going to be the mandate required? How specific is that going to be in a Strategic Concept? Or are we just going to rely on international law and allow the lawyers to argue about it after we have sent the bombers in?

(Mr Lloyd) Not just to say: are we just going to go for international law? It is quite important that we do go for international law. It is not just a question of letting the lawyers argue about it. It is a question of having a proper legal base. Let me remind the Committee. The concept of humanitarian emergency is something which does exist, of course, within the Charter of the United Nations. It is not something invented as a rationalisation, it is there. Within those terms, obviously any particular assessments of humanitarian need has to be specific and has to be in terms of the circumstances at the time. It is not possible to anticipate humanitarian crisis in advance, almost by definition of what we are saying, because any action would have to be relevant to that crisis and commensurate to the scale of the crisis. That is why anticipation in all circumstances simply is not possible, except simply to say that we must recognise that circumstances have arisen. It is not hypothetical. We can refer directly to what took place in the autumn of last year in Kosovo, where the situation on the ground did actively warrant action, the threat of action; and had that not resulted in response from Belgrade, it would have resulted in action which would have been justifiable in terms of international law with reference to the humanitarian need. In a sense, whilst it is very tempting to say that we can predefine every circumstance, the answer is that we cannot predefine the circumstances. What we can talk about are the general principles which under international law would allow us to act.

(Mr Robertson) May I pick up one point which Mr Blunt made, which is that you leave the thing vacant in the Strategic Concept, which is indeed what it does

[**Mr Blunt** *Cont*]

just now. There is no attempt to put in a legal base in the Strategic Concept. Then you get the lawyers in to argue after the bombers have gone in. As the Chairman of the Defence Council I cannot do that. I have to have a legal base before I can order the bombers in or I am personally liable in that capacity. A fairly onerous responsibility. All those who have held my position have had that as well. So there must be a legal base. We must act within international law. We would always do so. You can have a United Nations Security Council Resolution. That is certainly one form and that would probably be the ideal. We were faced last October, as Mr Lloyd has rightly said, with a humanitarian emergency. The UN Charter is quite clear that action can be taken in these circumstances. To bomb people to get them back to the conference table would clearly not be a legal base, but making sure that we do not create a situation whereby another humanitarian emergency is created would certainly be within the scope of the UN Charter. So there are a number of legal bases around the UN Charter itself: a Security Council Resolution; the OSCE has a mandate. We, as a country, certainly would always have to have a legal mandate before, as you say, the bombers go in.

Mr Hancock

303. I note the answer you gave to the Chairman's first point, but on that last point I would be interested to know: if there is no legality in actually bombing people back to the conference table, what about the threat of bombing to get those to the conference table? That would be an interesting one to ponder, would it not? That is what we have effectively done now, have we not?

(*Mr Lloyd*) May I respond to that. I think it is important that we do not let that pass as being a statement of reality.

304. I was responding to what the Minister said.

(*Mr Lloyd*) The certainty is this. If we do not see both the Belgrade and the Kosovar Albanians at the conference table, we will see an escalation of the violence that still continues in Kosovo. We should not have the view that there is no violence even now in Kosovo. Within those terms what we will see, it is absolutely certain, is escalation of the violence we saw, for example, in the massacres at Racak recently, when 43 people died but some 5,000-plus people disappeared from the area and ran off in temperatures of minus 15 into the mountains. It is not very hard to define, in the circumstances of Kosovo, the level of tension which exists; and that we would very quickly need to return to the levels of humanitarian emergency that we saw last autumn. Therefore, I do have to say, slightly pedantically, please do not cast this in the view of just being about threats that somehow do not need reference to international law. Everything which has been done in that sense has to be measured against the test of international law but also against the real situation on the ground. The situation is so fragile that anything which moves away from the negotiating table now will see—and I guarantee this to the Committee—increased levels of violence and increased levels of human emergency.

305. I understand that entirely. We will come back to Kosovo. On the answer you gave first, I would be interested in your view about the development of the Strategic Concept and how it gets brought together. How do we go to avoid creating a two-tier NATO, where there will be three or four big players who will be prepared to take fairly big decisions and the others may be dragged reluctantly to the agreement of action being taken.

(*Mr Robertson*) There are two issues there. One is the Strategic Concept and how it is determined. It is determined, like everything else in NATO, by consensus. As I pointed out, at the first meeting with the Permanent Joint Council with the Russians, the Russians only fully got a flavour of NATO when they heard the Defence Minister of Luxembourg lecturing the Defence Secretary of the United States of America, which has happened, because that is the way consensus is established. As we move through the Strategic Concept, I am not pinpointing Mr Brunei, the Defence Minister of Luxembourg, (and the Sports Minister of Luxembourg, as he happens to be simultaneously), in this way, because he is a very convivial companion and colleague. This is the way things are done and it will be the way in the Strategic Concept. The balancing that needs to be done in a multi-nation organisation will be achieved, I am sure, before the Summit takes place. We will not be left with a somewhat undignified and a rather incoherent situation, which applied at Madrid, where decisions were being taken as we actually discussed it. In terms of decisions to deploy force, those again are taken by consensus. Clearly there are some bigger military powers than others in NATO but unless everyone agrees to do something then nothing happens. The decision that was taken at Vilamoura at the informal meeting of NATO Defence Ministers at NATO last year in relation to Kosovo, was a decision taken round a table at lunchtime with all of the Defence Ministers there looking at a Security Council Resolution that made certain demands in that context, but the NATO Ministers believing that what was missing from it were the words "or else", and us saying that if we were going to avert what was manifestly a humanitarian catastrophe in the making the "or else" had to be supplied by NATO. However, it required the agreement of everybody by NATO round that table, which was achieved, and is one of the major benefits of being part of an alliance.

Laura Moffatt

306. I am very privileged because I am going to get the chance to take forward my questioning of yesterday to the Minister for Foreign Affairs on the Floor of the House. I want to discuss the new Strategic Concept of NATO and the way in which that may take us forward in areas which I believe are very fruitful and helpful. I want to talk about, in particular, weapons of mass destruction; but concentrating on chemical and biological weapons and leaving nuclear weapons to my colleague. We know that the United States appear to be very keen on having one of the new missions for dealing with proliferation of weapons of mass-destruction, although I have found that slightly

74   MINUTES OF EVIDENCE TAKEN BEFORE

17 February 1999]   Mr George Robertson, MP, Mr Tony Lloyd, MP,   *[Continued*
                    Mr Richard Hatfield and Mr Stephen Gomersall

[Laura Moffatt *Cont]*

strange because they are not that keen to adhere to the conventions on chemical weapons, as we now know. They are not very keen to allow inspection of their own pharmaceutical companies which slightly daunts. Nonetheless, they have said at various times that they are quite keen. What is the view of the United Kingdom Government? Would this be something that we would be whole-heartedly pursuing? Also, all that may entail, of course, which may take us down roads, which may commit us to all sorts of things.

(*Mr Lloyd*)   Britain would be very supportive and is very supportive of a weapons of mass destruction initiative within the context of NATO. That essentially is about information exchange. It is about pooling the knowledge that NATO members may have. I must as well put this into the context, of course. There is also considerable activity taking place in different international fora on the whole area. Also, if I may stick with chemical and biological weapons, it is important that you recognise that both chemical and biological weapons have an international basis by which they are, in any case, made illegal. We are working very hard, at the moment, in terms of a protocol for the biological weapons convention, which would bring in the same kind of verification system internationally as now exists for the chemical weapons convention. Obviously verification inspection regimes would not be something under the auspices of NATO. There would be, in the case of chemical weapons, an organisation for the convention of chemical weapons; and hopefully an equivalent organisation for biological weapons. So, yes, there is a role for NATO, but a lot of the important roles that need to be pursued in the context of non-proliferation will not be directly NATO responsibility because they are better done elsewhere.

307.   Okay. So would there be a role for NATO if it were found that people were not adhering to what they were supposed to be doing? At what stage would NATO become involved?

(*Mr Lloyd*)   I can only draw the parallel and say this: it is a matter of recorded fact that in the context, but not of NATO, Britain was involved recently in the destruction of the weapons of mass destruction capability of Iraq. Again, we have no doubt that this was the right decision to make in terms of undermining and weakening the capacity of Iraq at that time. Again it is perhaps worth stating, simply for the record, that of course we do know that Iraq has had a significant chemical and biological weapons capacity and still maintains and retains the capacity to recreate that. Therefore, there is a constant need to examine how we will respond to rogue states. We have taken military action against those rogue states and, as I say, were right so to do. Obviously within that there are other areas that we ought to be engaged in. There is a question as to whether NATO would choose to play a military role in those events, but as the Defence Secretary said earlier on, within NATO it is necessary to build consensus. That consensus at the time in respect of Iraq did not exist, which is why we acted separately and outside the NATO framework. I would also say to the Committee that there are other areas: non-proliferation of different types of technology, missile technology, nuclear supplies groups, with the Australia Group in terms of supplies for chemical and biological weapons programmes. Those are important, as well as the development of the inspection capacity within the chemical weapons convention and the need to make that same kind of progress for biological weapons. So within those terms, at the end of all that, the NATO role is an important dimension but it is not, by any stretch of the imagination, the area where most of the activity will take place.

Mr Cohen

308.   You know, of course, that Canada and Germany have suggested a "no first use of nuclear weapons" policy as a policy for an alliance. On what grounds does the United Kingdom Government apparently reject that when, when it boils down to it, we are a nuclear weapon state.

(*Mr Robertson*)   No, it is not. It has implications for a deterrent policy. The German Government have now agreed that this will not be pressed in the lead-up to the Washington Summit. But "no first use" is an issue we considered during the Strategic Defence Review. As Mr Cohen knows only too well, we have looked at our nuclear posture in some detail and have made very substantial changes to it, which have been widely welcomed in many parts of the world and make a lot of sense in today's contemporary circumstances. One of the areas we looked at, one of the suggestions which were put forward for de-escalation, was a declaration of "no first use". We believe that this might actually be the opposite of encouraging or reassuring and might detract from the concept of deterrence. Deterrence is essentially based on the doubt that is in any potential aggressor's mind, which has to be kept as uncertain as possible. A declaration of "no first use" would simplify any potential aggressor's planning because the clear implication would be that that potential aggressor could mount a substantial conventional, or a chemical or biological assault, without any fear of a nuclear response. So to add that into it would, we believe, be more dangerous than to leave the uncertainties that basically underpin the deterrent posture at the present moment. It was something we ruled out. Most of our allies have also ruled that out. I do not think that either the Canadians or the Germans are going to pursue this at the present moment before Washington. What I do think is that the Alliance after Washington should look, as we would do, at the existing nuclear posture; and make adjustments to some aspects of that to take into account contemporary circumstances. We would strongly oppose any declaration of "no first use" which is, at best, a declaration without real meaning. Secondly, if it had meaning, it would be to make the world more dangerous than it is just now.

309.   When the Committee had Ambassador Thomas Graham before it—and only four years ago he was the leader of the United States delegation at the Non-proliferation Treaty Conference—what he said was that if we are going to succeed with non-proliferation, what we desperately need is to lower the political importance of nuclear weapons. What first use actually does is increases, or says, that nuclear

[Mr Cohen *Cont]*

weapons remain something of considerable political importance. To that extent it actually encourages nuclear proliferation because if it is all right for the nuclear powers, why should not other countries have it? It encourages weapons of mass destruction as well because the theory, as you explained it, really boils down to uncertainty equalling stability allegedly, which is a very strange philosophy; but if that is the case then smaller countries will say, "Surely we need the uncertainty of weapons of mass destruction as well to create stability." Surely rogue states with leaders like Saddam Hussein are not deterred anyway by nuclear weapons. They carry on with their policies. As we have attributed them with a degree of lunacy, they are not going to be deterred by nuclear weapons.

(Mr Lloyd) The rogue states have to be dealt with as rogue states. That is right because they put themselves out with any rational calculation of the kind that this debate engenders. I must point out that in terms of the arguments of proliferation, the statement is beyond Mr Robertson's, that the original response is essentially between nuclear powers. There are guarantees which already exist for non-nuclear states. Those states which have signed up to the NPT, in fact, do benefit from what amounts *de facto* to a guarantee that they will not have nuclear equipment used against them. "No first use" is a concept which exists between the nuclear states or those that have abrogated their protection under the NPT.

(Mr Robertson) The point here is that to say you are not going to deal with a declaration of "no first use" is not to say we are going to use nuclear weapons first, which is what Mr Cohen appears to be implying. Far from it. We are not in favour of using nuclear weapons at all. There are essentially political weapons that are to be used only in the case of last resort; to be used only in the case of national survival. The degree of uncertainty that underpins a deterrent policy would be undermined by these declarations which, as I say, can be meaningless. First of all, you have to assume the other side are going to believe you. That is not necessarily guaranteed. Secondly, if they did believe you, this could lead them to take actions in a conventional sense or in an asymmetric sense, (in a chemical or biological context), which would allow them to take risks knowing that there was to be no penalty for doing that. So it is not something that makes any political or practical sense in the present circumstances. This is why it has never been part of NATO's policy and why it has now been abandoned by the Russians as well.

310. I allow your point but just to pick up again on Ambassador Thomas Graham's comments to this Committee, he made two other points. Firstly, he said that weapons of mass destruction, evil and deadly as they are, are not at the same level as nuclear weapons and the holocaust that nuclear weapons could make. Therefore, there needs to be a degree of proportionality. How can nuclear weapons be proportional in relation to biological and chemical weapons? That is the first point. Secondly, he outlined that there is a doctrine already, under international law of belligerent response, whereby international commitments are waived once there have been those

sorts of attacks. Why can that not be applied instead of having a first use policy?

(Mr Robertson) I could spend a goodly day here discussing the ins and outs of nuclear policy.

311. Maybe we should, not here, but the Ministry of Defence should be producing more on those issues.

(Mr Robertson) With the greatest of respect, we have done that. During the Defence Review we did look at every aspect of our nuclear policy at the present moment. We adopted some sensible suggestions which you will have noticed. We have reduced the alert state. The moves have been widely welcomed as being relevant. I hope they will give an example to the Russian Duma who might get round now to ratifying START 2 and allow for reductions in the huge arsenals that Russia and America have at the present moment. That is a very specific call I have made. Listen to not what we preach, but watch what we actually do. So we made very serious reductions in that. If you take the fire power of Britain's deterrent it will have reduced by something like 50 per cent since the height of the Cold War, so we are not ignoring the whole question of proportionality but in an uncertain world at the present moment nuclear deterrence provides an element of stability within that where everybody knows where we stand and people will not push back at the limit. I accept that there will be the Ambassador Thomas Grahams of this world and there are people who are in or out of the diplomatic or the military service who change their minds from time to time but there has been a continuum since Britain acquired its own national deterrent which came through the last election with a very firm commitment, which you and I fought the election on, to keep Trident. We are also committed to nuclear disarmament, a more urgent approach to arms control and what we did in the Defence Review was to bring up to date the nuclear posture and to reduce it where it can safely be done consistent with the concept of minimum deterrence.

312. One of the things that seems to be happening is that since the Cold War when there was a policy of clear deterrence, or that was the policy enunciated, there seems to be an increase in the options for the possible use of nuclear weapons, for example, we now have possibly against weapons of mass destruction, possibly against states who are associated with nuclear weapon states, rogue states. What is the justification for increasing the possibility of their use?

(Mr Robertson) That is not really correct. First of all, the Defence Review did something else apart from those aspects I have already mentioned: reducing the number of missiles per boat, the number of missiles in stock, the number of warheads in stock, the signing up to the Fissile Material Cut-off Treaty, the first nuclear state to ratify the Comprehensive Test Ban Treaty. In addition to all of that is a greater degree of openness about our nuclear policy than has ever been seen in this country, so open that there are still people going around claiming that we are being secret about some of the aspects that we have already published. One of the other aspects in response to the point you make is that we have not increased the relevance of the role of nuclear weapons, indeed we are now down to one system. The free fall bomb has now been eliminated

[**Mr Cohen** *Cont*]

in addition to the other variations that used to exist so there is one national deterrent and that is Trident. Submarines on patrol 24 hours a day, 365 days a year, are providing, I believe, an element of stability in an uncertain world but at the same time underlining the fact that this Government is committed not to no first use but to no use of nuclear weapons.

(*Mr Lloyd*) I think this is important. Of course, nuclear weapons themselves do have to operate under the framework of international law in exactly the way that we discussed this earlier on. A number of questions that Mr Cohen has raised about proportionality, about the validity of use, do still have to have reference to exactly the same questions as to the legitimacy under that international legal basis. It is a very important pre-condition on what is seen, as the question implies, as an almost total freedom to act under all circumstances. That freedom to act under all circumstances does not exist, it is very, very constrained.

Mr Cann: Could I just ask the Secretary of State, would he agree with me that the fact that we had the option of first use and the ability to deliver it saved the world from a Third World War over the last 50 years?

Mr Brazier: Hear! Hear!

Mr Cann

313. Would he agree with me that the certainty that is implied by the option of first use cannot be discounted and got rid of and the uncertainty of no first use option is not a good message to send?

(*Mr Robertson*) There are many views about how peace has been preserved over these years. I think in one respect the then Soviet Union and NATO both agreed that the nuclear balance was one which contributed to a period where aggression could not take place on either part. As I say, nuclear theology is a very intriguing matter, it is almost as time absorbing as religious theology. We now have one system. It has been endorsed by the British people in the election that took place but so too has our commitment towards reducing the nuclear stockpiles and to reducing eventually the role of nuclear weapons, their elimination as instruments, whether military or political. The Government is committed to doing that. In terms of what we have done in the last 21 months we have a very, very substantial record and I hope that other countries will take note of that. I recently met representatives of the Indian Government who came though London and I found myself in the position not of lecturing them about what they should be doing in the context of what they might regard as double standards; but I was able to tell them what we have done to make the changes to our nuclear posture, the reductions that we have been responsible for and that people on a wider basis should take note of that and welcome it as well.

Mr Hood: It is a very emotive subject and I am sure it is very intellectually challenging but I have to say that it is meaningless. Surely the deterrent is the fact that we have the nuclear weapons and if we are threatened by a potential aggressor they know that if they attack us then we will respond. I do not think that

this question of declarations of first use will do anything other than, as I say, challenge the intellectually obsessed with the subject. The fact that you have got the weapons and a potential aggressor knows that you have got the weapons is a deterrent and the rest is intellectual nonsense quite frankly.

Chairman: I think the Committee's view is almost unanimous.

Ms Taylor

314. Secretary of State, I think my question is most particularly directed to you. I wonder if you could actually look at some of the mixed or confused signals that some people seem to be getting and I am referencing in my question the new Strategic Concept. We are aware that we will be seeing this defined very clearly before very long. If you were to be given *carte blanche* what guidance on the new Strategic Concept would you wish the UK to give to all allied countries about NATO's military requirements? In that, how would you define our priorities in terms of modernising this process?

(*Mr Robertson*) In many ways the answer to your question is in the Strategic Defence Review because we set out to do what I believe NATO needs to do and what other countries may be already embarking upon and could pay attention to as well. NATO has to have forces that are more deployable, more mobile, more flexible, more sustainable than they are in many cases at the present moment. I believe that we have shown the way in which that can be done within a defence budget. It may be that some other countries will have to spend more on their defence if they are going to be able to make a contribution to what are seen as commonly agreed military objectives. We have shown the way in which forces can be modernised, can be reshaped to meet the modern world and I hope other people can take from that the British agenda. I do not preach or lecture but a number of countries have already come over and have been briefed by officials in our Department to that end. What we have specifically asked in the last few months inside NATO is for people to look at the closer integration of some of the multinational forces that already exist inside NATO. NATO has its own force structure but there are other organisations that have been created. One that involves the British is the UK/Netherlands amphibious force which works together, trains together and has got quite a considerable degree of capability. There is the Euro Corps that was formed by France and Germany and some of the other countries. There are the multinational forces inside NATO but outside the Allied Rapid Reaction Corps which is itself a multinational operation. There are other joint battalions, joint corps, that have been created. What I suggested at the Vilamoura informal Defence Ministers' meeting was that NATO really should take a greater part in bringing that co-ordination to bear so that if we do need to work and operate outside of NATO's area we have actually got embryonic structures that are there at the present moment. That is one of the suggestions that Britain has put forward and which has been taken up with quite a degree of

[**Ms Taylor** *Cont*]
enthusiasm and it is something that we intend to pursue.

315.   Can I ask a short supplementary. Is it feasible to actually say to us that once we have defined priorities in terms of the way of sustainability, flexibility, etc., that we can then say to all other European Union countries to do as you suggested in the MoD submission to the European Defence States, that we have got to articulate with greater speed and coherence, that we should be able to engage as Europeans in an enhanced capacity? It is asking them to behave in ways in which they have not behaved previously. We have had enormous disputes between us about how and when we should move in, and maybe Bosnia is the most obvious textbook example of that.

(*Mr Robertson*)   One of the Government's objectives at the present moment in terms of the European Defence Initiative that we are engaged in is to try and focus attention on capabilities in Europe, the ability to actually go into a crisis with troops which are properly trained, that have got the proper equipment, which can be sustained, so that they can fulfil the objectives which are stated. We cannot do that completely ourselves until the Strategic Defence Review is fully implemented and we have the heavy lift and we have sorted out our logistics, and we have properly repaired the damage to the Defence Medical Services. We are not able to do it fully now but we are better able to do it than some others are at the moment. So we have focused attention among our European allies on the need to address the capability gap which is no better demonstrated than by the fact that if there were to be air strikes against Serb targets, say next weekend, then we are talking about an air force of about 400 with over 300[1] of the planes supplied by America, so there is a capability gap and we have tried to focus on that. We have also said that there has to be a greater degree of political will among all of us in Europe to actually grasp some of these situations before they become disasters. Thirdly, we need to have a proper communication between the political will and the proper capabilities. That is what the Prime Minister's initiative was; it is actually commonsense, an expression of reality. It is not some sort of change of policy or new grand vision, it is based and rooted in the practical thinking that this nation is perhaps well-known for. The fact is that we Europeans have spent an awful lot of time debating institutions, creating institutions, creating wiring diagrams which show you who would be involved, who would not be involved, where the decisions are taken. Well, the stark reality is, you cannot send a wiring diagram to deal with a crisis, and what we want to do, and what I believe a lot of our allies are now facing up to, is to address that capability gap. The fact the Germans are involved in the Strategic Defence Review at the moment, the fact the French are professionalising their armed forces after so many years of conscription, the fact the Dutch Defence Minister brought a team across to the Ministry of Defence to see how we treated our defence review, the fact that Mr Carlo Scognamiglio, the new Defence Minister of Italy——

Chairman

316.   Who was that?
(*Mr Robertson*)   Carlo Scognamiglio.

317.   I am very impressed!
(*Mr Robertson*)   Not half as impressed as I am in being able to pronounce it! He is a new and formidable addition to the Defence Ministers of Europe who is himself conscious of the fact that he will need to address what Italy can do if Italy wants to play its part in the way he is absolutely determined it will. So we have shown a lead, a lot of people are addressing it but more attention needs to be focused on it.

(*Mr Lloyd*)   It is also fair, if I can just supplement that briefly, to say that of course the process began at St Malo has already led to considerable practical working together between the British and the French, but since then it has also engaged others, the Germans specifically, who are very important at the moment because of their joint chairmanship of both the WEU and of course the Presidency of the European Union. So it is having practical impacts on the ground in terms of the way we plan together literally almost as we speak.

Mr Hood

318.   Secretary of State, you said in July, "A certain line was drawn under the European Security and Defence Identity at the Amsterdam Summit, largely at British instigation, by preventing the merger of the WEU and the EU." What has changed the Government's mind between then and the Prime Minister's initiative in Pörtschach in October? To what extent was the UK's surprise initiatives, the Prime Minister's speech I have just referred to and the St Malo Agreement, an attempt to avoid any marginalisation in Europe vis-a-vis the single currency?

(*Mr Robertson*)   I am not as cynical as that. I think there are two reasons why the Prime Minister and the Ministers in the Government have looked with a new focus at the way in which Europe handles itself. One comes from the fact that the European Union has now decided it will appoint a High Representative on a Common Foreign and Security Policy, so the European Union is trying to sharpen up its act so far as political will is concerned about adopting positions, establishing policies that will perhaps guide the European Union in a world where it wants to have a foreign policy impact. That is a new dimension. There will be a personalisation of the Common Foreign and Security Policy, so that the famous question that Henry Kissinger once asked, "The Europeans say they want to be consulted, so where is the European telephone number?" will not arise. There will actually by the end of this year be a telephone number and there will be a personality involved in doing that. That in itself raises issues about what you then do about the policy decisions that you arrive at if you have inadequate capabilities for Europe to be able to act on its own if it wanted to do so, and if the Americans and the Canadians did not want to be engaged in that. So that was one factor

---

[1] *Note by witness:* figure should read 250.

[Mr Hood *Cont]*

that weighed in our minds. The second factor was this dawning realisation that Kosovo had brought to us, that actually when it came to the bill Europe on its own was not going to be able to intimidate President Milosevic from the kind of actions which led to the looming humanitarian catastrophe which was facing us at the end of last year. On paper I think there are 2 million troops in Europe in uniform but in reality a tiny fraction of them are deployable in any particular emergency. There are something like 7,000 fast jets[1] in the portfolio of the air forces of the European countries but a tiny number of them have a capability for nighttime bombing or for the kind of precision bombing which increasingly the legal authorities expect us to engage in. So we are coming face to face with this capability gap and the Prime Minister believed it was right we should start focusing attention on that, but we are using the agreements that were reached at Amsterdam with a lot of British input—the Common Foreign and Security Policy, the European Security and Defence Identity of NATO, and NATO is mentioned in the Amsterdam treaty for the first time ever in a European treaty largely at British instigation. So we are talking here about marrying up political will with genuine and real military capabilities and getting a sophisticated communication between the two so that when Europe decides on a policy and presses the button, the button is actually connected to something which will work in the situation. That is what the Prime Minister's initiative was all about. I think it took our European colleagues a little bit aback because we appeared to be more European than we had been but in reality it was very much a strong message of what we had been preaching before. I believe it has brought some of our colleagues much closer to NATO than they were before and the St Malo Declaration I believe did that on behalf of both Britain and France.

319.   Are you aware that there is a suggestion that the St Malo Agreement was an attempt by the UK to forestall possible efforts by Germany's new government to redefine or dilute traditional defence weapons?

(Mr Robertson)   No, it was not. We are working very closely with the new German Government. The new German Government recognised that it was the relationship between Britain and France that was perhaps at the core of how Europe was going to see itself in the future and that it made a lot of sense for Britain and France to try and put practical meaning behind the Prime Minister's initiative in terms of decision making and of capabilities and how to link the two together. It did not in any way upset the Germans who were very pleased to see the British and the French working in this area in particular so well and that fed in well to the discussions that then took place on a trilateral basis between the Germans, the British and the French and which has now encompassed the Italians as well.

320.   So what is the cost to the UK and to Europe as a whole of enhancing ESDI? What are the benefits?

(Mr Robertson)   There should be no cost to the United Kingdom because we already contribute to

NATO and potentially to ESDI in exactly the ways that they would expect it to be used in the future. It may cost some other countries some money because they may not within existing budgets be able to buy the equipment, do the training, get their troops up to the right level of readiness without some expansion of their budgets, although that is essentially a matter for them. In some cases they cannot do it without increasing the amounts that they spend on defence but in return for any investment in that area NATO will become much more effective and the European Security and Defence Identity will actually become more meaningful.

Mr Hancock

321.   Can I just ask you a quick question about the set up that you have created post-St Malo and the whole thing you have been talking about. It is a question of whether NATO in the command structures that we have got can deal with more than one situation arising in different parts in and out of the regions: Kosovo, Iraq and possibly the Kurds erupting in Turkey. So you would have one Arab region in Iraq with the UN Alliance to deal with political consequences. Is there now a structure which would be flexible and available enough to deal with three issues interlinked in that way?

(Mr Robertson)   We are doing that at the present moment. The Article 5 common security guarantee is still there and has to be there. We are dealing with a situation in Bosnia that is self-contained to Bosnia but it is a NATO led stabilisation force that is supervising that. There are some 34,000 troops there, not all of them NATO but under NATO command. In relation to Kosovo we already have NATO planes in the air engaged in overhead surveillance, we have a NATO extraction force in Skopje in Macedonia which has got European forces but again under NATO command. We are conscious clearly of the possibility, if there is an agreement to be reached at Rambouillet, of putting a very substantial land force of maybe over 30,000 in there. NATO is doing it at the present moment. What we have to have are flexible enough structures and sufficient military capability to be able to act when NATO chooses to do so in the way that NATO wants to do it. The limitation at the present moment is not structural or institutional, it is in terms of the military capability that is at hand and that is why all of us in Europe have got to address this capability gap because we have moved from the Cold War where we made very large investments in defence, essentially in static forces against a monolithic opponent, and now we are in a world where deployments are taking place all of the time, some of them by choice as we are in Iraq, in Kosovo, in Bosnia, but we are also engaged in a number of other areas, for example Sierra Leone where a ship of the Royal navy is presently located and is contributing to that effort as well. It is essentially a structure that will allow the flexibility to make the decisions that are required by the country or by NATO collectively.

---

[1] *Note by witness:* over 5,000 combat aircraft.

Mr Colvin

322. Secretary of State, there was confusion during the week of the St Malo Declaration because you made a very robust speech to the WEU rather bravely, because I remember you were suffering at the time from the most awful illness, and then the Prime Minister later on that week made a rather more European speech embraced in the St Malo Declaration. I am a little bit concerned about what you have said this morning about this High Representative appointed to personalise the CFSP. I just want to get your views on the future of the Western European Union if, as you have said this morning, both ESDI becomes more distinct and so too the CFSP develops. Is there eventually going to be a role for the Western European Union?

(Mr Robertson) That is a very interesting question and it is one that is exercising a lot of people today. It starts at the wrong end of the telescope. Essentially what you need to address are the capabilities and the effectiveness of decision making before you can start to get engaged in these wiring diagrams and the institutional changes that have obsessed the European Union.

323. We have that in NATO, do we not, it is really looking at the European dimension that I want to tease out.

(Mr Robertson) At the present moment there are procedures in place. The Amsterdam Treaty establishes a number of procedures along with the Berlin NATO Ministerial conclusions as well on the European Security and Defence Identity. At the present moment the EU has it within its power to make a recommendation in terms of military action in line with the Petersberg tasks, humanitarian, civil emergency, etc., and can task the Western European Union in line with these priorities to then use NATO assets under the European Security and Defence Identity to discharge the decision that was taken in the European Union. You only have to describe that, you only have to say it to realise how complicated and difficult that process is and it is perhaps one of the reasons why very limited use has been made of it since it was all set up. Once you come to the institutional arrangements when you have really focused attention on capabilities and decision making then there is a question mark as to what the role of the WEU should be. One alternative is that the WEU is simply merged with the European Union. That is what a number of our continental allies over the years have tried to do but it has got problems and difficulties associated with it. A second alternative would be to strengthen the WEU and give it the capability to be able to do the sorts of things that on paper it is supposed to be doing at the present time. That is one alternative but there again it might lead to some element of duplication. A third alternative is that you separate out the functions of the WEU so that its political role is subsumed by the European Union in association with arrangements that would allow the non-EU countries who are in NATO, or the neutrals, to have a part to play in it and you put its defence component into the ESDI of NATO. These are the three areas on which eventually decisions will have to be made. What the United

Kingdom has tried in our typically pragmatic way, characterised by Government Ministers as well as by Select Committees, is to get people to focus on what matters. Actually at the end of the day it does not become the priority what the organisation is if you cannot actually have aeroplanes that will drop the right bombs at the right place at the right time or you have not got the right ships to take your equipment and soldiers to the point of conflict. We should be much more focused on the capabilities and the willingness to take tough decisions than we should simply be about the nature of the institutions that presently serve us.

(Mr Lloyd) Of course, one of the great advantages of the St Malo Declaration and what has led on from there is that in fact we have avoided these theological debates and it has been a very practical process, a process that is designed to do what Mr Robertson has said, to deliver capacity at the sharp face rather than to engage in a debate about the future of institutions.

324. I accept the point about the theological debate but may I use the Secretary of State's analogy about the telescope. I agree that it is very important to focus on the practicalities of deploying the military to address difficulties but if you turn the telescope around it comes back to a question of national sovereignty. I am relieved, for instance, that we still have a Common Foreign and Security Policy rather than a single foreign and security policy rather than, to use an economic analogy, a single market instead of a common market. In so developing a single market we in Britain have sacrificed or pooled a very great deal of our national sovereignty. By having a CFSP rather than a SFSP, the ultimate sovereignty and control still rests with national governments and not with the European Union, and is that not the big issue that the Government has to address? Do we retain national sovereignty over foreign and security matters or do we pool it with our European partners which will ultimately lead, to a Single Foreign and Security Policy with a loss of national sovereignty?

(Mr Lloyd) But there is, as of now, no pressure to move from the Common Foreign and Security Policy. That is the position. It is intergovernmental, it is not within the competence of, for example, the Commission or some parallel organisation. If I can use this as an analogy, NATO has worked successfully by pooling national systems rather than, if you like, integrating those systems into one complete force. Certainly any discussion of Europe's security in the concept of its relationship with NATO or at the level we have just been debating would still include the concept of national control of armed forces.

(Mr Robertson) I think it is quite important to say that the St Malo Declaration has become a bit of an issue, and rightly so, because it was a watershed agreement in practical relations. If I can just clarify, having discovered a copy of it here, and actually as the addendum to the letter my Department sent to you about European defence says, it makes it clear that the British and French authorities agree that defence must remain intergovernmental, and a Common Foreign and Security Policy must remain intergovernmental, so there is a common objective there. The second thing is that it talks about not duplicating NATO structures,

[Mr Colvin *Cont*]

so in a way for the first time France is conceding that NATO is the cornerstone, ESDI within NATO is going to be the core capability, of the force that the European Union would be able to have access to in a much more straight forward way. So the principles of non-duplication of NATO, the importance of NATO and the necessity for having it based on national government decisions, is actually there very firmly in the St Malo Declaration and Mr Hatfield, who sweated way into the night to get that declaration finalised, will bear testimony to the fact it was a very important feature of what was ultimately published.

Mr Blunt

325. But, Secretary of State, you accept that the institutional framework is at least dynamic at the moment? In July you were telling us that a certain line was drawn under it at the Amsterdam Summit, by October the Prime Minister had gone over that line with his Pörtschach proposals, and at St Malo we were signing up to European co-operation within the institutional framework of the European Union on defence matters. As you have said, these things are in a sense theology and we should be looking at the practicalities, is that correct?

(Mr Robertson) The practicality is that it was my predecessor, who was called Michael Portillo in case people have forgotten, whose views on Europe are pretty well known, who signed up to the European Security and Defence Identity inside NATO.

326. Yes, but the institutional framework of how we control these things is at the moment up for discussion, the role of WEU and all the rest of it, and you are saying to us that this is the wrong end of the telescope, we should be looking at it as a practicality?

(Mr Robertson) I am simply saying that the institutions should serve the ability to deploy and to act rather than the other way round.

327. Therefore, when Mr Lloyd says to us there is no pressure as of now about changing the nature of the Common Foreign and Security Policy to a Single Foreign and Security Policy, and the Amsterdam Treaty says "might lead to a common defence", it is at least feasible that sometime in the future we could be looking at a Single Foreign and Security Policy or, as it says in the Treaty, a common defence?

(Mr Lloyd) If it helps the Committee, strike out the words "as of now" from my remarks. Does that help Mr Blunt? There is no pressure to reconsider this question.

328. But the pressure comes from exactly what Mr Robertson was telling us, which is that Europe has 2 million troops, has 7,000 fast jets without the right capability, that European Union countries spend as much on defence as the United States yet get about 30 per cent, 50 per cent, whatever figure one wants to put on it, a fraction, of the operational output of the United States. So surely within whatever new institutional framework is created there is going to be, in order to create what you call the requirement for greater political will in Europe and for that then to be linked into the ability to deploy forces in order for Europe to act, inevitably a move towards some form of Single Foreign and Security Policy?

(Mr Lloyd) No, that is not the case. Take the example of NATO, which I think the Committee would accept has been most successful in this. NATO has always operated on the basis of national structures which have been pooled together within the NATO framework, and secondly has always operated on the basis of consensus between national representatives, so as a model in actual fact it is there and it works. I really do think it is one worth examining.

329. But the legitimate criticism of NATO is that it has taken an awfully long time, and we are still far from actually achieving some commonality of equipment. NATO has standard operating procedures in the integrated military structure but it has been woeful in trying to get equipment programmes uniform, and that is a significant weakness of the NATO countries in actually optimising their military output. We are now looking at a proposal for having defence within the institutions of the European Union which has a single currency, a single economy, a single market, and it is a different institution, and surely the pressure is there to actually use the resources available to the European Union more effectively for defence, as the Secretary of State said, and does that not lead us to start at least considering a common defence in the Amsterdam Treaty?

(Mr Robertson) Common defence in fact appeared in the Maastricht Treaty for the very first time and that was a creature of the last Government, not this Government. Let me just put that point on the record. We have made it absolutely clear that we are not interested in some single European army, we are not interested in giving up national decision-making, and neither is anybody else in this field. What we want is a more properly co-ordinated approach at the European level for situations where the Europeans believe they have to take action, perhaps in circumstances where the Americans are not wanting to get engaged. So we are looking to a practical way forward to do what makes sense.

330. But there must be a contradiction there between Europe using the money it spends on defence effectively and sustaining the sort of political control we have over defence at the moment. There is an enormous price we are paying for sustaining the intergovernmental control over defence. It means you cannot move down the road of specialisation, we cannot move towards the Belgians doing one thing, the Italians providing other services, which would then mean that no one can ever have a veto because the United Kingdom, for example, would then lose key capabilities.

(Mr Robertson) We are obviously interested in greater collaboration. There is a number of collaborative projects which we are talking about just now and a number of collaborative projects which I have inherited as well. The Eurofighter is one of those and is likely to produce a very, very successful aeroplane a full 20 years after the first prototype was ordered by Sir John Nott, the Defence Secretary, in 1982. We can do a lot of these things better but it does not mean we give up national governance or we

[**Mr Blunt** *Cont*]

have some international security force based on the European Union.

Chairman: We have to move on. I personally would like a hundred year moratorium before we seriously discuss a common defence policy again. We will move on quickly.

Mr Cann

331. A very quick question. The French Government appears to believe that the St Malo Agreement means that we have called for higher levels of defence spending in Europe. Is that correct?

(Mr Robertson) That is returning to the answer I gave previously. If we are going to have the capabilities that are required in situations where Europe is increasingly becoming engaged then we have to have different force structures from those which apply in a number of the countries in Europe. It applies to us as well. The Strategic Defence Review was about reducing the importance of some of the capabilities we have at the present moment but acquiring new ones, so the acquisition of strategic lift, of planes that can carry large amounts of equipment very quickly into theatre, having deployable medical services, all of these things were designed to make sure that we were able to deal with tomorrow's problems and not yesterday's threats. A number of other countries will have to do so. Clearly those who have hollowed out their defence budgets very comprehensively are going to have to face the prospect that they will either have to spend more on getting that equipment that will allow them to engage or find themselves disengaged from the process. I do not know whether it is the French who think that. What we want to do, both the French and ourselves, and we spend almost exactly the same proportion of GNP on defence, is to focus other people's attention on getting the right capabilities for the kinds of tasks and missions that take place. Some people will have to spend more, some people will have to spend differently and reshape their forces and a lot of them are presently doing that and I think we are all comforted by that.

332. I rather thought that the SDR produced the capability of this country to act on its own in nearly every circumstance.

(Mr Robertson) The Defence Review makes it clear that we would normally be acting with others in coalition. There are very few situations where we can envisage us having by necessity to act on our own but it does give us that capability if that was to be the choice of the British Government and there are some situations already that have applied where we have done so.

Chairman

333. We are spot on time amazingly. I would like it if we could have half an hour asking questions on Kosovo and then two questions from Mr Hancock at the very end on enlargement. Firstly on Kosovo. Could I ask Mr Lloyd, could you give us some update on the current negotiations? If you were a betting man

what odds would you be prepared to bet on that there will be some agreement that might make the sending or deploying of NATO forces superfluous?

(Mr Lloyd) I think the question about NATO forces being superfluous is that hopefully it will not arise because it is our intention that there should be a negotiated solution arising out of that. Is that likely? I suppose, fortunately, I am not a betting man and therefore I would not speculate. We do know that whilst there has been progress in Rambouillet there has been no breakthrough and there still are very entrenched positions on the parts of the Belgrade authorities and the Kosovar Albanians. I think that is probably common knowledge anyway but let me make it quite clear that when the Foreign Secretary told Parliament yesterday that he was not in any sense promising that there would be a negotiated solution by the appointed time he was simply stating the very real fact that there is an awful long way to go and there still has to be real movement on the side of both the Kosovar Albanians and of Belgrade, a long way to go. Within those terms we have got to be very cautious. If that negotiating framework leads to some kind of acceptable conclusion then our commitment is that we would be prepared as part of the wider NATO framework to participate in ground troops being in Kosovo, but that is on the basis of their presence being acceptable to both sides, both to the Kosovar Albanians and to the Serbs in Belgrade.

334. Thank you. Before I ask Mr Blunt to come in I must say that I am very pleased that the MoD's website has given the list of those forces already deployed near and what might be deployed. I hope Mr Milosevic and his counterparts have full access to the Internet and perhaps other countries will be doing similar and that might have an effect on the eventual outcome of the Rambouillet negotiations if they can see that we are not simply talking but we are prepared to act if the negotiations grind to an inconclusive halt.

(Mr Robertson) I think you make a very valid point, Chairman, that negotiations are going on and the very fact that they are together at Rambouillet is a huge success for the Foreign Secretary and indeed for his French counterpart. To get them into the same room together was a super-human achievement. The fact that gradual small steps of progress have been made gives one hope. They need to know that NATO means business, that there is a reality behind the rhetoric that they are hearing and that the ACTORDS that were put in place last October designed to prevent a humanitarian catastrophe then remain in place and that is not some empty threat. We are ready to act if there are people who are determined to break up these negotiations or who refuse to recognise reality and who want to bring blood on the streets back to the Balkans.

Chairman: If the Serbs are obsessed by their 14th Century history then NATO is obsessed by its 50 year history and we would not want the anniversary to mark a diplomatic failure. I hope the Serbs and the Albanians are cognisant of the fact that in addition to the humanitarian reasons why there has to be agreement, I think NATO would want to be seen to be relevant. If we cannot solve problems in our own

[**Chairman** *Cont*]
background then people will see the Alliance as being the fifth wheel of a very heavy crutch.

Mr Blunt

335. Secretary of State, in the Strategic Defence Review in paragraph 89 you say: "On this basis we have set some broad bench marks for the scale of our plan. In addition to providing whatever military support is required to continuing commitments such as Northern Ireland, we should be able to: either respond to a major international crisis which might require a military effort and combat operations of a similar scale and duration to the Gulf War.... or undertake a more extended overseas deployment on a lesser scale (as over the last few years in Bosnia) while retaining the ability to mount a second substantial deployment—which might involve a combat brigade and appropriate naval and air forces—if this were made necessary by a second crisis. We would not, however, expect both deployments to involve war fighting or to maintain them simultaneously for longer than six months." I put this question to you in the House when you made your statement on Kosovo following a written question I had put to you earlier when you told me that: "The assumptions underlying the Strategic Defence Review were intended to guide force structure planning rather than decisions about individual deployments. A deployment to Kosovo would not invalidate these assumptions." Why not?
(Mr Robertson) Because they were, as I say, a guide to force structures. They would allow certain things to happen, and the illustrations are there and you have read them out. They guide that force structure because within that decisions can be taken that remain valid because of the circumstances that are involved in it. I noticed that in the House yesterday you actually said that we had a division in Bosnia.

336. A division minus.
(Mr Robertson) That is not what Hansard says but never mind. Your division minus can mean anything, it is not a division. We have a divisional headquarters because we command a multinational division out there but we have 5,000 troops. At the height of our involvement in Bosnia we had 13,000[1] troops in 1995 as part of the Intervention Force, we are now down to 5,000 and indeed there is a prospect during this year of further reductions. I would hope that given the level of commitment we might have to take on in Kosovo that we will see further reductions taking place in our commitments in that particular theatre. So the force structure was determined by a number of, as you say, guiding principles but they were not absolutely determined, that you have to do this or you have to do that. They provided a force structure within which choices can be made. Before making any decision about possible deployments in this contingency, and we might have to make a decision quite soon to put people into place, I have to listen very carefully to my military commanders who make an assessment as to whether or not it can be done within the force structure that we have at the present time, never mind the force

structure we will have when the Strategic Defence Review is implemented. It is their judgment that although there may be some short-term penalties we can still make those decisions based on what we are likely to deploy without in any way breaching the Strategic Defence Review calculations.

337. But what is the nature of these short-term penalties?
(Mr Robertson) There will be short-term penalties in terms of training, in terms of some of the restructuring which is necessitated by the Strategic Defence Review; some strain on individuals because although there is a generality of the troops who are engaged, some specialists—the logisticians, the engineers, the signals—tend to be used more regularly than others. So there might well be some short-term penalties but we have got armed forces which are used to being deployed, willing and often very keen to be deployed, so we do not take decisions which would in any way undermine seriously the kind of project we are involved in or indeed the overall force structures that should be at our command.

338. Except, Secretary of State, you have tried to say the figures about Bosnia were 13,000 when it was at its maximum, but in the SDR the assumption is based on "as over the last few years in Bosnia". When the SDR was published the numbers in Bosnia were broadly the same as they are now. The short-term penalties might arise out of a six months' deployment but Kosovo surely will need more than a six months' deployment of a military force in order for the settlement to proceed.
(Mr Robertson) Yes, but not necessarily at the level I was suggesting to the House last week. Remember, if I can just say this because it will save the time of the Committee, no final decisions have been taken on this and they will not be taken until there is agreement, so we are talking about contingency planning for a possible deployment if the circumstances are absolutely right. The United Kingdom's contribution will be made up, first of all, with the Allied Rapid Reaction Corps headquarters where we are the framework nation, and you are really talking there about 2,000 to 2,500 troops which will be deployed plus the United Kingdom's component which will not be radically different from those of other allies.

339. Which will involve a combat brigade, the Fourth Armoured Brigade?
(Mr Robertson) It will involve two balanced battle groups, but I make the point to you that initially there have to be large numbers of troops, first of all because of the ARRC headquarters, secondly——

340. Secretary of State, I accept all that, my concern is what happens in six months' time.
(Mr Robertson) It concerns me as well. I do not take your questions with any great hostility because clearly these are questions we are asking ourselves, and I hope I can enlighten you and members of the Committee that we did not act impetuously here, we are not simply acting because we always like to go to conflict, we are doing it because a careful

---

[1] *Note by witness:* figure should read 11,500.

[Mr Blunt *Cont]*

consideration was made of the timescale which would be involved, of the large number of troops which might be involved, and NATO works on the assumption that the ARRC headquarters is only deployed for a period of time, about eight months in Bosnia, and then it goes back because it is the Allied Rapid Reaction Corps, so it is not designed to be there on a semi-permanent basis. That would mean the troop commitment would be reduced in any event and the figures I gave for illustrative purposes last Thursday are being rigorously scrutinised at the moment to make sure they are the right numbers. They are maximum numbers rather than minimum numbers. Can I also point out to you, in terms of the specific point you make about the Defence Review, in the supporting essays which after all flesh out what is said in the Review itself, it says here at paragraph 5 on page 6.2, "It should be emphasised that the scales of effort are planning tools, they do not pre-judge the size of an actual commitment in particular contingencies which could be larger or smaller depending on the circumstances." So we made that sensible, commonsense caveat.

341. Secretary of State, no one would deny that is of course an entirely proper caveat but it is a guide to force structure planning and if we are going to find a combat brigade, even if the ARRC headquarters come out after six or eight months, remains in Kosovo alongside our deployment in Bosnia, it invalidates the assumptions made in the Strategic Defence Review. Lord Gilbert in the House of Lords last week did say that it would add greatly to overstretch in the Army. You alluded to the short-term problems which would come from various things, I would suggest will those not be long-term problems? If you are not going to look at the force structure of the Army in the wake of whatever happens in Kosovo, you are going to have a significant degree of overstretch particularly in the Army, just at the time you are trying to create a personnel policy which is essential to the success of the SDR?

(Mr Robertson) Mr Hatfield, who is feeling increasingly redundant, would like to deal with a couple of these technical issues and then I will give you a broad answer.

(Mr Hatfield) The first point I would correct is that in referring to the SDR planning assumptions you said the assumption was, as it were, based on recent force levels in Bosnia. That is not correct.

342. It says "over the last few years in Bosnia".

(Mr Hatfield) The actual assumption for force structure purposes was based on a medium level operation of about the peak of Bosnia. The reference to "over the last few years" was in discussing a broad range of circumstances which might come up, so the actual benchmark we set for force structure planning purposes was to be able to mount an operation of the same scale as essentially IFOR when it first went in.

(Mr Robertson) Let me make the point to you, as Secretary of State, if the Chief of the Defence Staff or the Chief of the General Staff had said, "We cannot deploy that number of people without unacceptable penalties on our training rotas, on the implementation of the Strategic Defence Review, or retention, then we would not be doing it.

Mr Blunt: I accept that, but——

Chairman: Excuse me but time is running out and I have seven people who want to speak.

Mr Hancock

343. Three quick questions. In none of the papers or speeches you have made or papers we have received from the MoD or at the recent NAA meeting in Brussels this last weekend, was the exit strategy for Kosovo explained or how you would achieve it. Secondly, what evidence is there that is available to you which leads you to believe that the UCK forces which have gone from Albania into Kosovo have any intention of settling for anything other than a completely free state of Kosovo? Do you have evidence to support the fact they are prepared to go for this partially autonomous region of Kosovo? Thirdly, on the bombing strategy, the big stick strategy, I would be interested to know if Milosevic pulled his troops back to barracks and played the game but the UCK did not, what would you do then? We have not had the answers to those questions.

(Mr Robertson) I will leave Mr Lloyd to supplement what I say especially on the political side of it. In terms of an exit strategy, the exit strategy is relatively clear if imprecise, and that is NATO forces may be required on the ground to police an agreement and when it is clear that that agreement is sustainable we get out. There are people who say we have no exit strategy for Bosnia, but actually British troops are down from a height of 13,000[1] to 5,000 and will be reduced even further from that. The totality of numbers in Bosnia has been reduced as well. So you cannot simply say, "If X happens we will all come out", because we are hoping that there will be an agreement at the weekend which both sides sign up to, both sides will co-operate with, which will be policed by a NATO force if that is going to be required. When that is sustainable, we will come out. Some people have said a three year period is likely to be the duration of that, to see whether that can be settled, that remains to be seen. I do not think we should try and fix in time terms what we are going to do. The only purpose of going in, if we go in there, is to make sure that both parties deliver on what they sign up to, we hope, at Rambouillet at the weekend. The alternative for those who want to see neat solutions or a neat exit strategy and to put it down on one side of paper is that we go back to the civil war and we get the carnage and the mass murders and we see the war crimes taking place and blood is spattered all across the Balkans yet again, huge numbers of refugees spraying out in all directions from that part of the world and that spreads into Macedonia and into Albania. We should not become mesmerised to the context of road blocks on the road from Pec to Pristina. What we are engaged in here is containing a conflict that has got all the ingredients of being one of the most brutal civil wars that we can see. Looking for an easy three line exit strategy frankly is beyond both of us.

---

[1] *Note by witness:* figure should read 11,500.

[**Mr Hancock** *Cont*]

344.   But the people in this country and the people in Europe are entitled to know that it could be a very long term deployment, more than three years.

(*Mr Robertson*)   The intention is that it will be of a duration of no more than three years but it would be foolish and irresponsible to say that it could not be longer.

345.   I understand that.

(*Mr Robertson*)   People of this country are intelligent enough to know that their future is tied up with the future of the Balkans as well. It is in our continent, it is a couple of hours flying time away, it is on the borders of states with which we have got close economic interests, so if the Balkans go out of control, if they erupt into flames again, it will apply just as decisively to mortgage rates in Portsmouth or in Hamilton as it will to the refugee flows that are pouring into Southern Germany. This is Britain, the NATO country, acting in our own self-interest, not as some sort of global policeman but very much as a matter of national interest.

(*Mr Lloyd*)   Can I just supplement that, if I may, I will try to be brief. There is a relevance to the three year time frame in any case because we need to look at the heads of agreement that were accepted by both parties before they came to Rambouillet and amongst those were first of all a demand for a ceasefire, a demand for a de-escalation of levels of forces and then specifically a three year interim agreement that would include autonomy for the Kosovar Albanians within the internationally recognised boundaries of the FRY. That is the relevance of the three year time frame, so to this extent what we are talking about is no discussion as to what the final constitutional make-up of the Kosovar Albanians will be within the FRY or elsewhere, that is beyond the remit here in Rambouillet, but it is a commitment to that three year framework that the interim agreement would operate. Within that the role of a NATO led force is to operate as a basis for stabilisation to allow other things to move forward. Amongst those other things is the need, for example, to hold elections amongst the Kosovans. A proper electoral base has not existed and in the end we cannot accept a situation when representatives appear, as perforce of circumstances they now must, on an ad hoc basis to be there for the indefinite future. We need to build up institutions like the judiciary and a local police force. All of that will go on within the framework that will be provided by a NATO led force. Mr Hancock asked specifically what guarantees could we give about adherence of the Kosovar Albanians to settlement within the FRY and the answer is nobody credibly could give any kind of assurance on that, that is not something that we can say now. What we can say is that the demand is very clear and for three years the interim agreement will stick. That is what the parties at Rambouillet are there to negotiate and that is what we demand of them. How do we police that? Again I cannot make any secret of a fact that is obvious to everybody, that, yes, we do have more ability to influence Belgrade than we have ability to influence the Kosovar Albanians but that does not mean to say that we would not take steps to restrict the activities particularly of the UCK, and

indeed are already taking steps to do that, to dry up the supply of finance to them, to do what we can to dry up the supply of weapons to them, those are important steps that we can and will take. Also we have made it quite clear that the potential for the use of force is there against any party which is prepared to risk the peace and to plunge Kosovo once again into the levels of violence that we have seen with these humanitarian consequences. I think that is a fairly explicit message, not only to Belgrade but also to the Kosovar Albanians.

Mr Brazier

346.   First of all a point for the record and then a couple of questions. When the Chief of Defence Staff came in front of the Committee, the Chairman was asking him questions and he was actually much more explicit than the White Paper was. I think I should just say for the record he said to us that "two medium scale operations, such as we are doing in Bosnia", and this was only six months ago in July, and he then said, "Of those two medium level operations, one would be with fighting ending in six months. I do not think we could sustain two for longer than that." When the Chairman pointed out the fact that this might be rather good news because we were in public session if anybody was listening he was even more specific: "We only have one line of communication at the moment and we need two. That is one of the principal reasons why the numbers in the Army—men and women—are actually going up, so that we can do that. We came to the conclusion that you could not sustain two operations for a very long time, therefore we pegged one and said we could only do it for six months." That is just an observation, I wanted to be clear that is all on the record from your senior military adviser. The question I really want to ask is this, and it follows on from Mr Hancock's questions: it took 100,000 soldiers to provide a pretty unsatisfactory level of peacekeeping in Palestine which had a very small population in those days. Let us suppose for a moment that these guarantees are not adhered to, the guarantee that is extracted out of the Serbs by the threat of bombing on the one hand out of the Kosovans to give a guarantee because they want to see us go, and that we come under fire from both sides, just how large a scale of commitment of troops do you think that NATO collectively, and that is likely to boil down to Britain and France bearing the bulk, is willing to make because frankly the sort of scale of deployment you are talking about at the moment is not a scale which could actually fight a war there?

(*Mr Robertson*)   We are not intending to fight a war. We are talking about supervising a peace agreement that has been signed up to by both sides. I think that is where other comparisons are not particularly valid. That is the assessment of the NATO military planners as to what would be required in that sort of situation. Any peace agreement would clearly involve a degree of disarmament on both sides that would reduce the potential for the kind of trouble that you are talking about. The configuration of the forces that we might send if the decision was taken to send them is especially configured after our experience of

[Mr Brazier *Cont]*

Bosnia to encourage both of the parties to accept what they have accepted. We are not sending Challenger tanks there because they just happen to be available or Warrior armoured vehicles, they are there because they have a very specific utility and they helped to reduce the conflict in Bosnia when they were deployed there at that time. There is quite a lot of experience collectively in NATO and in individual countries about how you go in to police an agreement like Dayton was and like we hope Rambouillet will be after the weekend.

347. But you surely acknowledge that the political difference to them is very, very different and from the point where Belgrade decided that they were not going to continue to back the Bosnian Serbs we were dealing with a far, far smaller scale potential problem on the one hand and the situation in Kosovo, as a number of commentators have pointed out—Sir Michael Rose as you probably know spoke out in the IOSI against us deploying troops there on the basis of a forced agreement—is that you have the alternative of securing borders, however unattractive that may be. There is a very strong case for saying that far from containing the problem the sending in of troops under an agreement that neither side really wants, although their arms may have been twisted to agree to it, could actually result in an explosion across the Balkans rather than actually solving the problem or containing the problem.

(Mr Robertson) You and former General Rose are entitled to your opinions and to your assessments but we have got to make our assessment as well. You might be right, we might be wrong. The NATO military authorities are the ones who have been doing the planning for us. They have a lot of local intelligence, a lot of local knowledge and experience to go by, so when they make an assessment that a force of around 30,000 would be sufficient, both to protect itself (because that is critically important) but also to act in the supervisory role that would be required, that is sound and sage advice. We have looked at this question of sealing the borders, but you only have to look at a relief map of that area to begin to see the problems which are involved in this so-called sealing of the borders. It looks fine on a map to draw a line down, but when you consider the number of troops which would be required to seal, for example, the Albanian-Kosovar border as it stands at the moment when the mountains are over 3,000 ft high and in deep snow at the present time, you begin to get the measure of just how unrealistic that prospect is and has been in terms of the military planning that has been done up to now. But, again, the parties which are sitting at Rambouillet may not be terribly happy with an outcome because if it happens it will be a mixture of the objectives of both sides, but they will have to sign up to it. It will involve a degree of disarmament which will itself reduce the threat. Both parties will know that there are further options available to NATO in self-defence if they choose not to adhere to the agreements which are there. Bosnia, as you say, was a much more complicated situation whereby you were trying to put together a country which had been torn apart, but our experience is much more simple even if more savage in the case of Kosovo, but sensible

decisions have been taken based on a very thorough analysis and I am content to go by the advice.

348. So decommissioning of some of the arms will be a condition of going ahead, will it?

(Mr Robertson) I am not going to go into any of the details of the negotiations at this stage, but part of the Holbrooke Agreement at the end of last year was— I would not use the word "decommissioning", that does not seem to be particularly useful at this point— a level of disarmament and de-escalation and returning of troops both into the Federal Republic of Yugoslavia and the Serbian Republic and away from Kosovo; that was all part and parcel of what the Serbs signed up to on a previous occasion.

Mr Hood

349. We were at the NATO headquarters a few weeks ago when it was really hotting up and there was a great demand by public opinion. In fact I commented there was more public support in Britain for strikes in Kosovo than there was in the previous months against Iraq. The Generals then told us that they had ways and means but the politicians had to deliver the end, the end game. Where they are now, we know what the end game is, we know we are trying to negotiate a peace settlement and NATO will go in and police that agreement hopefully for a short period, up to three years, but what is the end game if we do not have a peace agreement? Because, as the military was telling us when we were at NATO, okay, you can go and send your aircraft in and do your bombing, but what happens after that? What is the end game?

(Mr Lloyd) Of course, the question is a very real one but let me in answering it make this point very clear, the offer to commit troops is premised on there being an agreement, there is no suggestion under any circumstance that we will commit troops to fight their way into Kosovo to impose a peace from outside, because that would quite frankly be not possible. So it is within the context that there is agreement even before we begin to discuss that. I must say to the Committee that I will leave the Committee to speculate on what happens if we do not get an agreement, but what I will say to you very clearly—and I think this is relevant to Mr Brazier's line of questioning before because he made a point about the potential impact on the rest of the Balkans—as I said to this Committee some time ago, at the time of Racak just 43 people were killed and it saw something of the order of 5,000 people fleeing into the mountains. If there is no agreement the levels of violence which are always there—throughout the whole of this period of movement and negotiation deaths still continue—will explode. If that explodes, we will see a return to a ratchet type of violence, as violence itself begets violence, retaliatory violence of different kinds, and we will see the numbers of people who flee going back again to the kind of levels we have already seen. We do not even know, Mr George, but there are something in the order of 200,000 people displaced still within Kosovo itself, living in sometimes not very advantageous circumstances. Amazingly, there are only 20,000 who went to Albania and 20,000 Serbs

[**Mr Hood** *Cont*]

who moved elsewhere in Serbia, plus some 30,000 who fled to Montenegro. But the truth is, if we see a return to violence we will see a movement of people probably on a scale we have not yet seen. In terms of destabilisation of the whole region, we are beginning to move towards the levels that would produce huge pressures on Albania, huge pressures on Macedonia, and that has implications for the whole of that region. Within those terms, I do not think we can speculate what the next step is because at the moment the next step is to get an agreement in Rambouillet and that I think must concentrate all our efforts.

Mr Colvin

350. Are the Irish Guards, the King's Royal Hussars and the Fourth Regiment RA up to strength? If not, what is the shortfall and how is it going to be made good? With regard to the deployment of other troops, has NATO put a figure on the sort of numbers of troops that it is likely to have to deploy? You did not quite answer Bob Wareing's question in the House the other day when he asked about Russian involvement. I appreciate Partnership for Peace countries will no doubt be queuing up to deploy troops because of the need to prove their NATO worthiness, but what is the answer to the 3,000 Russian troops which has been suggested may be the Russian involvement?
(Mr Robertson) I have not heard the Russians were offering 3,000.

351. That was Mr Wareing's question which you did not answer in the House. Can we know about our own forces first? If they are not up to strength where is the shortfall going to be made good from? The TA?
(Mr Robertson) It may well be! It is quite remarkable that we have actually managed to do two hours——

Chairman

352. Two hours, 35 minutes!
(Mr Robertson) —— and not mentioned the TA! Not only that, Mr Brazier has actually asked me some very relevant and pertinent questions and he has not mentioned them at all! I think this must be a unique occasion. We understand there will be some back-filling of units required in these circumstances and how the Army deal with that will have to be based on the professional judgment by the Army. In a way it illustrates, does it not, the very point I was putting about the reserves before, that essentially we often now have to deploy people very quickly into theatre, where they are required to be in a state of readiness and a state of training which will allow them to be there in operations right away. One of the problems that our allies have in putting forward the numbers of troops they will want to put in is the fact they have so many people on lower states of readiness. Today's world demands high readiness troops and much more of them and they have to get them. We actually have them at the present moment, so back-filling may well be necessary with some of the units required, because as we said of the Defence Review it will take some

time for us to be able to get up to the recruitment figures which are very precise targets and to which we are very much committed. The numbers in total that NATO sees as part of this force would be around the 30,000 mark, in total, for all of those who would be there. The Force Generation Conferences are presently taking place with a view to making sure that we actually have these numbers and that they have got pre-positioned equipment so they can deploy very quickly if the decision was taken to do that. In terms of Russia and the Partnership for Peace countries, obviously we want them to be involved. Again, one of the great strengths of the negotiation which has taken place at Rambouillet is that the Russians are very active and full consenting members of the contact group and are part and parcel of the negotiations which are going on. When I met and was discussing this matter with the Foreign Secretary earlier this morning he was making the point that the Russians are deeply engaged in it and we hope that they will remain engaged very firmly in it and that they will play their part in any ground force that takes place within Kosovo.

Mr Cohen

353. In regard to this peacekeeping operating subject to the agreement, can you give us an assurance about the rules of engagement? They will not just be about self-defence, which is very important, but also the ability to stop a threatened massacre will trigger, so to speak, the rules of engagement. One of the problems of the current monitors is that they are not 24 hours and the slaughter at Racak, for example, took place at night. Will this whole operation be a 24 hour one?
(Mr Robertson) A 24 hour operation in Kosovo?

354. Yes. The monitors are not, that is the problem.
(Mr Robertson) The Kosovo Verification Force is there to verify the agreement that was reached. It is there in benign circumstances, they are not armed and clearly there are limits to what they can do. We are talking here about an Implementation Force along the lines of the experience that we have in Bosnia. There are going to be tanks there. It is very difficult to explain the role of tanks in today's conflicts but when I went to Bosnia immediately after the election I went to a little Serbian town called Beljanica to see the Royal Scots Dragoon Guards with their Challenger tanks and it was a pretty powerful message. There was not a great degree of violence in that town. Four or five Challenger tanks sitting there in a small village are unmistakeable in the message that they deliver. That is essentially what will be there but they will be there to supervise, we hope, an agreement that is the common consent of the various parties.

355. And the rules of engagement?
(Mr Robertson) The rules of engagement will be drawn up in the circumstances that apply when a decision is taken to deploy, as the rules of engagement were determined in Bosnia when the Intervention Force went in there.

[Mr Cohen *Cont*]

Chairman: Thank you very much. I understand you were at the Brit Awards yesterday and the fact that you did not have any water tipped over you indicates the theory that deterrence is working. Realising the state of violence in the British pop industry and British football then maybe a team made up of Vinnie Jones, Jarvis Cocker and the Manic Street Preachers would coerce even the Albanians into talk of submission. Thank you very much for coming. There are one or two other questions, perhaps we could drop you both a note. We are going to Kiev, Moscow and Bonn, three interesting cities to visit and then we will be producing our report hopefully in good time for yourselves, the Prime Minister and all the NATO leaders, which must be compulsory reading prior to the Summit actually taking place. Thank you very much for coming along and we know that you will keep us informed as to what is happening. Thank you.

WRITTEN EVIDENCE

Memorandum submitted by the Ministry of Defence on the Future of NATO

INTRODUCTION

The Committee asked for a paper setting out UK policy on the areas covered by the terms of reference for its Enquiry into the future of NATO, i.e.:

— "the development of NATO's New Strategic Concept prior to its adoption at the Washington Summit;

— to consider these issues particularly in the context of the international situation and changing emphasis in NATO's tasks from preparation for strategic attack to peacekeeping and other roles;

— to consider the process of the accession of the Czech Republic, Hungary and Poland to NATO, and case for further enlargement;

— to consider the continuing applicability of the North Atlantic Treaty and the Military structure of NATO to its new roles and any new Strategic Concept."

and any other factors which we consider to be relevant. This paper is submitted jointly by the Ministry of Defence and the Foreign and Commonwealth Office.

As the Strategic Defence Review made clear, membership of NATO will continue to provide the UK with its best insurance both against the new risks of instability within Europe and against the possibility that the political climate in Europe might change for the worse. The partnership between Europe and North America as been a uniquely effective political and military security Alliance for half a century; the forthcoming Summit will be an important event in the continuing development of the Alliance.

THE DEVELOPMENT OF NATO'S NEW STRATEGIC CONCEPT FOR ADOPTION AT THE WASHINGTON SUMMIT

The 1991 Strategic Concept set out the principal aims and objectives of the Alliance. Recognising that the strategic environment had changed since then, the July 1997 Madrid NATO Summit directed the North Atlantic Council in Permanent Session to examine, and update as necessary, the 1991 Strategic Concept, "to ensure that it is fully consistent with Europe's new security situation and challenges". The Summit further directed that "This work will confirm our commitment to the core function of Alliance collective defence and the indispensable transatlantic link." The Terms of Reference for this work were endorsed by Ministers in December 1997. The examination is being undertaken by nations through their national delegations to NATO, supported by the NATO International Staff and International Military Staff. Ministers received a progress report and discussed key themes of this work at their meetings in May and June 1998. They are due to receive a further report when they meet in December, and Heads of State and Government are due to endorse the updated Strategic Concept when they meet in Washington in April 1999.

The Government's overall approach to the updating of the Strategic Concept was set out in the Secretary of State for Defence's letter to the Chairman of the Committee reproduced as Annex B to the Third Special Report of Session 1997–98 (HC 903). As he made clear, the UK wishes to develop NATO's role as an organisation which reduces tension and is a force for good in the world. This means a NATO which:

— embodies and maintains the transatlantic relationship;

— prevents renationalisation of defence;

— contributes to managing other key relationships and engages Russia;

— remains an effective and flexible military instrument for dealing with threats and challenges to our security;

— through engagement with other countries in the region, spreads stability and democratic values, and;

— acts as Allies' primary forum for consultation on all issues of security concern.

The UK's aim is to ensure that NATO remains a dynamic, forward-looking, relevant organisation which continues to make this vital contribution to peace and security.

ISSUES RELATING TO THE UPDATING OF THE STRATEGIC CONCEPT IN THE CONTEXT OF THE INTERNATIONAL SITUATION AND CHANGING EMPHASIS IN NATO'S TASKS FROM PREPARATION FOR STRATEGIC ATTACK TO PEACEKEEPING AND OTHER ROLES

NATO and Allies will address the full range of Alliance activity in their examination of the Strategic Concept. The following issues will be particularly relevant.

Alliance Missions

The updated Concept must continue to fulfil its role as a guidance document for NATO defence and military planners across the full range of Alliance missions. Article 5 collective defence remains the core function of the Alliance; NATO planning should also take account of other (non-Article 5) contingencies where there is no threat of a direct attack on an Ally. Such contingencies could include, for example, crisis management operations and peace support operations, and may be conducted with the involvement of non-NATO countries. Non-Article 5 operations are not a Treaty obligation. A decision by NATO to conduct such an operation requires consensus from all Allies and, if an operation is agreed, each Ally is free to decide whether to take part in it and on what basis. The Alliance should continue to plan for the full range of missions through a single defence planning process and a single spectrum of military capabilities.

The updated Strategic Concept must also strike the right balance between, on the one hand, the positive developments in Euro-Atlantic security over recent years and the fact that NATO does not regard any state as an adversary, and, on the other, the continuing risks, whatever their source, posed by instability and the existence of substantial military capabilities in the hands of non-NATO members.

All NATO operations must have a basis in international law. The legal basis required in any particular case will depend on the particular circumstances. Article 51 of the UN Charter recognises the inherent right of self-defence, which includes the right to seek aid from elsewhere; friendly nations can give such aid individually and collectively. In other cases, a UN Security Council Resolution under Chapter VII of the UN Charter may be necessary to authorise the use of force.

Alliance Military Capabilities

The Alliance must have the military capabilities available to enable it to fulfil the full range of its missions referred to above. This means in particular that they must:

be structured, trained and equipped for combined, joint missions;

be deployable over extended distances;

be held at readiness levels which will allow the full range of missions to be undertaken in a timely manner;

have the sustainability necessary to support extended and possibly concurrent operations; and

be structured to permit, where necessary, longer term military capability to be built up by reinforcement, regeneration and reconstitution.

The force posture of the Alliance was set out in NATO's statement of 14 March 1997 that:

"In the current and foreseeable security environment, the Alliance will carry out its collective defence and other missions by ensuring the necessary interoperability, integration, and capability for reinforcement rather than by additional permanent stationing of substantial combat forces."

The NATO/Russia Founding Act stated (part IV, twelfth paragraph):

"NATO reiterates that in the current and foreseeable security environment, the Alliance will carry out its collective defence and other missions by ensuring the necessary interoperability, integration, and capability for reinforcement rather than by additional permanent stationing of substantial combat forces. Accordingly, it will have to rely on adequate infrastructure commensurate with the above tasks. In this context, reinforcement may take place, when necessary, in the event of defence against a threat of aggression and missions in support of peace consistent with the United Nations Charter and the OSCE governing principles, as well as for exercises consistent with the adapted CFE Treaty, the provisions of the Vienna Document 1994 and mutually agreed transparency measures."

The Strategic Concept should set out the requirements for Alliance military capabilities at the highest level; this guidance will then be taken forward by means of the Alliance's defence planning process.

Relations with non-NATO countries

As part of its reflection of the changed strategic environment, the updated Strategic Concept should also take account of its new relationships with non-NATO countries. Under the NATO Russia Founding Act, NATO and Russia are committed to developing a strong, stable and enduring partnership. NATO has established a distinctive Partnership with Ukraine, through the NATO/Ukraine Charter. NATO has launched the Euro-Atlantic Partnership Council and enhanced the Partnership for Peace programme; and is developing its Mediterranean dialogue.

For all NATO-led operations, the North Atlantic Council must remain the ultimate decision-making authority. We expect non-NATO members to continue to take part in future non-Article 5 operations, as in Bosnia. In such cases the views of other contributing nations must also be taken into account.

European Security and Defence Identity

NATO Ministers agreed at Berlin and Brussels in 1996 that the European Security and Defence Identity (ESDI) would be developed within the Alliance, under which NATO assets and capabilities could be made available for operations under the political control and strategic direction of the Western European Union

(WEU). Defence Ministers agreed in June 1998 to direct work to ensure that the key elements of the implementation of the Berlin and Brussels decisions are in place by the time of the Washington Summit. The results of this work should be reflected in the updated Concept to enable the practical development of the ESDI to continue in support of the overall aims and evolution of NATO.

Arms Control and Proliferation. The updated Concept should reflect both the progress in arms control and the challenges that remain. We will work to ensure that the Alliance's defence and arms control objectives remain in harmony. The proliferation of weapons of mass destruction and their various means of delivery constitutes a potential threat to the territory, population and forces of the Allies, and the updated Concept should provide a framework for the Alliance's response, in co-ordination as appropriate with other institutions, to such risks.

The role of other international organisations

The Alliance contributes to a security architecture of mutually reinforcing international institutions, and the updated Strategic Concept should recognise the role of other international organisations with a security remit, such as the United Nations, the Organisation for Security and Co-operation in Europe (OSCE), the European Union, and the Western European Union.

THE PROCESS IF THE ACCESSION OF THE CZECH REPUBLIC, HUNGARY AND POLAND TO NATO AND THE CASE FOR FURTHER ENLARGEMENT

The Alliance is on track for the Czech Republic, Hungary and Poland to accede by the time of the Washington Summit. All 16 Allies must accept the Protocols of Accession and the invited countries must then ratify. Following debates in both Houses, the UK formally notified the United States, as the depository power, of its acceptance of the Protocols on 17 August. Nearly all Allies have now completed their procedures. We expect all three invited countries to accede simultaneously after the process of ratification in all 19 countries is complete.

The process of full military and political integration began after the Madrid Summit, including

the agreement by the Invited Countries to complete a version of NATO's Defence Planning Questionnaire, prior to their accession;

the agreement of NATO Allies to allow an increasing level of participation by the Invited Countries in a wide range of NATO meetings (without decision-making powers), giving them increasing access to NATO procedures, systems, and issues, allowing for the development over the pre-accession period of effective political and military representation within the Alliance; and

the provision by NATO's Military Authorities of Interim Advice on the Minimum Military Requirements of the Enlarged Alliance (a copy of which, classified NATO CONFIDENTIAL, has already been passed to the Committee).

This has in turn led to:

the development by the Alliance, and the acceptance by the Invited Countries, of packages of challenging but achievable Target Force Goals. These are similar in format to the Force Goals, which have been agreed every other year by participating Allies, but outline the priority military requirements for integration into an effective enlarged Alliance. They assist the invited countries in planning, at the national level, the further preparation of their Armed Forces for membership; and

the development of capability packages and essential infrastructure programmes, as well as an "Interoperability Affirmation Programme", under SACEUR's management, reporting on progress on interoperability.

A further assessment of the resource implications of accession was included in the report on the Alliance's medium-term resource plan, noted by Defence Ministers at their meeting in June 1998; this confirmed the Alliance's earlier assessment that Alliance costs associated with accession would be manageable.

Further enlargement

NATO Heads of State and Government reaffirmed at Madrid that the door remains open to new members in line with Article 10 of the Treaty. The Washington Summit will review the enlargement process. The UK supports further enlargement when Allies collectively judge that further invitations would strengthen European security and the Alliance itself. No decisions have bene taken by NATO on the timing or composition of future enlargement.

THE CONTINUED APPLICABILITY OF THE NORTH ATLANTIC TREATY AND THE MILITARY STRUCTURE OF NATO TO ITS NEW ROLES AND ANY NEW STRATEGIC CONCEPT

The UK believes that the 1949 Washington (North Atlantic) Treaty remains applicable, relevant and valid as a basis for our security and that of our Allies.

NATO has developed a range of integrative mechanisms, principally the integrated multi-national command structure and the collective defence planning process, which have made a crucial contribution to Alliance cohesion and effectiveness, political and military, and thus to NATO's success as a whole. These mechanisms remain invaluable.

NATO is undertaking a process of adaptation of its military structures to ensure its continuing military effectiveness in the changed strategic environment. There are three main and linked areas of focus: the development of the Alliance's future command structure; the implementation of the Combined Joint Task Forces (CJTF) concept; and the building of the European Security and Defence Identity within the Alliance.

NATO Defence Ministers at their meeting in December 1997 agreed the new command structure as a whole, and in particular on the type, number and location of HQs. Since then, substantial progress has been made by the NATO Military Authorities in planning for the transition to the new structure. A detailed implementation plan is being drawn up, with a view to achieving full operational capability as soon as possible. Once implemented, the new command structure will be fully functional, militarily efficient, and cost effective; it will take account of ESDI and CJTF requirements (set out below), provide for the participation on Partner countries and facilitate the integration of the Invited Countries.

The Combined Joint Task Force (CJTF) concept will enhance NATO's ability to command and control multi-national and multi-service forces, generated and deployed at short notice, which are capable of conducting a wide range of military operations. They will also facilitate the possible participation of Partners, and, by enabling the conduct of WEU-led CJTF operations, will contribute to the development of ESDI within the Alliance. Two CJTF trials have now been completed, in November 1997 and March 1998. The next steps in implementation will be based on these and any subsequent trials, including trials and exercises for WEU-led CJTF operations and lessons learnt from the experience in Bosnia and Herzegovina. CJTF implementation will provide the Alliance with much greater operational flexibility.

Memorandum submitted by the Ministry of Defence on NATO's Involvement in Kosovo

Events in Kosovo represent a threat to peace and stability in Europe and produced a humanitarian crisis. NATO's efforts related to Kosovo have been focused on reinforcing the diplomatic efforts to find a peaceful and lasting solution.

At the Ministerial Meeting of the North Atlantic Council (NAC) on 28 May 1998, NATO expressed its concern at the situation in Kosovo and deplored the continuing use of violence. It also stated its support for a political solution which would provide an enhanced status for Kosovo, preserve the territorial integrity of the Federal Republic of Yugoslavia (FRY) and safeguard the human and civil rights of all inhabitants of Kosovo whatever their ethnic origin.

At that meeting NATO Foreign Ministers also outlined two main objectives with respect to the situation in Kosovo. These were:
— to help achieve a peaceful resolution of the crisis by contributing to the response of the international community;
— to promote stability and security in neighbouring countries, with particular emphasis on Albania and the Former Yugoslav Republic of Macedonia.

In pursuit of these objectives the Alliance decided to enhance and supplement Partnership for Peace (PFP) activities in the neighbouring countries of Albania and Macedonia with the objective of increasing stability and helping them to continue to develop their own forces and capabilities. NATO Ministers also approved an assistance programme to help Albania and Macedonia to secure their borders, upgraded a PFP exercise in Macedonia, scheduled a PFP exercise in Albania, established a PFP cell in Tirana to co-ordinate PFP activities and authorised a visit of NATO's Standing Force Mediterranean (STANAVFORMED) to the port of Durres. The last of these took place in early July.

Exercise Co-operative Assembly took place in Albania on 17–22 August and Exercise Co-operative Best Effort took place in Macedonia between 10–18 September. The exercises aimed to improve and exchange peacekeeping, peace support and humanitarian assistance skills at platoon level in a variety of settings; thereby fostering mutual understanding between NATO and partner nations. One of the objectives that flowed from this aim was to use these high visibility training events to improve the public image of Albania and Macedonia. The exercise in Macedonia held in the Krivolak Training Area had a special significance as the first exercise of its kind to be held in any former Yugoslav republic. The exercise were successful in achieving the political aims of demonstrating UK and NATO support for stability in the region as well as displaying NATO's capabilities.

Following their 28 May meeting, NATO Foreign Ministers also expressed strong support for the continuation of an international presence in Macedonia and supported the continuation of the United Nations Preventative Deployment Force.

At their meeting on 11–12 June, NATO Defence Ministers directed the NATO Military Authorities to assess and develop a full range of options for operations which might become necessary to reinforce or facilitate the efforts of the International Community to achieve a solution. This included possible missions to: disrupt a systematic campaign of violent repression and explusion in Kosovo; support international efforts to secure the agreement of the parties to a cessation of violence and disengagement; and to help to create the conditions for serious negotiations towards a political settlement. They directed the study to give priority options which were effective and readily available and to those which would prevent spill over into neighbouring countries.

At the same time the NAC decided that an exercise should be conducted with the aim of demonstrating NATO's capability to project power rapidly into the region. This exercise, known as Exercise Determined Falcon, took place on 15 June over Albania and Macedonia. The exercise involved over 80 aircraft (including 6 UK Jaguars and a Tristar) and all NATO countries took part excluding Iceland and Luxembourg.

At their June meeting, NATO Defence Ministers also decided to accelerate the provision of advice mandated by NATO Foreign Ministers in May on possible support for UN and Organisation for Security and Co-operation in Europe (OSCE) monitoring activity and on possible NATO preventative deployments in Albania and Macedonia. Since then, NATO has considered a wide range of options relating to the Kosovo crisis. Contingency planning for possible air operations was largely completed in early September. Planning for a possible ground force deployment also continued.

On 24 September the NAC approved the issuing of an Activation Warning (ACTWARN) for both a limited air option and a phased air campaign in Kosovo. The ACTWARN took NATO to an increased level of military preparedness and allowed NATO Commanders to identify the assets required for potential NATO air operations. The Secretary General also expressed the strong support of all Allies for the United Nations Security Council Resolution 1199 that was adopted on 23 September. The Resolution made clear that President Milosevic must:

— stop repressive actions against the civilian population;

— take immediate steps to alleviate the humanitarian situation;

— seek a political solution to the Kosovo crisis based on negotiations as must the Kosovar Albanians;

Allies subsequently agreed, following a report by the United Nations Secretary General on 5 October condemning the continuing destruction and killing and emphasising the need for urgent steps to prevent a humanitarian disaster, that the use of force could be justified without the need for a further UNSCR.

On 13 October, the NAC were briefed by the US Special Envoy, Mr Richard Holbrooke on his diplomatic efforts to end the crisis. He stressed that such progress he had been able to make up to that point had been crucially due to the pressure exerted by the Alliance in the previous few days and that NATO should maintain that pressure in order to ensure continued progress. In the light of this, the NAC decided to issue activation orders (ACTORDS) for both limited air strikes and a phased air campaign in the Federal Republic of Yugoslavia. Execution of the limited air strikes was delayed for 96 hours to allow a final opportunity for diplomacy to succeed so that the use of military force might be avoided.

On 14 October Mr Holbrooke announced details of an agreement. The key points were:

— full compliance with UNSCR 1199;

— a substantial and intrusive OSCE verification mission of around 2,000 personnel;

— aerial verification by NATO, with FRY air defence systems either removed from Kosovo or placed in cantonment sites;

— agreement to reach a political settlement with the Kosavar Albanians by 2 November, including broad self government in Kosovo, elections to key posts overseen by the OSCE, a Kosovo police force and an amnesty.

Agreements establishing the verification missions were signed by President Milosevic and representatives of NATO and the OSCE on 15 October 1998. NATO subsequently decided to extend the delay before limited air strikes could be launched until 27 October 1998 to give time for further evaluation of the FRY's performance.

NATO is planning to establish a small NATO co-ordination centre in Macedonia, the principal task of which will be to liaise with the OSCE, and update them on the results of NATO surveillance. This co-ordination centre will require some 100 service personnel from Allied nations.

LESSONS

It is too early to draw detailed lessons from Kosovo about NATO's role in conflicts beyond its own borders. But NATO's role in addressing the Kosovo crisis shows the Alliance's continuing commitment to promoting stability and preserving international peace and security which is a vital interest of all its members.

Memorandum submitted by Humphry Crum Ewing, Research Fellow, Centre for Defence and International Security Studies on the Future of NATO

BACKGROUND AND OVERVIEW

To visit Hungary, Poland and the Czech Republic and to talk with Hungarians, Poles and Czechs involved in the arrangements for joining NATO is to form a picture of what joining NATO means to them that differs significantly at a number of points from how the enlargement of NATO to include them is perceived in London, Brussels and Washington.

These differences include:

— a much deeper and more widespread sense of generalised "Insecurity" and a more active concern for "security" than we in the West now feel;

— a much more "military" attitude than that to be found in many or most of the present 16 members;

— a concern that NATO, in its new Strategic Concept, should keep as its priority objective its original specific character of a regional alliance for mutual defence and that its concepts should not change towards those of a "security" organisation tasked to go firefighting more widely;

— an unwillingness to understand and accept that their defence budgets should recognise the distinction between the (relatively large) expenditure required to bring their armed forces up-to-date in any case and the (relatively small) expenditure required simply because of adjustments to the requirements of NATO membership;

— a timescale for the modernisation of their armed forces that looks ten to fifteen years ahead and more as compared with western expectations and assumptions for their achieving this in five to ten years at the most;

— an enthusiasm for further enlargement and a determination to work from within NATO to push on with this as rapidly as possible.

Each of these prospectively perceived significant differences is discussed further in Part B below.

Both Hungary and Poland are working away at all aspects of preparing for NATO membership and for subsequently playing a full part in the work of NATO. In both cases this is despite changes in Government.

In the case of the Czech Republic the change in Government this summer has resulted in much of the detailed work going onto hold, although there is no falling back from the desire to assume membership.

There is a deeply felt desire throughout the region to "re-enter" Europe, but there is strong hostility (usually not articulated) to Germany and also no desire to exchange Russian hegemony for American hegemony. The cash, personnel and resources that flow into the region on a large scale from the US do however serve to push anti-Americanism under the carpet.

It must be emphasised that the process is perceived, and almost invariably spoken of there, as being one of "re-entry into Europe" and not one of "entry"—a distinction which all too many in the west seem unwilling to comprehend and recognise.

This process is seen as taking the form of memberships of the EU and of NATO. These are what matter; memberships of the Council of Europe, OSCE, and Partnership for Peace are all very well in their respective ways but (to mix the metaphors) they are perceived as cosmetic sidetracks.

Funding from the EU directly and via the EIB has an important and fairly high profile part in ongoing reconstruction. The role of the EBRD is almost invisible. This funding has undoubtedly contributed to the fact that a "detailed and expert level assessment . . . [by and for NATO since March 1997 . . . (including site visits) showed that the infrastructure of the prospective new members was much better than had hitherto been assumed"—thus contributing to lower estimates of joining costs.[1] It has also to be said that the infrastructure (of motorways, railways and so on) in former East Germany has been enormously improved in the past nine years or so, since the East was assimilated to the West. By its geographical location the infrastructure of East Germany is fundamental to planned arrangements to reinforce the joining countries. Former East Germany, an important erstwhile member of the Warsaw Pact, has of course already become, by unification, a member *de facto* of both NATO and the EU.

---

[1] Paragraph 14 point 3 in *Studies of the costs of NATO enlargement: note by the Ministry of Defence, March 1998*. House of Commons Deposited Paper 6278. Hereafter cited as "the MoD NATO enlargement costs study, March 1998".

The sense of generalised "insecurity"

There is a generalised sense of insecurity felt at most levels of opinion and in all the countries which I have assessed in the region. It is no longer that the Russians may return at any time, although there is a consciousness that history teaches that there is a danger of their doing so at some time in the future. The sense that membership of NATO carries with it the US nuclear guarantee against Russia is a dormant issue in the region, however much its logical consequences may trouble members of the US Senate. The fear is not of an invasion by the Ukraine—the neighbour with relatively substantial armed forces. It is not that the conflicts in former Yugoslavia will spread as such into Europe proper. The latent hostility to Germany already mentioned reflects fears about economic, social and cultural imperialism rather than about military conquest or territorial aggrandisement.

In positive terms there is a real fear of the flow of refugees, of economic migrants, of seekers after what might be called "ethnic re-unification" (as the counterpart of ethnic cleansing) all in numbers with which the individual countries and their fragile economies will be unable to cope. There is a desire to retain frontiers as ring-fences and as means of control, as water-tight compartments as it were, necessary to ensure that the ships of state remain afloat. There is a sense that no one of the countries of the region is strong enough to be certain of standing alone against these pressures but that it *may* be possible if they all co-operate with one another and that it *will* be possible to do so as members of Europe.

This generalised sense of insecurity grows above all from the history of the region, not only since 1945 but going back 150 years and more, and particularly from a shared (and selective) recollection of the failure of the Collective Security arrangements of the 1920s and 1930s[1] to protect the successor states of the Austro-Hungarian, German, Russian and Turkish empires after 1918.

In its immediacy this pattern of past misfortunes and present fears differentiates the historical-cultural ethos of Central and Eastern Europe from that of the west, where historic anxieties about security have been rendered "unthinkable" by half a century of stability.

The popular attitude towards "military" issues

Some of the same historic and cultural factors which contribute to the sense of insecurity also contribute to a stronger adhesion to the military virtues and respect and admiration for the profession of arms than is now the case amongst most people in Western Europe.

In this sense the enlargement of NATO to the East—particularly the addition of Hungary and of Poland—will bring into its military resources substantial additional strength in terms of basic soldierly capabilities, the will to fight and the willingness to undertake routine military duty.

I recognise that in propounding this view—that this enlargement at least will enhance and not weaken the military effectiveness of NATO—I go to some extent contrary to received opinion. This different assessment follows largely from a different view as to the relative importance of the contributions to military effectiveness of men and their morale on the one hand as compared with machinery and its technology on the other.

The new NATO Strategic Concept: a regional alliance for mutual defence or a much more widely focused "security" organisation?

There is a strongly felt belief, albeit one that is hesitantly expressed at this stage—i.e., while the countries are still applicants and not yet members—that the new NATO Strategic Concept should focus firmly on the character of the Alliance as a regional arrangement for collective self-defence and that it should not branch out too far into becoming a generalised security organisation tasked to act more widely as an international firefighting force.

Persistence in this line, i.e., a limitation to mutual self defence rather than acceptance of a wider security role, would place NATO on a course which departs from that envisaged in the implicit bargain between the US Administration and the US Congress, namely that if the Congress will continue to fund the US to underwrite NATO then NATO will assume from the US a larger role in the dangers (particularly the risk of casualties) involved in acting as the world's policeman.

I would suggest to the Committee that this is a real antithesis in contemplating the future of NATO and that it should give some attention to the implications for the United Kingdom of taking one position rather than another on this issue.

---

[1] For example Locarno, the Little Entente and the Anglo French guarantees to Poland in 1939.

A distinction in defence budgets between bringing forces up-to-date in any case and the strict costs of joining NATO

The MoD NATO enlargement costs study, March 1998 follows some (but not all) earlier studies of likely costs by distinguishing between costs of modernisation which new members will be required to meet "to fulfil NATO obligations" from "the overall cost of modernising and restructuring new members' armed forces (required in any case)".[1]

While this differentiation is an important one, which may seem clear enough in theory (at least to us), it is not one which anyone in the region is willing to accept to the extent of applying it, or indeed really able to understand. This lack of comprehension is an inexorable consequence of endogenous insouciance about financial details aggravated by 50 years of living and working in a centrally directed economy, in which costs, in our sense of the term, have had no meaning.

So far as the countries of the region are concerned therefore all costs of military modernisation will continue to be perceived as costs of joining NATO and dialogue about such costs will continue to be distorted by such asymmetric assumptions.

The timescale for modernising armed forces

The general western view is that it might take as long as 10 years to complete the transition. The view in the region is that it will take 10 to 15 years or more. Such a proportionate difference in projected timescales leads to a different view about the cost of the process, particularly when discounted to present values. Put at its simplest the figure taken by the Committee in its Third Report[2] of £110 million (or double that) over 10 years for the UK's contribution translates crudely as £11 million a year (or £22 million). Over 15 or 20 years it becomes £6 million to £7 million a year. An exercise in discounting to present value the costs to be incurred in future years produces a lower figure still.

Figures reached on such a basis must be tentative or, at best, illustrative but I am reasonably confident in putting to the Committee the view that costs will be stretched over a period that is relatively much longer than that envisaged in early prognostications.

Further enlargement: scope and speed

Where, following my discussions in the region, I differ most strongly and most confidently from current western assumptions is in relation to pressures for relatively rapid further enlargement. My differences here lie in the opposite sense to those which I have about the timescale of military modernisation for joining members.

The western view and particularly the American view may be fairly summarised I believe as "Let's digest this lot, see how long it takes and how well it works out and then it will be time enough to think about the possibility of adding one or two more."

The view of the newcomers, as regularly and explicitly expressed in neighbourly dialogue, is that they will act as strong advocates within NATO for further enlargement as soon as possible, and indeed that the process of further enlargement will be an important determinant in the more measured process of modernisation.

Put at its simplest the question of whether Slovakia is inside NATO or outside it will be highly relevant to the military planning and requirements of all three joining countries; the position of Romania will be highly relevant to Hungarian planning and of Lithuania to Polish planning.

Attitudes to "the Open Door" form a further real antithesis in contemplating the future of NATO. Because the consequences of "the Closed Club" vs. "the Open Door" are so much less amendable than decisions on the words of doctrine this point of difference is even more important than that on Strategic Doctrine. I would again suggest to the Committee therefore that it should give considered attention to the implications for the United Kingdom of taking one position rather than another on this issue.

SOME OTHER RELEVANT REGIONAL CONSIDERATIONS

The Russian financial collapse, unless retrieved reasonably quickly, will also move the future of the (detached) Kaliningrad oblast further up the East European (and Baltic) regional agendas.

In the minds of those in the regional prospective membership of the EU is much more closely linked with prospective membership of NATO than it is in the minds of those who are already members of either or both.

To present views on EU membership would go beyond the scope of this note, but the note would not be complete without drawing attention to the fact of this perceived linkage and to the weight attached to it in the region.

---

[1] Para 3b Point 2.
[2] Para 88.

The fact that Slovenia and Estonia, for instance, are approved applicants for membership of the EU but not of NATO is regarded as incomprehensible and, by those concerned to make difficulties, as clear evidence of an aversion in Western Europe to accepting "re-entry" from those in the East.

The defeat of the Meciar Government in Slovakia at the General Election there at the end of September should have important consequences, provided that the former opposition groups can hang together to form a stable government. Such a change of regime will be seen in the region as entitling Slovakia (separated from the Czech Republic since 1992) to re-enter negotiations for membership of both NATO and the EU from which it was excluded by reason of the financial and political conduct of the Meciar regime.

The change of Government in Germany (following the General Election there which took place while I was in Berlin) will, I believe, have significant but at this stage unpredictable effects within the region, on the enlargement of NATO, on its future strategic doctrine and on its overlap with the membership of the EU. It would however already seem clear, in general terms, that there has been (a) a generational change (b) a sweeping change in personalities (c) a transfer of weight in the *Bundestag* due to the proportional representation element in the German electoral system from the parties of Western Germany to those of Eastern Germany. It is also realistic to assume that the forthcoming transfer of the German capital back to Berlin will mark a renewed phase of Germany's historic *Drang nach Östen*, with all that this implies for the future orientation of NATO.

INTERIM CONCLUSIONS

The shadow of Russia over Central and Eastern Europe has diminished, partly because of the elapse of time since Russia withdrew its forces from the region, partly because its economic and financial incompetence has reduced respect as well as fear. For the time being at least chaos has replaced subjection as the ultimate threat to security in the region.

Contrary to some fears, including those discussed in the Committee's Third Report, the inclusion of the three joining countries will enhance rather than diminish the effective military strength of NATO, so far as its present and immediately foreseeable tasks are concerned.

Programmes for military procurement will focus on refurbishment rather than replacement, will proceed at a much slower pace than is sometimes envisaged and will be altogether lower key—with emphasis on C4I and IT generally rather than on state-of-the-art platforms and weaponry. There will be no bonanza for the world's defence manufacturing industries.

The whole process of reconstruction and up-dating will require a much longer term than first hopes have assumed. The time horizon will be ten to fifteen years and more, not five to ten years at most.

The joining members will exercise continual pressure from within NATO for future extension to proceed faster and further than the present members anticipate and, apparently, wish.

There are considerable implications for the US relationship with NATO as such and with its individual nation members; this will follow in part from an eastward movement in NATO's centre of gravity, but also from differences in underlying views about strategic concepts.

It is still too early to assess sufficiently precisely the nature and extent of the new pulls and the new pushes within NATO. Therefore, while it is not sensible to try to prophesy now and in detail their full implications, it will be important to seek to understand them correctly as they do emerge and not to be taken by surprise by them.

STATUS OF THIS MEMORANDUM

This Memorandum has been prepared following a visit by the writer in September 1998 to Vienna, Budapest, Warsaw, Berlin, Dresden and eastern Germany, Prague and the Czech Republic more widely, in the course of his work on programmes of research at the Centre for Defence and International Security Studies, Lancaster University (CDISS) on *Russia and Related Issues* and on *The Future of NATO*. He would like to record his appreciation of the help he has received from those whom he met and talked with in the course of his visit; from colleagues at CDISS working with him on these programmes; and from many others who have talked freely with him under the Chatham House rule.

Memorandum submitted by John Roper, Associate Fellow, International Security Programme, Royal Institute of International Affairs on the Future of NATO

I should like to address the questions implicit in the Committee's terms of reference for this enquiry, by attempting to define the probable problems of European Security in the twenty-first century, and to examine NATO's comparative advantage in dealing with these problems.

NATO's problems as it looks into its own second half century, as well as into the twenty-first century are, in some large measure, the problems of its own success. The first half century of its existence has seen it make such substantial contributions to the solution of the problems of security in Western Europe, as they were seen, at its creation, half a century ago that it needs to redefine its role in a radically changed security environment.

In some ways its most remarkable success, which was never its primary objective, but was never totally absent from the thinking of its member states, has been the creation of a "security community" among those of its members who are also members of the European Union. The concept of a "security community", which was developed in the 1950s by the Czecho-American political scientist Karl Deutsch, refers to a group of states who cannot imagine the use of military force to settle disputes among themselves. The combination of the security umbrella provided by NATO, the culture of military transparency and co-operation that has developed underneath that umbrella together with the process of integration that has occurred within the European Union has eliminated the principal security problem facing Western European states in the first half of the twentieth century—namely the risk of conflict between themselves.

NATO's other success, its contribution in creating the strategic environment which lead to the end of the Cold War has gone a long way towards eliminating the principal security problem that confronted Western Europeans in the second half of the twentieth century. The existing European members of NATO, with the exceptions of Greece and Turkey, no longer perceive direct threats to their own territory in the near future. It is probably also the case for the three states, the Czech Republic, Hungary and Poland who are due to join the Alliance next year, but less so, at least in terms of perceptions, for many of the would be candidates for membership.

The twenty-first century looks therefore very different from the twentieth century in that it will be one in which Western Europe is an area of relative stability in an uncertain world. The security tasks which now face Western Europe can be seen as three.

> The extension of the "security community" which exists in Western Europe eastward through the enlargement of NATO and the European Union, and the development of a network of bilateral and multilateral relationships with those states which are likely to be early members of NATO and the EU as well as those for whom membership will occur later if at all.

> To contribute to security in its own immediate neighbourhood, not only for altruistic reasons, but because the spillover effect of disputes in its neighbourhood, including the flow of refugees.

> To make contributions to security further afield. This may be to respond to indirect threats to its own security, but may also be to accept its global responsibility.

There is relatively little controversy about the first two tasks, although the enlargement of the European Union may well be more difficult to achieve because of short-sighted views of those who will not be prepared to make the short-term economic structural adjustments in the interests of long term security. For the second, NATO in former Yugoslavia has already demonstrated its efficiency as an instrument of military co-operation, once a political settlement had been reached.

The third task is not yet so widely accepted. Does a prosperous and relatively secure Europe feel it has any responsibilities for global security? Does it feel an obligation to constrain proliferators of weapons of mass destruction, to punish perpetrators of genocide or other crimes against human rights, to bring humanitarian aid to victims of natural or man-made disasters or to balance the development of some new potentially hegemonic power which might in the long term provide it with a challenge? The twentieth century has seen a decline almost to vanishing point of any residual European imperial pretensions or responsibilities. They will not return and do not seem to have yet been replaced by any particularly strong vocation to use military force to right wrongs in the rest of the world.

This issue of contributing to global security is linked to the more fundamental question of what sort of player Europe, and more specifically the European Union, intends to be in world affairs. Whether it intends to be a regional power concerned that there is no trouble on or adjacent to its frontiers, or to be more ambitious and contribute to global security, it will need to consider what instruments it will require to influence developments. If it wishes in addition to diplomatic and economic instruments to be able to use, or have the capacity to use, military force elsewhere in the world, there will be a need to develop appropriate forces, a military command structure and political arrangements for the direction of such forces. Some of these issues have been recently raised by the Prime Minister, while making it clear that NATO remains the instrument of choice for the military implementation of policy.

In considering these long term challenges to European countries it is also important to consider Europe's future security relationship with the United States, its indispensable ally during the Cold War. It is clear from recent United States studies, including their most recent Quadrennial Defence Review, that their planning for future major military action to face possible challenges is centred outside Europe, with the Gulf and North East Asia being two particularly risky areas. While few at present would expect European forces to return to North East Asia, a contingency in the Gulf would lead to American expectations of active European cooperation, with consequential strains on the North Atlantic Alliance if this did not occur. Moreover, if Europe wants to be able to influence the actions of the United States in the exercise of its power, military as well as non military, in the world, it has to have the capacity to be a partner in action as well as discussion. In the longer term the continuation of United States interest in European Security may be linked to the preparedness of Europeans to take an interest in wider issues of global security which form the predominant concern of the United States.

The conclusion of this position is that NATO should consider its role in providing a continuing mechanism for military cooperation in this wider field. It is the instrument of choice of the military professionals in all West European countries as well as, I believe, in the United States. As well as being the mechanism for cooperation between Europeans and Americans for dealing with security problems within our continent, (a diminishing task) it could also become the instrument for cooperation between Western Europeans and Americans outside out continent on the new agenda of trans-regional security.

This may be considered to some to be a move too far, with overtones of great power neo-imperialism. This argument must be considered and the widest involvement of the UN and the other permanent members of the Security Council is clearly desirable. The alternative is to leave a single super-power making its own decisions on the imposition of global order. I distrust monopolies whenever I see them, and, as a friend of the United States, would advocate this new role for Western Europe and NATO above all as being as good a way as I know to keep the Americans honest. This is, I believe, not only in our interest and that of the world but also in theirs.

Memorandum submitted by Dr Jonathan Eyal, Director of Studies, Royal United Services Institute, on the Future of NATO

Membership in the Alliance was viewed by the leadership of Poland, the Czech Republic and Hungary as an act of "historic justice", erasing the divisions on the European continent and rendering the collapse of the Soviet empire irreversible. Once the hurdle of the membership has passed, however, some of the real problems with NATO's enlargement are becoming more obvious. In broad terms, the problems with the new members are as follows:

Support for NATO's missions. This is strongest in Poland, and weakest in the Czech republic. The reasons are mainly historic. There is a virtual unanimity in Poland that if the country does not become a member of the Alliance it would ultimately be dragged into another game of spheres of influence in Europe. The Polish military also enjoys a favourable image, despite the brief period of the military dictatorship in the early 1980s. In Hungary, support for membership in the Alliance is weaker although there is a broad agreement between both government and opposition that it is necessary for the country's security. Support for the Alliance remains weakest in the Czech republic: the Czech armed forces have a poor image internally, for they are regarded as having being unable to defend the state either before the Second World War or during two communist take-overs, in 1947 and 1968. Furthermore, pacifist movements are more widespread in the Czech republic than anywhere else. Nevertheless, latest opinion polls indicate a rising support for Czech participation in NATO's task, although from a relatively low base.

By far the thorniest issue is that of defence expenditure. There is no agreement on how much the process of adaptation will cost. But it is already clear that both the Central Europeans and the existing NATO member states have an interest in claiming that someone else will pay the bulk of the adaptation costs. Ways around the problem can be found. First, the Central European military has to spend money on modernisation of its ancient equipment anyway; governments in that region will therefore argue that they are not about to spend anything more, and may even be able to save money by entering the Alliance. Furthermore, the entire project could be spread out over a period of years, and credits can be obtained on soft terms from Western defence manufacturers, effectively postponing payment for the military bills even further. And, finally, all the Central Europeans are insisting on "off-setting" agreements, which mean that Western military companies will have to invest in local economies, thereby allowing politicians to claim that they are actually creating jobs and saving indigenous defence industries from extinction. But three major caveats remain. Defence is just about the only discretionary item of government expenditure which can be cut without much outcry; grappling with budget deficits and/or exploding social security and health expenditure, every government has sought to save on military spending. In the immediate flurry of enthusiasm after NATO's Madrid summit last year all Central European countries promised to spend more on their defence budgets. With the exception of Poland, this enthusiasm has now subsided. Much of the Hungarian air force is grounded due to lack of cash, and the problem is even trickier in the Czech republic, where a Socialist government enjoys a tenuous parliamentary majority and is internally divided about the allocation of the country's resources.

Political control over the military is, supposedly, not a problem. There is no chance of a military coup in any Central European country, or even of a major insubordination. But this is merely a facade masking much trickier issues. The reality is that a proper civilian control over the armed forces is yet to be established. Civilian defence ministers uneasily co-exist with general staffs, which are still dominated by men in uniform. Most of the threat assessments are being done by military personnel, rather than civilians, as in all NATO countries. Parliaments exercise only a perfunctory control over military affairs. The lack of defence experts in civilian life and of defence correspondents capable to report such matters in the media compounds the isolation of the military from society at large. And the absence of women or ethnic minorities in the services as well as the reluctance of young men to perform military service does not help either.

Although the Central Europeans will be eager to send representatives to NATO headquarters, the plain fact remains that they have neither the quality of staff nor a sufficient number of officers speaking English or French, the working languages in the Alliance. An accelerated programme of English language teaching is underway, but it will take years to bear fruit.

Furthermore, the entire military establishment in Central Europe is not capable to absorb the sheer quantity of information and decisions which are being taken in the run-up to NATO membership. A hugh amount of documentation and intelligence-sharing facilities needs to be set up. More importantly, massive defence contracts need to be negotiated, and it would be highly surprising if corruption does not follow, as it has done in almost every NATO country. Expect some high profile corruption scandals in the years to come; the only hope is that they will be revealed after most of the decisions about the adaptation of the military have already been taken.

Finally, one of the key political problems which will emerge almost immediately is who actually decides on security policies. Once members in the Alliance, the Central Europeans will have a permanent representative on the North Atlantic Council. That person may come from the foreign ministry, but is expected to work closely with the military staff, and co-ordinate policies with the defence and finance ministries. The new members will therefore be expected not only to iron out the traditional difficulties between prime minister and head of state (potentially acute in Poland and the Czech republic, although not in Hungary), but also between various government departments, and especially diplomats and the military. The tussle which now accompanies the conduct of the negotiations for membership in the European Union does not give any reasons for encouragement that the process of co-ordination will be either smooth or swift.

The Government is committed to a process of enlarging the North Atlantic Treaty Organisation to the former communist countries in Europe, provided that the process does not add security obligations which no existing member state in the Alliance is either willing or able to fulfil, the countries which join contribute to the security of all and the Alliance is not diluted either in scope or in it functioning capabilities. There is little doubt that the position is both logical and comprehensive. But it is equally clear that it is a list of *desiderata*, an ideal situation which is unlikely to coincide with European realities for many years to come.

Despite all the genuine efforts to present the process of enlargement as a technical exercise in which those best suited to join are invited and those not yet ready are told what they need to do to quality, the debate about enlargement has assumed the air of a beauty competition. Britain is not to blame for this outcome: both the present and the previous Administration have made strenuous efforts to avoid such an impression, but London had no control over the French behaviour with Romania, the Italian noisy support for Slovenia, or the blunt announcement of the US that it would accept only three countries in the Alliance.

Regardless of the claim that the first wave of enlargement should be small in order to be both digestible and acceptable in Europe, the truth is, as the Foreign Secretary mentioned on the eve of the Madrid summit, that an enlargement that includes Poland, the Czech Republic and Hungary is not particularly small.

Nor is it particularly coherent. Hungary will have no territorial continuity with other Alliance members; Ukraine will border on NATO at some points but not others. More importantly, while everyone claims that the real security challenges of the continent are at Europe's flanks, the enlargement remains a Central European affair.

Finally, the claim that the current enlargement process is but one of several to come is not credible in the countries which are asking to become members. Theoretically, the Alliance was open to new members since its inception and, indeed, accepted new states at various times. But these countries joined during the period of the Cold War when "our gain" automatically the communist bloc's "loss" and when the desire to assume commitments and reward those willing to help the West was at its highest. It is difficult to see how a new consensus could be created for another enlargement in a few years, how the US Congress could be persuaded to ratify another wave, and how the Russians could be persuaded that, yet again, this should not threaten their interests. Theoretically, the possibility of another enlargement will always be there, and the political difficulties can be overcome. Taken together, however, the probability of all these obstacles being ignored by the government of the member states in the next few years (particularly since Germany will lose interest in another enlargement) remain very slim indeed. Furthermore, even if the best will exists to integrate new countries (particularly former neutral states), the prospect looks remote for the leaders of the former communist states in eastern, southern and northern Europe, and is meaningless to them in political terms.

As a consequence, Europe will have to live with five different categories of states and security arrangements:

(a) countries that are both in the EU and NATO, or will soon belong to both institutions;

(b) countries that are in NATO but have no early hope of joining the EU;

(c) states that are in the EU and have no immediate desire to join NATO;

(d) countries that are not member of either institution but will continue pressing for both;

(e) states which are excluded from both institutions, but which know that it is particularly this exclusion which gives them importance.

The classification is controversial, but it is already clear that Turkey belongs to category b, the neutral states in the EU to category c, Romania and the Baltic states in particular in category d, and Russia and Ukraine are in the final classification. The existence of this seemingly confusing pattern of security arrangements allows for a measure of flexibility, and does not necessarily prevent joint European action when this is required. Furthermore, various instruments for dealing with individual cases have evolved and are being designed with the full co-operation of the British Government. But the security challenge will remain most acute in the countries which are likely to experience a "double rejection" from both NATO and the European Union. And, curiously, they also happen to be the most vulnerable countries on the continent.

Slovakia, Romania, Bulgaria and the Baltic republics are, to one extent or another, in the same category. But even in this classification, some caveats are in order:

Technically, they all are countries which may join both NATO and the EU, but not in the immediate future. In practice, however, the situation of Romania and Slovakia and Bulgaria is quite different: while the Baltic states are both small and economically developed (and therefore have a good chance of joining the EU, particularly in the case of Estonia), Romania, Slovakia and Bulgaria have no hope of being among the front-runners in the EU. The danger of a "double rejection" is therefore not only looming; it is a reality.

In both Romania and Slovakia, the credibility of the authorities depends (although in different ways and with potentially different outcomes) on the question of integration into NATO and the EU.

They both contain large ethnic Hungarian minorities, a potential source of trouble for NATO and the EU whether Slovakia and Romania join these institutions or not.

They border on Ukraine, and therefore offer another sensitive dimension to European security arrangements.

When Czechoslovakia broke up at the end of 1992, there was unanimity in the West that the two halves of the old country should be treated on an equal basis. There was also great understanding of the sensitivity of the Slovaks to any apparent slights on their national honour and standing; indeed, all Western states were determined to include Slovakia in both the EU and NATO, despite the fact that from the start the Slovaks were economically weaker than their Czech former partners. In effect, Slovakia excluded itself from both institutions, through the policy of its Prime Minister, Mr Vladimir Meciar, and his association with extreme nationalists in his country. Britain led the way in co-ordinating a EU response to the rapid deterioration in the respect for human rights and constitutional norms in Slovakia and, although it has been accused by the Slovak government of adopting a "hostile" attitude, the UK has preserved. Meciar's removal as a result of the latest elections in that country has vindicated Britain's original position, but has not made our policy any easier. One of the first acts of the British government after the parliamentary elections was to impose a visa regime on Slovak citizens, a necessary measure given the rise in the number of asylum applicants from that country, but one which has hardly inspired confidence in Slovakia's ability to integrate within either NATO or the EU. The introduction of new immigration legislation in the latest Queen's Speech may alleviate the problem with the visa regime in the future. Measures which the Slovak government has undertaken to prevent discrimination against its Roma minority (the main source of the bogus asylum applications in the UK) will help as well, but tangible results will take years. The dispute about the visa regime is, of course, of little practical importance for the security relationship. But it has a huge psychological impact inside Slovakia. And it is difficult to see how the Slovak government can make huge strides in its desire to join either the EU or NATO in the years to come. A crisis of expectations is therefore inevitable in Slovakia.

Romania failure to join NATO in the "first wave" has caused bitter disappointment. The option of integration into the West has not been given up, but it is coupled, at least in opposition circles, with ironic remarks in the direction of Western governments, and a rising political debate within the country, questioning Western motives and good intentions. The current Romanian government has conducted such an aggressive campaign to join NATO because it assumed—correctly—that success on this score is just about the only achievement it could offset against the pain of economic reform. Failure on this campaign was followed by the utter failure of economic reform; the bickering coalition in Bucharest is unlikely to survive for much longer, and elections are almost inevitable next year. To make matters much worse, it is difficult to see how these elections could produce a stable administration; the political scene is deeply fractured, and just about the only parties which seem to be gaining in popularity are the extreme nationalists. Relations with the ethnic Hungarian minority will not worsen immediately. But any chance of further improvements are probably gone. It is hard to see how the Government could make new concessions on the subject of minority language teaching or the use of minority languages in various countries, beyond what has already been tabled in parliament. Bereft of any concrete security links, Romania will build up its connection with Turkey. Romania will be careful that this should not be seen to be happening at the expense of Greece, but there is little doubt that, when it comes to keeping Russia in check—which is a Romanian obsession—the Romanians see in Turkey their only reliable local partner. Economic interests (including a sizeable Turkish investment in Romania) merely complements this trend. It will be hard to prevent Greece from seeing such developments to its disadvantage, and another layer of problems could be added on NATO's southern flank. Finally, there will be little appetite for sending peacekeepers to various future operations in the region, unless these are tied to NATO and offer realistic prospects—in the Romanian leaders' minds—for Romania's future membership in the Alliance. Negative developments in Romania will have a direct effect on Ukraine and Hungary, and may yet embolden the Serb leadership to resist Western efforts in Yugoslavia. Romania is the biggest former communist state in Central-Eastern Europe after Poland, and the only country with a considerable military potential in the region (albeit plagued by inefficiencies). For historic reasons, there is a consensus in Romania over defence which will guarantee a relatively high military expenditure level. And, with Romania less pliant to Western policies unless it sees an immediate and tangible return, the southern flank of the Alliance will become even more difficult to manage. A way around the problem exists, but it will require the commitment of additional Western resources. It is obvious that Romania cannot officially be treated differently from other countries which have failed to be included into this wave of enlargement. But it is equally evident that in many other respects it will have to be treated differently from, say, Bulgaria, which has recently revived its interest in military integration. Britain has performed an important role in this process of calming the Romanians down and ensuring their co-operative behaviour. The Romanian military has always been suspicious of the French despite all the honeyed words between Paris and Bucharest. France is not yet in NATO's integrated military command structure and the failure of France to resolve this issue before the Madrid summit has weakened Romania's own position, a factor which the generals in Bucharest are unlikely to forget. Further afield, the Romanian military's relationship with the Germans is almost non-existent; the British are the most important partner from the Romanian viewpoint. Military co-operation programmes with Romania have been expanded, and the Romanians were gratified by the recent visits to their countries of the Prince of Wales and the Foreign Secretary. Nevertheless, NATO will not be able to discriminate openly between the PfP arrangements with—say—Bulgaria, and those with Romania. A more intense bilateral relationship between Britain and Romania will provide the country with an added edge in its military contacts with the West. It may also provide useful terrain for exercises for the British armed forces, particularly if the locations in Poland prove both expensive and environmentally sensitive, as they will most certainly do in the future.

For all the familiar political reasons, NATO cannot and should not forsake the possibility of further enlargements. At the same time, the Alliance is unable to offer either a concrete timetable or a firm guarantee of membership to any particular country. When the Cold War ended, every Western government agreed that just about the worst possible outcome would be one in which certain countries were excused from both NATO and the EU at the same time. For a variety of reasons—and which the West does not necessarily carry the blame—this worst outcome is now a reality, precisely in the countries which are least stable on the continent. Enhanced PfP arrangements, greater military co-operation and soothing speeches are fine. But they have a strictly limited "shelf-life"; in not more than two years from now Western security dilemmas with the countries which have suffered this "double reject" will intensify. Any internal crisis in these countries will automatically affect NATO: it will force Hungary—against its current will—to raise the issue of the Hungarian ethnic minorities in Slovakia and Romania, and will compound the Alliance's difficulties on its southern flank. These dangers can only be avoided if the NATO summit in Washington next year goes beyond the vague promise made to Romania and Slovenia at the Madrid summit in 1997. How to phrase this promise in such a way that it offers concrete advantages to potential new members while not committing the West to any new obligations is now the biggest immediate problem.

Memorandum submitted by Professor Cedric Thornberry, Visiting Professor at the Centre for Defence Studies, King's College London, on the Future of NATO

INTRODUCTION

It is a privilege to have the opportunity to address the Committee, especially on a subject of such importance: one that will affect security concerns—and wider issues of international relations—long into the future. My remarks will chiefly focus on what sometimes seem to be two inter-related questions—the future of NATO, and the future of international peacekeeping in a regional context. These are matters of which I have some direct experience, having worked closely with senior personnel of the UN and NATO in international peacekeeping and peacemaking, and in the planning and management of such operations in Africa, Asia and Europe. Though concentrating on these two matters, it is also necessary, I believe, to note the urgent importance of creating in Europe a joint civilian/military structure to deal with, in a closely co-ordinated way, and under effective political direction, all aspects of the various types of emergency that may threaten the security and stability of the continent in the years ahead.

NATO—FROM MILITARY PACT TO REGIONAL SECURITY ORGANISATION?

The North Atlantic (Washington) Treaty is best-known for its collective guarantee to the Parties if an armed attack were to occur against one or more of them in Europe or North America (article 5). This is, indeed, its sole major operative provision—apart from some benign generalities about the development of the parties' free institutions, and a vague agreement amongst them that "separately and jointly, by means of continuous and effective self-help and mutual aid, [they] will maintain and develop their individual and collective capacity to resist armed attack". This seemingly insignificant undertaking has, however, led to the creation of NATO's historically unique, internationally-coordinated defence machine. It should also be noted that there is no authority under the Washington Treaty for NATO to do many of the things it has been doing in recent years in Bosnia, and recently threatening to do to Serbia, including in its province of Kosovo. Such actions would be those of a regional security organisation—which NATO is not at this time. NATO is, instead, a military pact. The Treaty can, of course, be revised.

NATO's PfP (Partnership for Peace) programme has been actively carried forward in recent years, in accordance with the PfP Framework Document of January 1994, by which the participants declare themselves "resolved to deepen their political and military ties and to contribute further to the strengthening of security within the Euro-Atlantic area". I have had the continuing opportunity to help conceptualise and run several NATO/PfP peacekeeping-training exercises, have discussed with senior military officers from NATO and PfP countries, and have been impressed by how successful the programme appears to be in developing co-operation between NATO's sixteen (soon to be nineteen) nations and almost all of the remaining countries of Europe. Their enthusiasm for participation has been notable at senior political and military levels. I have often been told how the morale of the speaker's armed forces has been boosted by the programme. Even neutral Switzerland's officers have been reviewing their role and activities, and have begun training for new kinds of task (in which I have also had the privilege to participate). The positive approach in some states to the usually complicated and sometimes difficult issues surrounding democratic control of the armed forces has also been striking. This is a matter that continues to assume great practical importance, especially—as I have seen in practice—in countries of the former communist bloc such as Armenia and Georgia. (This is a programme which is usually conducted by civilians and it remains to be seen how successful it will be.) Overall, my (layman's) impression is, that the PfP programme has reinvigorated NATO, which might otherwise have been bemused by the ending of the Cold War.

While the case has been made for wider or much wider NATO membership in the near future, and many of the applicant PfP countries vociferously do not wish to settle for less, it can equally be said that many of their perceived needs can be met within the list of objectives set out in article 3 of the PfP Framework Document:— transparency in national defence planning and budgeting, democratic control of the military, maintaining a readiness level for UN or OSCE operations, joint planning with NATO for peacekeeping, search and rescue and humanitarian operations, and inter-operability. It seems to me that, in political reality, it is unlikely that the "collective guarantee" would appreciably add to the security of PfP states who were not NATO members. The cost of NATO membership for many applicant countries, as well as for existing members; the danger of dilution of the remarkable operational co-ordination capability, not least in the field of logistics; as well as the degree of enhancement some applicant countries must first conduct, suggest a cautious approach to further enlargement. In any event, as it seems to me, it is logically necessary to consider what NATO should be doing next century, before finalising any answer to the question of its membership.

Thus, noting that in some respects a re-invigorated NATO has, since the end of the Cold War, already burst its bonds and gone beyond the confines of its Charter, I should like to consider a possible concept of what the organisation's role might look like ten years from now. Before doing so, however, I would look at the interesting invention called "international peacekeeping", and the related provisions of the UN Charter. NATO's evolution must of course be in accordance with the Charter. Its operational tasks will—surely—be largely concerned with peacekeeping. Some weaknesses already evident in its early practice should be corrected as soon as possible.

INTERNATIONAL PEACEKEEPING AND THE INTERNATIONAL SECURITY ENVIRONMENT

Despite historically-unprecedented barbarities during this century, international law has shown a general desire of the community of nations to abandon the former practice of unregulated resort to force, the period showing a consistent trend in favour of settling disputes by peaceful means. The exceptions to this under the UN Charter relate to force used in self-defence (which today is narrowly defined by the World Court, to avoid abuse), and in enforcement action taken in accordance with Chapter VII of the Charter. It should be emphasised that merely calling a military action "peacekeeping" does not make it so. Recent years have seen interventions by local "Big Powers" of dubious legality in Africa, among the countries of the Commonwealth of Independent States, and in the Caribbean.

Impatience with any social order—especially, its procedural requirements—and the temptation on the part of the strong to take unilateral violent action against the weak, instead of utilising the wide range of peaceful means of dispute settlement, is not unusual. In international affairs, unilateral forcible intervention usually assumes some disguise, but it is almost always unlawful, disrupting the stabilising efforts of statesmen over the years to create an international rule of law to which all—superpowers and lesser nations—will be subject. Recently, there have sometimes been pressures from the remaining superpower to by-pass the UN Security Council in appraising the possible use of force. But failure to comply with existing rules must inevitably bring about a wider condition of disrespect for the law and, with it, a tendency to anarchy—dangerously incompatible with the growing need to come to terms with globalisation in all its forms, and to try to curb its excesses.

BRITISH PARTICIPATION IN UNITED NATIONS' PEACEKEEPING

The UK has actively participated in both UN and NATO peacekeeping. Curiously, neither the UN Charter nor the North Atlantic Treaty make any reference to the term. It was invented by the UN during the 'fifties and 'sixties to describe its *ad hoc* attempts to control or stabilise situations of recent inter-state conflict—especially in the Middle East. (Copy of an article in the *International Herald Tribune* of 11 June 1998 tracing this evolution, and marking the fiftieth anniversary of international peacekeeping, is attached).'

The UK served in just one of the initial sixteen missions of the first forty-one years of international peacekeeping—with UNFICYP in Cyprus. Since the Namibian operation in 1989–90, however, and the ending of the Cold War, the UK has been much more active, participating in fourteen of the next twenty-seven. Thus, through 1996, the UK had contributed military and other personnel to UN operations in Cyprus, Namibia, Angola, Western Sahara, Rwanda, Cambodia, ex-Yugoslavia, Georgia and Kuwait-Iraq. Britain has also taken part in Chapter Seven enforcement action under Security Council mandate in Iraq, and in the NATO operations, also in accordance with Security Council mandates, in Bosnia—in IFOR and SFOR. Britain has not only taken a more active part in international peacekeeping; its personnel have seemed well-adapted, physically and mentally, for its special demands. Having worked with UK personnel in diverse operations in Cyprus, Namibia and Yugoslavia, then in NATO/PfP exercises and staff college training, a high quality of understanding and technique has shown itself among British participants. This may perhaps derive from the experience of providing "aid to the civil power" not only in Northern Ireland, but in several decolonisation phases in recent decades. The requirements of this kind of national soldiering come closest, perhaps, to those of UN peacekeeping. It has also been good to observe that the UK, in its approach to the modalities and requirements of international peacekeeping, has adhered to the principles of international law, especially as set out in the Charter of the United Nations.

UN PEACEKEEPING, ITS STRENGTHS AND WEAKNESSES

A Security Council determination that a peacekeeping force shall be established is usually arrived at under Chapter VI of the Charter, dealing with "Pacific Settlement of Disputes". Nearly fifty Chapter VI UN peacekeeping operations have taken place—in Africa, the Americas, Asia and Europe—and, at the time of wiring, seventeen are in the field. In the former Yugoslavia several UN peacekeeping operations (in Bosnia, Croatia and Macedonia) have co-existed with IFOR and SFOR, the NATO missions in Bosnia. They have received little attention from the media but have been quite successful—for instance, the UN Transitional Authority in Eastern Somalia (UNTAES, 1996–98) and the UN Preventive Deployment Force (UNPREDEP 1992) in Macedonia.

UN peacekeeping is, however, at a rather low ebb at present, partly because of a (political) crisis of confidence, especially in the US, since operations in Bosnia and Somalia. This is illustrated by current figures: there are about 15,000 personnel in current UN peacekeeping operations, at a cost of about $1 billion annually, in contrast to the situation in July 1993 when there were nearly 79,000 personnel at a cost of about $3.5 billion. The UN's potential is further affected by the failure of a number of countries to meet their financial obligations, and especially by the failure of the US to pay both its regular budget and peacekeeping assessments.

Between 1989 and 1992 a kind of international euphoria overloaded the UN's limited and fragile peacekeeping resources. This coincided with a trend in the Security Council to act in an unfocused way, with the Secretary-General being given broad and sometimes incompatible mandates, without the necessary resources or support. The Secretariat, moreover, had problems in adapting quickly enough to its new operational and managerial duties. When, to cap it all, several deeply intractable conflicts were dumped on the UN's doorstep by the Council, the earlier crisis of over-confidence had, by 1995, become an equally exaggerated crisis of under-confidence. Thus the Dayton Accords, for example, foresaw no role for the UN.

These pendulum swings of mood often disguise the reality of UN peacekeeping, its strengths and weaknesses. In fact, it continues to achieve a great deal, despite the present adverse circumstances, and a number of recent operations have been highly successful. With the experience of nearly fifty varied missions and the support of its 185 members from all parts of the world, the UN has also the legitimacy that only a universal organisation can possess, and is able to mount integrated operations involving civilians, police and a full range of specialist personnel, as well as a military component. The Secretary-General, and through him, the Head of mission, be s/he civilian or military, can also rely on a long tradition of exclusive authority over the individuals and contingents placed under his/her command. By contrast, problems of co-ordination and co-operation have been central and endemic in the IFOR/SFOR missions. However ingeniously the situation is dealt with, it is operationally very unsatisfactory to try to run military and civilian missions as separate though parallel entities. It also contravenes one of the basic principles of UN peacekeeping—unity of command—confirmed and re-confirmed in the experience of numerous international operations. Some have also felt that the NATO missions have at times been insufficiently responsive to their political mandate and the situation on the ground.

On the debit side, UN peacekeeping is habitually under-funded—not only because many governments often do not pay their bills, but because the budgets adopted by UN inter-governmental committees tend to be so meagre that they adversely affect operational competence and even the security of personnel (e.g. mission communications, mine-resistant vehicles, other vital equipment). Moreover, while universality usually enhances legitimacy, including a mission's reputation for impartiality, the converse of this is that it may present problems associated with the political, economic and cultural diversity of its world-wide elements. This can affect external confidence in a mission and its cohesiveness. The question should also continue to be pressed upon the UN Secretary-General whether the structure and nature of the UN Secretariat is appropriate to backstop, manage, command and control operations in demanding circumstances.

In a few people's minds the desire seems to exist to try to replace UN peacekeeping, which it is difficult for any one state or small group of states to control—in part because of the universal role of the Security Council— with some form of regional action, which it is not so difficult for powerful states, with their own agendas, to hi-jack. It will be important for the Security Council to continue to exercise cautious oversight of such activities. But regional arrangements, and the security they can effectively help to guarantee, have an important part to play in a shrinking world. They cannot displace UN operations, whose authority, impartiality and detachment can rarely be challenged. The UN, it should also be added, makes mistakes—peacekeeping is not an easy discipline—but neither NATO nor any other of the recent participants in regional operations can afford to blunder around, disregarding the elementary lessons of several decades. Re-inventing the wheel comes expensive in these days of rising defence costs and critical legislatures.

REGIONALISM, PEACEKEEPING AND NATO

We have made this *tour d'horizon* of international peacekeeping because, in common with many western analysts, we conclude that peacekeeping, or some future derivative, will become increasingly familiar to all concerned with international strategy and security. It may, indeed, emerge that it is one of the most important forms of civil-military action. Any re-formulation of the strategic concept of NATO—and it has already been noted that it needs to be up-dated—should reflect this likelihood and encourage planning for its further development—as, in another context, the recent British defence white paper did.

Since about 1992 growing attention has been paid to the possibility of using regional organisations to deal with issues of international security. It is said that the countries of a region have a more direct and vital interest in their own locality and will accordingly be more willing to make political and economic commitments to resolve its problems. The converse of this is that they may have *all too direct* an interest in the internal affairs of their neighbours. Encouraging regional involvement in a country's problems could provide an excuse for otherwise illegal interference—a cloak for the local bully. Especially concerned at any enhancement of "regionalism" in the security sphere would be the small neighbours of large and powerful states. Leaders in the Caucasus republics energetically promote the idea of UN peacekeeping and strong NATO links as essential means to help correct the neighbourhood imbalance. Intrinsic to UN peacekeeping has been the principle that a mission should not be driven by the interests and resources of one state only, or even those of one group of states. The League of Nations and the UN have taken evolutionary strides beyond the hegemonic machinations of the nineteenth century Great Powers in the Concert of Europe.

Nevertheless, the UN Charter (in articles 52–54, Chapter VIII) specifically approves "regional arrangements". It requires states that are parties to them to try to settle their disputes through such arrangements before bringing them to the Security Council. The historic reason for Chapter VIII of the Charter was the nature of the relationship at the time of its drafting of the US to the other States of Organisation of American States. The Charter also contemplates the Security Council using these arrangements for enforcement action under its authority—though emphasising that no such action would be permitted without the authorisation of the Council. It also requires that the Council be kept "full informed of activities undertaken or in contemplation under regional arrangements or by regional agencies for the maintenance of international peace and security".

While the North Atlantic Treaty endorses the Purposes and Principles of the UN Charter, NATO is probably not a "regional arrangement" within its meaning, as we have concluded earlier. It does not have the kind of machinery necessary "for dealing with such matters relating to the maintenance of international peace and security as are appropriate of regional action". Instead, the NATO treaty—the "Washington Treaty" of 4 April 1949—creates a defence alliance around the collective guarantee of article 5. This of course does not prevent the Security Council from delegating to NATO, or indeed to any other group of countries, functions under the Charter—as it has previously done in the case of Kuwait/Iraq and Bosnia—including enforcement functions.

The Treaty contains a provision for the review of its terms ten or more years after it came into force. The parties could, if they so wished—subject to the provisions of the UN Charter and the norms of international law—change the nature of the alliance, enable it to operate out of area, or provide for a wider membership. (The US Secretary of State was recently reported as suggesting that NATO could even undertake policing duties through much of Africa—a suggestion that was also reported to have met with some criticism). As regards further accessions to the Treaty, article 10 states that these must be European States (though the parties could also amend this provision.) Amendments to the Treaty would, as required by the general law of treaties, have to be unanimously approved by the membership.

The nearly-fifty years of close association between the military personnel of NATO's sixteen nations has not abolished their national differences. But they have brought about a mutual harmonisation and familiarity among the military establishments of NATO which are impressive to one used to the UN, with the strengths and weaknesses that sometimes go with its variegated, universal nature. In part, it is due to the widespread proficiency in English of NATO officers and to standardisation of equipment, acronyms, etc. NATO strongly conveys the image of an efficient defence alliance. In comparison to the UN, it is well-funded. It has also been noticeable how interest in peacekeeping on the part of senior military personnel has grown during the past six or seven years (including among the US military—though there are many different, sometimes polarised, viewpoints in that army, even at general officer level.)

Can the widespread desire of defence staffs in the western world in general, and in NATO in particular, to play a major part in future international peacekeeping be accommodated within "international constitutional law"—i.e. the Law of the UN Charter, including the pre-eminent role of the Security Council?

In 1993 the witness participated on behalf of the UN in planning with the military planning staff of NATO-AFSOUTH a joint UN-NATO operation throughout ex-Yugoslavia, then thought quite imminent. Planning went smoothly and few problems arose in integrating—on paper—UN civilian and NATO military operations, though it was clear that logistical and budgetary planning would be byzantine. But it was impossible to complete the planning because, while the NATO personnel endorsed the principle of the subordination of the military to civilian/political control, they were not authorised, they said, to accept such a concept in respect of a joint UN/NATO operation in ex-Yugoslavia. More precisely, the US military were not so authorised. Of course, it was unimaginable that the US military would reject one of the most basic of western democratic principles. Further discussion elicited that their concern was that civilian control in the field could slide into micro-management, interfere substantially with command and control, endanger the security of the force, and adversely affect the attainment of mission objectives. These are real fears and one can recall some real dangers to which they might have related. They needed—and still need—to be effectively addressed, at the highest political and military levels, if regional peacekeeping with a NATO force is ever to become an effective reality. There should be no more IFOR/SFOR structures. It is difficult, however, to see how to respond without unkindness to the other main concern brought forward at that time—that the US could not allow anyone other than an American to lead such an international undertaking.

If, as suggested, the Washington Treaty were amended to enable NATO to become a regional organisation, as broadly described in Chapter VIII of the UN Charter, this could permit Europe—however that geographical concept were precisely defined—to begin to put together an effective regional security structure—under WEU, or other, auspices. But such structure would have to have competent mechanisms for the control, management, solution of disputes, as recent experience in the Balkans has shown. The kinds of dispute and problem which a regional structure should have authority to address must be able to include internal conflicts and humanitarian disasters, whether natural or man-made. *Via* the military aspect of the alliance, it would have a coercive security capacity. But that capability has to be closely harnessed to the continent's political objectives. There could be no question of the military "floating free". It is not their task to make policy—a truism that it should be unnecessary to repeat. For the last fifty years UN peacekeeping has been firmly attached to the Security Council's political objectives. A senior political adviser has been number two to the Force commander in the more military kind of mission; with a civilian special representative heading others. These models work—at least, when the senior mission personnel have sufficient professional experience and are personally compatible. Bosnia and other contemplated operations have shown how much a regional security organisation will require continuity of management and support, and how crucially it will require logistical planning and provision. The old military adage can never be too often repeated: "amateurs talk strategy—professionals talk logistics". To which one would like to add "and co-ordination".

The subject is "the future of NATO" and it would therefore seem inappropriate to attempt to describe the various possible aspects of an overall political/security architecture for Europe.

CONCLUSIONS

(a)   NATO's continuance, its enlargement to the frontiers of Europe or, anyhow, a further enhancement of the Partnership for Peace (PfP)—are assumed for this presentation

(b)   In principle, however, NATO should undergo a steady transformation, finally assuming further roles in a new European or Atlantic-European regional configuration

(c)   NATO would be changed from being a military pact to being a constituent part of a regional security organisation, in accordance with Chapter VIII of the UN Charter

(d)   This organisation could be based on OSCE, as well as upon NATO, and would deal with any security matters or humanitarian problems jeopardising continental stability

(e)   NATO's international peacekeeping modus operandi would reach prevailing international standards and benefit from extensive experience accumulated since 1948

(f) Future NATO functions would take place within such political, geographical and functional framework, thus also strengthening operational co-ordination.

(g) However, NATO could exceptionally be tasked by the Security Council, and in accordance with the UN Charter, as regards issues arising out of the new organisation's area

(h) Regional security arrangements would not be allowed to undermine, in any manner, UN responsibilities for international peace and security, but instead strengthen them.

Memorandum submitted by Randolph C Kent on the Future of NATO

It is clear that NATO has the capacity to provide significant assistance to those affected by disasters and emergencies. To date, NATO has begun to develop a disaster early warning system as well as an ability to respond to various types of disasters within Europe. However, there are four sets of issues that NATO will have to consider particularly carefully as it embarks upon such undertakings; the types of humanitarian crises that will have to be confronted within the foreseeable future; appropriate civilian-military planning structures; key operational issues affecting civilian-military activities; and geographical reach.

HUMANITARIAN CRISES OF THE FUTURE

The agents of future disasters will encompass a broader range of hazards than now, from terrorism to infrastructural decay, from global warming to economic collapse. Moreover, these hazards are likely to become more inter-active. Future disasters and emergencies may well reflect the interplay among seemingly diverse factors such as technology, the environment and security.

A considerable amount of attention has been paid to individual disaster agents and, to a lesser extent, to the contexts in which such agents may impact. Little if any attention has been paid to how different types of disaster agents and potential areas of impact inter-relate and how they can trigger large-scale catastrophes.

If NATO is truly to play a significant role in supporting humanitarian assistance in the future, it will have to have a more developed concept about the types of humanitarian issues that will have to be confronted in the future. Towards that end, greater attention must be made by member-states to develop integrated and coherent futures analyses leading to scenario-building and training as well as to integrated early warning and monitoring systems.

APPROPRIATE CIVILIAN-MILITARY PLANNING STRUCTURES

In the context of NATO's future support role in humanitarian assistance, greater attention will have to be given to the ways that the military components of NATO interact with a broad spectrum of civilian actors. This issue has become a common-place in civilian-military discussions, but has failed to result in the sorts of arrangements that future humanitarian crises will require.

The military and civilian sector, particularly when it comes to non-governmental actors, will have to pay far greater attention to ways of planning together and to ways, in the midst of operations, of adjusting such plans collaboratively. Planning in this context often has less to do with methods than mind-sets, and for this reason various ways to acculturate the main actors into their respective operational and planning modalities might well be the principal consideration.

Towards that acculturation objective, NATO could develop secondment policies that could reach out into the non-governmental sector as well as other areas of the humanitarian world. It, too, could develop inter-institutional planning processes to ensure close military-civilian planning—as has recently been initiated between humanitarian and military actors in the United Kingdom, under the auspices of MOD.

KEY OPERATIONAL ISSUES AFFECTING CIVILIAN-MILITARY ACTIVITIES

Related to above, NATO could take the lead in addressing the sorts of operational difficulties that arise now and may well arise more frequently during times of difficult humanitarian crises. Such issues span a range of considerations, including the military's approach to its primary projection role, utilisation of military resources *in support of* civilian operations, security and exit strategies.

In each of the complex emergencies involving military force, including NATO's involvement in the former Yugoslavia, these sorts of issues have affected military-civilian relationships, to the detriment of both. These considerations reflect certain core institutional perspectives, procedures and dynamics; but that said, there are ways to deal with such operational issues as there are ways to deal with the intricately related issue of planning.

Two obvious but hitherto poorly implemented approaches to deal with such operational concerns begins with troop training, manuals and education at the level of military academies and staff colleges. While these sorts of solutions have always been accepted in principle, they have never been fully accepted as directly relevant to the core concerns of the military. This assumption, like other issues related to the military ethos, will have to be changed. Similarly, more concerted efforts will have to be made to relate the operational procedures and activities of the military into those of major humanitarian players.

GEOGRAPHICAL REACH

The geographical limit of NATO engagement is an issue that will be central to a review of NATO's future. Depending upon that decision . . . or perhaps even despite it . . . NATO's role in support of humanitarian activities could eventually prove to be an important example to other regional and national organisations around the world which may require military support for humanitarian initiatives.

In that regard, the planning perspectives as well as operational modalities that NATO and civilian counterparts should develop could serve as useful models and bases for training elsewhere in the world.

Memorandum submitted by Michael MccGwire on the Future of NATO

In April 1999 Poland, Hungary and the Czech Republic will become full members of NATO.

Notwithstanding the sharply polarised US debate that surfaced in 1995–97, future membership for these three states had effectively been decided in the White House by October 1993.[1] After that (as Clinton remarked in Prague in January 1994), the question was no longer whether, but how and when?

Washington makes no pretence that NATO enlargement is other than a US-led policy,[2] and within the Clinton administration, it is recognised that the drive came from the White House. The policy was initially opposed by the Pentagon and by the relevant specialists in State, until enlargement was made a test of loyalty to the President. So, too, did NATO members' support for enlargement become a test of loyalty to the alliance and (since it was a US-led policy) to America.

In sum, NATO was presented with a *fait accompli* regarding the three new members, with little opportunity for substantive discussion or dissent. In one sense, that is water under the bridge. In another, it is a precursor of what lies ahead. The Clinton administration sees enlargement as the unfolding of a policy formulated in 1993–94;[3] a continuous process, rather than an exploratory step with a pause for reassessment.

It is most unlikely that the British Government will call for such a pause. But as the Defence Committee urged caution over the question of further enlargement, its members may wish to take this opportunity to review the question of European security and the future of NATO from a new base line, one that is more favourable to long term decisions on European security than existed five years ago.

THE POLICY ENVIRONMENT

Some of the improvements in the decision-making environment reflect the passage of time and/or the reduction of uncertainty. Others are the result of inviting Poland, Hungary and the Czech Republic to join NATO.

— In terms of American electoral politics, the Polish vote is probably the most important single ethnic group, while the other two have some significance. Their satisfaction increases Clinton's freedom of action regarding enlargement.[4]

— Germany wished to escape the role of frontier zone. It also favoured some kind of Western institutional structure, rather than the spread of German hegemony. Those preferences have been met, allowing a less subjective assessment.

— The Founding Act is in place. We are now in a better position to foresee how Moscow will respond to different NATO initiatives and how this will affect Western policy objectives in the longer term and/or in other areas.

— We have a clearer idea about the political, economic and ethnic situations in the newly independent states, and the relations between those states.

— London and Paris are no longer at odds with Washington over Bosnia, allowing European members of NATO more latitude to challenge the US-led policy on enlargement, should that be desirable.

---

[1] James M Goldgeir, "NATO Expansion: the anatomy of a decision" *Washington Quarterly* 21:1, 1998, pp. 85–102
[2] The State Department is on record insisting "that the US Government has been the driving political force behind NATO's enlargement process." See letter of 1 April 1996 from the Chief Financial Officer of the State Department to the General Accounting Office, commenting on Report GAO/NSIAD-96-92 NATO ENLARGEMENT (6 May 1996) for the Committee on International Relations, US House of Representatives.
[3] The word in Washington is that there will be another five new members in time for the Presidential elections in the year 2000: Slovenia, Roumania, and the three Baltic states.
[4] Traditionally Republican, the ethnic vote turned against Bush in 1992. Clinton won 12 of the 14 states where ethnic voters were concentrated, delivering 186 out of a possible 192 Presidential electors, one third of the total. This pattern was repeated in 1996.

At this stage in the enlargement process, we need to focus on two questions:
— How will the three new members be integrated into the existing alliance structure?
— What are the implications for further enlargement of this increase in membership?

In addressing those questions, we need to be sensitive to a critical flaw in current policy, a flaw that originates in the American domestic policy process. Under the rubric of "enlargement", NATO is pursuing two competing and contradictory objectives.

The original rationale for NATO enlargement was that the spread of liberal democracy would bring stability and peace in Europe.[1] It was seen as an evolutionary process and would possibly include a democratic Russia, who would in all circumstances participate as partner in a larger security regime embracing greater Europe.[2] The White House had an Inclusive objective—co-operative security in a Europe reaching from the Atlantic to the Urals.

Outside the Clinton administration, the most important political support for NATO enlargement came from the "unilateralists".[3] This hard line viewpoint was strongly represented in the Republican-dominated Congress elected in November 1994.[4] It was against partnership with Russia and stressed rivalry, even enemity.[5] The long-term objective was Exclusionary, its variants ranged from containing Russia, to establishing US preponderance, if not hegemony in Central and Eastern Europe.

This contradiction has been obscured by the fact that NATO enlargement had changed from being a means of promoting security in Europe and become an end in itself. As a result, NATO policy has been and continues to be shaped by competing objectives that are largely mutually-exclusive.

— One involves the inclusive concept of co-operative security IN Europe—a greater Europe extending from the Atlantic to the Urals—which sees Russia as an essential partner in that endeavour.

— The other involves the exclusionary concept of the defence (retitled "security") OF a Europe that will be co-extensive with a steadily expanding NATO. It sees Russia as a rival at best, and more often as an enemy.

The Republican majority in Congress[6] is the reason why the exclusionary concept prevailed so frequently in the last four years, notwithstanding the inclusive rhetoric emanating from the White House and NATO HQ in Brussels. For example, only when Yeltsin was facing defeat in the 1996 Presidential election did NATO moderate its line that the emerging security structure in Europe was no business of the Russians.

INTEGRATING NEW MEMBERS INTO THE EXISTING STRUCTURE

While all three new members will be fully covered by the terms of the Washington Treaty, the detailed nature of their integration should reflect the wider purpose that the policy of enlargement is meant to serve. This becomes difficult to achieve if, as described above, the policy is pursuing contradictory objectives. Outlined below are the logical (but mutually exclusive) implications of the competing concepts. Three background conditions are relevant to both.

— Whatever the concept, NATO will continue as a fully-functioning US-led military alliance, which provides leadership and a resource base for PfP, CJTF, an the like.

— The Treaty's requirements are very general and, in practice, each member of NATO has a unique relationship with the Alliance. For example, France, Denmark and Norway do not allow foreign troops on their territory. France and Spain are not part of the integrated Military Structure. Iceland is an exception to most things. The so-called 2+4 agreement (1990) obliges NATO not to station nuclear weapons or foreign troops in the eastern part of a reunified Germany.

— Since the dissolution of the Soviet Union, the Vise-grad states have enjoyed a higher level of national security than at any time in the last eighty years or so. Nor is there any immediate threat to that

[1] "Enlargement" was coined by the White House in August–September 1993 as a post-Cold War organising concept to echo and replace Kennan's powerful concept of "Containment". It was to be an evolutionary process, a global exercise in geoeconomics, the natural enlargement of the Free World's community of market democracies, through free trade. Enlargement and engagement were inextricably linked to America's domestic renewal and retaining its place as the world's largest exporter. The concept had Republican support.

[2] In respect to Central and Eastern Europe, NATO was the obvious vehicle for this global US policy. It followed the Cold War practice of using the US military as a highly biddable instrument of socio-economic policy in the world-wide struggle with Communism.

[3] This label includes the advocates of a global Pax Americana, the conservative isolationists' who favour external intervention to instil American values, and the coalition of interests which continues to see Russia as an enemy and is intent on denying Moscow any influence beyond its borders.

[4] NATO Enlargement was one of the ten principles in Congressman Newt Gingrich's "Contract with America".

[5] In March 1994, Senator Lugar (a moderate Republican), declared that the US had "to get over the idea that it was involved in a partnership with Moscow". This is a tough rivalry, he insisted. Michael Cox, *US Foreign Policy after the Cold War* (London: RIIA, 1995) p.67.

[6] See, for example, the ten conditions imposed by Senator Helms in September 1997 as the price for his support of NATO enlargement, and the terms attached to the Senate resolution (30 April 1998) on ratifying the Treaty Protocols enabling the accession of three new members. (*Basic Paper* No.27, May 1998)

security. There is, therefore, no inherent urgency about the process (as opposed to the principle) of military integration.[1]

The Exclusionary concept implicitly sees NATO as an offensive bridgehead. The implied objective is to progressively incorporate as many countries west of Russia's borders as possible into a fully-integrated, well-armed collective-defence alliance.

The three new members are therefore welcomed as an important first step in this direction. As they now represent the new front line, NATO would set out to fully integrate them into the alliance infrastructure as soon as possible.

The exclusionary objective does not prohibit co-operation with Moscow, should that facilitate the concepts immediate or wider purposes. But it does exclude any self-imposed constraints on further enlargement or on the deployment of forces and development of infrastructure.

The Inclusive concept is concerned that enlargement should not work against the objective of some larger security regime either by drawing new lines across Europe or by estranging Russia and encouraging competitive alliance building. It wants to avoid the image of NATO as an offensive bridgehead and to emphasise the fundamental change in NATO's nature and purpose.

Those concerns can be met without creating the impression that the newcomers are second class members. In order to "blur" the new line across Europe, the extension of NATO's physical infrastructure would be highly selective. NATO would make a formal commitment to refrain from deploying nuclear weapons or stationing forces on the territory of new members, subject to obvious provisos.

The extent to which new members were integrated into the military structure of NATO would be a matter for discussion. The existing NATO command structure and the partial integration of forces reflects evolved practice and is not a treaty requirement. In treaty terms, there is no reason why the new members should not enjoy the full protection of Article 5, without making fundamental changes in the existing military structure.

Current NATO Policy

The NATO costing study indicates that it intends only to invest in upgrading C3, air reinforcement infrastructure and integrated air defence. The "Founding Act" states that it is not NATO's "foreseeable intention" to deploy nuclear weapons on the new members' territory.

This would seem to suggest that NATO is pursuing the inclusive concept. However, NATO also:

— refuses to commit itself to no nukes on new members' territory, even with the necessary let-out clauses and despite the precedent of East Germany;

— insists on its right to bring Estonia into NATO, despite Estonia's geographical location and vital strategic (actual and historical) significance for Russia;

— thought it appropriate to stage a joint NATO-Ukrainian landing exercise in the Crimea in August 1997. The original scenario involved countering a "separatist uprising" supported by a neighbouring state [read Russia].

Once again, NATO falls between two stools. Its declaratory policy is co-operative security and its rhetoric is inclusive. But it is unable to harvest the political benefits in terms of NATO/Russian relations because of the continual slippage into collective defence concepts, where Russia is "the enemy." Nor can it explain how the security of Estonia will be enhanced (let alone guaranteed) by membership of NATO.

THE QUESTION OF FURTHER ENLARGEMENT

The public debate in 1995–97 reflected many different agendas, but it centred around four distinct points of view. These can be visualised as occupying a 2x2 matrix, comprising the type of objective (inclusive or exclusionary) and whether for or against enlargement.

These four viewpoints are summarised in highly simplified form below. Thereafter, the discussion focuses on the implications of further enlargement for the inclusive concept of European security, since that concept is declared NATO policy, and also that of the British Government.

Arguments

Among those who subscribe to an exclusionary concept of security, opposition to enlargement comes from those who fear dilution or overstretch. For proponents of enlargement, the best way of enhancing European security is to extend NATO's borders as far east as possible, preferably up to the Russian frontier. There is no better time to do it than now, when Russia is still in disarray.

---

[1] The requirement that their forces be able to operate with existing NATO forces in peacekeeping/enforcement operations is already covered by the provisions of PfP.

Among those who subscribe to the inclusive concept of security, there is a deep divide on the question of further enlargement. Although this reflects differing judgments on the relative priority to be given to various factors in the security equation, the rift is fundamental.

Setting aside the influence of US electoral politics, the original impulse for NATO enlargement was Wilsonian liberalism, a belief that the spread of democracy and market economies would bring political and economic stability and ensure peace and security in the region. Enlargement is seen as an evolutionary process. As Russia is already embarked on the path of democracy and marketisation it has no reason to feel threatened by this process. If Moscow does feel threatened, ways can be found to reassure and propitiate it as necessary.

Those within the inclusive camp who oppose enlargement acknowledge the importance of democratisation but see constructive engagement with Russia as a fundamental prerequisite for long-term security in Europe.[1] The existing (but fraying) co-operative relationship derives from the post-cold-war settlement with Moscow, which was "extraordinarily favourable to the West."[2] The enlargement of NATO is seen by Russians of all political complexions as breaching the terms of that settlement.

The withdrawal of Russian co-operation could negate Western attempts to contain conflicts such as those in the former Yugoslavia. It could bring to a halt the process of dismantling Russia's nuclear arsenals. If Russia felt threatened and withdrew its co-operation, the nature of Russia's political and strategic interests in the former Soviet Republics would change. Meanwhile, the constraints on Moscow pursuing those redefined interests would be weakened or removed entirely, as the security of the homeland assumed its traditional place at the head of Moscow's concerns.

Attitudes

In very general terms, one can differentiate between the attitudes underlying the opinions of the opposing wings of the inclusive approach to European security. The proponents of enlargement tend to idealism. Coming form Wilsonian liberalism, that is to be expected and is reflected in their concern for the aspirations of medium and small states and their urge to right the wrongs of Yalta and/or the Soviet Empire. They think that a new approach will escape the constraints of the past and have relatively short time horizons.

The opponents of enlargement tend to realism. They have a traditional view of world affairs based on the lessons of history, which in the case of Europe are particularly rich and relevant.[3] They believe that the security of individual states, large and small, depends on the security of the encompassing region. The latter has priority and depends in turn on co-operation by the relevant major powers. In evaluating policy options, their historical perspective demands long time horizons.

Outcomes

The proponents of further enlargement can point to the fact that the first stage has been largely accomplished, without the dire consequences predicted by the opponents. It has been possible to meet Russia's need for special treatment through the Founding Act, the Permanent Joint Council and (separately) the G8. Despite much huffing and puffing, Moscow is in no position to oppose the reality of continued expansion.

Predictions that the prospect of NATO membership would provide positive incentives have meanwhile been proven correct in relation to political and economic reform in the newly-independent states and the resolution of internal and external inter-ethnic claims. The certainty of membership has been successful in removing the pressure to rebuild national defence capabilities and has been an influence for lowered military requirements and reduced defence expenditure.[4]

The opponents of further enlargement acknowledge these short-term benefits but point to the facts of geography, history, emotion and long-term time horizons. There are good reasons why Moscow should rationalise membership for the Visegrad states as a special case and equally good reasons why Moscow should refuse to see it as signalling acquiescence to further enlargement. Otherwise, where does this "evolutionary" process stop? From the Russian viewpoint, if Romania and Bulgaria, why not Armenia and Georgia, even Azerbaijan?

Meanwhile, Moscow sees the former Soviet Republics as in a different category to the east European states. The Soviets entered eastern Europe in the process of defeating Nazi Germany and withdrew voluntarily, if under

---

[1] An unexpected characteristic of this wing of the inclusive camp is that its members come from both sides of the Cold War divide between "hawks" and "doves".

[2] Michael Mandelbaum, *The Dawn of Peace in Europe,* (New York: Council on Foreign Relations Press, 1996) paragraph 60–61. Mandelbaum points out that as Moscow took part and acquiesced in all the events that produced the settlement, it has a measure of legitimacy in Russian eyes, which "is a priceless asset to the West."

[3] John Lewis Gaddis notes that "historians—normally so contentious—are in uncharacteristic agreement, with remarkably few exceptions" about NATO enlargement. They see it as "ill-conceived, ill-timed, and above all ill-suited to the realities of the post-Cold War world". Gaddis, 'History, Grand Strategy and NATO Enlargement', *Survival* 40:1 1998, p. 145.

[4] Jorgen Dragsdahl, 'NATO resists pressures to militarise Central Europe' *BASIC PAPERS* No. 28, July 1998.

economic and political duress, in 1989–90. While Moscow sees the inclusion of Warsaw Pact members in NATO as a breach of trust, those countries are in no way comparable to the former Republics of the Soviet Union. The latter (for the most part) had been part of a single state entity which, at the time of its dissolution in 1991, had existed some 200 years.[1] They now constitute Russia's *de facto* national security zone. Latvia and Estonia are of particular significance in ethnic and strategic terms.

The opponents of further enlargement do not see Moscow's acceptance of *force majeur* at this stage as a valid indicator of Russian behaviour in the next 10–20 years. They point to the almost universal Russian resentment over the extension of NATO. Resentment is a slow-burning fuse and a powerful political force. It was 15 years after Versailles that Hitler came to power. It is argued that resentment over the extension of NATO "could make the overturning of the post-Cold-War settlement a central aim of [Russian] foreign policy, no matter who is responsible for conducting it."[2]

Alternatives

Proponents assert that for the "grey zone" between NATO's new boundary and the Russian frontier "there is no alternative" to further NATO enlargement.

This ignores the unappealing alternative of a Europe divided along a line following the former border of the Soviet Union. Although not likely at this juncture, it could yet emerge as a pre-emptive response to the exclusionary concept of European security and the explicit threat of an evolutionary (read inexorable) enlargement of NATO. In this scenario, NATO would face a Pan-Slav alliance that for strategic reasons had incorporated Moldavia and the Baltic states.

Opponents note that there are other alternatives, albeit largely unexplored. These alternatives mainly build on the *de facto* nuclear-weapon-free-zone that extends from the Arctic to the Black Sea, and the possibility of a mutual security belt covering the remaining non-aligned states in that zone. They include sub-regional co-operative agreements, special arms control regimes, great power guarantees and so forth. The need for critical mass is another argument against further enlargement.

These embryonic schemes embody the truism that the micro-security of individual states in this "grey zone" depends absolutely on macro-security in greater Europe. They reflect the utilitarian principle of the greatest good for the greatest number and distinguish between the aspirations of states at this point in time and the long term interests of their people.

For example, which will best ensure Estonia's long-term security? Membership of NATO? Or membership of a tightly-bound northern-Baltic neutral and nuclear-free coalition comprising Finland, Sweden and the Baltic States?

To conclude

In its report on NATO Enlargement the Committee said that "opponents of enlargement have to accept a certain political logic to further enlargement and, like King Canute, [we] acknowledge that to attempt to turn the tide back could prove to be a stubborn waste of political energy".

In March 1998, ratification was the only sensible recommendation. The decision to enlarge NATO had been presented to Parliament as a *fait accompli*; the "first stage" was being achieved without dire consequences for European security; there was a certain political and geographical symmetry to the new alignment, which did not directly threaten Russia; and to have failed to fulfil the raised expectations would have had very serious consequences.

Our present situation is rather different, not least because the easy part is now behind us and the difficulties lie ahead. Any further enlargement will confirm that NATO is embarked on a "process" that is seemingly open-ended. That process will increasingly encroach on what Russia sees as its national security zone, the former Republics having particular geopolitical and strategic significance.

While nominally inclusive, the influence of hard-line Republicans means that NATO;s declaratory policy is often exclusionary, as is policy-on-the-ground. The hard-line tendency in US policy will almost certainly increase if Moscow reacts strongly to further enlargement, leading to action-reaction and growing confrontation.

This prospect would be less disturbing if the policy of enlargement was the result of a structured political-military assessment of the long-term requirements for European security. But we now know that this policy emerged during the first nine months of the Clinton administration from a White House seeking ways to counteract the domestic effects of its involvement in Somalia and inaction over Bosnia. The policy was strongly

---

[1] For example, Estonia and Latvia were wrested from Sweden in 1721, and had only enjoyed independence in the interwar years, 1918–39.

[2] Mandelbaum, *op. cit* p. 61. He points out that "NATO expansion is, in the eyes of Russians in the 1990s, what the war guilt clause was for Germans in the 1930s. It reneges on the terms on which they believe the conflict with the West ended. It is a betrayal of the understanding they thought they had with their former enemies."

opposed by the Pentagon and the relevant specialists in State. And when presented to NATO, it was initially opposed (for their separate reasons) by Britain and France.

Nor is it reassuring that in June 1997, 50 former US senators, cabinet secretaries and ambassadors, as well as US arms control and foreign policy specialists, took the most unusual step of writing an open letter to President Clinton stating their belief that "the current US-led effort to expand NATO . . . is a policy error of historic importance."[1] In May this year, similar misgivings were expressed by a comparable group of British notables in an equally unusual letter to the Prime Minister.

The decision to publicly criticise one's Government is not taken lightly by people of that background and experience. Nor was the letter to Clinton the first time that experienced US professionals had formally expressed their concern about NATO enlargement.[2] On both occasions the signatories included former Cold War warriors, the last people to be solicitous about Moscow's sensibilities.

Given the genesis of the policy of enlargement, its foreseeable consequences, and the calibre of dissenting opinion, the Committee might consider replacing the image of Canute, helpless before the tide, with the more activist metaphor of someone travelling by river. At various stages they have the opportunity to review their plans and decide whether it is wise to continue down stream, given what expert opinion and the available evidence suggests might lie ahead. At each stage, they have to ask themselves whether they would be better advised to haul the boat out of the water and travel towards their objective by some other means.

I suggest that we are at such a stage in respect to NATO enlargement.

It may have made political sense in late 1993 for the British Government to have gone along with the non-specific, inclusive policy of NATO enlargement that was being pushed by the new Clinton administration. It was perhaps understandable that the Labour Government should have chosen to take NATO enlargement as a "given" in its strategic defence review. But with the intricacies of the SDR behind us, the Defence Committee should now press for an urgent inter-Departmental review of this US-led policy.

It may be that NATO enlargement is not a "policy error of historic importance". But, given the implications for European security, it would seem essential that Britain should develop its own, properly-staffed view of the matter, rather than acquiesce to such policies as emerge from the US political process.

THE FUTURE OF NUCLEAR WEAPONS

Writing in 1993, Sir Michael Quinlan raised the question of whether the world still needed nuclear weapons. He concluded that it did and that Western policy on nuclear possession should continue unchanged.[3]

Since then there has emerged a significant body of authoritative international opinion, which outspokenly favours the elimination of nuclear weapons. This includes a sizeable number of very senior retired military officers, Presidents and Prime Ministers. There are substantive reasons for this development, which suggests that it is now time to revise the questions posed in Quinlan's article.

An important catalyst for new thinking about this question was the view which emerged in the wake of the Gulf War that the USA's main objective should be to prevent the proliferation of nuclear weapons.[4] Elimination was one way of achieving that objective and would bring other benefits. Besides removing "all kinds of risks of catastrophic destruction" America would then "be free to enjoy two extraordinary strategic advantages: first, as the least threatened of major states, and second, as the one state with modern conventional forces of unmatched quality". This led to the conclusion that it would be very much in the interests of the USA if all nuclear weapons were "taken off the table of international affairs"—if only one knew how.[5]

The revisionary process had meanwhile been at work on some of the assumptions underlying the Western policy of nuclear deterrence. A re-examination of decision-making by all parties involved in the Cuban Missile crisis made several of the original participants—notably Robert McNamara—realise we had come much closer to a nuclear exchange than people realised at the time. This led him to conclude that the indefinite combination

[1] Eminent and highly respected individuals made up this bipartisan group. The five senators included Sam Nunn, a long standing expert on defence. Arthur Hartman and Jack Matlock, ambassadors to Moscow 1981–87 and 1987–91, were among twelve signatories of that rank. Professors Richard Pipes and Marshall Shulman (former members of the NSC, but on opposite sides of the US debate on Soviet policy in the 1970–90 period) both signed the letter, as did Robert McNamara, Secretary of Defence in the Kennedy and Johnson administrations, and Paul Nitze, who was President Reagan's arms control supremo in the 1980s and a leading member of the hawkish 'Committee on the Present Danger' in the 1970s.

[2] In May 1995, a group of retired senior Foreign Service, State Department, and Department of Defense officials wrote privately to the US Secretary of State expressing concern about enlargement. A copy of the letter was subsequently published in the *New York Review of Books*, 21 May 1995, p. 75.

[3] See "The future of nuclear weapons: policy for Western possessors", *International Affairs*, 69:3, 1993, pp. 485–596. Quinlan had recently retired as Permanent Under Secretary of the Ministry of Defence.

[4] The idea was floated initially by Les Aspin, then Chairman of the House Armed Services Committee and subsequently US Secretary of Defense.

[5] *Reducing nuclear danger: the road away from the brink* (New York, Council on Foreign Relations Press, 1993) p. 5. Joint authors: McGeorge Bundy, Special Assistant for National Security Affairs, 1961–66; Admiral Crowe, Chairman of the Joint Chiefs of Staff 1985–89; Sidney Drell, nuclear physicist and long-time advisor to the US government.

of nuclear weapons and human fallability would inevitably lead to a nuclear exchange. McNamara's personal conviction was reinforced by academic analysis of various situations and incidents in the 1960–85 period, highlighting the inherent danger of inadvertent and/or accidental war.[1]

In other words, nuclear deterrence was not and never had been risk free. Furthermore, access to Soviet archives cast serious doubt on the core Western assumption: that Soviet policy in the Cold War years was driven by an urge to military expansion. This underlined the claim that nuclear weapons had kept the peace, leaving the central truth that it was the existence of nuclear weapons which made nuclear war possible.

This led to the question of whether, in the post-cold-war security environment, as should adopted "the firm and serious policy goal of a nuclear-free world?[2] In addressing that question, there emerged a new awareness that the policy-choice was not between the seemingly-stable, low-salience, nuclear world which we currently enjoyed and some future, hypothetical, nuclear-free world. We had to choose between two unfolding processes; we had to compare likely outcomes over time. Neither policy would be risk free.

Risk is the product of the consequences of a calamity and the likelihood of its occurrence. In a nuclear world (such as we have known this half century) the worst case is a full-scale nuclear exchange. In a non-nuclear world, the risk would be nuclear breakout, leading in the very worst case to the limited use of nuclear weapons. Opinions may differ on the comparative probability of the worst case occurring under the different policies. But in terms of risk, we can be certain that any disparity would be insufficient to balance the incomparable calamity of a nuclear exchange.

It was this kind of thinking that persuaded experienced military men like Field Marshal Lord Carver and USAF General Lee Butler to support the goal of a nuclear-free world.[3]

There were other reasons for this re-evaluation, including the 1995 Review Conference on the Nuclear non-Proliferation Treaty. Preparation for the Conference engaged the attention of officials and politicians, raised public awareness and prompted new analyses by non-governmental groups. These included the Washington-based "Project on Eliminating Nuclear Weapons of Mass Destruction,[4] and the international "Canberra Commission." The latter was specifically tasked by the Australian Government to develop concrete proposals on how to achieve a nuclear-free world.

Another spur was the growing danger of nuclear proliferation, in part a byproduct of the dissolution of the Soviet Union, but also a corollary of the two-tier structure of the NPT. Added to the opinion that elimination would be in US interests and to the technical demands of the START dismantling process, this stimulated new research and increased investment in the science and technology of verification, which was still low on its learning curve. It was concluded that a nuclear-free world was within the bounds of feasibility.

The Canberra Commission published its report in August 1996, soon after the ruling by the International Court of Justice that "the threat or use of nuclear weapons (would) generally be contrary both to the rules of international law applicable in armed conflict and in particular to the principles and rules of humanitarian law."[5] The Commission's report described practical measures to bring about the verifiable elimination of nuclear weapons and called on the five nuclear powers "to give the lead by committing themselves unequivocally" to that goal.[6] It was followed in December 1996 by a "Statement on Nuclear Weapons by International Generals and Admirals" (including 19 from the USA and 17 from Russia) supporting the principle of "continuous, complete, and irreversible elimination of nuclear weapons".

In February 1998, "The State of the World Forum" released an open statement that had by then been signed by over 100 former civilian leaders and senior officials (including 52 past Presidents and Prime Ministers) from 48 states (including the major powers). Noting that "immediate and practical steps" towards a nuclear-free world had been "arrayed in a host of compelling studies", the statement called on the five nuclear powers to commence

---

[1] For example: Bruce G Blair, *The logic of accidental war* (Washington DC: Brookings Institution, 1993); Scott D Sagan, *The limits of safety organisations, accidents, and nuclear weapons* (Princeton, NJ: Princeton University Press, 1993); Peter Douglas Feaver, *Guarding the Guardians: civilian control of nuclear weapons in the United States* (Ithica: Cornell University Press, 1992)

[2] This was Michael Quinlan's formulation. The qualifiers were needed to distinguish this course of action from rhetorical pronouncements during the previous 25 years.

[3] As CinC Strategic Air Command (91–92) and CinC Strategic Command (92–94), General Butler had been responsible for all USAF and USN nuclear deterrent forces.

[4] The Chairman of the Project's Steering Committee is General Andrew Goodpaster, currently co-Chair of the Atlantic Council and formerly SACEUR (1969–74); the 17 members include Robert McNamara (US SecDef 1961–68), Amb Paul Nitze (Arms Control Supremo 1981–89), Gen Charles Horner (CinC N American Aerospace Defence Command 1992–94), and Gen W Y Smith (Dep US CinC Europe). This multi-year project was launched by the Henry L Stimson Center in 1994 and has published ten reports to date. The most relevant to this discussion is the Steering Committee's Second Report *An Evolving US Nuclear Posture* (Dec 1995). It advocates "an up-front, serious commitment to the long-term objective of eliminating all weapons of mass destruction" combined with an "evolutionary" nuclear posture of careful phased reductions.

[5] The Court was unable to "conclude definitively whether the threat or use of nuclear weapons would be lawful or unlawful in the extreme circumstances of self-defence, in which the very survival of the state would be at stake."

[6] The Canberra Commission also concluded: "There is no doubt that, if the peoples of the world were more fully aware of the inherent danger of nuclear weapons and the consequences of their use, they would reject them. . ."

"the systematic and progressive reduction and marginalisation of nuclear weapons" and declare "unambiguously that their goal is ultimate abolition". The statement was launched with a powerful speech by General Lee Butler, in which he explained how he had come to reject the theories and doctrine he had subscribed to throughout his service career, with particular emphasis on the "treacherous axioms" of nuclear deterrence.[1]

In June 1998, the Foreign Ministers of eight good friends of the Western nuclear powers issued a joint declaration supporting the Canberra Commission's conclusions on the danger of nuclear war and calling on all nuclear-weapons states to commit themselves "unequivocally" and "now," to the "speedy, final, and total elimination" of their nuclear weapons capability.[2]

These various statements differ in their details and emphases, but share the conviction that the continued existence of nuclear weapons imperils mankind. They all stress the crucial importance of the five nuclear powers making an unequivocal (rather than rhetorical) commitment to the elimination of such weapons and the need to back words with action. They consider that such a commitment would have a radical influence on the problem of proliferation. Some believe it would have a transformative effect on the international system.

Judging by the *Strategic Defence Review* the British Government remains unpersuaded by these arguments. It seems not to agree that nuclear weapons imperil mankind, noting merely that "the world would be a better place if such weapons were still not necessary."[3] Nor is the Government prepared to make an unequivocal commitment to the goal of a nuclear-free world,[4] which it considers can only come about when the conditions exist "in which no state judges that it needs nuclear weapons to guarantee its security."[5]

This is a legitimate point of view, and the Government is under no obligation to present a case other than its own.[6] But it is under an obligation not to misrepresent the alternative policy, as it does when it says that "the condition for complete nuclear disarmament does not yet exist." The context implies that proponents of the alternative policy think it does exist, whereas they have always been explicit that elimination will be an evolutionary process, taking 20–30 years, or longer.

The Government also has a responsibility not to use words that mislead the public as to the policy it is actually pursuing. Reading of its "commitment to the elimination of nuclear weapons", one would assume that the Government supported the various statements referred to above. That is, unless one knew that some such form of words had been used since 1970, the year the NPT entered into force and (coincidentally) the build up of nuclear arsenals began in earnest. Past usage has ensured that in sophisticated circles, "commitment" to elimination is understood to be rhetorical, unless it is qualified by a term like "unequivocal.[7] The average reader is not aware of that convention.

There is a third, important point. The question of whether Britain should adopt "the firm and serious policy goal" of eliminating nuclear weapons is of a different order and in a different category to questions concerning the utility of an independent British deterrent or the number of Trident war-heads. In the short-to-medium term these questions are not interdependent. A decision to adopt the goal of a nuclear-free world would need have no early effect on the other category of questions.[8]

---

[1] For extended extracts from his speech at the National Press Club, Washington on 2 February see *Disarmament Diplomacy* (London: Acronym Institute, No. 23, Feb 1997) pp 24–30.

[2] "A Nuclear-Weapons-Free World: The Need for a New Agenda," Joint Declaration in Dublin by the Ministers of Foreign Affairs of Brazil, Egypt, Ireland, Mexico, New Zealand, Slovenia, South Africa and Sweden, 9 June 1998. This said (*inter alia*) "we are deeply concerned at the persistent reluctance of the nuclear-weapon States to approach their Treaty obligations [under the NPT] as an urgent commitment to the total elimination of their nuclear weapons."

[3] Quotations from the *SDR* come from paras. 3, 20, 22 of the *Supporting Essay on Deterrence (etc)*.

[4] In this part of the *SDR*, the term "unequivocal commitment" is only used in respect to Britain's obligations under the NPT, where the reference to nuclear disarmament can be construed in different ways.

[5] China has always favoured the elimination of nuclear weapons, as has India. In January 1986, genuinely concerned about what he saw as the very real and growing danger of nuclear war, Mikhail Gorbachev made a formal proposal (repeated in October that year at Reykjavik) that all nuclear weapons should be eliminated by the year 2000. Through 1992, Russia continued to advocate (unequivocally) complete nuclear disarmament.

[6] The *SDR* is uninformative in this respect, but there appears to have been no significant change in the long-standing policy inherited from the Conservatives. Nuclear deterrence is needed to keep the peace unless (or until) there is a fundamental change in the nature of the international system, such that no state sees the need for nuclear weapons. Failing such a change, the Government doubts the very feasibility of a verifiable nuclear-free world and, even if it were achievable, it would not necessarily be desirable. In such a world, the possibility of conventional war between major powers would re-emerge, leading (most likely) to the reconstitution of nuclear arsenals, and (possibly) to nuclear war. In sum, stay with the devil you know, make comforting noises about nuclear disarmament, but no unequivocal commitments to a nuclear-free world.

[7] This convention was confirmed implicitly by the careful wording of a statement by Baroness Symons in the Lords (note 19, below). Quoting the Papal representative's call "for an unequivocal commitment to the abolition of nuclear arms", she said she was "happy to repeat that the Government was committed to the global elimination of those nuclear weapons." Note the elision of "unequivocal."

[8] One explanation for the new Government's reluctance to debate the question of eliminating nuclear weapons could be that it (wrongly) perceives nuclear matters as a single ball of string. It is loth to tamper with the ball lest the rationale for a British nuclear capability starts to unravel.

To Conclude

Writing in 1993, Sir Michael Quinlan, recently retired as Permanent Under Secretary of the Ministry of Defence, posed two questions. First, did the world have to have nuclear weapons at all? Second, were there adequate reasons for NT adopting the firm and serious policy goal of a nuclear=free world?[1]

Quinlan answered both questions in the affirmative and it is reasonable to assume that this was Government policy at the time. Lip service notwithstanding, the *Strategic Defence Review* gives no reason to suppose that Government policy has changed in this particular area.[2]

One explanation for the new Government's reluctance to debate the question of eliminating nuclear weapons could be that it (wrongly) perceives nuclear matters as a single ball of string. It is loth to tamper with the ball lest the rationale for a British nuclear capability starts to unravel.

Since 1993, a series of international reports and declarations have reached a different conclusion and answered documents has been the range and calibre of the signatories and the depth, spread and relevance of their political and professional expertise.

This does not mean they are necessarily right. But it does suggest that their conclusions deserve serious consideration. Five years down the road, Quinlan's questions should be revisited in open debate.

When addressing this issue, it is important that the global question of the future of nuclear weapons be treated as quite separate to questions concerning the British deterrent, which are not directly related. The global question can only be analysed by envisaging the unfolding of the alternative policies (each with its attendant consequences, good and bad), and comparing the risks over time.

Supplementary Memorandum submitted by Michael MccGwire on the Future of NATO

There appears to be a consensus within NATO officialdom and among European members of the alliance that following the accession of Poland, Hungary and the Czech Republic in April 1999, there should be a moratorium on further invitations.

Such a policy, providing time for digestion, restructuring and evaluation, can be supported by almost all parties to the debate. Many of the strongest proponents of enlargement urge caution at this stage, as do most governments.

The adoption of such a policy at the Washington Summit is threatened by the US political process. For their different reasons, the hard line Republicans in Congress and the White House favour further invitations.

The danger lies in the White House tactic of making unilateral statements about future membership, which take on the garb of irrevocable NATO commitments.

To counter this threat requires that pre-emptive statements on the need for a moratorium be placed on record by European members and publicised internationally, preferably before the end of the year. The following example is worded to attract maximum support from both sides of the debate.

> "At the NATO Summit in April 1999, Poland, Hungary and the Czech Republic will be confirmed as members of the alliance.
>
> Even though there is a certain logic to their membership in geopolitical and strategic terms, to incorporate these former Warsaw Pact countries into NATO's evolving mission structure will require significant adaptation by all parties.
>
> The last five years has been a time of continual change for NATO: PfP, the Euro-Atlantic Partnership Council, the push for enlargement, the Dayton accords (and Kosovo), the Founding Act with Russia, joint operations with 'partnership' forces, and now the new Strategic Concept.
>
> There is a pressing need for time to digest these structural developments, to analyse the growing body of experience and to consider how best to move ahead.

---

[1] See note 1. For an up-to-date version of Quinlan's argument see *Thinking about nuclear weapons,* (London: Royal United Services Institute, 1997) For a rebuttal of Quinlan's original argument, see MccGwire, "Is there a future for nuclear weapons?" *International Affairs* 1994, 70:2, pp. 211–228.

[2] This conclusion is supported by the carefully worded statements of Baroness Symons, when she took the "opportunity to present . . . the Government's position on nuclear disarmament." (*Hansard,* 17 December 1997, cols. 684–89). She claimed that a speech in the UN First Committee by the Papal representative calling for the world "to move to the abolition of nuclear weapons through a universal non-discriminatory ban" was mirrored in the government's manifesto commitment to "mutual, balanced and verifiable nuclear disarmament." The Government would "work for the global elimination of nuclear weapons" by pressing for "multilateral negotiations towards mutual, balanced and verifiable reductions." (See also note 16 above). This Lords debate was noteworthy for having one Prelate (the Lord Bishop of Oxford) opposing a nuclear-free world, one Field Marshal (Lord Carver) in favour, and two Field Marshals (Lords Carver and Bramall) advocating the elimination of Britain's nuclear capability.

It is also clear that enlargement beyond NATO's newly created eastern border will involve political complications of a different order to those encountered to date.

In the period leading up to the April Summit, it is important that all NATO members should avoid any statements, collective or individual, that imply that the alliance is committed to further enlargement at this juncture in time."

Memorandum submitted by the French International and Defence Studies Group, European Studies Research Institute, University of Salford, Manchester

Any assessment of France's attitude to NATO must begin by stressing:

(i) the nationally self-conscious French outlook on all foreign and security issues;

(ii) the importance of history in informing French defence and security debates and perspectives (See the 1995–96 Rapport d'Information of the French Senate Foreign, Defence and Armed Services Committee on "The Future of Military Service").

We have followed the format of the Defence Committee's terms of reference for the inquiry into the "Future of NATO" as outlined in Shona McGlashan's letter of 19 October 1998.

THE DEVELOPMENT OF NATO'S NEW STRATEGIC CONCEPT PRIOR TO ITS ADOPTION AT THE WASHINGTON SUMMIT;

The international situation since the end of the Cold War has placed France on a new fault line running to the South rather than to the East in which NATO's southern flank is perceived to be of particular sensitivity. Instability along the North African coast with the risk of both rogue states (Libya) and internal violence (Algeria) is perceived as an external menace to France. Some fear the acquisition of WMD capability among these states will place southern cities (e.g., Marseilles, Nice) within range of ballistic missiles (rumoured to be of Chinese, North Korean or Iranian provenance). Connected to this, Islamic fundamentalism is seen as presenting internal threats (a Moslem immigrant community of 1.3 million) via terrorism (see Paris metro bombings and Air France hi-jack in 1994–95). For many French commentators and politicians, NATO's southern flank is perceived as a potential barrier to the new "threat from the south".

What arises from this, for the Committee's inquiry, is France's interest in harnessing NATO to the new French strategic requirement of providing collective or common security to the south.

TO CONSIDER THESE ISSUES PARTICULARLY IN THE CONTEXT OF THE INTERNATIONAL SITUATION AND CHANGING EMPHASIS IN NATO'S TASKS FROM PREPARATION FOR STRATEGIC ATTACK TO PEACEKEEPING AND OTHER ROLES:

Peacekeeping

France appears an enthusiastic participant in supranational peacekeeping roles (rather than peacemaking) which fits with the "historic mission" of the "armies of the Republic" e.g., 1992: 10,000 French military personnel engaged in global peace-keeping operations).

Humanitarian Interventions

This remains a central plank in the rationale of the French armed forces and is likely to facilitate co-operation if conducted under NATO auspices.

TO CONSIDER THE PROCESS OF THE ACCESSION OF THE CZECH REPUBLIC, HUNGARY AND POLAND TO NATO, AND THE CASE FOR FURTHER ENLARGEMENT

Because of the historic "German problem" for France, Russia has been France's ally in the last hundred years more often than her enemy (Franco-Russian treaties of 1894, 1935, 1944), the Cold War notwithstanding. De Gaulle encapsulated this in suggesting that France, unlike Britain, had no serious conflicting interests with Russia. Therefore in any process of accession to NATO by states in East-Central Europe from 1999 onwards (and subsequent further enlargement) to include, hypothetically, the Baltic Republics, France must be expected to show greater concern for Russian sensitivities, because of the proximity of these states to Russian borders. It should be expected that any case for further enlargement towards Russia's borders may encounter French opposition.

TO CONSIDER THE CONTINUING APPLICABILITY OF THE NORTH ATLANTIC TREATY AND THE MILITARY STRUCTURE OF NATO TO ITS NEW ROLES AND ANY NEW STRATEGIC CONCEPT

(i) France's attempts to adjust the focus of NATO's orientation from a predominantly eastward threat assessment to a more southerly one found expression in the 1995–97 drive by President Chirac to claim for France the NATO AFSOUTH command. The French presented it as a condition for reintegrating the military command and nuclear planning group. From December 1995 France stated its readiness to return fully to NATO provided Alliance structures were reformed and a new equilibrium established over duties and responsibilities between the US and NATO-Europe. The obstacle to agreement was the command at Naples (CNCSOUTH). Chirac's premature declaration in early September 1996 that the US was ready to concede French aspirations was contradicted by President Clinton's rebuttal of 26 September 1996.

(ii)   The consequences for France's policy on forthcoming enlargement. France has given assurances that she will not place obstacles in the way of NATO's internal reform prior to the projected expansion of April 1999. However, what is already apparent is a cooling of French enthusiasm for NATO in general; a weakening of French support for US-led NATO enforcement of the Dayton accords; and renewed French reticence about supporting US policy positions out of the NATO area (viz 1998 Israel-Palestine Wye Accords; UNSCOM enforcement in Iraq). The best that it seems safe to forecast for the very near future at a policy level is a France, to quote Defence Minister Alain Richard, "in, but not integrated" (2 December 1997). At a technical level this may mean in practice, the participation of French officers on the staffs of CJTF's for instance, which would be a case of France practising what the respected defence correspondent Jacques Isnard called "à la carte co-operation with NATO". This was made clear by General Douin, until recently Chief of the French Defence Staff, who declared bitterly: "France won't return to NATO like an errant school-boy to class" (*Le Monde* 5 December 1997).

(iii)   This Franco-American divergence may put Britain in a privileged position as one of the bridging stones between the European and Atlantic pillars (particularly in the light of the Prime Minister's recent support for a strong European foreign policy backed by a real "defence capability").

CONCLUSION

(i)   Though a pause has occurred in France's attempts to "rebalance" the location of power and tenure of commands in NATO, there has been movement within the French decision-making process.

(ii)   The rebuffs of 1997 appear to have weakened Jacques Chirac's presidential prerogatives in his previously "reserved domain" of foreign and defence policy.

(iii)   Dialogue henceforth with France should engage as much with the Foreign Ministry and Prime Minister's Office as it should with the Elysée.

(iv)   We would underline the assurances of the French Foreign Minister, Hubert Védrine (who increasingly dominates government thinking on security), that France is not reverting to isolation but rather will go on struggling to persuade her NATO partners of the desirability of moving towards a genuinely rebalanced alliance (J Howorth, *Brassey's Defence Yearbook 1998*, pp. 130–51).

(v)   Belgium is likely to support constructive British leadership and mediation in this continuing project. This was indicated by the Belgian Ambassador to London, Lode Willems, who commented that Tony Blair's enthusiasm for a European "defence capability" would be seen by the Belgian government as a step in the right direction.

(vi)   All of this suggests considerable scope for British "defence diplomacy" to play a constructive role in the development of NATO.

Letter from the Ministry of Defence on the Committee's recommendation that the Government invite NATO to make publicly available declassified versions of the studies on the military and financial implications of NATO Enlargement

I am writing to follow up the Committee's recommendation in its Third Special Report of Session 1997–98 (HC 903) that the Government invite NATO to make publicly available declassified versions of the studies on the military and financial implications of enlarging NATO which we gave the Committee on a classified basis. You will recall that the Defence Secretary undertook to draw NATO's attention to the Committee's request but noted that the matter was one for collective decision based on consensus among allies, and that the reports were not the property of the Government (Official Report, 17 July 1997, column 750).

The UK Delegation to NATO accordingly asked for collective consideration of the Committee's request. The NATO International Staff have now responded that discussions among Allies have led them to conclude that there is no consensus to release these documents nor to attempt what would inevitably be a difficult and time-consuming process of preparing a declassified version for public release. Although formal release by NATO is not possible, national authorities are of course free to draw on the reports as fully as they deem appropriate, bearing in mind the sensitivity of their comments, in briefing their respective Parliaments and public opinion on the implications of NATO enlargement. We have accordingly reconsidered whether there is any more information which we could release the studies beyond the considerable amount that we made public in our initial memorandum to the Committee (pages 88–91 of the Committee's Third Report of Session 1997–98, HC 469) and in the second response to the Committee's report (the Committee's Third Special Report of Session 1997–98, HC 903). We do not, however, believe, bearing in mind the position of other Allies on the question of publication, that there is any significant information that we can release.

Memorandum submitted by Sir Michael Alexander on the Future of NATO

The issues facing the drafters of the New Strategic Concept, and of any associated Declaration to be finalised in Washington in April, must, I imagine, include those set out below. The list makes no claim to be inclusive nor to deal with all the matters on which the Defence committee will need to touch.

THE ISSUES ARE:

— reconciling the Alliance's conflicting roles as an instrument of collective defence and as an instrument of collective security;

— suggesting the basis on which the Alliance expects its relationship with Russia to develop in the period ahead;

— defining the areas, both geographical and functional, within which the Alliance should operate; sketching the basis of any new transatlantic bargain;

— indicating how the Alliance sees the evolution of its relationship with the European Union as the latter acquires a defence identity;

— defining the conditions on which "coalitions of the willing" (including the participants in a European security and defence identity—ESDI) could deploy NATO's military assets;

— securing agreement on the circumstances in which the Alliance could act autonomously rather than as an instrument of the "international community" i.e., the Security Council;

— finalising the admission of the three new members and dealing with the question of further enlargement;

— confirming on-going adaptations to NATO's military arrangements as well as defining the role of nuclear weapons in NATO strategy.

COLLECTIVE DEFENCE V. COLLECTIVE SECURITY

The tension between these two aspects of NATO's role goes back many years and has been analysed many times. It still causes trouble in the minds of politicians, commentators and planners. It will continue to do so in future. This is because, while it is politically essential for the Alliance to meet both requirements, the two are fundamentally irreconcilable—at least on the classic definitions of collective security. Collective defence looks outward, collective security looks inwards. Collective security aims to make collective defence unnecessary. This conflict did not matter greatly before the Nineties since up until 1990 collective defence was overwhelmingly more important for NATO. But it does matter now. The problem underlies many of the issues touched on later in this note.

Throughout the period when the military threat was unambiguous and the priority of NATO's defence role unchallenged, proper deference—but no more—was shown to the idea of collective security (c.f., the 1967 Harmel Report). Latterly, however, collective security has become a dominant concern: the prominence given to peacekeeping, crisis management, the projection of stability etc reflects the shift. This change in emphasis, already evident in the 1991 Strategic Concept, was unavoidable. To have remained focused on collective defence when there appeared to be no threat would have resulted in the rapid atrophy of the Alliance. In any case it would have been politically unacceptable for the Western world's primary defence organisation to have ignored indefinitely, e.g., the crisis in the former Yugoslavia.

But, as always, doing a straddle involves discomfort. The military requirements of the two roles are different: over a period providing the force structures, the planning and the equipment needed for crisis management and humanitarian tasks will tend—to downgrade the provision made for defence tasks. The habits of mind associated with reliance on "coalitions of the willing" to deal with individual crises will tend—again over a period—to undermine the "all for one, one for all" assumption which has lain at the core of NATO's collective defence success. Rendering the "partnership" relationship with states outside NATO increasingly indistinguishable from full membership will, equally, tend over time to undermine the coherence of the Alliance. (Complaints are already audible from the three new members to the effect that the Alliance they are joining is not the collective defence—against Russia—organisation for membership of which they applied at the beginning of the decade.)

No amount of statesmanship would have avoided the emergence of this dilemma at the end of the Cold War. It is one consequence of the success of the West. What matters now is that governments recognise the problem and keep it in focus, e.g., in drafting the New Strategic Concept. If governments think exclusively of collective security e.g., of greatly increased (including perhaps Russian) membership and of primarily peacekeeping and humanitarian roles, it will become progressively more difficult to retain the credible defence capability which is NATO's *raison d'etre*. (If that capability is allowed to degrade much below present levels NATO wide, it will be extraordinarily difficult to restore.) This could in time have the paradoxical consequence of undermining the US engagement in Europe on which Europe's post-war security and stability has been founded (see cap 3 below).

I hope therefore that the Washington documents will contain a detailed and plausible analysis of the need for NATO to retain a credible capability for collective defence (c.f. our own SDR.)—caps 2, 3, 5 and 8 below refer. Such an analysis will provide the necessary counterpoint to the, no doubt, more extended analysis of the requirements of collective security. I hope, incidentally, that the latter can avoid references to the indivisibility of security in the North Atlantic region. For many years yet security in the real world risks being only too divisible.

NATO AND RUSSIA

The NATO-Russia Founding Act (1997) states that "NATO and Russia will work together to contribute to the establishment in Europe of common and comprehensive security." The implication that these are two separate, balancing entities with a common interest in stability in Europe is exactly right and properly reflects the continuing importance of Russia. It should be the basis of the mutual relationship for a good many years to come. NATO countries and Russia share membership in many international institutions; NATO and Russia will want to work together in dealing with many–hopefully most—international crises of concern to both. But to hold open the prosect of Russian entry into NATO in the foreseeable future would be to give a decisive thrust to NATO's drift away from its collective defence role. In appearing to favour Russian membership, the Clinton Administration has risked undermining NATO's principal appeal to the US viz. That it is a military organisation with the capacity to act effectively in military as well as crisis management and humanitarian situations.

Many object to this approach to the NATO/Russia relationship on the grounds that the balance of power approach to European security (and indeed to international security generally) has been overtaken by events; and that to juxtapose NATO and Russia, whether explicitly or implicitly, is to encourage political recidivism in Russia. But my own view is that balance of power thinking, however retrograde it may seem at the end of the twentieth century, is alive and well in most of the world's capitals (notably in Moscow). It will remain so until the global village has a global policeman—a development still two or three generations away. Acknowledgement of this by NATO could well cause trouble in and with Moscow. But the prime causes of the crisis in Russia lie elsewhere and could easily, in the short term, result in administrations there with programmes inimical to the interests of Western Europe. Some would argue this is already happening. NATO, for its part, may in any case be driven to pursue policies which will be highly unpopular with the Russians, e.g., bombing Serbia or renewed strikes against Iraq (for which NATO will be blamed).

There is no point in trying to plan for all the twists and turns which lie ahead in the NATO/Russia relationship: the PJC is there to deal with them. NATO's policy will have to be formulated flexibility and with due regard for the evolving situation in Russia. But I hope that the participants in the Washington summit will recognise that this partnership, above all, will be governed by "realpolitik"; and that the present political establishment in Russia, despite—or even perhaps because of—their country's current weakness, are still far from accepting either that a stable and prosperous European reaching to Russia's border is in its interests; or that Western concern for Russia's own stability is genuine. As and when these facts can be acknowledged in Russia, collective security in Europe will begin to become a reality.

THE ROLE OF THE ALLIANCE; THE TRANSATLANTIC BARGAIN

US engagement in the Alliance, and therefore in Europe, since 1949 has been based on the proposition that continued stability and security in Western Europe, founded on committed US military power, has been in the US national interest and has justified a substantial national effort. It is evident that this proposition is, post the Cold War, decreasingly defensible in Congress—which in any case has along history of doubting the fairness of the transatlantic bargain c.f. the endless debates on burden sharing. As a result the voices in Washington arguing for a new bargain—Alliance involvement in the defence of Western interests outside the NATO area in return for a continued US commitment to Europe—have for some time been growing louder. They now include Administration spokespersons. The European response has been, and is likely to remain, unenthusiastic—for the usual reasons.

I hope that the Alliance debate on this issue, which will not be resolved in April, can be reasonably frank. The issues involved are too important to be swept under the carpet. It is essential that the North Atlantic community begins to develop some commonality of view about what are its vital interests in a global context; what it is prepared to do to advance or defend them; and where. US opinion formers need to be persuaded that there are at least some out-of-area interests which a significant part of the Alliance (not just the UK) would be prepared to defend by force; and that the Europeans are capable of formulating and acting upon vigorous and relevant security policies. European opinion, for its part, needs to be persuaded that US decision makers take Europe seriously and will not simply ignore it even when Europe is expected to carry the can (c.f., Holbrooke in Kosovo). The Europeans also need to know that they can rely on the US, e.g., that US support in logistics and communications will be available for European led operations even if US involvement is minimal.

One can, as always perceive potential threats to the transatlantic relationship beyond simple disagreement on policy (which in its essence is about the collective defence/collective security issue). The increasing coherence of Europe (a strong Euro will tend to increase the cost of US forces in Europe) is one problem; trade (bananas, BST etc.) is another; the future of the defence industry (which could be a uniting or a highly divisive factor) is a third. I hope, therefore, that the overwhelming importance of maintaining the transatlantic relationship will be the subject of more than merely lip service in Washington. For the US, Europe is still the only credible and worthwhile partner when global security is at issue; for Europe, engagement with the US is vital not merely for the sake of Europe's internal security and stability but also as a means of influencing the policies of the global superpower and encouraging it to resist the temptations of solipsism (c.f. the theory of rapid dominance).

I suspect that efforts in April to define precisely the areas in which the Alliance could or should act will be counter-productive. The future it is too unpredictable and current differences too great. It will probably be better to seek to lay down a basis of principle and priority which will encourage member states to think harder about what their vital interests are going to be over the next generation and thus to facilitate the assembly of "coalitions of the willing" when those interests are seen to be at stake.

NATO AND THE EUROPEAN UNION

The declaration issued by Alliance Heads of Government in Rome in November 1991, to accompany the Strategic Concept, contained a lengthy passage on what was then called "the European security identity and defence role". This was part of the package which had enabled France—as is often overlooked—to participate fully and from the outset in the quadripartite group which wrote the then new Strategic Concept. The hopes expressed in the Declaration for the enhancement of the role and responsibility of its European members within the Alliance and for the emergence of a European security and defence identity (EDSI) have been slow of realisation. Progress has of course been made—including very recently—but Spain is only now about to join the integrated military structure and France, bizarrely but predictably, still seems a considerable way from doing so.

What is known as "functional integration" is facilitating a continuing rapprochement between France and Nato by removing the actual obstacles to co-operate while leaving the shibboleths in place. The shibboleths will have to be addressed at some point but probably not in April. Full re-engagement will only come, if ever, when there is some kind of consensus on the transatlantic bargain (see cap 3. above)—French withdrawal from the policing of the no fly zones in Iraq being an unhelpful augury—and when there is more evidence as to how ESDI is going to interact, or be allowed to interact, with Nato.

HMG has—as it has always had—a major interest in ensuring that co-operation between Nato and ESDI is smooth and mutually beneficial. Hopefully the Washington documents will reiterate forcefully the Alliance's interest in this. But whether the aspiration is realised will depend largely on how demanding the French choose to be; and, more importantly, on how tolerant the US is. I hope the US Administration will see it as being much in their interest to encourage the emergence of a genuinely effective European Union defence identity.

"COALITIONS OF THE WILLING"

It seems clear that much of the Alliance's future activity will be governed by "variable geometry", by groupings which are "separable but not separate". Some of the necessary infrastructure is already in place or planned, notably the CJTF concept, and will presumably be referred to in the Washington documents. For reasons already described, this development will not necessarily strengthen the Alliance but has long since become unavoidable. However it may be important to re-affirm, on the one hand, that operations carried out in Nato's name will always be subject to consensus, regardless of who actually participates; and, on the other hand, that consensus will not be gratuitously withheld. It is as crucial, of course, that this be acknowledged by the larger members of the Alliance as by the smallest.

NATO AND THE SECURITY COUNCIL

NATO's ability to act out of area independently of the UN seems bound to be a contentious issue in the run-up to the April summit. The US and the UK will agree neither that a UN mandate for NATO action is always essential nor that NATO should ever appear to be little more than a sub contractor for the Security Council. France, supported by Germany and others, will argue that NATO should only act, out of area in pursuit of goals agreed by the "international community".

For the cynic, the UN issue is at root a diversionary tactic available to members of the Alliance, considering that their vital interests are not engaged in a given crisis, to delay or inhibit those who do consider such interests are engaged or who may favour a looser definition of what constitutes a vital interest. If NATO did agree that its vital interests were engaged—say in some repetition of a Rwanda 1994 situation—one may doubt whether scruples about Security Council approval would delay matters for very long. The same goes for a "coalition of the willing" involving some or all of the leading NATO players. Article 51 is there to be used.

That said, NATO Heads of Government will be looking for language to obscure these underlying realities and to make it easier for consensus to emerge. "Due respect" will be paid to the rules of international law and to the position of the Security Council. Specific description of Security Council procedures and mechanisms for authorising international police actions will be avoided. Approving references will be made to the role of the OSCE. NATO's intention to deal with crises which directly threaten the security of member states will be underlined without spelling out where such crises might arise or what form they might take. It will be understood, though not stated, that Alliance lawyers will be free to create legal justification, e.g., "imminent humanitarian disaster", to permit threats of the use of force despite the absence of explicit UN authorization. And so on. This is a difficult and controversial issue but in the last analysis NATO governments, and least of all France, are not going to get into a position where military action they may wish to take can be vetoed by NATO non-members, however important.

THE NEW MEMBERS: FURTHER ENLARGEMENT

The three new members of the Alliance will have been admitted before the Washing summit assembles— possibly as early as February. Presumably the actual date will depend on the speed with which the more important of the still outstanding issues can be sorted out: Poland's demand for a special place as a "big" country; the legal and constitutional framework within which Hungary will join; the defence budgets in all three countries, but especially in the Czech Republic, where the economic position continues to deteriorate; security clearance procedures for personnel tasked with NATO duties; etc., etc. But none of these issues will be allowed to hold up incorporation for long. It has already been agreed that the three new members should be in a position to participate in discussion of the New Strategic Concept and in co-ordination of Western strategy for the new round of CFE negotiations (another neuralgic topic, incidentally, in the context of the NATO/Russia relationship).

As regards further enlargement, it seems clear that no new invitations will be issued in April. But there is continuing controversy about the formula to be used to give encouragement to those who missed out in Madrid in 1997. If, which I would have preferred, Romania and Slovenia had been admitted then, it would have been somewhat easier to handle the problem now. As it is the Alliance faces an awkward choice between disappointing Romania and Slovenia if it fails to indicate some kind of preference for their candidatures next time round and disappointing e.g., Bulgaria, Slovakia, and Lithuania if it does do so. Although the names are different, the problem is much the same as that which caused such dissension in Madrid. Postponement is probably the best policy but he commitment to further enlargement will need to be unequivocal. I would have liked to see it stated that special considerations (undefined) applied to candidates formerly part of the Soviet Union. But this would presumably be unnegotiable.

NEW MILITARY ARRANGEMENTS: THE ROLE OF NUCLEAR WEAPONS

The process of updating and simplifying NATO's command structures and employment plans is ongoing. This will no doubt be reflected in the Washington documents. On a related subject, it would be useful if the Alliance could provide evidence that it was grappling effectively with the problem of the growing gaps among member states in military technology—particularly, but not only, across the Atlantic. The rest of the Alliance's efforts to sustain military co-operation will become nugatory if interoperability falls below a certain level.

As regards nuclear weapons NATO would do well to follow the example of the SDR and, alongside a continuing reduction on the number of nuclear warheads deployed and in their potency, pursue a policy of greater transparency about the numbers, capabilities and roles envisaged. In the long run, given that nuclear weapons can be reduced but not eliminated, ever greater transparency offers the best hope of controlling the dangers posed by military nuclear technology while retaining its war deterring potential. NATO should make "greater nuclear transparency" one of its slogans. But "no first use" declarations would add little if anything to the stability of the NATO/Russia relationship in this field and would in any case be unnegotiable with Moscow. It is good, therefore, that the German government seem to be backing away from a "no first use" debate. The temptation to indulge in one will probably resurface, e.g., in Ottawa: HMG should continue to oppose it.

Memorandum submitted by Lord Kennet and Mrs Elizabeth Young on the Future of NATO

The mew NATO Strategic Doctrine that the US is proposing, as is clear from the public actions and pronouncements of many US officials over many months, fully reflects the conditions that Senator Jesse Helms imposed as legally binding on the Clinton Administration in the course of the Senate agreeing to the Enlargement of NATO (Senate Resolution, etc., of April 30, 1998; passim).

The Helms conditions include:

— NATO not to be subject to the United Nations Security Council or to the UN Charter, even when acting out of area;

— NATO to defend our interests and shared values' wheresoever in the world they may be at risk;

— The US Senate to be informed of the sufficiency of the defence budgets of the European members of NATO, and US funding of NATO to be reduced annually;

— There to be a "fire break" in relations between NATO and Russia (in spite of the Founding Act) and NATO only to "brief" Russia on its decisions, not to consult.

The following comments pick up the numbering above.

The most fundamental of these conditions is the first: the removal of NATO from the ambit of the United Nations and its Charter, and therefore effectively from international law. Given Britain's full and long-standing membership of the UN and our status as a Permanent Member of the Security Council (not to mention the fact that loyalty to the United Nations figures in the Constitution of the Labour Party), such a proposal should not be seriously entertained by this country.

Relations between Britain and the United Nations and Britain and the United States are a matter of foreign rather than of defence policy, but the absence of a foreign policy statement preceding the Strategic Defence Review (SDR) has effectively placed the topic in the defence area. That the SDR resulted in the specific formulation of an "expeditionary capability" implies a willingness to take part in activities beyond the NATO area, presumably either as NATO actions or as participation in so-called "coalitions of the willing". But the general assumption has been that Britain would not act outside United Nations authority, except possibly in cases of truly urgent humanitarian necessity.

And indeed a few weeks ago the Government accepted that "overwhelming humanitarian necessity" might allow military action out of area which was not specifically authorised by the United Nations Charter or by the Security Council. However, the Foreign Office later made quite clear (see Written Answer from Baroness Symonds to Lord Kennet, 16 November 1998) that this could lawfully happen only in "exceptional" circumstances, "on a case by case basis". "There is no general doctrine of humanitarian necessity in international law".

And when NATO threats were made to Milosevic, in spite of anticipated objections from Russia and China in the Security Council, retrospective approval was subsequently sought and obtained from the Security Council. Nevertheless the United States's Mr Holbroke Claimed that these at the time unauthorised threats to Milosevic amounted to a precedent for a new NATO doctrine: but his claim was denied by several European members of NATO. The value of the "precedent"—similar to Helms condition 1.—would have been to ensure that neither Russia nor China, nor indeed France, should be able to "meddle" in American or NATO policy. (The word "meddle" is routinely used by American officials in this context.) The same doctrine in a non-NATO context has just been seen in operation against Iraq, when the US and Britain formed a "coalition of the willing" of two, under US leadership.

It is by no means clear that Europe's "interest and values" do always today, or in the future always will, coincide with those of an increasingly unilateralist United States. The US fails to pay its dues to the United Nations; widely claims extraterritorial jurisdiction; in the view of the EU misuses the World Trade Organisation; fails to go along with "Kyoto" or with the ban on anti-personnel landmines; displays double standards in the Middle East concerning ownership and production of weapons of mass destruction; attempts for domestic political (anti-Iranian) reasons to disrupt the commercial development of the Caspian oil province; increasingly uses capital punishment; and so on. The US is also apparently intending unlawful actions in the military field, such as the offensive militarisation of space: laser weapons for deployment in space are being developed.

And in the opinion of many governments, the US attitude to the existing disarmament and arms control agreements to which it is a party is often cavalier. Thus, the spirit of the Comprehensive Test Ban is breached by computerised "virtual reality" nuclear weapon testing; the text of the Non-Proliferation Treaty is being breached (articles 1, 4 and 6); the (US-Russian) ABM treaty would not survive the deployment of the national anti-ballistic missile defense system Congress is seeking to fund; and the production of tritium for military purposes is being resumed.

The geographical scope of "out-of-area" NATO must also give rise to misgivings. Partnership-for-peace "activities, and activities 'in-the-spirit-of-Partnership-for-Peace'" are already, and increasingly, carried out, often at American expense, in areas very far from the North Atlantic. It looks as though they may very well link up fairly soon with the exercises which are already carried out, in the Far East under some "Pacific Rim" title, in which even the UK already occasionally participates. The geographical area of operation of the US-Japan Security Agreement is not known, but appears elastic. Certainly many of these activities do not seem compatible with Mr George Robertson's admirable "Defence Diplomacy" which the SDR also advocated.

European electorates, particularly East European electorates, are unlikely to want to increase their defence budgets, particularly at the expense of health, education and environmental reclamation (see polls carried out in Poland, Hungary and the Czech Republic by USIS researchers in 1997.) From the West European point of view there is probably already too much militarisation of relations between NATO and the countries of Eastern Europe, between NATO and the ex-USSR countries right into Central Asia, and bilaterally between the United States and all these countries. (About the last of these, the NATO allies are not informed.) Russia of course prefers the OSCE to NATO and indeed the Conservative Government explicitly (Mr Portillo in Kiev, autumn 1996) restricted NATO out-of-area action to that authorised by the United Nations Security Council or by the OSCE.

The need of all arms industries—American, British, Russian, North Korean, Israeli—to promote their product and to sell it abroad has brought about a competition in taxpayer subsidy for arms exports, and substantial lobbying. (The US arms industry thought it worth while to spend some $50 million lobbying in favour of NATO expansion—an exercise our own Ministry of Defence has stated it is unaware of).

In the UK, the arms industry receives, or benefits from, state money from a Defence Sales Fund, from a Defence Military Assistance Fund, from a Defence Policy Fund, and of course in the mainline of Defence Procurement itself. It is also supported by the FCO and the DTI. ECGD is said to be currently handing over roughly £1 million a day to British Aerospace because Saudi Arabia is not meeting its commitments. All of which suggests that no more in this country than in others is tax-payer money always spent on what is, nationally or globally, most important or most rewarding. What would be rewarding is the solution of soluble problems, including the reduction of lethal conflict. Conflict is how people react to injustice and frustration. The arms we and others hand over, whether by sale or only too often otherwise, feed the conflicts that kill people who would prefer to live.

None the less, Condition 3 indicates Senator Helms' belief, which is shared by many members of the US Senate, that the European members of NATO are not contributing enough to the maxi-NATO they see as part of the global strategy of the United States in the execution of its role of "sole military super-power".

This global strategy comprises:

— the ability to fight two major regional wars at once, in which the opponent is assumed to be able to field weapons no less effective than those fielded by the United States;

— the establishment of "Full Spectrum Dominance" by 2010, to include Space Dominance, Information Warfare Dominance, and both Nation-wide and Alliance-wide Anti-Missile Defenses;

— the operation of a Defense Counterproliferation Program, pre-emptive if necessary, and, according to Presidential Decision Directive 60 (of November 1997), possibly making use of nuclear weapons, against others' Weapons of Mass Destruction;

— a "Revolution in Military Affairs" that leaves us Europeans at the wrong end of a "technological disconnect" (the phrase is that of the German General Klaus Naumann, recently Chairman of the NATO Defence Committee);

— a Central Intelligence Agency costing some $28 billion a year;

— ensuring, through direct funding and through military collaboration, a permanent "military edge" in the Middle East for Israel, including newly "enhancing" Israel's "deterrent capability", funding its anti-ballistic missile defenses, providing real-time space-derived intelligence, etc. etc.;

— the permanent maintenance of an (increasingly unwelcome) military force of 100,000 in the Far East;

and also of

— some tens of thousands of people in this country conducting intelligence activities some of which do not appear to be monitored by British nationals and which may well include commercial surveillance.

Russia remains opposed to NATO enlargement, as do the majority of the well-informed in the United States and in this country. That there is apparently now to be a pause in expansion is good. But the globalisation of NATO no longer depends on its explicit expansion now there are bilateral military agreements between the United States and the Baltic and other ex-Soviet States, and what is now being sought in the revision of the Strategic Concept is allied consensus of the legitimacy of NATO's—and the United States'—global role, as an alternative to the United Nations system.

This is misconceived.

In the long run Russia is a rich country with massive natural resources and China has a huge sense of its historical importance. Japan is increasingly loath to accept American economic direction. The Euro now faces the Dollar in the financial markets. The imposition by the US of injustices or frustrations on other societies through unrestricted Free Markets will undermine any empire it may seek to set up. Not even a militarily Full Spectrum Dominant United States will be able to run an economically globalising and socially fragmenting world. The United Nations and the rule of as much international law and collaborative effort as we can get is the only way ahead that is likely to be sustainable in anything but the shortest run.

When the Helms mandatory conditions became public knowledge last Spring, the British Government claimed they were purely a domestic matter for the Untied States. It is now clear they are also a matter for European Government and Parliaments. Our own Government is today facing a newly actual choice between increasing military co-operation with our European neighbours on the one hand—as recently advanced by the Prime Minister—and on the other automatic support for United States military decisions. Hitherto it has usually accepted the latter, and at the recent North Atlantic Assembly meeting in Edinburgh the Chairmen of two House of Commons Select Committees, along with two US colleagues, successfully tabled amendments which deleted references to the United Nations from the Assembly's main Resolution, thus causing the Resolution to place the authority of NATO above that of the UN.

The sum up, there is now no longer a fence for us to sit on. We the British have explicitly to choose, within NATO, between a Helms-led United States and our European neighbours; and in the wider world, between a Helms-led United States and the United Nations. For Britain to remain the uniquely subservient ally of the one member of the Security Council which is systematically enfeebling the United Nations itself and the existing structure of international law, befits neither our history nor our interests.

Memorandum submitted by CND on NATO's Strategic Concept

INTRODUCTION

CND is opposed to NATO primarily because it is, and appears intent upon remaining, a military nuclear alliance with an aggressive nuclear doctrine. We are also concerned about its future direction and the implications this could have on future European as well as global security, particularly with relations with Russia.

Rather than taking up the Committee's time expressing views which have undoubtedly been expressed by other people on the dangers of current and future expansion plans, particularly if NATO starts to move into the baltic states, we would like to devote this submission to "nuclear weapons and NATO"—the one area that will undoubtedly receive little, if any attention, during discussions about NATO's future role.

NUCLEAR WEAPONS AND NATO

"Kosovo is not only an immediate crisis—it is also an illustration of the complexity of today's security challenges. We cannot overcome these challenges with yesterday's formulas and recipes. For NATO, thus, celebrating its 50th anniversary can only mean looking ahead; getting ready for the challenges of the next century. NATO's evolution throughout the 1990s laid the groundwork. The Washington Summit will bring together the different aspects of NATO'S adaptation and set out the way ahead."[1]

NATO NUCLEAR DOCTRINE

"We reaffirmed the fundamentally political role of the Alliance's nuclear forces, as described in the Strategic Concept: to preserve peace and prevent coercion and any kind of war. Nuclear forces play a unique and essential role in the Alliance strategy of war prevention. Their presence ensures uncertainty in the mind of any potential aggressor about the nature of the Allies' response to aggression. Thus, they contribute uniquely to demonstrating that aggression of any kind is not a rational option. We recognise that, in the current security environment, the circumstances in which any use of nuclear weapons might have to be contemplated are extremely remote. We confirmed that the Alliance's nuclear forces will be maintained at the minimum level sufficient to ensure achievement of Alliance political goals." [Final Communiqué, Ministerial Meeting of the Defence Planning Committee and Nuclear planning Group, NATO Press Communiqué, 17 December 1998].

Current NATO nuclear weapons policy was launched at the Rome Summit in November 1991—a month before the collapse of the Soviet Union

Current NATO nuclear weapons policy is "yesterday's formula" stuck deep in the depths of Cold War ideology and desperately needs revising.

Dramatic changes have occurred in the world security environment. NATO no longer faces the threat of all out war in Europe. The conflicts are now of a social, political, economic and environmental nature both within and outside the NATO area, both intra-state and inter-state.

Nuclear weapons can have no role to play in any of these types of conflict. What use are they in dealing with the problems in the Balkans, for example?

There are a number of things wrong with NATO nuclear policy. Below are the major points:

— NATO retains the unexamined belief that nuclear weapons prevent conflict. Rather than entering into a long, theoretical discourse about "deterrence" a practical examination of the types of conflict NATO may be facing in the twenty-first century is needed and the question asked—"what if any role will nuclear weapons play?" In each scenario. In CND's view the answer in every conceivable scenario would be "none". Most nations have never subscribed to "nuclear deterrence" and have never sought to obtain a nuclear arsenal. Most nations rely upon conventional forces backed up by diplomatic, legal and economic methods. Why should the NATO alliance be any different?

— NATO rationale for retaining nuclear weapons was used last year by Pakistan and India to justify their nuclear ambitions. After all, if NATO continues to emphasise the importance of nuclear weapons why should states in regions that are in a far more perilous position be expected not to seek to acquire nuclear weapons for their own defence?

---

[1] Speech by NATO Secretary General, Dr Javier Solana, Rome, 25 January 1999.

— NATO belief that nuclear weapons can be used as a form of "political backmail" as demonstrated in such phraseology as *"maintained at the minimum level sufficient to ensure achievement of Alliance political goals"* displays a belief in the political usefulness of nuclear weapons that you have the power and status to get what you want or else. The proliferation of such a belief is not to be encouraged.

— NATO's retention of nuclear weapons breaches the nuclear Non-Proliferation Treaty (NPT) on two counts. Articles I and II outlaw the passing on of any information by any nation concerning nuclear weapons or the possession of such weapons to any other nation who is not a declared nuclear weapons state. NATO has done the opposite by including non-nuclear weapon member stated in its nuclear doctrine—turning them all into *de facto* nuclear weapon states. Article VI obliges all nations to work towards attaining a world free of nuclear weapons. NATO is doing the opposite by continuing to attach political and military importance to nuclear weapons.

NATO's NUCLEAR STOCKPILE

NATO currently has at its disposal some 150 US free-fall nuclear bombs for use by NATO aircraft. These are stored in Germany, Great Britain, Italy, Turkey, Belgium, the Netherlands and Greece.

NATO also has at its disposal, if required, the one operational British Trident submarine, the two operational French Triomphante submarines and several US Trident submarines totalling a further 400 plus nuclear weapons.

This makes NATO the fourth largest possessor of nuclear weapons in the world.

Basing of nuclear weapons on the soil of NATO members and the pivotal political and military role nuclear weapons continue to play in NATO defence and foreign policy, changes the status of those countries from being non-nuclear nations within the nuclear Non-Proliferation Treaty to being nuclear nations: a breach of Article I and II of the NPT.

Yet, the tactical nuclear weapons deployed for NATO use have no military role. They are seen as a very visible sign of America's continued commitment to NATO and European security—the glue that keeps America and NATO together.

This is made clear in the Strategic Concept where it states that *"nuclear forces based in Europe and committed to NATO provide an essential political and military link between the European and North American members of the Alliance . . . "*[1]

A recent Canadian Parliamentary Committee investigation was told during evidence gathering that, concerning NATO, tactical nuclear weapons deployment "political value far exceeds any potential military value these weapons might have."[2]

The current Strategic Concept encompassed a view that "with the radical changes in the security situation" NATO's nuclear forces could be dramatically reduced in size and roles. This led to the withdrawal of all NATO nuclear weapon except the 150 or so that remain on NATO soil today.

This conclusion should be extended when NATO publishes its new Strategic Concept in the spring in Washington. NATO should remove the last remaining nuclear weapons deployed for use by NATO forces on European soil. This would display, as with the current Strategic Concept, the de-emphasise of the political and military value NATO has attached to nuclear weapons and instead a greater commitment as an alliance to rid the world of nuclear weapons.

This would also provide a much needed buffer zone between Russian nuclear forces and NATO. De-emphasising their importance within NATO doctrine would also send the clearest signal to Russia and the world that a belief in nuclear weapons as weapons of war is in the past and not of the future.

EXPANDING THE NATO NUCLEAR CLUB

One reason why NATO's expansion is seen by Russia as a threat is because NATO can now deploy weapons along the Russian border. The *de-facto* nuclear weapons free zone that existed in the past between these two neighbours will no longer exist and will be further eroded by future expansion.

The often quoted reassurance NATO gave to Russia in this regard was:

> *"The member states of NATO reiterate that they have no intention, no plan and no reason to deploy nuclear weapons on the territory of new members, nor any need to change any aspect of NATO's nuclear posture or nuclear policy—and do not foresee any future need to do so."*

[1] Paragraph 56, NATO's Strategic Concept.
[2] Frank Miller, US Assistant Secretary of defense for International Security Policy in evidence before the Canadian Parliamentary Standing Committee on Foreign Affairs and International Trade during their investigation of Canada's policy on nuclear non-proliferation, arms control and disarmament.

What NATO has not offered is a legally binding reassurance that will allow the continuance of the *de-facto* nuclear-weapon free zone in Eastern Europe.

Nation's who choose to join NATO cannot pick and choose from the protocols of accession. As was explained in the "Principles of Enlargement":

> " . . . *new members will enjoy all the rights and assume all obligations of membership under the Washington Treaty; and accept and conform with the principles, policies and procedures adopted by all members of the Alliance at the time that new members join . . . "*

Therefore, there is nothing to stop NATO at some point in the future forcing Poland, Hungary and the Czech Republic to live up to their NATO obligations to accept the deployment of US tactical nuclear weapons on their soil. There is also nothing to stop any of these three nations demanding that nuclear weapons be deployed on their soil as is their right as full members of NATO.

One must also presume that the air forces of Poland, Hungary and the Czech Republic will train with other NATO air forces in the use of tactical nuclear weapons just in case the need ever arises.

Whilst NATO retains it's aggressive pro-nuclear weapons policy, any expansion of its membership will be seen as an expansion of the NATO nuclear club and in Russia as a direct threat to its security.

No-first use

Adopting a policy of "No-First Use" when coupled with the removal of all remaining nuclear weapons from NATO soil would be an important confidence building measure that NATO member states poses no direct threat to Russia, are committed to nuclear disarmament and no longer regard nuclear weapons as a valuable political and military bludgeon.

A policy of "No-First Use" was hinted at in the London Declaration of 1990 (which began the drafting of NATO's current Strategic Concept) where nuclear weapons were described as "truly weapons of last resort".

The logical next step would have been a declaration that only in the instance of a nuclear strike against NATO would nuclear weapons usage be contemplated, i.e., a "no-first use" policy. A policy vociferously opposed by the United States, Britain and France.

The Strategic Concept that appeared later the following year, the one currently in circulation, watered down this view by stating that circumstances arising where their use may be contemplated were now "*even more remote*". This still leaves open the option for NATO to use nuclear weapons in any circumstances including using nuclear weapons first or in response to a conventional conflict occurring.

If this policy is retained and possibly expanded, there is no reason why Russia in particular should not continue with its policy of increased reliance on nuclear forces as opposed to conventional ones as the principal means of response to any future aggression.

Arms control and disarmament

The aim of the nuclear Non-Proliferation Treaty (NPT) is to "*pursue negotiations in good faith on effective measures relating to cessation of the nuclear arms race at an early date and to nuclear disarmament, and on a treaty on general and complete disarmament under strict and effective international control*" under Article VI. This aim can never be fulfilled if NATO retains its current policy of reliance upon nuclear weapons as an essential component of its defence and foreign policy.

The policy choices that NATO makes regarding the deployment and conditions of prospective use for nuclear weapons will increasingly impact the health of the NPT regime. If NATO members continue to support policies that assign a high political value to nuclear weapons, for instance as an essential bulwark of Alliance cohesion, the cost in terms of the effectiveness of global non-proliferation efforts will be significant . . . Presently, NATO policies favouring reliance on nuclear weapons and attaching a high political value to these weapons benefit the Alliance very little, but the cost of these policies is becoming very high in terms of the non-proliferation efforts they impede.[1]

The set of principles and objectives designed to strengthen, promote and implement the NPT regime agreed at the 1995 NPT Review Conference have to date failed to be endorsed by NATO as an alliance.

NATO should formally adopt and include within its Strategic Concept a clear commitment to the main Principles and Objective agreed by NPT members that—as a body NATO is committed to the "*determine pursuit . . . of systematic and progressive efforts to reduce nuclear weapons globally, with the ultimate goal of eliminating those weapons.*"

---

[1] Letter from Ambassador Thomas Graham Jr., to NATO Heads of State, 2 November 1998. For a full copy of the letter, see Appendix A.

No-one should underestimate the significance of such a commitment by NATO as an alliance.

The need for such a commitment by all nations and all defensive alliances was made clear by the Canberra Commission:

> This commitment would change instantly the tenor of debate, the thrust of war planning, and the timing or indeed the necessity for modernisation programmes. It would transform the nuclear weapons paradigm from the indefinite management of a world fraught with the twin risks of the use of nuclear weapons and further proliferation, to one of nuclear weapons elimination.[1]

Not only should NATO be seen to be committed to this objective, NATO should be seen to be fulfilling it.

This is why CND believes that as a precursor, a sign of its commitment to the NPT, NATO should declare a policy of "no-first use" and withdraw all NATO-assigned nuclear weapons currently based on NATO territory.

CONCLUSION

Nuclear weapons have no role to play in NATO or any nation's defence.

As the Strategic Concept currently states:

> "The Alliance's arms control and disarmament policy contributes both to dialogue and to co-operation with other nations, and thus will continue to play a major role in the achievement of the Alliance's security objectives. The Allies seek, through arms control and disarmament, to enhance security and stability at the lowest possible level of forces consistent with the requirements of defence . . . "

The removal of all US tactical nuclear weapons from NATO bases and a policy of "no-first use" are essential first steps in a process of de-emphasising the importance of nuclear weapons within NATO. These measures should be the first concrete signs of a commitment enshrined in any new Strategic Concept to nuclear disarmament.

NATO should be committing itself, through its revised Strategic Concept, to nuclear non-proliferation and to achieving a world free of nuclear weapons instead of pursuing new rationales for retaining and threatening to use its nuclear arsenal.

Memorandum submitted by the Slovak Republic on the future of NATO

NEW NATO STRATEGIC CONCEPT

The Slovak Republic, in its evaluation of the North Atlantic Treaty Organisation, starts from two fundamental aspects of the NATO development that are to become also a part of the new NATO strategic concept:

> Continuity in fundamental questions about the NATO operating, and

> Paying respect to the Euro-Atlantic area security situation changes.

Continuity

Common values such as democracy, human rights and the rule of the law.

Fundamental elements of the allied security policy: dialogue, co-operation and collective defence.

Attributes of the joint defence system, integrated command structure, necessary defence planning process and political and military consultations.

NATO as political and military organisation.

Principle of Alliance's openness.

Changes

Process of the internal adaptation of the Alliance, whose aims have been defined at the Madrid summit, such as maintaining military efficiency and its ability to face various events, protection of the Transatlantic alliance, development of the European Security and Defence Identity within the Alliance. A component part of the internal adaptation is finalisation of a new command structure and the implementation of the CJTF concept.

---

[1] Canberra Commission, Report of the Canberra Commission on the Elimination of Nuclear Weapons, Commonwealth of Australia August 1996, Canberra. Available on the web at http//www.dfat.gov.au/cc/cchome.html.

Process of external adaptation presented in particular in the process of NATO enlargement, as well as in the process of the Partnership for Peace Programme improvement together with creating a new relationship frame-work between NATO and the Russian Federation.

The Slovak Republic is expecting:

that NATO stays open to other countries;

the process of enlargement will not be connected with creation of new dividing lines;

to become centre of the Co-operative European Security System;

to create political and military support for the process of building the European Security and Defence Identity;

to continue in the efforts to involve the Russian Federation into the system of the European security, striving to change the Russian attitude towards the Alliance (as a condition of a reciprocal co-operation at a qualitatively higher level);

to continue deepening the Partnership for Peace Programme and creating conditions for the partner countries to participate more widely in the NATO programmes through EAPC;

to create political conditions for crisis management.

THE SLOVAK REPUBLIC'S VIEW ON THE INTERNATIONAL SITUATION AND CHANGES, LAYING STRESS ON PREPARATION OF THE DEFENCE OF THE ALLIANCE

Since the Strategic Concept was adopted by the Alliance in 1991, further positive changes have taken place in the security situation in Europe. The process of removing political division of Europe, once presenting a fundamental source of the military confrontation threat, is going on. Through implementing the agreements on control of armament and disarmament and strengthening of confidence and safety, the armament level has dropped down significantly, while the military transparency and mutual confidence have grown. Although at different levels, the changes of establishment of plural democracy, respecting human rights, free market economy and the rule of law are taking place in Central and East European countries. The security system on the basis of increasing the defence co-operation, political consultations and economic integration is being created progressively. The effort of countries to enter the European and Euro-Atlantic structures also plays an important role, because one of the fundamental conditions is the settling the discrepancies with one's neighbours, the roots of which often date back to the last century. However, certain threat to stability may be caused by the feeling that some countries will be left out of this process.

At the same time, the existence of the security challenges, risks and their evaluations contained in the Strategy Concept is being confirmed. However, these have been specified and extended on the basis of the concrete development and, to a certain degree, their hierarchy is changing too. In any case, its a deal that the new environment does not change the mission or security functions of the Alliance, but, on the contrary, underlines their validity.

Existing potential threats, challenges and risk cannot be ignored. The development of the situation in Bosnia confirmed the member states' requirement for capacity to deploy armed forces out of the NATO member states' territory, and for the other countries, it proved that NATO is the best structure to prepare and co-ordinate approaches and to solve the problem on it's own. The variety of risks calls for flexible approaches, non-existence of such limits which would restrict the specific kind of operation, as well as absenting restrictions for the kind and scope of the used armed forces. The Kosovo conflict has revealed the fact that the wide international support in these operations could be negatively influenced through a divergent interpretation of the UN mandate.

The Slovak Republic anticipates that the possible participation of the member countries in operations beyond Article 5 will be embodied.

ENLARGEMENT OF THE ALLIANCE BY THE CZECH REPUBLIC, THE HUNGARIAN REPUBLIC AND THE REPUBLIC OF POLAND, AND FURTHER PROSPECTIVE ENLARGEMENT

The resolutions, taken by the NATO summit in Madrid, about inviting the Czech Republic, Hungarian Republic and the Republic of Poland and non-inviting the Slovak Republic for negotiations bring some changes into the evaluation of the security situation, nevertheless, in any case, it doesn't mean any decline of its security position. There are the following reasons for that:

The selective NATO enlargement being realised in its variant without the Slovak Republic, although it does not mean any full-fledged area security stabilisation of the Central-European territory, it represents an important phase of the process of stability transfer into Central Europe. It started by the integration of three states into the military-political group, the which the Slovak Republic strives to enter as well.

All the three invited countries are neighbours to Slovakia, which with a dominant part of its borders is becoming neighbour to the most efficient security system of Europe.

Accepting common values and consensus principle inside the Alliance creates, at the same time, conditions for eliminating such ambitions of its members, which can not be accepted from the Slovak Republic's national interests point of view.

THE ALLIANCE REMAINS OPEN FOR THE SLOVAK REPUBLIC FOR THE NEXT WAVE OF ENLARGEMENT

In valuation of the further development in the process of the NATO enlargement, the Slovak Republic starts with the following presuppositions:

The development so far has confirmed that for the decision to invite any country into the Alliance, the international context of the enlargement process is of crucial importance, whereas the reasons for the individual countries striving to achieve the security guarantees are less determining for such resolutions.

Although the Alliance lays stress on the peace operations beyond the Article 5 of the Washington Treaty in the first place, it will remain an integrated political-military alliance with its central interest in an effective collective defence, and that is the reason why a strict choice of countries for the enlargement process can be expected.

The time dimension of the next enlargement process will be significantly influenced by the experience of incorporating the three new members into the Alliance.

Progressive and gradual enlargement that would provide enough time for integrating new members can be expected.

It is necessary to respect the fact that the enlargement of NATO and EU are two processes supporting each other and the development of both organisations' enlargement is not wished to differ from each other.

One of the main determinants of the enlargement process is the fact that not all the countries who would wish or need it can be involved, so that further strengthening of the Partnership-for-Peace Program, the co-operation within EAPC, extending security relations with the Russian Federation and Ukraine, as well, are found to be tasks of so great importance as the own enlargement.

Presently, it is not possible to estimate the ambitions of the NATO enlargement in their southern dimension (Slovenia, Rumania) or in their northern dimension (Lithuania).

CONTINUITY OF APPLICABILITY OF THE WASHINGTON TREATY AND ITS MILITARY STRUCTURE

The Washington Treaty document is based on formulating the common values, there is no identification of an enemy, it respects the sovereign decision rights of all members and has been formulated flexibly enough, which enables the Alliance to adapt itself to the international conditions in change. This is why even the integrated military structure has been changing according to changes in the strategic environment during the whole existence period of the Alliance.

The CJTF conception presents nowadays crucial component in the internal adaptation of the Alliance. The conception is understood as an expression of the necessity to strengthen the European defence potential of NATO through WEU which is supposed to become a defence body of EU. It expresses the way how to improve the co-operation with WEU and considerate the process of the ESDI creation. At the same time, it enables the possibility to expand PfP towards a larger political and military co-operation, including some peace-keeping operations.

The implementation of CJTF causes a transformation towards smaller but more flexible and mobile forces ant are capable of a quick and effective response tow a wide scale of potential contingencies in development of the political and military situation.

At the same time, a progressive adaptation of the up to the same time predominantly static command structure of the Alliance is going on.

From the Slovak Republic's point of view this refers primarily of the most to a concept enabling the partner countries to be involved in operations, including the participation in their preparation.

ESDI

We consider the framework of the Transatlantic security system as the fundamental condition for ESDI's success.

We consider the settlement to reciprocal relation between EU and WEU at least as much important a the previously named condition.

It is an expression of the reality that EU will become more and more a centre of decision-taking to influence the every-day aspects of the life in Europe. This will particularly be a successful realisation of the currency union, which could be a moving force for the political union as well. However the sinew of the national identity and the will to protect the national sovereignty is still being in effect, which slows down the realisation process of a common foreign and security policy.

While there is no real political unit in Europe existing but several integration levels within the EU structure, it will be difficult to co-ordinate the European countries' defence efforts.

WEU

The previous information shows that WEU will continue to embody the European defence identity within NATO and the base for the European defence co-operation within EU. It will have an important role as a uniting element between NATO and EU.

For WEU, the Washington summit will have a significant importance in confirming and approving the creation of an own security and defence identity. In this way, Europe will take over more responsibility in the framework of the Alliance. NATO's internal adaptation will concurrently contribute to strengthen its capacities necessary for providing crisis management under the leadership of WEU.

From the point of view of the WEU it will be also important to strengthen the foreign and security policy. In accordance with the Amsterdam Treaty, EU will be allowed to use the WEU in order to carry out crisis management in terms of the tasks of the Petersberg meeting.

On account of the initiatives by France and Great Britain, a new area of the European security and defence has been opened, which will have effect on the WEU as well. Nevertheless, the appeal for taking an effective reaction on the situation will depend on the following:

firstly: the European readiness and will to participate in the crisis has to be expressed in a much clearer way;

secondly: strengthening European defence capacities.

COMPREHENSION OF TRANSATLANTIC DIMENSION OF THE ALLIANCE

Transatlantic alliance of Europe and USA will have an important role for European security in the future.

There is a mutual relation: when there is stabile and peaceful Europe, then the USA are also more secure. As far as the USA prosper, Europe prospers too.

The aim should be to build a relationship in which Europe and USA could act together in presenting and defending their common interests in and outside of Europe and in which they would also develop those things that are special.

Although a strong Transatlantic connection is very important at the present time, there also exist certain risks concerning the Euro-Atlantic territory as a whole and these include:

certain problematic areas in Transatlantic relations caused by the pressure to run an independent economic policy and a rise of unilateral protective arrangements as a consequence of this;

tendency leading to a relative decrease in the participation in the defence of Europe considering the increase in diversification of economical and political interests of the USA in the world.

Memorandum submitted by the Ministry of Defence on the St Malo Agreement

The Committee asked for a note on the implications of the declaration on European defence issued at the British French Summit at St Malo on 3–4 December 1998. I attach a copy of the declaration, which is in the public domain.

The Prime Minister opened a debate on European defence and security issues at the informal European Union Summit at Portschach in Austria on 24–25 October 1998. The Government believes that the European Union needs a more unified and influential voice in world affairs, articulated with greater speed and coherence through the Common Foreign and Security Policy (CFSP), and that the development of the security and defence dimension within the EU would reinforce its capacity and standing.

In order to achieve this, the Government believes that the EU must develop the political will and the appropriate tools to be able both to decide and to act quickly and effectively to achieve common goals. The Amsterdam Treaty will create new CFSP instruments, but Europeans also need to enhance our ability to act and develop defence capabilities which are able to cope with future crises, as we are doing through the Strategic Defence Review.

Our opening of this debate has been welcomed by our European partners and by the United States. It is possible that, as the debate develops, it might turn out to have institutional implications, particularly for the Western European Union (WEU). But that is not the premise on which we have started. We want the debate to focus on practical questions of how to improve Europe's ability to decide and act.

We do, however, have certain guiding principles. The Government believes that the capacity for Europeans to act together where the United States and Alliance as a whole are not engaged should be enhanced, building on the existing European Security and Defence Identity arrangements. But the Alliance will remain the foundation of our collective defence and will be the instrument of choice when Europeans and Americans want to take action together. We also want to avoid unnecessary duplication: the new European effort should both reinforce CFSP and strengthen the European contribution to NATO and in turn NATO as a whole. And we want to ensure that other European countries are actively involved in the process, recognising the existing positions of WEU Observers and Associate members, and Associate Partners.

The Committee also asked how the desire for a clearer European identity within NATO, and for the European Allies to take on more of NATO's missions, squares with the Secretary of State's evidence on 14 January 1998 that the proportion of the burden carried by the European Allies was right. Mr Robertson provided this answer in response to a question about NATO budgets. But as the above makes clear, the Government's aim is to ensure that defence expenditure is clearly directed towards strengthening both European defence capabilities and the EU's CFSP. A more effective ability for Europeans to respond together to crises will be good for Europe and for NATO. The European-led NATO extraction force in Macedonia is a clear demonstration that there is no contradiction between these aims.

The debate is at an early stage, but it is already clear that there is a lot of common ground between partners on the issues that we have raised. In particular, we have found that we share with the French the same view of the objectives we want to achieve and the key principles we want to preserve. The two Governments therefore felt that it would be helpful to the Wider European debate to set out that agreed view in a public document at the St Malo Summit. We are continuing to discuss these issues with all our EU partners and NATO allies.

BRITISH-FRENCH SUMMIT, ST MALO, 3-4 DECEMBER 1998

DECLARATION ON EUROPEAN DEFENCE

The Heads of State and Government of France and the United Kingdom are agreed that:

The European Union needs to be in a position to play its full role on the international stage. This means making a reality of the Treaty of Amsterdam, which will provide the essential basis for action by the Union. It will be important to achieve full and rapid implementation of the Amsterdam provisions on CFSP. This includes the responsibility of the European Council to decide on the progressive framing of a common defence policy in the framework of CFSP. The Council must be able to take decisions on an intergovernmental basis, covering the whole range of activity set out in Title V of the Treaty of European Union.

To this end, the Union must have the capacity for autonomous action, backed up by credible military forces, the means to decide to use them, and a readiness to do so, in order to respond to international crises.

In pursuing our objective, the collective defence commitments to which member states subscribe (set out in Article 5 of the Washington Treaty, Article V of the Brussels Treaty) must be maintained. In strengthening the solidarity between the member states of the European Union, in order that Europe can make its voice heard in world affairs, while acting in conformity with our respective obligations in NATO, we are contributing to the vitality of a modernised Atlantic Alliance which is the foundation of the collective defence of its members.

Europeans will operate within the institutional framework of the European Union (European Council, General Affairs Council, and meetings of Defence Ministers).

The reinforcement of European solidarity must take into account the various positions of European states.

The different situations of countries in relation to NATO must be respected.

In order for the European Union to take decisions and approve military action where the Alliance as a whole is not engaged, the Union must be given appropriate structures and a capacity for analysis of situations, sources of intelligence, and a capability for relevant strategic planning, without unnecessary duplication, taking account of the existing assets of the WEA and the evolution of its relations with the EU. In this regard, the European Union will also need to have recourse to suitable military means (European capabilities pre-designated within NATO's European pillar or national or multinational European means outside the NATO framework).

Europe needs strengthened armed forces that can react rapidly to the new risks, and which are supported by a strong and competitive European defence industry and technology.

We are determined to unite in our efforts to enable the European Union to give concrete expression to these objectives.

Memorandum submitted by Ambassador Thomas Graham, President of the Lawyers Alliance for World Security

I appreciate this important opportunity to provide input to the Committee's consideration of the conditions under which the United Kingdom would support the use of nuclear weapons by NATO. While the Cold War has ended and the prospect of a deliberate Russian nuclear attack on NATO targets has receded beyond probability, there are still many threats to the security of the Alliance and its member states. Excessive reliance on nuclear weapons for decades has left the world with thousands of nuclear weapons ready for launch, tons of weapons-usable fissile material at risk for theft or diversion, and numerous states questioning whether or not nuclear weapons are necessary to assert international relevance. These conditions have greatly complicated and increased the risk of nuclear proliferation.

In many ways the danger of a major city in the United States, the United Kingdom, or somewhere else being destroyed by a nuclear weapon is greater now than before. The NATO Alliance clearly commands the destructive power to deter those who can be deterred, but the prevention of proliferation to undeterrable actors has become a chief security concern that will require revision of NATO's Cold War doctrine regarding nuclear weapons. NATO's policy of reserving the right to use nuclear weapons first may have been appropriate during the Cold War, but now it is contrary to our international commitments associated with the Non-Proliferation Treaty, the NPT, and a direct contradiction to our non-proliferation efforts. In 1995, in association with the effort to extend the NPT indefinitely, the United States and the United Kingdom, as well as the other three nuclear weapon states, undertook a formal commitment never to use or threaten to use nuclear weapons against non-nuclear weapon state parties to the NPT, now some 181 countries, unless they attacked in alliance with a nuclear weapons state (no exception was made for chemical or biological weapons). In 1996, the World Court found this commitment to be legally binding. It is difficult to reconcile a NATO first use option with this commitment. The only states which this commitment does not apply to are Russia and China, because they are nuclear weapon states and India, Pakistan, Israel and Cuba because they are not NPT parties. Surely we would not wish to initiate a nuclear war with Russia or China, thus if we are to be faithful to our international commitments, the United States, the United Kingdom, and France—the three nuclear weapon states in the Alliance—the first use option rationally applies only to India, Pakistan, Israel, and Cuba, while it significantly damages our worldwide non-proliferation efforts. It is not easily justified when considered in this light.

The right to use nuclear weapons first was thought to be important to the defense of NATO during the Cold War because of the former Warsaw Pact's superiority in conventional forces. But since the fall of the Soviet Union and the dissolution of the Warsaw Pact, it is NATO which maintains conventional superiority in Europe greater than has ever been enjoyed by any force in history. Continued insistence that the most powerful conventional force in the world would need to use nuclear weapons first strains NATO's credibility, as well as the belief by the world's non-nuclear weapons states that their own security does not require a nuclear weapons guarantee.

The civilized world's principal defense against the proliferation of nuclear weapons to irresponsible states, terrorist organizations, or criminal conspiracies in the Nuclear Non-Proliferation Treaty (the NPT). In order to preserve this necessary foundation of post-Cold War security, NATO's nuclear strategy must be consistent with the non-proliferation priorities of its member states which are all states parties to the NPT. Concluded in 1968, the NPT is the legal framework that establishes the international norm against nuclear proliferation and serves as the foundation for all other efforts to control weapons of mass destruction. When it was being negotiated, many predicted that there could be as many as thirty nuclear weapon states by the end of the 1970s, and who knows how many today, if the trend toward nuclear proliferation had been left unchecked. The NPT gave the world a thirty year respite from further proliferation. While three countries—India, Pakistan, and Israel—remained aloof from the Treaty they were careful not to openly defy the regime; until India and Pakistan did so earlier this year.

Overt nuclear proliferation in South Asia, amid fervent denunciation of the NPT as a discriminatory and even racist regime, and other ominous developments, now threaten to upset the delicate balance on which both nuclear non-proliferation and disarmament depend. The original NPT signatories in 1968—and all of the countries that have joined since to form a nearly global non-proliferation community—agreed that the number of nuclear weapon states in the world should be limited to the five states that already possessed nuclear weapons. The nuclear arsenals of the five were not approved by the NPT; they are specifically challenged by Article VI and their ultimate abolition is mandated by the Treaty. However, the performance of the nuclear weapon states in moving toward nuclear disarmament has been insufficient in the eyes of many non-nuclear weapon states. Many of those that have voluntarily foresworn the nuclear weapon option on the conditions that only five states would have nuclear weapons, and that those five would work toward disarmament, may reconsider their own commitments in light of changes in these conditions. Many have said as much, and if any leave the Treaty regime, more would surely follow.

The threat of use of chemical or biological weapons is not a valid reason to retain a first use policy. First, because the added deterrent value that nuclear weapons give beyond NATO's overwhelming conventional superiority is debatable. Second, because continuing to invest high political value in nuclear weapons erodes the nuclear non-proliferation regime, as described above, and impresses on the world that weapons of mass destruction are necessary instruments of policy. Third, because if we violate our international commitments not to threaten to use or use nuclear weapons first against non-nuclear weapon states because we face chemical or biological weapons threats, we are inviting other states which also face serious chemical and biological threats, such as Iran, to acquire nuclear weapons themselves. Fourth, chemical and biological attacks are unlikely to cause a level of damage proportional to a nuclear responses. Fifth, assuming a truly disastrous chemical or biological attack were perpetrated against a NATO member state, one that would be proportionate to a nuclear response and that could not be stopped without resort to nuclear weapons, the longstanding international legal doctrine of belligerent reprisal would recognize our right to step outside our international commitments in self-defense. NATO's first use policy does not protect us against chemical or biological attacks, it makes nuclear proliferation, and other weapons of mass destruction proliferation, more likely.

The world is at a fork in the road with regard to nuclear proliferation. If the NPT is to be preserved, and the number of states and other groups armed with nuclear weapons is to be limited, all of the Treaty's states parties must work together towards its fundamental goal: the ultimate abolition of nuclear weapons. One milestone will be the Third Preparatory Committee Meeting this Spring for the year 2000 NPT Review Conference. The first two Preparatory Committee Meetings ended in diplomatic disaster, and the third is likely to do the same unless the nuclear weapon states do more to live up to their disarmament commitments. But the NATO Summit, which will happen at almost the same time as the NPT Preparatory Committee Meeting, is likely to reinforce the overly high political value of nuclear weapons by not revising the outdated, Cold War language which pervades the old NATO Strategic Concept document and which extols the value of nuclear weapons. This could lead to a diplomatic train wreck which would gravely endanger the NPT and it should not happen; NATO's strategy review preceding the Summit must be a real review, and those who already realize the dangers of consistency only for the sake of consistency must speak out to make it so. The far too high political value of nuclear weapons, a relic of the Cold War, continues. The Indian Prime Minister said, in effect, after the tests last Spring, that *India is a big country now that we have the bomb.* If this high political value of nuclear weapons is not lowered, nuclear weapons will simply be too attractive politically and the 1945-era technology too simple to acquire for many nations to continue to forswear them. Nothing would do more to lower the political value of nuclear weapons and strengthen the NPT regime than to limit the role of nuclear weapons to the core deterrence function of deterring their use by others—in other words, a pledge by NATO that it will not introduce nuclear weapons into future conflicts—that it will follow a no first use policy.

Canada and Germany have both asked the question of whether or not it is time to revisit NATO's first use policy in light of the end of the Cold War and changed security threats and requirements. This is a timely and important question. If the NATO Summit re-affirms the antiquated, Cold War language of the current Alliance Strategic Concept document without revision, and more importantly if it retains the unqualified first use option, this will have a negative impact on the Third Preparatory Committee Meeting for the 2000 NPT Review Conference which will occur at the same time. The first use policy does not protect the Alliance, but if it does not change, it may contribute to greatly increasing the threat of widespread nuclear proliferation. I was in the United Kingdom last month where I much enjoyed meeting with the Defence Committee among other meetings. Over the last fourteen months I have also led delegations to Bonn, Paris and Ottawa to discuss this important issue, I will be visiting the capitals of Belgium, the Netherlands, Norway, Germany, France, Spain, and Italy early this year. I am undertaking this effort because I believe NATO will adopt a no first use policy; it is only a matter of when. The issue is too important and close to the surface to go away. But there is considerable danger if we wait too long to take this action. If we continue to insist that despite the greatest conventional military advantage the world has ever known and thousands of nuclear weapons available if that conventional advantage were to be somehow not enough, we must explicitly retain the option to use nuclear weapons first, we are sending a clear message to the world: nuclear weapons are essential for security and greatness. The world is beginning to understand this message and before long it may be impossible to convince twenty, fifty, or a hundred nations otherwise. In such a world, security and greatness would be beyond the reach of all.

Memorandum submitted by the Ministry of Defence on NATO's involvement in Kosovo

(15 February 1999)

The situation in Kosovo remains a threat to the peace and security in the region, raising the prospect of a humanitarian catastrophe. The focus of international efforts remain on the political track. NATO is taking sensible contingency preparatory measures to ensure that it is ready to respond as required.

On 13 October 1998, NATO approved an Activation Order (ACTORD) for limited air strikes and a phased air campaign which would be executed after 96 hours. Against this background, President Clinton's special envoy, Richard Holbrooke, was able to reach an agreement with President Milosevic on 14 October. The key points of this agreement were:

— full compliance with United Nations Security Council Resolution 1199;

— an Organisation for Security and Co-operation in Europe (OSCE) verification mission of around 2,000 personnel with substantial and intrusive powers;

— aerial surveillance and verification by NATO, with Former Republic of Yugoslavia (FRY) Radar and Air Defence Systems either removed from Kosovo or placed in cantonment sites and not operated;

— agreement to complete negotiations on a framework for a political settlement by 2 November.

NATO military commanders also secured undertakings from Milosevic on 24-25 October that he would draw down Serb security forces in Kosovo to pre-March levels by 27 October. On the basis of an assessment that FRY security forces were complying to a significant degree with this undertaking, although compliance was not complete, the North Atlantic Council (NAC) decided not to take military action, but extended the ACTORD until further notice, with a further NAC decision required before any action could be taken.

The NATO air verification flights started on 17 October (two UK Canberra aircraft were made available to participate in the operation). The aims of the operation are threefold:

— verification of the cease-fire by all parties through the use of unarmed and unmanned aerial vehicles;

— assessment of the situation through the collection, validation and analysis of data;

— reporting of compliance to the North Atlantic Council, United Nations and the OSCE.

Under the agreement signed between the FRY and the OSCE, the security of the Kosovo Verification Mission, whose task is to verify the maintenance of the cease-fire, is the responsibility of the FRY authorities and the OSCE. However, a NATO Extraction Force has been established in Macedonia, to extract OSCE verifiers in an emergency if other precautions (in particular early unassisted evacuation by the verifiers themselves) fail. The United Kingdom is contributing a Warrior Company Group. Our overall commitment to the force for the first six months (after an initial surge of enabling personnel) is about 390 personnel.

Following the killing of 45 Kosovar Albanians at Racak on 15 January 1999, Generals Naumann and Clark, the Chairman of the NATO Committee and the Supreme Allied Commander Europe (SACEUR), visited Milosevic on 20 January to give him a clear message to comply with the October agreements.

On 20 January, in the light of the deteriorating situation, SACEUR decided to reduce the notice to employ NATO aircraft for air strikes under the existing Activation Orders (approved in October, and which remained in effect, but which required a further Council decision to trigger air strikes) from 96 hours to 48 hours. In response to this, the UK redeployed four Harrier GR7 ground attack aircraft and an additional tanker aircraft to Italy to join other UK and NATO forces. The total of NATO aircraft committed to the NATO operation numbers over 300, with the UK contributing eight Harrier GR7s and two tankers.

On behalf of the NAC, the NATO Secretary-General issued a solemn warning on 28 January to Milosevic and the Kosover Albanian leadership, supporting the diplomatic efforts of the Contact Group, demanding compliance by the Parties with their existing commitments to the international community, demanding agreement to the proposals to be issued by the Contact Group for completing an interim political settlement, and making clear NATO's determination to halt the violence and support the completion of negotiations on an interim political settlement for Kosovo, thus averting a humanitarian catastrophe. Steps to this end included acceptance of both parties of the summons to begin negotiations at Rambouillet by 6 February 1999 and completion of the negotiations of an interim political settlement within the specified timeframe; full and immediate observance by both Parties of the cease-fire and by the FRY authorities of their commitments to NATO, including by bringing VJ and Police/Special Police force levels, force posture and activities into strict compliance with the NATO/FRY agreement of 25 October 1998; and the ending of excessive and disproportionate use of force in accordance with these commitments.

If these steps are not taken, NATO has said it is ready to take whatever measures are necessary in the light of both parties' compliance with international commitments and requirements. The NAC agreed on 30 January that the NATO Secretary General may authorise air strikes against targets on FRY territory. In reaching his decision on military action, the NATO Secretary General will take full account of the position and actions of the Kosovar leadership and all Kosovar armed elements in and around Kosovo. He will also consult Allies before taking his decision.

Proximity talks in Rambouiilet near Paris started on 6 February 1999. Whilst these are taking place, work continues at NATO on military preparations. In addition to activity in the areas described above, planning is underway to prepare for a possible NATO ground force to implement any peace agreement.

Together with our Allies, we are making contingency preparations to be able to respond and deploy rapidly, if required, and following a peace agreement. As part of these preparations, the UK decided on 11 February to send to the Balkans region the vehicles and other heavy equipment of the units that would form the leading elements of any deployment. The majority of the personnel from these units will remain at home bases, and a decision whether or not they are deployed later will depend on how the situation develops. Some 200 UK logistics personnel are deploying to Greece and Macedonia the region in advance of the arrival of the heavy equipment. The measures the UK and its Allies are taking represent prudent military contingency planning, and do not prejudge any decision to proceed with an operation, a decision which would have to be taken by the UK and its Allies on the basis of a satisfactory outcome to the Rambouillet proximity talks.

Memorandum submitted by the Ministry of Defence answering the Committee's questions on NATO Enlargement and Kosovo

(5 March 1999)

Q1. *Will NATO be better able to deliver its "new missions" as a result of enlargement?*

A1.   Countries invited to join NATO must be ready and willing to assume the responsibilities and obligations of membership, and to contribute to the full range of Alliance missions. Before the Madrid Summit, the Czech Republic, Poland and Hungary had already demonstrated their commitment to enhancing European security. Forces from all three were deployed in the NATO-led operations in Bosnia, the most prominent example of NATO's "new missions". They were leading contributors to Partnership for Peace and to co-operation and dialogue, with NATO members, their immediate neighbours and across Europe. In addition to their proven commitment to NATO's "new missions", the Alliance's decision to invite these three countries to accede also took account of their ability to fulfil obligations related to Alliance collective defence.

 The invited countries will therefore bring with them the expertise they have developed as NATO Partners, as well as their wider political contribution. As the Committee's Third Report of Session 1997–98 (HC 469) recognised, it will take some years for the three new Allies to integrate fully into the Alliance's military structures. We share the Committee's conclusion, however, that the three invited countries were the most ready of the aspirant countries to join the Alliance, and contribute to the full range of Alliance activities and missions. Their capacity to contribute to the range of Alliance missions will, moreover, increase in line with progress on integration, and with the more general evolution of the Alliance's military capability in support of these missions. NATO will be stronger as a result of the accession of the three new members.

Q2. *Does the UK have a clear policy on further enlargement?*

A2.   The Government strongly supports NATO's Open Door policy set out in paragraph 8 of the Declaration issued by the Madrid NATO Summit on 8 July 1997, which continues to govern the Alliance's approach to its further enlargement. This confirms that the Alliance will continue to welcome new members in a position to further the principles of the Treaty and contribute to security in the Euro-Atlantic area. HMG's support for this approach has been set out on a number of occasions, for instance in the Prime Minister's statement to the House on 9 July 1997 (*Official Report*, columns 937 to 938), and the Memorandum submitted in October 1998 for the current Enquiry.

Q3. *What is the UK's view about the future of Partnership for Peace?*

A3.   The UK strongly supports the Partnership for Peace and its progressive development as an extremely valuable part of the European security environment. Following the decision at the NATO Foreign Ministers meeting at Sintra in May 1997, important steps have been taken to strengthen all aspects of the Partnership. These include the further development of the Planning and Review Process, and the establishment of Partnership Staff Elements in the military Structure of the Alliance Work is also continuing on developing the Political-Military Framework for NATO-led Peace Support Operations which will set out the principles which will govern future Partner participation in such operations: we expect this to be agreed at the Washington Summit.

Q4. *Is the UK's influence within the Alliance being diluted by enlargement—we now have no UK-based NATO command centres, and fewer senior officers at SHAPE?*

A4.   The UK will continue to play a leading role in the Alliance, based on the quality as well as the quantity of our armed forces and our commitment to Alliance political and military objectives. The EASTLANT Regional Command will continue to be based at Northwood; we continue to command the ACE Rapid Reaction Corps (ARRC), NATO's only large, deployable high-readiness reaction force in Europe and be the main contributor to the ARRC headquarters; and we will continue to paly a leading role in both SHAPE and SACLANT. At SHAPE, the posts of Deputy Supreme Allied Commander Europe (DSACEUR) and Chief of Staff (COS) will be shared between UK and Germany ensuring that there is always a UK member of the SHAPE Command team. At SACLANT we will continue to hold the post of Deputy Supreme Allied Commander. In Europe, as part of the command structure review a new command, RC North, will be formed from the amalgamation of the two existing North European Major Subordinate Commands. The new command will be the senior European command position in the Alliance and the posts of Commander and Deputy will be held rotationally between the UK and Germany. This level of representation reflects the very considerable contribution the UK makes to NATO, both in the Northern region and more widely, and will not be diluted by enlargement.

Q5. *What advice has the Secretary of State received on the consequences for overstretch in the Army of:*

> *a six-month deployment to Kosovo?*

> *an indefinite deployment to Kosovo?*

A5. The Secretary of State concluded, after considering all advice, that maintaining a deployment in Kosovo in parallel with a significant commitment in Bosnia and the Army's other responsibilities will be very demanding. There are likely to be effects on tour intervals, training and the rate at which we are able to implement some aspects of the SDR, all of which could contribute towards increased overstretch. A deployment in Kosovo will nonetheless be manageable, although we will look to reduce the number of troops deployed as soon as is militarily prudent to do so. For example, troop numbers shall fall markedly once HQ ARRC completes its tour. We shall also be examining the scope to reduce further our military contribution in Bosnia.

Q6. *On what advice did Lord Gilbert make his statement about a deployment to Kosovo adding greatly to overstretch in the Army [Lords Hansard, 11 February 1999, Column 389]?*

A6. Lord Gilbert made his statement on the basis of the analysis and conclusions outlined in the answer to the first question above.

Statement submitted by the Russian Ambassador on relations between Russia and NATO
(26 November 1998)

Next year the NATO will celebrate its 50th anniversary.

It is natural that on such occasions one feels duty bound, to point out achievements of any organisation and almost totally ignore its inherent faults.

Since Russia assesses the nature of the NATO and its performance in these 50 years differently than its members it is not prepared to join the chorus of voices to praise its half a century's record. My intention today is to address the present and the future rather than the past as well as the alliance's relations with Russia.

It is generally agreed that the world situation in the 90s has dramatically changed in comparison with the circumstances, which propelled the NATO to existence.

In evaluating the present geostrategic situation, particularly in Europe, one can conclude that on the threshold of the 21st century we have together rid the world community of a heavy burden—the global confrontation between two opposing political systems which was the main driving force of the Cold war.

In its place a new process has begun, one of transition to a multipolar world order with a growing variety of political, economic and cultural structures. This process leads to a closer interweaving of interests and consequently to the realisation that partnership in interstate relations is essential.

These changes have affected the military sphere too. Today it is an established fact, except in the minds of some kremlinologists, that Russia and the NATO no longer regard each other as adversaries. This is turn has reduced to practically zero the probability of large-scale military conflicts in Europe. Moreover, a partnership in maintaining peace and security on the continent has begun to take shape.

The NATO-Russia Founding Act is a telling example. It is a document of great international significance and it will, if properly put to use, play an important part in European relations.

Certainly, the situation in Europe and in the world at large is still far from stable. While the simplistic stereotypes of the Cold war era are receding, the risks and threats in the world, albeit of a different nature, are unfortunately not diminishing.

In spite of the fact that the line of military confrontation between the two blocs has been erased from the map of Europe, there are still forces striving to draw new dividing lines. Regional hostilities emanating from ethnic, national or religious differences are dangerous breeding-grounds of tension. We must also take account of the threats posed by the growth of religious fundamentalism and by the spread of international terrorism and drug trafficking.

Devising effective responses to these new challenges and threats to the security of Europe should therefore be major priority for us all.

It is often heard from the NATO quarters that the alliance is at a watershed today and is reforming itself. Work over an updated version of its strategic concept for the XXI century is referred to. We agree that this work has tremendous importance and could have far-reaching repercussions not only for the NATO but beyond it.

In the new circumstances in Europe the NATO, no doubt, has a real chance to transform itself from a predominantly military bloc to an organisation truly at the service of peace and stability in Europe, as part of a new security architecture evolving in Europe through efforts of all states of this continent.

Russia, as is known, put forward a concept of a security architecture for Europe in conformity with the principles of the Helsinki Final Act, signed by all European states, US and Canada, and based on the Organisation for Security and Co-operation in Europe (OSCE), the only international organisation on the European continent that comprises unlike the NATO, all states of Europe and fully reflects their interests in its activities, ensures that all have equal rights irrespective of their membership in various alliances, military or otherwise.

The NATO could certainly play a constructive role in this process. The Russia-NATO partnership could substantially contribute to overcoming the remnants of the division of Europe and to meeting jointly new challenges and risks to peace and security.

However, for that this military alliance must, in our view, evolve in the direction of a political body and shed its threatening posture towards non-member states.

Relations with the NATO are a very sensitive subject for us in Russia. How to build co-operation with the alliance remains constantly under close scrutiny nationally and by the Russian public and state institutions, it is in the centre of political battles and will be even more so as the parliamentary elections of 1999 and the presidential campaign of 2000 draw closer. We are fully conscious that the character of the Russia—NATO relations will in many respects determine the tendencies in the European politics today and in the next century.

At present our relations are legally and politically based upon the Founding Act on mutual relations, co-operation and security between Russia and the NATO. The way to the signing of this document was not easy. It involved tough negotiations and required a strong political will on both sides to elaborate mutually acceptable formulas. Certainly, the Founding Act remains a compromise document. However, under the present circumstances it is optimal from the point of view of interests of both sides. its major achievement is that a limit was put to possible negative consequences of the NATO expansion toward Russia's borders which we continue to strongly deplore.

The understanding that has been reached on permanent consultations and co-operation within the framework of the NATO-Russia Permanent Joint Council provides a basis for extending co-operation and for arriving at mutually acceptable solutions to the existing problems between Russia and the NATO. Actually the PJC is already working. We effectively co-operate in facilitating the peaceful settlement in Bosnia. We discuss and bridge gaps in our approaches towards resolving acute international crises, find common ground on ways of strengthening the non-proliferation regime.

It is, however, too early to speak in terms of a qualitative breakthrough in the NATO-Russia relations. Both sides approach almost diametrically the role and the place of the NATO in the construction of the system of European security. The Kosovo crisis too revealed substantial disagreements between Russia and the NATO.

Whereas Russia sees the OSCE as the key organisation for maintaining security and stability in Europe the NATO clearly aspires for making the alliance the core of security on our continent. One can speak of a forced export of the NATO—centered security ideology and of a tendency to repudiate other security attitudes. Even ideas about the convergence of different security approaches is frowned upon.

The NATO ideologues seem to draw rather strange conclusions from the radically changed situation on the continent.

Instead of reuniting Europe the reforms proposed could in fact lead to deepening the divisions on the continent and to a resurgence of tensions.

Three main dangers which could jeopardize mutually advantageous co-operation between Russia and the North Atlantic alliance should be acknowledged.

First and foremost a rather determined pursuit by the NATO of its "open door" policy. The implementation of existing plans, in their present form, could surely be a destabilising factor in European relations.

Especially sensitive is the idea of admission to the alliance of former Soviet republics, in the first place the Baltic States. It is an open secret that if anyone of these states is enticed into the NATO we shall have to reconsider or relations with the alliance.

As a sort of compensation for the NATO eastward enlargement Russia is offered the assurances, mostly verbal, that the NATO is undergoing evolution from a largely military bloc to more and more a peacemaking organisation and that its expansion therefore should not be seen in Russia as menacing her borders or interests in Europe. Surely we take note of these assurances. But we remember the well known maxim formulated by our renewed actor and theatre director K Stanislavsky: "If you see a gun hanging on the wall in the first act of a play the gun will certainly fire in the third act". Thus Russia deems it necessary to be ready for any eventuality.

Secondly. What gives rise to serious concerns in Moscow are efforts of the NATO to appropriate a political and military role globally especially a new assertive role for itself in regions beyond the geographical zone of responsibility of the alliance as set forth in Articles 5 and 6 of the Washington Treaty. Some of the NATO members are even inclined to project force freely without any constraint from the UN Security Council beyond NATO's frontiers as the sine qua non of effective security. If these ideas are put in practice the planned functional and operational expansion of the NATO will result in legal nihilism with as yet unforeseen consequences of the world order.

Foreign Secretary Robin Cook recently quite rightly stressed in his article: " . . . We must uphold the sanctity of international law and the United Nations. If we abandon them, we lose the only objective standard by which a country can steer its course. The rule of the strongest would be substituted for the rule of law". This statement is very consonant with democratic Russia's attitudes.

However, in Kosovo the NATO members have in fact transgressed the sanctity of international law by declaring their readiness to use armed force without the specific authority of the UN Security Council against a sovereign nation and over an internal conflict. The appropriation by the NATO of the right to decide to what extent UN Security Council Resolution N 1199 is to be implemented, without any doubt, is unacceptable. Such right belongs exclusively to the Security Council, which upon consideration of the reports by the UN Secretary-General may come to certain conclusions and undertake appropriate measures, if necessary. This provision acquires vital importance when the question arises about adopting decisions on such a serious matter of principle as pressure by the use of force.

By adopting the decision to use force against Yugoslavia on 13 October, the NATO, in fact, laid claim to the prerogatives of the Security Council upon which in accordance with Article 24 of the UN Charter was conferred the primary responsibility for the maintenance of international peace and security.

Moreover this NATO decision contradicts both the NATO-Russia Founding Act and its own legal basis— Washington treaty which remains so far unamended.

In conformity with Articles 5 and 6 of the Treaty the use of armed force can be possible only in case of an armed attack against one or more states-members of the NATO in exercise of the right of individual or collective self-defense recognised by Article 51 of the Charter of the United Nations. The use of force is to be limited by the area of operation of the NATO, namely by territories of any of the parties of the Treaty in Europe and in North America. Belgrade, as everybody is aware, did not invade any NATO members or their territories.

In Article 7 of the Washington treaty it is clearly stated that the treaty "does not affect and shall not be interpreted as affecting in any way the rights and obligations under the Charter of the Parties which are members of the United Nations, or the primary responsibility of the Security Council for the maintenance of international peace and security".

Thus a possibility of force operations of the Alliance beyond the framework of Article 5 of the Washington Treaty bypassing the UN Security Council would in our view:

— signify a revision of the basic principles of the UN Charter by a group of states;

— lead to erosion of the UN Security Council Charter prerogative on the use of force, enforcement measures and its major responsibility for maintaining international peace and security;

— signify violation of existing law and order based on the central role of the UN.

We hope that our NATO partners will take one more look at what their plans and decisions might entail, especially within the framework of the ongoing review of its strategic concept in preparation for the 50th anniversary of the Alliance. I would like to remark in passing that Russia is kept unawares even of the basic elements of the drafts discussed. Seems to be another example of how secretive diplomacy can be.

Meanwhile, it should be clear that any strategic concept of the Alliance disregarding Russia's position and interests, prepared without consultations with Russia will miss its aim, if the aim is increased stability in Europe, and may become a breeding ground for added distrust. The prospect for the Washington summit next year would in this case be bleak indeed.

Thirdly. What could impede mutual co-operation between Russia and the NATO is the clear intention of some of our partners to turn the Russia-NATO Permanent Joint Council into a debating club or a useful reference to prove Russia's presumed acquiescence to the NATO policies. That would in our opinion not only undermine the Founding Act but will make the Council useless for us.

So far as Russia is concerned we shall firmly pursue the constructive line for turning the Russia—NATO Council into a decision making body capable of taking practical actions aimed at the implementation of appropriate provisions of the Founding Act.

It is our conviction that, in spite of the problems that exist, the NATO-Russia Founding Act, is not misused, provides extensive opportunities for creating an atmosphere of trust in Europe. It can facilitate settling existing differences in our relations as well as establishing efficient and productive machinery for co-operation between the military and political establishments of Russia and the NATO member states. Only in this way can we complete our common task of building up a community of free and democratic states in Europe and safeguard durable peace. Russia is determined to move in this direction.

Memorandum submitted by the Romanian Ambassador on the Washington Summit (23-25 April 1999) and the Continuation of NATO Enlargement

To become, as early as possible, a member of the Alliance has been a firm objective of Romania. Since the Madrid Summit, Romania has enhanced its capacity to add to the security and the stability NATO stands for, as well as to the cohesion of the Alliance. Based on its steady efforts to meet the accession criteria and NATO acknowledgement thereof (paragraph 8 of the Madrid Declaration), Romania percieves itself as a credible aspirant to such a status. Romania's first choice would be to receive an invitation to join NATO at the forthcoming Washington Summit.

If, for reasons inherent to the Alliance itself, no new invitations are to be extended by the 1999 Washington Summit, the "second best choice" favoured by Romania consists in:

— a differentiated listing of the eligible aspirants, starting with Romania and Slovenia;

— preservation of the principles according to which the eligibility of Poland, Hungary and the Czech Republic was judged, in 1997, as the yardstick for future invitees;

— approval of a NATO accession Schedule for the designated countries, to stipulate:

   — the year 2000 to be set as the timeframe for launching new invitations to start membership negotiations with the most deserving aspirants;

   — a reasonable horizon for the completion of accession procedures by the years 2002–03, once the absorption of the three new members has been carried out in its key dimensions;

   — assigning to the North Atlantic Council the task of conducting periodical reviews of the progress made by the aspiring countries (see Annex 1);

— launching a set of guidelines and practical measures (a "Madrid plus Package", or a "Membership Accession/Action Program"/MAP/), aimed at enhancing the ability of the eligible aspirants to shoulder NATO's efforts to project stability and security beyond its current area, as well as their preparedness for integration into the Alliance;

   — the achievement of the Program's goals would only be beneficial if MAP were to be jointly pursued by NATO and each aspiring state;

   — designed for all eligible aspirants, MAP should also include parts (components) tailored to the degree of performance level, already reached by each individual candidate.

— once MAP has been adopted by the Washington Summit, its expeditious implementation would be most desirable line of action. The identification, by NATO and each aspiring country, of the best ways to do so, as well as the setting up of an appropriate calender could be rendered as the first steps of an *Upgraded Individual Dialogue (UID)*;

— the UID should focus on:

   — designing a specific accession-preparation strategy meant to cover all the dimensions of the process (political, economic, military, etc.);

   — establishment a well-defined mechanism for progress evaluation;

   — singling out the areas where assistance and closer co-operation are needed for the attainment of MAP's goals;

   — co-ordinating other tracks of the aspirant's relationship with the Alliance, such as PfP (see Annex 2).

Besides the UID, other forms of upgraded co-operation between NATO and each candidate could be considered (see Annex 3).

ANNEX 1

PERIOD REVIEWS BY THE NORTH-ATLANTIC COUNCIL OF ASPIRANTS' PREPAREDNESS FOR INTEGRATION INTO NATO

— Reviews of the aspirants' preparedness (including that of their Armed Forces) to assume the responsibilities and obligations of membership will be made by NAC Ministerials.

— NAC reviews could be organised bi-annually/annually.

— The first of them could be included on the agenda of the NAC Ministerial of December 1999, or Spring 2000, at the least.

— An evaluation in the "19+1" format of the progress made by each candidate should replicate the evaluation pattern applied within NATO for its Member States.

— NAC Ministerial should be entitled to:

(a)   extend invitations for starting membership negotiations (when the progress made by a given aspirant is judged as appropriate);

(b)   decide on the steps and duration of the negotiations.

ANNEX 2

CO-ORDINATION OF MAP AND PFP ACTIVITIES

— As was the case with Poland, Hungary, and the Czech Republic, after the Madrid Summit, the PfP activities for the eligible aspirant countries should be tailored to the membership goals.

— The Alliance could equally envisage new steps aimed at testing the ability of eligible aspirants to contribute to the security of the Euro-Atlantic area, such as:

— defining new, upgraded, Partnership Goals for the eligible aspirants (the attainment of the goals possibly being an early litmus test assessing their ability to contribute to the coherence of the Alliance);

— subject to the conclusions of NAC review meetings, involvement of the best performing eligible aspirants in NATO exercises and other activities, other than the standard PfP or NATO-led PfP exercises.

ANNEX 3

SPECIFIC FORMS OF CO-OPERATION

— Focus on Specific Programs for achieving designated Interoperability Goals with NATO.

— Regular work sessions with various NATO Committees, in accordance with proposed and accepted programs.

— Attendance of certain NAC meetings (at the level of Ambassadors, Foreign and Defence Ministers and Heads of State and Government) and other NATO Working groups and Committees meetings.

— Attendance of certain Military Committee meetings (at the level of Military Permanent Representatives, General Chiefs of Staffs).

— Enhanced consultations, in the "19+1" format, on current regional security issues and accession preparedness.

— Participation of observers at NATO and Applicant Countries' military exercises, intended for testing Forces preparedness for article V-type missions.

— Periodical visits in each applicant County by NATO teams for Programs Assessment, as part of a "feed-back" mechanism.

— Organisation of military exercises, in the "19+1" format, on the national territories of the designated applicant countries.

— Expertise assistance given by various NATO bodies for increasing Forces Interoperability of the Applicant countries (e.g., for the Defence Planning Questionnaires, achieving Interoperability Objectives/PARP, etc.).

— Funds allocation from the NATO Security Investment Program (NSIP) for modernising infrastructure assets to be made available for NATO/PfP missions by the Applicant countries.

— Access to NATO information systems currently available for NATO member countries only.

— The increase of the number of slots at NATO schools for diplomats, political-military experts, and military personnel working in the field of Euro-Atlantic integration, as well as offers for preparation studies and the internships within the Alliance's military structures (e.g., NATO HQ, Strategic Commands, Regional and Sub-regional Commands).

WEDNESDAY 24 MARCH 1999

Members present:

Mr Bruce George, in the Chair

Mr Crispin Blunt	Mr Mike Hancock
Mr Julian Brazier	Mr Jimmy Hood
Mr Jamie Cann	Mr John McWilliam
Mr Harry Cohen	Laura Moffatt
Mr Michael Colvin	Ms Dari Taylor

Examination of Witnesses

RT HON GEORGE ROBERTSON, a Member of the House, Secretary of State for Defence, REAR ADMIRAL SIMON MOORE, Assistant Chief of the Defence Staff (Operations) and MR CHRIS HOLTBY, Secretariat, Ministry of Defence, were examined.

Chairman

356. Secretary of State, thank you very much for coming. I know it has been a terribly worrying time for you. These are very grave times in which we are living. It is unfortunate that, because of the juxtaposition of the continuing crisis in Kosovo and the problem that we were going to spend most of our time on Bishopton, with regret I will say to our colleagues from Bishopton that we do not think it would be appropriate to deal with the problem of Bishopton in what remained of the time after dealing with Kosovo, so I extend my profound apologies to them, especially those who have travelled all the way from Scotland and Bristol to attend. I have spoken to Mr Dromey who fully concurs with the decision that we have made. People from Royal Ordnance know better than anybody the importance of the problems of dealing with external crises and I appreciate, Mr Dromey's decision on this. Again, profuse apologies. Could I welcome you, Secretary of State, in these difficult circumstances. What I propose to do with your permission is to spend at least an hour on the question of Kosovo and then we will leave you to get on with dealing with the problems at hand. Would you like to make an opening statement?

(Mr Robertson) Thank you, Chairman. I appreciate that and I too apologise to those who were and are interested in the future of Royal Ordnance at Bishopton. I asked to come here because I want to get that issue clarified and I am not reneging from that. I hope to have the opportunity of coming to you before you come to your conclusion on that subject, but this is one of the gravest days that we and our NATO colleagues face. I am happy to be in front of the Committee today because I think it gives an additional opportunity, on top of the Prime Minister's statement yesterday and cross-examination to the House, to get what information I can prudently give to the House at this time. In addition to that of course there is coincidentally tomorrow a debate in the House on defence, the Armed Forces in the world, which will again provide an opportunity for the House of Commons in plenary session to discuss that. I will be opening that debate. There are opportunities but the Defence Select Committee is by far the most

appropriate body here for going over some of these details in as much as we can give them. I am accompanied here by Rear Admiral Simon Moore, who is the Assistant Chief of the Defence Staff (Operations), and Chris Holtby, who is from the Ministry of Defence's Balkan Secretariat. Given that we are here at short notice, I hope that we can help you with what information you need. I will say a few words in introduction to provide some further detail on what the Prime Minister said yesterday in the House. As this Committee will already know, last October NATO threatened to use force to secure an agreement from Serbia to a cease fire and an end to the repression that was then taking place in Kosovo. At that time diplomatic efforts, backed up by the threat of NATO military action, led to the creation of the OSCE's Kosovo Verification Mission. The establishment of that mission enabled tens of thousands of Kosovars to return to their homes. We have said to them and to President Milosevic that we would not tolerate the brutal suppression of the civilian population and we must continue to honour that promise to the thousands of innocent civilians who only wish to have an opportunity to live in peace. At that time Milosevic gave an undertaking to the United States envoy, Richard Holbrooke, that he would withdraw Serb forces so that their numbers returned to the level before February 1998. That is roughly 10,000 internal security and 12,000 Yugoslav Army troops. He has not fulfilled that commitment. Indeed, we believe that the numbers have increased and that there are now some 16,000 internal security forces and 20,000 Yugoslav Army troops in Kosovo with a further 8,000 army reinforcements poised just over the border. On the 30 January this year (just a few weeks ago) NATO warned President Milosevic that it would act in order to avert a humanitarian catastrophe which was likely (and still remains likely) if he failed to come into compliance with the October agreements if the repression was continued and if there was no peace agreement. Despite the intense diplomatic efforts which we have all seen he has so far failed to meet any of these requirements. The NATO position is absolutely clear. Our overall political objectives remain to help achieve a peaceful solution to the crisis

[**Chairman** *Cont*]

by contributing to the response of the whole international community. More particularly, NATO made it clear in a statement of the 30 January that its strategy is to curb the violence and support the completion of negotiations on an interim political settlement. That remains our aim but President Milosevic has failed to respond to the most intense diplomatic efforts and the time has now come for NATO to act. Our military objective—our clear, simple, military objective—will be to reduce the Serbs' capability to repress the Albanian population and thus to avert a humanitarian disaster. Military action has the agreement of all 19 NATO nations and to achieve the military objective NATO has available some 200 fast jet aircraft. The United Kingdom has eight Harrier GR7 aircraft equipped with Paveway laser guided bombs. In addition, the United Kingdom is currently providing one air to air refuelling tanker which will support all NATO aircraft and provide a significant multiplier to the NATO force package. At sea we have one of the most potent of weapons available to NATO. HMS Splendid, which is equipped with Tomahawk land attack cruise missiles, is in the area and available for operations. The United Kingdom Tomahawk land attack missile is the conventionally armed, submarine launch missile with a range in excess of 1,000 nautical miles. This Committee will already be familiar with the capability of this weapon system from its operations in the Gulf. In addition, HMS Iron Duke and HMS Somerset are in the Adriatic along with NATO vessels from Germany, Greece, Italy, the Netherlands, Turkey and the United States and a French task force. On the ground there are forces from six NATO nations already in Macedonia: the United Kingdom, France, Germany, Italy, the United States and Norway, but these will not deploy to Kosovo without the consent of both parties following the acceptance of a peace deal. In all some 13,000 troops are immediately available. While at this stage I would not wish to speculate on what elements may be involved in any initial military actions, I would like to stress that whatever action is taken, that action is taken on behalf of all NATO allies with the aim—the clear and, I believe, justified aim—of averting a humanitarian disaster.

357.   Thank you very much. I thought whilst you were making your statement that we could divide the areas of questioning into discrete sections, but I reached the conclusion that we that would be totally impossible so I am afraid, Secretary of State, that you are going to have to face questions moving swiftly from one area of your responsibility to another. The long build-up whilst negotiations have been proceeding turned out to be a fruitless effort on our part but has given us the opportunity of building up sufficient forces for whatever military and political strategy is going to unfold probably over the next few days. Are you satisfied, Secretary of State, that we have sufficient forces *in situ* to meet all of the potential actions that Milosevic might take? It seems to me that ground forces are rather limited in number, particularly in the light of the size of the Yugoslav National Army forces. Are you confident that they will at least be able to defend themselves should there be any of his getting

his retaliation in first either by moving into Macedonia or moving into Bosnia, with a lot of ammunition stored in Bosnia? Are you satisfied that we have sufficient forces at our disposal to meet that wide range of possible contingencies?

(Mr Robertson) Yes, I am. I would have had to be before we embarked upon anything like this. Many members of this Committee, indeed the whole Committee, know Lieutenant General Sir Mike Jackson who is the Commander of the Allied Rapid Reaction Corps, and I of course take his judgement on these matters. He is some 20 miles away from the Kosovo border and he is satisfied that force protection is maintained. Can I make the point that if the Yugoslav Serbian forces attack NATO troops that are in Macedonia or in Bosnia, they will be attacking people who are engaged in peacekeeping operations and who represent no threat to him. It would therefore be a gross violation of international law to do so and would lead to an immediate and considerable response and in self-defence from us.

358.   Are you satisfied that our air force contribution is sufficient?

(Mr Robertson) Yes. We have supplied to SACEUR what SACEUR required from this country. The force configuration is a matter of the judgement of the Supreme Allied Commander Europe and we have supplied what he required from us. To go into what our capability is and what his objectives are would be to disclose operational information. It sounds like a small component of the total number of planes that are there, but they have got the particular qualifications that SACEUR wanted as part of that package and they have to be seen in terms of the overall package there as well. In addition, within the last brief period we were able to add HMS Splendid to what is available to SACEUR in the circumstances that he might decide they could be useful.

359.   And we would have the ability, I presume, to increase our number of aircraft swiftly should occasion merit it?

(Mr Robertson) SACEUR is in command. We are in a situation that is virtually unprecedented. There is a similarity to Bosnia when an activation order was passed, but the Secretary-General of NATO last night passed over the activation order to SACEUR and SACEUR therefore request what we have. We have clearly got other commitments which are something that applies to us and not necessarily to everybody else, but we are capable of supplying what he believes is necessary and it is a decisive contribution to the force that is there should it be necessary for that force to be used.

360.   Would you have at your disposal the number of aircraft that other allies are contributing, or is that classified?

(Mr Robertson) We are contributing what we need to contribute. They have particular characteristics in terms of the precision guided weapons that are on board which have been seen in action recently and which have proved their capability. It is precisely the number that SACEUR wanted from the United Kingdom. There will be planes from 13 air forces in

[**Chairman** *Cont*]

the air as and when SACEUR makes the decision to deploy them if diplomacy has completely failed. It is worth making the point to the Committee today, and to anybody else who might be listening in the outside world, that at any point President Milosevic can stop the violence, can go back to the levels that he promised to keep to, or the levels of forces that he promised last October, and he can sign up to the Rambouillet agreement which is an agreement that will safeguard the positions of the Serbian Kosovars and indeed the long term future of his country.

361. I presume that at the last minute, should he be prepared to do so, he would have to come up with something serious and not simply delaying what appears now to be the inevitable.

(Mr Robertson) Absolutely. We are only interested in him being serious about stopping the violence. That is the criterion. There is a lot of loose talk around in some parts of the media, although I have to compliment our own media for a very balanced coverage of what are ominous circumstances. Talk about our bombing Serbia is loose and inaccurate. The targets will be military targets exclusively. The military objective is precise and clear and that is to diminish the ability of the Serbian forces to continue with the violence against the civilian population that they have bene involved in.

Mr Colvin

362. Secretary of State, the media have also been critical about the legal basis for the use of force. At the moment that rests on United Nations Security Council Resolutions 1160 and 1199 which are under Chapter VII of the UN Charter, which covers action in respect of threats to the peace, breaches of the peace and acts of aggression. I should have thought that was enough, but could you reassure the Committee that you do not feel that any further Security Council Resolution is required in order perhaps to give a more unambiguous authority for all necessary means to be used to deal with the present situation?

(Mr Robertson) No, we do not think it is necessary. We think that there is a sufficient authority in existing Security Council Resolutions and indeed the use of force in international law can be justified as an exceptional measure to prevent an overwhelming humanitarian catastrophe. Since it is commonly agreed that that is what we are facing there is no doubt about the legality of the operation we are involved in. Speaking as I do on behalf of the United Kingdom and as Chairman of the Defence Council, I have a particular personal responsibility in this regard which would turn into a legal one if it came to it. I am satisfied that the Resolutions lay down very clear demands, especially Resolution 1199, which, as well as the exceptional circumstances, give us an absolute legal base.

363. You have referred to the humanitarian problem, but are our soldiers on the ground going to be equipped and trained for dealing with the refugee problem? That is going to be severe and is likely to increase maybe as a result of air strikes. We are going to get more refugees fleeing the country, are we not?

(Mr Robertson) The refugee crisis will undoubtedly grow. It is already quite significant. It is estimated that 20,000 people inside Kosovo have been displaced since last Sunday, since the breakdown of the negotiations. That is growing with every day that passes, with every bombardment that takes place. The number of those displaced in Kosovo alone inside the country and into the outside world is now 420,000. That is 20 per cent of the population there. These population movements are considerable. I was in Macedonia three weeks ago. At that time the number of refugees coming across the border was very small and they were actually being accommodated by the Macedonian people in an amazing act of hospitality to their brethren across the border, but that is now turning into a very significant tide. If violence at the present level by the Serbs were to continue that would certainly turn into a very large number. Yesterday I was with Mr Akis Tsohatzopoulos, the Defence Minister of Greece, who was paying a visit to me in this country. The Greeks already are host to a very large number of refugees from Kosovo and fear very significant increases in those numbers. Into Albania, into Macedonia, into Bulgaria and Romania, and even right up into Germany, which has already got something like 400,000 Albanian refugees as a whole, we are talking about a pretty significant flow of refugees destabilising many of these countries. That is one of the ways in which it affects us.

364. I can understand the hospitality in Macedonia where a quarter of the population is Albanian, but I understand that the Macedonians have now closed their frontier which, from a practical point of view, would seem a fairly difficult thing to do. What instructions have been given to our forces on the ground there?

(Mr Robertson) It is actually a very simple thing to close the border because there is only one road that goes from Macedonia into Kosovo. It divides into two beyond the border but these are not super highways. There are humanitarian agencies in Macedonia now and our forces will clearly look, as they would always do, to help wherever they can with the refugee flows. It may not be our particular job to do so but, as I say, there are 12,000 to 13,000 troops in a small country. Remember that Macedonia is the size of North Yorkshire and has a population roughly similar to Greater Manchester. It has the youngest Prime Minister in Europe, aged 33, and the oldest President in Europe, who is 83. They are taking on a huge challenge and when I met the Prime Minister I could not help but be impressed by the way in which they have recognised their place in the world so suddenly and been willing to take on these huge burdens that have come from being host to very large numbers of foreigners.

Mr McWilliam

365. I hope, Secretary of State, and I am really speaking through you to a wider audience, that everybody understands how impressed we have all been by the diligence, patience and hard work of the contact group in the run-in to the Rambouillet

[Mr McWilliam *Cont]*

agreement. Indeed, their patience was beyond what we thought was reasonably possible. Can you satisfy me that the rules of engagement for our forces are sufficiently robust to enable them adequately to defend themselves?

(Mr Robertson) I can. I cannot go into details because we never do. General Jackson is now in charge of the ARRC in the area and there is nobody more robust practically anywhere you can imagine than General Jackson. Being there in residence, so close and with a large number of British troops, both in the Ark and in the potential implementation force, I think he recognises that. We are not ignorant of the risks. Of course there are risks involved in this whole operation and it would be foolish to deny it. Our people are in what is going to be a very dangerous territory. We know that, but the alternative to doing that is not doing anything at all and that would be much worse.

Mr Hancock

366. With 50,000 Serbian soldiers either in or around Kosovo, once we attack the opportunity for them to give instant payback to the Kosovars is obviously a very great incentive on their part. They will be able to dish out a lot of punishment very quickly. What is the plan to safeguard the interest of those Kosovars who are very close to where the Serbian soldiers, the regulars in the Yugoslav Army and the Serbian police, are at the present time. Secondly, is there a proportion of the air power available to protect the interests that we have been able to secure in Bosnia and possibly elsewhere if the Serbs in those parts of the former Yugoslavia decide that they will support the Milosevic position?

(Mr Robertson) I do not wish to say anything about what we would do in self-defence of our forces. Essentially one of the key components would be the determinance of what the other side might expect. We have got of course the capability to act in self-defence of our forces. I do not believe that anybody in Belgrade mistakes the message of what an attack upon NATO would mean for them. It is not something that I think they would easily contemplate, but if they did it, they would have to face up to the fact that we would react very strongly indeed. I do not think we should go beyond that. He would be taking on the North Atlantic Treaty Organisation and 19 countries who are united in this endeavour. This is not an operation that involves the United Kingdom alone. There are 18 other countries that are part of it. You asked about the percentage of air power———

367. No. I asked specifically about how we would protect the Kosovars who are on the ground very close to the 50,000-odd regular Yugoslav and Serbian police who are in Kosovo today.

(Mr Robertson) We would clearly take that into account if that was the situation. The air verification operation has been ongoing since October and we have therefore got information that comes back as a result of that. We are conscious that we do not want to add to the miseries of those who are in that location, but we would obviously still be conscious of our own force protection necessities.

368. Would it be right for me to assume that many of the strategic military targets we will be aiming at are Yugoslav forces already in Kosovo?

(Mr Robertson) You are talking about where the air targets might be?

369. Yes.

(Mr Robertson) I cannot answer that question. I make the point that they will be military targets. The military objective is clear without any doubt and that is to reduce, diminish, his capability of attacking the civilians. A lot of planning has gone into this. If you remember, the first threats were made last October. We have done a huge amount of work in both the civilian side of the Ministry and the military side of the Ministry as well as through the NATO planning procedures so that if it comes to using military action in the next few days we know what it is we need to hit, we know how to hit it and we know with just how much force to hit it.

370. Would you assume that HMS Splendid would take part in the initial attack of what would probably be several hundred Cruise missiles?

(Mr Robertson) We are not saying anything at all about HMS Splendid other than the fact that she is in the area.

Mr Blunt

371. Secretary of State, to what level do you believe we need to reduce the Yugoslav National Army and the internal security troops in order to prevent them suppressing Albanian citizens of Kosovo?

(Mr Robertson) By enough to stop them doing it, to reduce their opportunities of doing it.

372. Can I put it to you that a prolonged air campaign may enormously degrade the number of functioning armoured vehicles, but it is going to be very difficult with an air campaign to go beyond reducing them to effectively an infantry army, which would surely still be sufficient to continue what is happening in Kosovo today, and indeed it might make the clearance rather more bloody? What appears to me to be happening is that since President Milosevic decided that he was going to defy NATO, and he appears to have taken that decision about a week ago, he then appears to have given order to clear at least northern Kosovo and that is why we are now seeing this enormous swathe of refugees from the ethnic cleansing which would appear to be going to get worse. My concern is that in a sense, however much we bomb the Yugoslav National Army, if Serb will holds then it is going to be impossible with air power to achieve our objective which is degrading his military capability so that he cannot oppress the local population.

(Mr Robertson) You have to make a number of calculations in this which involve the diplomatic, the political and the military elements in this. There is no computer into which you can put all the information and it will give you a printout that says, "Do this, this and this, and it will produce an outcome". We are dealing with somebody whose unpredictability

[**Mr Blunt** *Cont*]

matches his brutality. Therefore we must act on the basis of what we think is right and what we can do in the knowledge of what he has done in the past and how he has reacted in the past. I fear that he and maybe some other people in Belgrade misunderstand NATO's intention or NATO's will and determination, and that that may be leading them into making false decisions. If that is the case then they will only discover when things to start to happen that they are wrong. This is not a secure dictatorship. There are democratic elements inside Serbia although they are oppressed and they may well find it difficult to articulate their case, but once things start, if it gets to that, then they will have to make a calculation as well. We are setting out to reduce his military capability to conduct that violence in the only way that is open to us at the present time. We have got weaponry and we have got the means that we are confident can do that job.

373. It would appear from the reports that we are getting of the political situation in Serbia that even the liberal Serb parties you are referring to, seem to be, as one might expect, rallying patriotically to the leadership, and so precisely what role the opposition plays is open to question and I do not think we can expect the reaction from them that you imply. You spoke about the unpredictability of this exercise. Would it not be more predictable and would not the military advice be that you could actually predict and control the outcome if you were prepared to take the decision to conduct this operation as a land/air operation with both ground forces and air troops and then you could predict the outcome?

(Mr Robertson) I do not think so. It is a pretty unanimous view of the military commanders that we should not get involved in a land campaign because the sheer numbers that would be involved are so considerable and that is why, when I spoke to our troops on a hillside in Macedonia three weeks ago, I gave them the commitment that they would not fight their way into Kosovo. We have the capability. The North Atlantic Treaty Organisation has got the capability for strategic air strikes that we believe can have a significant effect on the military capability of the Yugoslav forces to commit the levels of violence that they have been engaged in up to now and to challenge their political will to go ahead with something that is clearly not in the Serbian national interest. In a way this is a reminder to them that the Rambouillet agreement actually has something very substantial for the Serbs within it, but they seem incapable of understanding that, of seeing that, because some of them clearly do not believe that the international community means business. The frustration of NATO is shared by others who have traditionally in the past been more understanding of Serbia. The Russians have tried to get the message over that the Rambouillet agreement is in the Serbian best interest, but have not been able to do so. Our objective is to stop the violence, not to bomb them back to the negotiating table. It is not our objective to do that. It is to stop the escalating violence that is going to create these refugee flows at the humanitarian disaster which we all see looming in front of us.

374. But unless we are prepared to use ground force, the military capacity of Serbia, particularly its armoured forces and its armoured infantry forces that it would need to take on a NATO army or armed force attack in Serbia are not needed by Serbia. There is no threat to Serbia of that happening. I am obviously including Kosovo in this. If the Yugoslav Army is reduced to the status of an infantry force, and it is not realistic I believe to expect air power to go further than that, we are going to be left with the slaughter and the ethnic cleansing continuing to happen in Kosovo, possibly in greater numbers than we have now, and then I fear that the humanitarian crisis will worsen. I wonder how we are going to react to the enormous pressure that will come, since we will have 25,000 troops in Macedonia, to act to bring the situation to a conclusion, which we could do if we had the will to deploy the very large number of ground forces that you indicate.

(Mr Robertson) I know you were yourself in the army and in reconnaissance, which is even further ahead sometimes than the front line. I do not know how willing you would be—presumably you are still on a reserve list—if I were to call you back in order to lead——

Chairman: And Mr Brazier!

Mr Blunt

375. Perhaps I can answer that point.

(Mr Robertson) It is not a frivolous point. The people who would have to do it have rejected that as an option but the Serbian threat, or any other military threat, is made up of a capability and an intention. Of course every last soldier in the Serbian Army with a gun and a bayonet could *in extremis* cause carnage. The capability may be there. The question is whether the intention would be maintained. Creating a desert and calling it peace, creating carnage in Kosovo and calling it part of Greater Serbia, is not going to be an achievement. Milosevic at the moment has got all of the controls. He is the driving force. He has got no competition. Our objective here is not to try and get into his mind. It is to use strategic precision bombing on military targets to reduce his ability to order the kind of ethnic cleansing that we have seen up to now.

Laura Moffatt

376. Secretary of State, I know that we all feel—I certainly do myself—that we have the moral authority to take some action, but I think that there is a difficult question, as Mr Solana quite clearly says, that we are not waging war with the Yugoslavians. We would all accept that. What troubles me is that if you were a Serb on the ground and bombs started to fall, you might have a different view, and with the closure of the only independent radio station during the night there is little or no information getting to them for them to understand that this is truly a humanitarian act to stop aggression towards people on the ground who are in the most dire conditions. What can we do to try and improve that situation? How can we make people on the ground understand that this is truly to stop aggression?

[**Laura Moffatt** *Cont*]

(Mr Robertson) I think it will be clear, if it comes to that, that our targets are military and do not involve civilian or urban targets. That is a message that will get through despite the fact that the media is state owned and controlled. The other fact is that in this day and age it is actually almost completely impossible to control media, especially in the centre of Europe where satellite footprints extend beyond it. I did a programme near midnight last night for BBC World who claim some vast audience in hotels all over the world, and presumably in Belgrade, but who say they have information to suggest that it is actually there in the Serbian military information command centre as well. There is a message that has to get through at an international level that this is happening, that we have no argument with the Serb people and that what is being done in their name has almost certainly not got their support. They may want to hold on to Kosovo and it has a precious status in their history. They may believe that it is right that they should stand up to what is portrayed as external aggression. But I cannot believe that the Serbian people that I have met over the years, the ordinary Serbs, would be party to the kind of violence, the bombarding and the destruction of villages, the massacre of innocent elderly men, women and children because they happen to be close by what is believed to be a KLA stronghold, or would subscribe to that. That is a message that we have to get across. If military action has to be taken, it will be taken with the heaviest of heavy hearts. It will be taken with precision guided weapons, and it will be taken against only military targets with a very clear objective, not to bomb common sense or even self-interest into the mind of President Milosevic, but to reduce the military capability that is being used against a civilian population.

Mr Hood

377. Secretary of State, I agreed with the Prime Minister yesterday when he told the House that doing nothing was not an option. Some of the comments that are made about expressing worries about this and that seem to come from an area where people are maybe looking at it not as positively as you would expect them to do in the seriousness of the situation. But when we visited the NATO headquarters as a Committee a few weeks ago, we had discussions with the military there and they talked about the need to have an end game. We had a discussion about the ways and means and whether there was an end game. This is probably the reason why it has gone on so long to get agreement round what that end game is. The Prime Minister told the House yesterday that to send ground troops you would be talking about a figure of 100,000. I find it difficult to understand, if air strikes are not successful, how we can move on from there without putting ground troops in. To say we are not going to put ground troops in and just rely on air strikes is an area where I need to be convinced that air strikes are going to succeed. What is the end game, Secretary of State, if the air strikes do not succeed?

(Mr Robertson) We would not be undertaking the possibility of the sanction unless we were confident that we could inflict significant damage on his military

capabilities and his ability to repress the population. That is the limit to what we can do. That is the limit to what international law allows us to do. That in itself is quite significant. Putting ground troops into that part of the world is not just a daunting military challenge; it is human challenge as well. It might even be a legal challenge. The objective here we are confident is inside international law, achievable and, given the capabilities of all NATO acting together, likely to be able to reduce significantly this military machine and therefore the ability to go ahead with that. Into that you have to feed the ingredients of his political will, the political will of the forces there, to take that and not to question it. Mr Holby has just been pointing out that a member of the Serbian Parliament which rubber-stamped the decision yesterday in the way that it does actually stood up and said that there was no fighting in Kosovo. Partly they are starved of information, partly they do not want to know the information, but we have got an obligation to get as much in as possible. I go back to this argument about the footprint of the BBC World Service or other television providers. The Internet is now a method by which people can have an access to the outside world. We have to get over the message that there is actually an end game here which makes sense. The end game is the Rambouillet agreement. If you look at the ingredients of that, and I am very proud of the achievement of the Foreign Secretary and his French opposite number at Rambouillet, they put together an agreement which provides for Kosovo staying not just inside Yugoslavia but inside the Federation and guarantees the integrity of the Federal Republic of Yugoslavia. The Kosovo Albanians have signed up to it. The people who were standing for independence, some elements of whom were fighting for a greater Albania, said, "We are willing to compromise our objectives and sign up to it." There is an end game there for Milosevic to take and he is being advised to take it by the Russians, never mind by the NATO countries as well. We have to have a degree of confidence on what it is we can realistically do. It may be that Admiral Moore—I know he is a sailor—might want to give you an impression from somebody who serves in the forces about the prospect of a land invasion force incursion into Kosovo.

(Rear Admiral Simon Moore) The idea is a very difficult one, as the Secretary of State has said, but in many terms. First of all, where you are operating is very difficult; secondly, it would be very difficult to supply the armed forces, and thirdly it would be very difficult to get the whole of the act together in sufficient time to make a difference. Therefore, the reliance on a strategic air campaign is absolutely the right strategy at the moment.

378. At the moment. What happens if it does not work? What happens if it does not drive Milosevic to the negotiating table to accept a peace deal? What happens then?

(Mr Robertson) NATO would then have to consider it. The international community would then have to consider what was to be done about it. The precise objective that is set there and which we think can be achieved is to cause huge damage to the

[**Mr Hood** *Cont*]

structure that he has there and which he is presently using against the Kosovar people. It is all too easy to say "what if, what if, what if?" down the line. What if Albania burst into flames? What if the refugees have crossed into Macedonia: you will crush that government? What if Bulgaria and Romania are destabilised? There are a lot of possibilities here. What we are doing at the moment is acting in order to stop some of the repercussions that will certainly happen if what is happening at the moment goes on. Macedonia is a very young democracy. It is a part of former Yugoslavia, finding it difficult in that part of the world, but I think making huge strides forward. Albania is in total crisis at the present moment. The destabilisation of Albania if this conflict goes on will be even greater. I was in Romania and Bulgaria. I think the Committee has been out to that part of the world as well. These are fledgling democracies. The Balkans aflame are going to burn more than just Belgrade and those who are in the immediate environs. The international community is acting here to stop the conflagration. There is something ironic that the Century started with a war that commenced in Sarajevo and here we are, nine months away from the end of the 20th century, trying to put out the fires in exactly the same part of the world. Maybe we have learned during the Century that sometimes you have to act quickly in order to make sure that it does not get out of control and destabilise the whole country.

Ms Taylor

379.   Secretary of State, you are very clear that we have a capability of defining military targets and actually taking them out. This is the whole basis of what you are suggesting to us. Can I ask you to restate that so that I can here it once again from you? I know you have been saying it and you said it to Crispin Blunt and others. I want to be sure in my mind that that is exactly what you are saying: "We know where these targets are, we can isolate them, and we actually can take them out." We all know that Milosevic is waiting for civilian casualties to make his statement: "This is what Britain is doing to us. This is what NATO is doing to us." I would really like you to restate that for me please.

(*Mr Robertson*)   There is no casualty-free conflict in this day and age. There is no way that you can insure against casualties on either side. But you can use the increasingly sophisticated weaponry that is available. We have already shown members of the Committee—and I think the Committee is coming in to look at more information today—what happened in Operation Desert Fox. We can show the world from some of the photography there, the battle damage assessment on Iraqi military targets during Operation Desert Fox just how forensic and how accurate the weaponry is that is available against military targets. We are confident that with the meticulous planning that has gone into it President Milosevic's military machine is going to take a very considerable hit and therefore reduce the chances of further violence against civilians. He is well armed, both on the ground and in terms of equipment. A lot of it is quite old but still very reliable. It was supplied in some cases by

western governments, including ours, who were supplying the former Yugoslavia quite legitimately—I do not think any criticism can be made of that—and we therefore know its capabilities. The forces of Yugoslavia have shown over the years that they are brave and they do not easily give in, but what is being done in their name and the name of Serbia is a disgrace and a stain which, if they knew about it, I am sure they would hold back. If Milosevic is hell-bent on taking his country, as he has over the years, into these disasters one after another, at some point the people of Serbia are going to say "Stop". It has already happened in the last 18 months. The demonstrations we all saw in Belgrade gave us great heart. They were finally suppressed but the people of Serbia are not all sheep. I cannot believe that they themselves would back a President who has been so nationally suicidal as this one has been.

380.   That is very persuasive but how about the other side of that coin? The Kosovar fighters: have we actually got arrangements with the Kosovar fighters that during this NATO intervention they will actually not take advantage of it?

(*Mr Robertson*)   We cannot have that. They are engaged in their own particular battle. They have gone the distance in terms of compromising their overall objectives at Rambouillet. We have no more hold over them than we have over the Serbs, but the heavy artillery, the ability to destroy villages, to wipe out communities, is very much in the hands of the state apparatus of Yugoslavia and of Serbia. The call to stop the violence is one that goes to both sides. We are not here saying that the guns that are fired from one side are better than the guns fired from the other side, but the overwhelming force is on the side of the Serbs. It is also worth making the point that there is information in print in public that there is quite a bit of dissatisfaction inside Serbia with what is going on, that they are finding t difficult to call up the troops in the numbers that they are requiring at the present moment. The Chief of the Defence Staff was removed from his job within the last six months because he would not co-operate in every detail with President Milosevic. There are indications that some people question this suicidal policy and hopefully in the next few hours more people will be giving that message.

381.   If we are so competent, Secretary of State, everybody is asking, why have we not picked Milosevic up? What is it that this man has got, what capabilities has he got, that he can keep on avoiding being picked up by us? We can talk about competence all the way along the line. Why is he not at The Hague?

(*Mr Robertson*)   If it were that easy, Ms Taylor, then all of those who are indicted for war crimes would be in The Hague. If you are running a state like Yugoslavia or Serbia today, you are pretty well protected in personal terms. I think the bombshell that would be required would be immeasurable. Those who are indicted, those who are responsible for war crimes, will eventually be at The Hague—I can say that with confidence—and they should not sleep easily in their beds thinking that they have got away with it or they will not eventually have to face justice. In the last two

[**Ms Taylor** *Cont*]

years since I have been in charge we have been responsible for a very significant number of people picked up as indeed have other nations. A very significant number are facing proper justice at The Hague. Some have been discharged, some have been found not guilty, but other people have faced the justice of the international community for crimes beyond belief and description. Ultimately all of those who have been responsible will be there as well.

Mr Cohen

382. Secretary of State, I know you have said it this morning and the Prime Minister said it yesterday, that this is being undertaken with enormous reluctance. Can you give a judgement about the possible loss of life involved in such military action, including possibly to British service men and women? How does that compare to what would happen in the humanitarian disaster if no action was taken? Also, could you say whether NATO has consulted Russia and what their reaction is likely to be to air strikes? Finally, is there any proposal to take this matter back to the UN for discussion there?

(Mr Robertson) The question of loss of life and of casualties is one of the biggest issues of all we face. I am a civilian, I am a Member of Parliament like you are. I have no military background, no military career, but at the end of the day i have to take decisions based on the advice that is given to me by people who have faced action, who have been in conflict, and who are properly conscious of the responsibility for the young men and women who are in their charge and whom they send into these dangerous situations. They will tell me that there is the prospect of casualties. They rightly warn that we cannot have a casualty-free war. This is not a war, but any conflict that involves military action is not going to be casualty-free. It is one of the risks that you have to balance against the large scale loss of life that would be the consequence of doing nothing. Indeed, the strategic consequences of political and every other term that would flow from the fact that where there was a conflict we stood back and did nothing about it. That is a balance that has to be taken and the air crew and ground crew who are in Italy today facing the prospect of being sent into action know that well. They face it with remarkable courage. I salute their bravery and I do not send them into action with anything other than the realisation that the alternative is much worse.

Chairman

383. Having clarified their legal status, I presume there will be no formal declaration of war.

(Mr Robertson) It is not a war.

384. If a NATO pilot is shot down or vice versa, what under the Geneva Convention or anything else can downed pilots demand under international law?

(Mr Robertson) The full protection of the Geneva Conventions. The Geneva Conventions are not tied to a declaration of war. All parties to any conflict must be bound by the Geneva Conventions and we would expect that Yugoslavia would do that if there was any

situation that arose there at all. This is not a war. We are not declaring war on Serbia. We are not bombing Serbia. We are damaging the military capability to destroy civilians in that part of the world, but those who do that, and after all they are acting not just in accordance with international law but in the interests of international law, would get the full protection of the Geneva Convention.

385. Will you be taking it back to the UN?

(Mr Robertson) Russia is clearly a factor in this. We must remember that Russia is a full member of the contact group, so that all the processes that we have been engaged in up to now Russia has been fully subscribing to. The Security Council Resolution 1199 that laid down the demands on Milosevic last October were subscribed to by the Russians as well. They were involved in the outskirts of Rambouillet as part and parcel of the structure that led up to it. So far as we know, they have recommended very strongly to President Milosevic that he accepts these agreements as being in his own best self-interest and indeed in the interests of the wider area. The Russians have said that they object to military action. They seem to think that more negotiations will produce an outcome. I do not know whether they are sanguine about the violence that continues while these so-called talks take place, but they are perfectly entitled to their view. We disagree with them and that is why we are taking action. It is action taken in pursuit of UN Security Council Resolutions, two of them but particularly 1199, which laid down the demands which are quite clearly being flouted by Milosevic today. You asked about taking it back to the UN. Clearly, if the Rambouillet agreement were to be signed up to, we would want to enshrine that in the UN Security Council Resolution. In the meantime there is more than adequate legal standing without going back. The situation is of considerable urgency, given the nature of the bombardment that the Kosovar villagers are suffering at the moment.

Mr Brazier

386. Secretary of State, you stated NATO's objective very clearly several times. How will we measure the success of the operation?

(Mr Robertson) It will be a matter for the NATO military authorities to look at the battle damage that has been done, to make an assessment about how much of the air defences and other targets have been hit. Then we watch on the ground what the forces are doing. I do not think you would want me to venture into the territory about what we would attack because that would be of some help—limited help but some help—to those who might be the ones involved in the action on the other side.

387. Of course not, Secretary of State, I would not do that. Without asking in any way for you to indicate what sort of targets we are talking about, my question really is, will you measure the success in terms of damage to targets, whatever they may be, or in terms of Serbian behaviour afterwards?

(Mr Robertson) The objective is to reduce the capability so that he will reduce the level of violence,

[Mr Brazier *Cont*]

so we will make assessments based on that, both at a political and at a military level about that. I would not want to go beyond that at the present moment. A lot of planning has gone into this whole operation. Another thought that comes to mind in relation to Mr Cohen's question, which relates to this, is that we of course have updated the United Nations Security Council at every stage on what is going on here.

Ms Taylor

388.   Secretary of State, this "what if" question: is there a chance that NATO's action now could lead to a north/south partitioning for Kosovo with the north being in Serbian control, being ethnically cleansed, and the south a UN protectorate? Is there a chance that we could end up with this outcome and would you be content if that were the outcome?

(Mr Robertson)   The answer to that question is no. The answer to the first question is that it is impossible to tell. The Rambouillet agreement is the ideal. That is what was negotiated. The Kosovar Albanian side have made very substantial concessions on what we know to be their objectives in agreeing to that. That keeps the integrity of the Federal Republic of Yugoslavia and allows a huge degree of autonomy for those who are in there, more autonomy than they previously had under the old Yugoslav constitution, which is where all this started when Milosevic tore it up. It may be that President Milosevic is undertaking a de facto partitioning at the moment. Mr Blunt raised that possibility at the beginning. That is not our intention, but it is difficult to read his mind in every regard except that we have seen in the past that he respects military power. We know that his regime depends on the military structures and that in the past when he has believed that we have threatened that military power, he has been prepared to back off, both in the Bosnian conflict, and indeed in the earlier part of this conflict. That is an ingredient that has to be taken into account when we go down that route. The Rambouillet agreement did not allow for partitioning and we believe that, just as the Serbs and the majority of the Albanian population used to live in peace and contentment inside the autonomous Kosovar structures under the old Yugoslavia, it is not impossible for them to do it again.

Chairman: It has been said that Milosevic is both the arsonist and the fire brigade. He will have to prove that the second part is going to be valid in future because he is the one who can stop the carnage in his own territory.

Mr Blunt

389.   Secretary of State, you suggest that my reserve service might be called upon.

(Mr Robertson)   This was not a serious remark.

390.   Let me make the serious point that I want to, that if I found myself back in an armoured reconnaissance squadron with the full weight of NATO air power and artillery support available to those forces taking on a JNA, I would be rather more sanguine about my chances of survival than I would

have been when I was facing the Eighth Guards Tank Army on the German border. I actually think that if there was a proper land/air campaign with the enormous difficulties of all the support that the Rear Admiral mentioned, the number of casualties on the table would not be as high as one would expect. It would be a situation rather akin to the battle in Kuwait. The Government have ruled that out as an option for the time being.

(Mr Robertson)   NATO has ruled that out.

391.   What I would like to explore is the relationship with the KLA who are an armed force on the ground. In your words, Secretary of State, you said that the KLA had gone the distance by reducing their aspirations from that of independence, but for a very long time the Kosovars have sought by democratic means to pursue their right of self-determination and any democratic opportunity for that was denied to them by the Serbians. So I believe what they are fighting is a justified liberation struggle. They have now gone the distance, in your words, at an international conference. What is our relationship now with the KLA? Surely, in a sense we are now on their side? I do not understand what the NATO Secretary-General means when he says, "We urge in particular Kosovar armed elements to refrain from provocative military action", when it is their people who are being ethnically cleansed and are the victims, in your words, of crimes beyond belief and description. Is there now an opportunity to at least co-ordinate our military actions with the KLA? What do you think is going to be the future of our relationship with armed elements on the ground in Kosovo?

(Mr Robertson)   The provocation that the UN Secretary-General was talking about was the offensive actions taken by the KLA who are a part of the Kosovo Albanian population which collectively signed up to the accord. It is right to say they should not be engaged in provocation. Up until Racak earlier this year the KLA were responsible for more deaths in Kosovo than the Yugoslav authorities had been. The call all along has been for the end to violence on both sides and seek the diplomatic channel. They signed up to their cause including the disarmament aspects of the Rambouillet agreement and I think that is a very significant move and I hope they hold to that and there are not wilder elements that seek to break up the unity that appeared at Rambouillet. We recognise the threat to the Kosovar Albanians. That is why we are willing to take action. We are not siding with the KLA whose longer-term objectives we may not subscribe to at all.

392.   Again as part of the agreement they have now signed up to objectives which we do support.

(Mr Robertson)   But I do not think that puts them on our side if they are doing things that we would disagree with there. What we are doing here is trying to protect the civilian population of Kosovo. That is what they say they are doing as well. We are willing to take that action because the other side is not willing to see the commonsense or even the self-interest that would be involved in signing the agreement. I do not think it would be right and proper for NATO to say, "They have signed up to the agreement, we will therefore take their side on that." Our objective has got

THE DEFENCE COMMITTEE

151

24 March 1999]

RT HON GEORGE ROBERTSON, MP, REAR ADMIRAL SIMON MOORE
and MR CHRIS HOLTBY

[Continued

[Mr Blunt *Cont]*

to be very clear and very narrow when dealing with another sovereign state and that is the emergency situation of averting a humanitarian catastrophe, not taking sides in an armed struggle.

Mr Cann

393. You have made it very plain that it is military targets only and we are going to use precision on those targets. We all accept, of course, that civilians must be avoided at all costs. There is no point protecting civilians in Kosovo if we kill civilians in Serbia. So we come down to the question of accuracy. The Harrier GR7s, for example, have got a very good track record but there have been doubts expressed about the accuracy of Tomahawk missiles and if the track record is anything to go by we will be using those first to take out their capability to damage our aircraft which we will use later. How confident are you a) in the accuracy of Tomahawk missiles and b) since it is the first time a British submarine will have fired any in anger whether they are trained in their use?

(Mr Robertson) I am not saying whether we are using Tomahawk missiles at all, but if you are asking about the capability of the system, test firing took place in September of last year and very clearly verified accuracy over very long distances of this particular system. Since I have got an Admiral here it seems to me appropriate for him to answer that particular question.

(Rear Admiral Moore) It is a very capable system but the missile is so good and so intelligent itself that in fact the crew prepare and fire it and the missile is then programmed to go to the target. It is the missile system in which the accuracy lies more than in the residual capability of
the submarine.

394. But the missile itself is 100 per cent accurate? 90 per cent? 95 per cent?

(Rear Admiral Moore) I do not think we want to go into that at this stage but it is a very accurate system.

Chairman

395. We are looking at pictures afterwards.

(Mr Robertson) There are unclassified pictures from Operation Desert Fox that leave you in absolutely no doubt at all that this is a formidable system both for the punch that it has and the accuracy that can be deployed and therefore the lack of collateral damage that would affect people who are not party to a conflict. Anybody who has seen the unclassified pictures of the Ba'ath Party headquarters in central Baghdad with 11 Tomahawk cruise missile holes like holes on a golf green destroying everything within that building but leaving no damage at all outside the building will realise that when we are talking about this, it sounds cold, it sounds clinical and there are some people who are deeply uncomfortable about even entering into a conversation about it, we are now at a time when international law and public feelings demand precision in what we do and therefore the attacks, if they take place and they have to take place, will be against military targets with some of the most precise weapons that have ever been invented.

Mr Colvin

396. The evidence of the previous stand-off crisis showed that Milosevic's position has not been weakened but strengthened domestically and I am not convinced that the air strikes that are now planned are going to do anything more than strengthen domestic support for him. No doubt he can invoke Article 51, the self-defence article, to justify the calling up of we read in the papers one million reservists to reinforce his 209,000 regular troops. There are an awful lot of "what if" questions this morning but what provision has been made by NATO for calling up additional troops to cope with a ground operation when we know perfectly well from previous experience of fighting in Yugoslavia the ratio of defenders required especially if you have got a sympathetic civil population on your side who do not receive regularly CNN and Sky News and the all the rest but are bombarded with domestic propaganda from Milosevic? What provision has been made for the numbers that are going to be required? Has any estimate been made of the numbers of ground troops that would be required if a ground operation were required? I think the Prime Minister's estimate yesterday of over 100,000 was the understatement of the year, quite frankly. You are talking about ten times that, are you not?

(Mr Robertson) The Prime Minister gave an estimate and the NATO military authorities have done a lot of planning on the basis of it. It is certainly in excess of 100,000. You have to work out yourself where they are going to come from. You cannot call up reserves and you cannot use conscripts because if you were ever to get engaged in that sort of conflict, and we are not planning to get engaged in that sort of conflict, you have got to have troops that can protect themselves from day one and not build themselves up. We are dealing with an urgent situation and that is why the NATO commanders have taken the role that they have taken. They said before Operation Desert Fox that any bombing on Iraq would consolidate Saddam and make him stronger as a result of that. In fact, he is much weaker. His military machine was damaged very substantially and he could not even produce a civilian casualty to parade on the streets to show how wanton we had been in the bombing that he claimed we were engaged in. So the damage has been done. He is not stronger, he is weaker and there is a lot of evidence coming out of Iraq in the past few weeks that he has been executing senior army officers because they themselves are now questioning what he is doing and may well be organising coups against him. So I do not think this assumption that dictators are strengthened by the fact that military targets are attacked holds water at all. Milosevic is finding it very difficult to get people to be called up. There were demonstrations the other day in Belgrade of mothers of existing soldiers complaining bitterly about them going to Kosovo. There is a huge reluctance to get engaged in this conflict because there is no appetite for that sort of fight. I do not believe that NATO attacks if they happen on military targets are going to do

[**Mr Colvin** *Cont*]

anything to increase the strength of Milosevic and will perhaps persuade the population that this man has yet again got them engaged in a murderous conflict from which they can only lose.

397. Has he called up his home guard?

(Mr Robertson) He is trying to call up people at the moment. He has called a state of emergency and he is calling them up but even the public information that is available shows how difficult he is finding it to do that. If people are actually refusing to be called up, if conscripts are unwilling to turn up that in itself is the tip of an iceberg of collapsing morale that is in there. There is a risk, of course, that it will consolidate Milosevic. That is not something we discount and say pooh-pooh to, but this is a country in the centre of the Europe, a relatively sophisticated country and I do not believe that the people of Serbia want to be dragged down this track of national suicide again and to be pilloried by the whole world community for the destruction of villages, the destruction of human beings, the perpetration of atrocities. There are indications that people among the civilian population in Serbia will blame Milosevic for it and certainly will not support him.

Mr McWilliam

398. Secretary of State, do you believe that Milosevic really does think that the slaughter of Serbs in Kosovo in the fourteenth century is an excuse for slaughtering Kosovans at the end of the twentieth?

(Mr Robertson) I do not think that is the reason he is doing but it is a method of orchestrating support. Sadly, Serbia is not the only part of the world where history is brought out as a convenient means of masking homicidal tendencies on behalf of today's generation. What we have tried do in Bosnia, what we are again trying to do in Kosovo is to draw a line to tell those who would use violence in order to achieve historical missions or day-to-day land aggression that they cannot get away with it and the international community will simply take a stand. We were successful beyond many people's forecasts in Bosnia and a civil society is reappearing there and I think

growing with every day. In Kosovo we are again drawing the line if Milosevic wants to choose the path of peace and a future of security for his own people inside the Federal Republic of Yugoslavia, but if he is hell bent on war then we must respond because the consequences are too horrifying to contemplate.

Chairman

399. Thank you very much for coming. It has been a rather depressing overall experience despite your well-received presence, Secretary of State, and whatever the degrees of support to Government policy—and I think there is a very substantial majority that do support Government policy than those that do not—whenever British forces and NATO forces are deployed and their lives are threatened then we can unanimously endorse the view that we wish them well and we hope they can return to normal duties as quickly as possible. We hope that we will be able to discuss Bishopton with you so our office will be in touch with yours, Secretary of State, early afternoon. Once again, apologies to the people who came down. We would like to have a brief chat to them afterwards before they leave.

(Mr Robertson) I am grateful to you for your indulgence. I think it would have been wholly inappropriate to have crammed it in and anyway the Government wishes its Parliament to be involved as fully as possible and tomorrow's debate will allow that. Mr Brazier on my extreme left took umbrage at something I did not actually say about the role of reserves and the implementation force. I can assure the Committee and him that as the reserves have played a distinguished and essential role in Bosnia I contemplate that when, as I hope, we have an implementation force in Kosovo we will need and will require and will value the reserves there.

Chairman: I attended a ceremony at Lichfield Cathedral on the last formal occasion of the Third Battalion Staffordshire regiment where they marched through the town. I think you had better act very quickly to save them from complete break up. Even at this late juncture there is still time! Thank you very much.

Printed in the UK by The Stationery Office Limited
4/99   399474   78344

ISBN 0-10-222699-7

9 780102 226997